FREE-BORN JOHN

Pauline Gregg began her writing career with books on the social and economic history of England. At the same time she was becoming closely involved in the seventeenth century through her work on the Leveller Movement, which had been the basis of her doctoral thesis. *Freeborn John*, her biography of John Lilburne, the Leveller leader, resulted in a more intensive study of the period which led her to the heart of the struggle – King Charles himself. She was married to the late Russell Meiggs, the historian of Greece and Rome, has two daughters and seven grandchildren and lives in Bristol.

Also by Pauline Gregg

King Charles I (Phoenix Press)

A Social and Economic History of Britain 1760–1980

The Chain of History

The Story of the Main Links in the Chain of Man's Development from the Stone Age to the End of the Nineteenth Century

The Welfare State: an Economic and Social History of Great Britain from 1945 to the Present Day

Oliver Cromwell

Black Death to Industrial Revolution: a Social and Economic History of England

FREE-BORN JOHN

A Biography of John Lilburne

Pauline Gregg

'I neither love a slave nor fear a tyrant'

**PHOENIX
PRESS**

A PHOENIX PRESS PAPERBACK

First published in Great Britain
by J.M. Dent in 1961
This paperback edition published in 2000
by Phoenix Press,
a division of The Orion Publishing Group Ltd,
Orion House, 5 Upper St Martin's Lane,
London WC2H 9EA

A CIP catalogue record for this book
is available from the British Library.

Printed and bound in Great Britain by
Clays Ltd, St Ives plc

Preface

ALL WHO STUDY ENGLISH SEVENTEENTH-CENTURY HISTORY become rapidly aware of the importance of the pamphleteers, whose vociferous self-expression vitalizes so much of the period. My first debt is to them, and I acknowledge it in full. Of all the historians to whom students of the civil wars are indebted, two stand out from the rest—Samuel Rawson Gardiner and Charles Harding Firth. I owe much to both.

Professor R. H. Tawney, under whom this work was begun, guided and helped me in many ways, for which I am most grateful. To R. W. Southern, Chichele Professor of Modern History in the University of Oxford, Dr C. M. Fraser, of King's College, Newcastle-upon-Tyne, and Mr Mervyn James, of Hatfield College, Durham, I am very grateful for help in building up a picture of the Lilburne manor. I am much indebted to Mr Theodore Gang, of King's College, Newcastle-upon-Tyne, who spent much time in examining for me the records of Lilburne baptisms and burials. I should like also to record my thanks to the vicar of St John the Baptist church, Eltham, and to Miss A. M. Lane, who kindly showed me the parish registers of St John's.

Above all, I am deeply grateful to Mr Christopher Hill, Fellow of Balliol College, who read an untidy manuscript, corrected much of my ignorance, and answered questions out of his unrivalled knowledge of the seventeenth century.

Towards many institutions I feel a sense of warm obligation, particularly to the Bodleian Library, with its friendly and efficient staff, and to the North Library of the British Museum, where the Thomason Tracts are read.

For helping with illustrations I am indebted to the co-operative staff of the Print Room in the British Museum and the Department of Fine Art at the Ashmolean Museum, to Mr Edward Milligan, the Librarian of the Society of Friends, and Miss Dorothy Coates, the Librarian to the Marquess of Bath. For permission to use photographs I am grateful to the Trustees of the British Museum, the Curators of the Bodleian Library and of the Ashmolean Museum, the Library Curatorship Committee of the Society of Friends, and to the Marquess of Bath.

To Mr A. J. White, a very patient editor, and his staff at Harraps, particularly Mr D. D. Bird, I am glad to record my thanks; and also to Mr F. J. Bradford, the Art Editor. If these thanks could be taken to cover also our earlier collaboration I should be happy.

In Tutorial Classes at High Wycombe we used to talk much about Lilburne and the Levellers, and I am delighted to thank again all the members of those classes, not only for their enthusiasm, but for the new light which their often practical approach threw upon the activities of Lilburne and his friends.

As always, I am grateful to my family for patience and forbearance, and to my husband, Russell Meiggs, for the help and criticism which he has never failed to give at every stage, in spite of his own pressing commitments.

Above all, I want to thank Mr Ian R. Lilburn, Coull House, by Aboyne, Aberdeenshire, a descendant of Free-born John, for his generosity in allowing me to take advantage of his researches into family history. My knowledge of John Lilburne's children comes from him, and I am deeply grateful for the genealogical table which he has prepared for this book. In the chapter notes I make acknowledgment to him by name.

Finally, I want to acknowledge a more elusive debt—to all those who, like John Lilburne, have believed that the cause of freedom was worth a lifetime's struggle. Many of these we know by name or through their works; some are unrecorded. But the lives of all of them lie deep in our inheritance; their spirit is part of the fabric of our society. To all these, in humility, I dedicate this book.

P.G.

Holywell Manor,
Oxford
March 1961

Contents

Preface to the 1986 edition

For some years no biography of John Lilburne – other than the present one, which was first published in 1961 – has been available, in spite of the fact that interest in the English civil wars of the seventeenth century has never been greater and that a growing number of books on various aspects of the subject continues to appear.

Yet no study of the period is complete without reference to Lilburne and the contribution which he and his party, the Levellers, made to political thought and to the central idea of democratic government. The Leveller party, in particular, has featured not only in discussion among historians but has been taken up by politicians and others of left-wing views. Some historians doubt Lilburne's influence with the army; the *Agreement of the People* is fertile debating ground; political activists claim affinity with the Levellers. Whatever view one takes it is clear that today, when the idea of democracy is synonymous with liberty over much of the world, the career of the man who spelt it out to the English people over three hundred years ago cannot be ignored.

When, at the same time, personal freedom is threatened and curtailed in many lands, Lilburne's continuous fight against tyranny, as he saw it, regardless of the consequences to himself, is fully relevant. He may not always have been right; he was often provocative and exasperating. But his activities never passed unnoticed. Indeed, he sometimes held centre stage – and how he enjoyed doing so! – rubbing shoulders with Cromwell both as friend and enemy, approaching Charles I when he considered it expedient to do so, stage-managing his own trial for life as though he were producing a play. His political democracy might not be as fully fledged as ours today, yet as agitator supreme he had no equal then or now.

Lilburne's chief weapons were words, spoken and written: if this reissue does nothing more than introduce the reader to Lilburne's magnificent seventeenth-century prose it will have achieved something worthwhile. But I hope it will also bring to new life the man himself and the Leveller movement he led.

Despite the passage of a quarter of a century I do not wish to alter my original assessment of John Lilburne, and I am very glad that this biography is again available. For this new paperback edition I have added recent publications to the final page of the Bibliography.

To all those who keep alive the memory of Free-born John and the Levellers – in particular Tony Benn, the WEA Oxford Levellers Branch and all who fight for Freedom.

Pauline Gregg
February, 2000

CHAPTER ONE

The Hixons of Greenwich

My father wore a gold Chain as the badge and livery of a very Illustrious and Noble Earl.

My mother was a Courtier borne, bred, and brought up and ended her days at Court.

JOHN LILBURNE, *Letter to the Apprentices*, May 10, 1639, published in *The Prisoners Plea for a Habeas Corpus*, April 4, 1648

THE ANCIENT ROYAL PALACE OF GREENWICH LAY ON THE south bank of the Thames five miles east-south-east from London in the Hundred of Blackheath, in the county of Kent. Round it lay the villages of Deptford, Woolwich, Charlton, Plumstead, Lewisham, Eltham. Humphrey, Duke of Gloucester, had in 1433 been licensed to build a mansion here, crennelled and embattled, and a tower in stone and lime.[1] His successor, Margaret of Anjou, named the palace Placentia, or Pleasaunce.[2] The Friars Observant, who observed the rule of St Francis, were established at Greenwich by Edward IV, and their chapel stood by the river to the west of the royal buildings.

Under the Tudor monarchs Placentia reached the height of its splendour. Henry VII enlarged it handsomely, in particular by a brick frontage to the river, and here his second son, Henry, was born on June 28, 1491, and eighteen years later was married to Catherine of Aragon in the Friars' church. On February 18, 1516, their daughter, Mary, was born here, and christened two days later in the same chapel. Because it was his birthplace, or because of its easy reach by river from London, Placentia, or Greenwich Palace, as it came to be called, was one of the favourite palaces of Henry VIII.

It occupied about seventeen acres. On the north it was bounded by the Thames, on the south by the high road to

[1] The notes will be found together at the end of the book (pp. 361–398).

Woolwich, which separated it from the park. On high ground within the park stood Duke Humphrey's tower, which had been substantially repaired in 1525. On the east was a narrow way to the river, and on the west the Friars' road ran from the park to the Friary. The water-terrace and river-steps of the north frontage were on ground built up from the river, and here, direct from the Thames, were the stairs and water-gate which constituted the main entrance to the Palace. On the landward side the chief approach was from the east over Shooter's Hill —the way taken by Anne of Cleves in 1540, when the brush and furze of the common were specially cut to make a way for her. She, and other important visitors approaching from the land, came in by the Friars' road, and entered the Palace precincts by a door leading from the stables to the Friars' church, and then went in by the great water-gate. This led to an outer court, from which opened the great hall, lying east and west. On the east were the chapel and vestry; to the rear were three courts —the conduit court, where a special balcony was constructed for Anne Boleyn to watch the cockfighting, the cellar court, and the tennis court. To the south-east was the tilting-yard, with a tower for viewing the tournaments; to the south-west were the gardens and orchard, the cemetery and garden of the friars. In the south-east corner, beyond the tiltyard, the boys of the chapel choir were lodged, and temporary buildings for banquets and apartments for royal visitors were erected. Here also were the still-house, the brewery and bakery, the laundry, and the other services essential to make the Palace virtually self-contained, as well as some of the lodgings of the permanent staff of the Palace, containing, perhaps, a parlour, kitchen, buttery, barn, and yard, besides bedrooms.[3]

Greenwich Park contained much fine timber, as well as the hawthorn bushes which were the object of many royal maying expeditions,[4] and was kept well stocked with deer. Nearer the Palace were the well-cared-for orchard and gardens beautified by fountains and architectural ornaments and a profusion of simple and sweet-smelling flowers, for tending which the Keeper of the Orchard and Gardens at Pleasaunce was in the reign of Elizabeth paid £18 5s. a year and the gardener £7 4s. 2d.[5]

The responsibility for keeping the Palace ready for the immediate occupation of the sovereign and his guests fell to several members of the royal household. The office of Keeper of the Manor of Pleasaunce with Greenwich Park and Tower was held successively by gentlemen close to the Crown—by a Cecil, a Sackville, the Earl of Northampton—whose salary of less than £20 a year was augmented by leases of land and tenements in the district.[6] The actual work of the Palace and its grounds was done by humbler people—by the Keeper of the Standing Wardrobe, by keepers of gardens and orchard, of venery and falcons, by yeomen of the armoury, and by the yeoman of the pastry, who had charge of game, hare, and wild-fowl in the manor for wages of 8d. a day and 26s. 8d. yearly for livery.[7]

To the Keeper of the Standing Wardrobe fell the task of caring for the furniture, carpets, hangings, and other permanent furnishings of the Palace. It was a post which Thomas Hixon, who became Keeper or Gentleman of the Standing Wardrobe in 1593, in succession to Thomas Mayneman, was proud to hold.[8] He was privileged to live and board with his family within the royal Palace,[9] was supplied with livery, with the services of a man to help him, and the salary of 8d. a day in addition. His total salary was £27 5s. a year—three times as much as the Wardrobe Keepers at Oatlands or Richmond, more than twice that of the Keepers at the Tower, more than his colleagues at Windsor and Westminster—more even than the Keeper of the Orchard and Gardens at Greenwich. He was more highly paid, too, than the Master of the Queen's Barge, who received only £16 8s. 1d. a year, and the Chief Waterman, who received £18 1s. 1d.[10]

Thomas Hixon had had a good life.[11] After a brief period as Groom of the Chamber an increasing restlessness led him to take service for the Protestant cause under Henry IV of France —in spite of his marriage to Margaret Manley, a gentlewoman, the daughter of Thomas Manley of the county of Chester.[12] His growing family brought him again to Court, and to the pleasant office of the Standing Wardrobe at Greenwich, with the comfortable apartment within the Palace precincts.[13]

Greenwich was a good place for rearing a family, with clearer, cleaner air than the capital [14]: of the Hixons' eight children, only two died young.[15] From the hill on which stood Duke Humphrey's tower they could look over the great sweep of the Thames that almost turned the opposite shore into an island.

The shipyards of Woolwich and Deptford could be clearly seen, and the hammer-blows, the shouts, and the songs of the workmen rose up from the banks. The river was thronged with ships of all kinds—men-of-war, trading vessels, barges for goods and passengers, the Tyneside colliers bringing the popular ' sea-coal ' for the growing population of the capital, and innumerable small pleasure-boats. Over the fields their masts could be seen rising as if from the grass, and their sails floated swiftly through the meadows. The cries of the water-men, with the songs and even the banter of their fares, mingled with the noises from the shipyards and the sounds of unloading coal. To the north-west the Tower of London and the huddle of the City were seen, and farther away the Palace and Abbey of Westminster rose from the river. From here there was little to mark the new industrial developments round London, and the narrow streets of Southwark and Wapping held close their little factories for the manufacture of paper and alum, glass and beer and soap.

Nearer at hand were the lush grazing meadows preserved from tillage for some of the most profitable pasture in the country. Trees edged the ditches that cut the great meadows into a patchwork of smaller fields, emphasizing their pattern. Taller poplars lined the roads that connected the farms and villages. A couple of miles to the south-east lay the Palace of Eltham, abandoned by Queen Elizabeth in favour of Greenwich, its great hall with its lofty gable roof and double bay windows standing high amid its trees, as it had done since its completion by Edward IV in 1479. From Greenwich hill the road that connected it with its little village of Eltham could be clearly marked.[16]

In these villages south of the Thames many Hixons lived, and Thomas and his family worshipped in the little church of St Alphege, to the west of Greenwich Palace. But at first there was no record of their names, for the parish registers began only in 1615. They do not record the marriage of Thomas Hixon and Margaret Manley, nor the births of Robert, Humphrey, Thomas, John, William, Elizabeth, Margaret, and Catherine, nor the deaths of the eldest son and the daughter Elizabeth.[17]

The Hixons shared with many friends and colleagues the daily life of Greenwich Palace. Among the people who lived by personal service to the Tudor sovereigns there was always a new story to recount or an old one to remember. The revels of Henry VIII loomed large in the narrative, and the splendid show when the Emperor Charles V landed at Greenwich at six in the evening on June 2, 1522. Thomas Hixon was too young to remember Catherine and the two Annes, but the old men told him of the gaiety of Anne Boleyn when she first came to Greenwich, of Campeggio and the great Wolsey, who came to argue with Catherine and went away unsatisfied, of the gay Christmas and New Year kept by Henry and Anne, of their daughter, Elizabeth, who had been born here on September 7, 1533, and christened in the Friars' church. But as Catherine left Placentia for Eltham, so Anne left for the Tower and the scaffold, and in due time Anne of Cleves came riding over Shooter's Hill.

And now they were all dead, and Edward and Mary were dead too, and not even its close personal associations with Henry VIII had protected the Friary from dissolution with other monasteries. But Greenwich was still the favourite palace of the monarch, and in the first year of her reign the City Companies had welcomed Elizabeth by sending to Greenwich a quota of 1400 men-at-arms, who marched down from London and mustered in the park in their arms. Twenty years later there was a far different episode on the Thames, when a young man, boating with friends between Greenwich and Deptford while the Queen was on the river, accidentally shot and wounded one of the royal oarsmen. The Queen remained calm, but her pardon was not granted until four days later, when the young man stood at the gibbet by the waterside with the rope round his neck.[18]

Whenever the royal barge brought Elizabeth down from Westminster, Thomas Hixon and his assistant were prepared. Daily they tended the great hangings of arras with their stories from the Old Testament, the tapestries woven with classical as well as Biblical themes, the great bedsteads with their richly wrought curtains in cloth of silver and crimson damask, the fine sheets and counterpanes, the chairs and stools and cushions, many covered with cloth of gold, with silver and crimson satin, bearing the royal arms, or occasionally the cypher of an Anne or a Jane. They inspected and dusted the portraits; they cleaned and polished the silver and the pewter.[19]

Visitors from home and abroad thronged the Court at Greenwich. A German traveller named Paul Hentzner came in 1598,

and took very careful note of the Queen and all about her.
He spoke afterwards of her floors " after the English fashion
strewed with rushes " [20]—too wide a generalization for those
who knew well the great and small carpets within their care.
Not only famous people, but many ordinary visitors from other
parts of the country, came to see the Queen and the Court,
and many young men fringed the retinue of her courtiers.
Thomas Hixon's own wife was from Chester. His second son,
Humphrey, married Mary, the daughter of John Bradshaw of
Lancaster, neighbour to the family who produced the regicide.
His son Thomas married Anne, daughter of John Marselyne,
bachelor of divinity of Raydon, in Suffolk. John married
Elizabeth, daughter to Sir Thomas Cave, of Stanford, in
Northamptonshire.[21]

Now, in 1599, Thomas Hixon's daughter Margaret was to
marry Richard Lilburne, a young man from County Durham
in the service of the Earl of Northumberland.[22] His three sons
had married well. He could not be so sure of this marriage.
Durham was far away, and the Lilburne family home of
Thickley Punchardon might be as outlandish as its name.
Plague was endemic in the North, and with bad harvests and
indifferent husbandry much of Northumberland and Durham
was virtually waste land. Moreover, Richard Lilburne, although
likeable enough, was only sixteen years old.[23] But he was a
gentleman, an eldest son and well-connected, bearing the arms
of the ancient Lilburnes of Northumberland and Durham—
three water bougets sable upon a silver ground. His grandfather, magnificently accoutred, had attended Henry VIII at
the Field of the Cloth of Gold,[24] and his personal and landed
property was not inconsiderable. He had come to Greenwich
to see something of the Court and the capital, and would remain,
for a while at least, with the Court. So, on October 29, 1599,
Richard Lilburne of Durham and Margaret Hixon of Greenwich were married in the church of St John the Baptist,
Eltham,[25] within the orbit of Elizabeth's Court, and in the full
flowering of the Elizabethan Age.

Edmund Spenser died in the year they married, but in that
year alone they might have been present at first nights of
Dekker's *Shoemaker's Holiday*, of Ben Jonson's *Every Man
Out of his Humour*, of Shakespeare's *Twelfth Night*, *Henry V*,

and *As You Like It*. In an age when families preserved and
passed on their chests of viols and when every barber's shop
kept a cittern for the use of waiting customers, they would
have been unusual if they had not played a musical instrument
and sung at sight to the music of Byrd, Morley, Palestrina, or
of Thomas Tallis, who lay buried in the church of St Alphege.

They had both grown up in the sense of security which
followed the execution of the Queen of Scots in 1587 and the
defeat of the Spanish Armada the following year. They were
perhaps unaware when they married that they had also
witnessed the end of an era with the passing of the great seamen
and statesmen of Elizabeth. The sinking of the *Revenge* and
the death of Grenville in 1591 was a fitting postscript to the
story of the Sea Dogs. The burial of Hawkins and Frobisher
in 1595, and of Drake himself in the following year, were
less sensational. The passing of Walsingham in 1590 and of
the aged Burghley a year before their marriage affected them
less than the slaying of the poet Christopher Marlowe in a
tavern brawl near by, and his burial in St Nicholas Church,
Deptford, sometimes called West Greenwich, on June 1, 1593.

They would have been more than usually prescient young
people if they had been aware of the formation in the year of
their marriage of the East India Company and of the sailing
of the first of the Company's fleets from Torbay in the following
year. Nor could the birth of Oliver Cromwell in the year they
married have meant anything to them; nor, perhaps, the birth
of a second son, Charles, to James VI of Scotland in the
following year. They were more sharply aware of the career
of Robert Devereux, Earl of Essex, the Queen's favourite in the
year they married, but executed for treason two years later.

The rising prices of articles of common use—coal, soap,
salt, starch, leather, fruit, books, and wine—rarely affect the
young, and never directly affect those who are provided for
by great households; but the Parliamentary discussions—
particularly those of 1601, when the Parliament summoned to
contribute to the cost of war instead denounced monopolies—
could hardly pass unnoticed by those who lived within the
sight and influence of Westminster.

But, in spite of portents, it was only when the Queen lay
dying at Richmond—having gone upstream instead of down

on her last journey—that they felt they had come to the end of an epoch. Mixed with grief at the passing of a monarch who had been at the centre of their lives for as long as most of them could remember were the questions which all members of her household were bound to ask. Would James of Scotland succeed his cousin ? Which of her palaces would he favour ? Which of her household servants would he retain ? Anxiously James's progress from Edinburgh to London was watched by all his subjects, and more particularly by those whose living depended directly upon the sovereign. On the whole they were all pleased with the easy good nature of James; they marked his promises, his love of the chase, his profuse awarding of knighthoods. The presentation of a petition for the reform of church ritual signed by a thousand Puritan clergymen led to the Conference at Hampton Court in 1604, where James displayed his erudition and skill in debate and showed a shrewd knowledge of English affairs.

James talked also to his first Parliament, which, determined to make a stand at the beginning of the reign, challenged the King on cases of privilege and Parliamentary returns. It won on both issues, and proceeded to question the royal interests in purveyance and wardship. When James refused its proposals it recorded in the *Apology of the House of Commons* the " liberties and privileges " which were the right and due inheritance of the Commons of England, and which included free election, freedom from arrest, and freedom of speech. James's reply was testy. He found in his Parliament, he said, " nothing but curiosity, from morning to evening, to find fault " with his propositions. It continued to do so. James's every effort to raise money outside Parliament was obstructed by the House of Commons, even when approved by his judges and sanctioned by his Ministers. Thus began the battle of principles and words between King and Parliament. Richard Lilburne was close to the main actors. How deep was the impression made on him by this talk of " liberties and privileges " ? How much of the spirit of these years did he pass on to his sons ? Was his later Puritanism then engendered ? Or, thinking of his home so near the border lands, did he follow with greater interest the proposal for a union between England and Scotland ?

When he was not hunting or otherwise on the move James
kept his Court mainly at Whitehall or Hampton Court, but
his queen was frequently at Greenwich. Two of his daughters
were born here, and in 1606 Christian IV of Denmark came
to Greenwich to visit his sister, Queen Anne. But Thomas
Hixon, now many times a grandfather, had played his part
often enough in Court affairs, and in the same year—it was
the year following the unmasking of Guy Fawkes—he resigned
his office of Wardrobe Keeper, and his eldest surviving son,
Humphrey, succeeded him.[26]

Humphrey and his brother Thomas both had large families,
but his brother John was childless and would remain so. That
Margaret and Richard Lilburne were still without issue was
possibly owing to their extreme youth when they married, or
perhaps to the loss of children in the bad plague years at the
beginning of the century: their family was to come fourteen
years after their marriage.

In 1605 John Lilburne, father of Richard, died, and was
buried in the family church of St Andrew's, Auckland, on
March 30.[27]   Richard went with his wife to assume his
responsibilities as eldest son and to take over the family home
of Thickley Punchardon. While in the North the Lilburnes'
three eldest children were born. There was first a girl, Elizabeth, then Robert in February 1614, and John in 1615. Richard
was probably not at home at the time of the heraldic visitation
of Richard St George, Norroy King of Arms, in 1615, for his
brother, George, signed for him when reporting Robert, aged
two, John, and Elizabeth.[28]

Robert was the only one of the Lilburne children to be
born in the family home and recorded in the family church:
he was baptized at St Andrew's, Auckland, on February 2,
1614. Elizabeth, the eldest child, was born on one of the
frequent family visits to relations at Newcastle or Sunderland.
John Lilburne was born at Sunderland in 1615 in time to be
included in the statement to Norroy King of Arms.[29]

Shortly afterwards the Lilburnes again came south. While
they had been away the aged Salisbury and the young Prince
Henry had died, the Princess Elizabeth had been married with
much pomp to the Elector Palatine, and a Parliament of 1614

—the " addled " Parliament—had failed to come to terms with the King. Robert Carr, establishing himself as King's favourite, had ruled as Viscount Rochester and Earl of Somerset, but was already—after the scandals attaching to his marriage with Lady Essex and the murder of Sir Thomas Overbury—waning before the rising star of George Villiers, who became Earl of Buckingham in 1617. Sir Thomas Roe had sailed up the Amazon in 1610–11, and a first shipment of tobacco had been received from Virginia in 1614. The Lilburnes probably returned shortly after the death of Shakespeare in April 1616, and before the Lord Chief Justice Coke fell from power in November of that year.

During the Lilburnes' absence James had given Greenwich Palace to Queen Anne: they may have returned in time to see her lay the foundation-stone in June 1617 of the new house in the park designed by Inigo Jones. Certainly the Lilburnes' youngest son, Henry, was born at Greenwich in 1618. He is the only one of the Lilburne children to appear in the parish register of St Alphege, being baptized here on October 21, 1618,[30] in the same month that Sir Walter Raleigh was executed in Old Palace Yard. Nine months later Henry's grandfather, Thomas Hixon, was buried in the church on July 10, 1619 [31]: it may have been his failing health which had brought the family again to Greenwich. A little more than a year after Henry's baptism his mother also died, and was buried in Greenwich parish church on November 15, 1619, four months after her father.[32] A mourning family composed the memorials to father and daughter which were placed over the door and on the north wall of the church where so many generations of household servants lay buried.

With the death of Thomas Hixon and of Margaret Lilburne within a few months of each other, the Lilburne associations with Greenwich came to an end. Richard Lilburne travelled by sea with his three sons and his daughter to Newcastle, and thence by road to the family home in Thickley Punchardon. But years later, when part of the Manor and Palace of Greenwich were sold during the Commonwealth, a lodging near the tiltyard was sold to Edward Sexby,[33] a friend and agent of John Lilburne in many matters. Is it fanciful to believe that John, always sentimental, was buying his grandparents' house through his friend?

CHAPTER TWO

The Lilburnes of Durham

I am the Sonne of a Gentleman, and my Friends are of rancke
and quality in the Countrie where they live.

JOHN LILBURNE, *A Worke of the Beast*, 1638

FEW SHIPS VENTURED INTO THE NORTH SEA BETWEEN NOVEMBER
and March, so it was probably in the late spring of 1620, some
six months after the death of Margaret Lilburne, that the
Lilburne family set sail from the Thames on the three-hundred-
and-fifty-mile voyage to the Tyne. They passed the familiar
sights of the river, the pleasure-boats and the trading vessels,
perhaps looked back where the *Golden Hind* still lay at anchor
off Deptford, saw an East Indiaman unloading spices for the
East India Company, heard the loud-voiced, burly coal-
heavers boarding the Newcastle colliers that lay at anchor in
the river, and saw them shovelling the coal into the wooden
vats, which they emptied over the ship's side into the waiting
lighter. They passed the royal dockyard at Woolwich, and
soon left the homely river and turned into the North Sea on
the turbulent journey to Newcastle. The voyage would not be
smooth, even in the kindest weather, but shipwreck was not
common, and the risk of pirates, though real enough to be
exciting, was not as great as if they had been sailing in the
Channel.

If they could have disembarked at Sunderland they would
have been nearer their home, but not only was the harbour of
Sunderland in ill-condition to deal with large ships, but the
bar at the mouth of the Wear was so choked with sand and
rubbish that most ships of any size preferred to dock at Newcastle.[1] Moreover, Richard's younger brother, George, was
established at Newcastle as merchant and town counsellor.
So, about two weeks after leaving the Thames, they negotiated
the Black Middens and turned into the deep haven of the Tyne,

" indeed a river to be out-done by few in the whole kingdom." [2]
They passed the little village of Tynemouth and saw Tynemouth
Castle, the eleventh-century monastery fortified in the reign of
Henry VII, standing apparently unassailably on its high rock
to the north of the estuary. In years to come Henry Lilburne
would test its impregnability in the desperate encounter in the
Civil Wars which cost him his life.

The Lilburnes sailed past Jarrow, with its monastery, the
home of Bede, past the salt marshes to the south where coal
was already being used to dry out the salt for the prosperous
salt industry, past numerous little villages, until they ran into
Newcastle and were at last in Lilburne country.

The Lilburnes were originally a Northumberland family,
taking their name from the villages of East and West Lilburn,
in the parish of Bamburgh, County Northumberland, which,
in turn, derived from the Lil-burn, or -bourn, one of the streams
which watered the parish. By the beginning of the thirteenth
century a family of landowners were resident at Lilburn who
were using the name of the village as their own, and the name
became common in deeds. A Robert of Lilburn was one of the
twenty-four knights who, in 1245, surveyed the boundaries
between England and Scotland.[3] In the following century the
family spread over the county, but it was John of Lilburn who,
in the early fourteenth century, raised the family both to fame
and to the ranks of the great landowners. He was the nephew
and heir of Christine of Lilburn, through whom he inherited
" livery of the manor of Lilburn as one knight's fee " on
October 26, 1324.[4] He was knighted, becoming the first Sir
John Lilburn, at the King's Court at Christmas, 1315, and a
few months after was appointed Constable of Mitford Castle.
He added considerably to his lands, including the barony of
Stamford and Dunstanburgh, and was appointed Constable of
Dunstanburgh Castle in 1323, where he built the famous
Lilburn Tower, part of which is still standing. He was Com-
missioner of Array in Northumberland in 1325 and Sheriff of
Northumberland from 1327 to 1329.

Sir John Lilburn attended the Parliament at York in
February 1328; to the Parliament summoned to meet on
November 12, 1384, his grandson, another Sir John, was called.
This Sir John was resident at Shawdon when a son was born

on February 22, 1387. Sir John rode to Alnwick and invited
Henry Percy, first Earl of Northumberland, and the Abbot of
Alnwick Abbey to be the child's godparents. The Earl was
actually present at the child's baptism at Bolton church—
evidence of the family's powerful connexions.[5] The grandson
of this Sir John became Constable of that very Alnwick Castle
to which his grandfather had ridden in 1387 to summon a
Percy to a Lilburn baptism.

By this time Lilburnes were already settled in the neighbouring county, for a William Lilburne is recorded about 1380 as
holding land at Thickley, in County Durham, by right of
his wife. In 1434 another William, brother of the Constable
of Alnwick Castle, received by grant of Robert Ogle of Bothell
" the manors of Thickley Punchardon and Shildon, co. Durham
and all his messuages, lands etc. there." [6] The reason for the
grant is obscure, but William and his descendants remained at
Thickley Punchardon and were independent of the Northumberland Lilburnes. William's great-granddaughter, Margaret,
married a Claxton. His great-great-grandson, Bartholomew,
attended the Field of the Cloth of Gold and left magnificent
body armour and other effects to his sons.[7] One of these sons,
John, married Isabel Worthy. The three sons of this John
and Isabel were Richard, George, and Joseph.[8] It was Richard
who now, fifteen years after the death of his father, was
returning, a widower with four children, to Thickley Punchardon.

Although none of the later Lilburnes reached the eminence
of the first or second Sir John, they had, by the seventeenth
century, spread widely over the northern counties, not only as
landed squires and poorer peasants, but as merchants, industrialists, teachers, and preachers, playing their part in
industry, commerce, and local government.

In Newcastle and Sunderland they established themselves
firmly on the back of the expanding trade and industry of the
district. A fifteenth-century Richard Lilburne was a Newcastle
merchant.[9] A sixteenth-century Thomas was important in the
town,[10] while another sixteenth-century merchant, Robert
Lilburne, on March 27, 1539, appeared at a muster of the town
of Newcastle carrying a bow and wearing " a cot of playt " [11]
and " a steill bonet." But the greatest benefits from the
merchant connexion were reaped by Sir Thomas Lilburne,

who in 1633 was working the flourishing Benwell Mine, among the most important on Tyneside,[12] and by George Lilburne, younger brother of Richard of Thickley Punchardon. George was town counsellor of Newcastle in 1600, and was probably here when his brother came north in 1620. Later he moved to the rising town of Sunderland, where his expansive energies had more scope, and by investing in collieries, obtaining leases of others, and selling them at a profit, as well as by trade in general, he prospered and became wealthy.[13] One of his daughters, Isabel, married Benjamin Ellison, a Merchant Adventurer and member of a successful and wealthy Newcastle family.[14] Another daughter, Elizabeth, later married a dissenting minister of Easington named William Pell.[15]

In Yorkshire, meantime, another branch of the family had produced another Richard, a schoolmaster of Kirkby Wharf. This Richard became a Roman Catholic in August 1603 or 4 [16]—a circumstance never mentioned by the Durham Lilburnes, perhaps because of their own Puritan leanings, or because it was not an occurrence to meet with much publicity, even within the family.

Newcastle was new after the Conquest. In the seventeenth century the town was still surrounded by the strong stone wall which had been built against the Scots. A walk ran on top of the wall, and under it, on the river side, one of the most striking features of the approach by boat was the series of water-gates inhabited by coal-merchants and shippers of various kinds.[17] For Newcastle was already famed for the sea-coal with which it provided much of England, including the capital, and the Low Countries. During the sixty years from 1565 to 1625 the shipments of coal from Newcastle probably increased at a more rapid rate than at any other period in their history, being about 400,000 tons at the later date. Between Richard Lilburne's first departure to Greenwich and his return with his family in 1620 coal shipments had about quadrupled.[18]

The collieries stretched along both sides of the river, mostly to the west of Newcastle and near enough to the river to make shipment easy. Many of the pits were new, and most of the mining was deeper than it was when Richard Lilburne left the North as a young man for the Court. Seams which had been abandoned when the surface coal was exhausted had been opened up and dug more deeply with the help of new pumps, and now a line of new pits, most of them more than fifteen fathoms deep, stretched along both banks of the river for nearly eight miles west of Newcastle.[19]

In the hospital of St Mary in the west gate was the Royal Grammar School, founded by Thomas Horsley, alderman and mayor of the town in 1525 and 1533, who left his lands for the purpose. Here John Lilburne was to go to school under the mastership of Francis Grey.[20]

From Newcastle the Lilburnes travelled twenty-five miles by road to Bishop Auckland, where they were in the heart of Lilburne country. So many Lilburnes lay buried in the church of St Andrew's, Auckland, that the porch was named the Lilburne porch.[21] In the market-place stood the Grammar School, of which Richard Lilburne was governor—one of "twelve discreet and honest men" who were by statute appointed.[22] The school had been founded by King James in 1604 in perpetuation of an earlier school for instructing youth in Greek and Latin grammar and other good literature. In it the Lilburne sons would begin their education.

Bishop Auckland was a pleasant town situated at the confluence of the rivers Wear and Gaunless, the hills enclosing it rising steeply from the town and their lower slopes bright with gardens. Its castle was begun by Anthony Bek, Bishop of Durham, in the fourteenth century, and Newton bridge over the Wear had been built in 1388. It was still within the coal-producing area, though here the collieries were neither so thick nor so fruitful. Lower down the Wear they clustered more thickly, and Sunderland owed much of its importance to the export of coal from its river, which in 1620 had risen to about 35,000 tons a year.[23]

From Bishop Auckland a ride of three and a half miles south-east brought the family to their home at East Thickley, or Thickley Punchardon, a small township containing little but the Lilburne manor. It was said to have acquired its distinctive name from Hugh de Pountchardon, who in the fourteenth century had been granted by Bishop Anthony Bek the lands which were acquired by William of Lilburne in 1434.[24] The neighbouring manor of Shildon was part of the original grant, but in the time of Richard Lilburne it was probably

already leased to the Bellasis family.[25]   Thickley itself is
recorded as being held by Richard Lilburne's father of Prince
Charles at one knight's fee of 40s. a year.   It consisted of 200
acres of arable land, 100 acres of meadow, and 200 acres of
pasture, with two messuages.[26]   Two messuages only would
suggest a certain measure of enclosure and depopulation, or
perhaps merely of depopulation in the bad years at the end of
the previous century.   With 300 acres of pasture and meadow,
the Lilburnes were perhaps cattle or hay merchants, a supposition supported by the well-watered and rolling nature of the
country round Thickley.   The arable may have been held as
a separate farm.   Richard's grandfather, Bartholomew, who
bequeathed the splendid body armour to his sons, left an
inventory which included also farm and household goods and
animals, but did not mention either the nature or extent of his
holdings or any substantial quantity of stock, his concern seeming to be with domestic animals and those with young—perhaps
those that were tended more immediately at the house and by
the family.   These included six kine with calves or in calf, 29
wethers and ewes, 14 hogs, a sow and three pigs, and a mare
with her follower.   There was a quantity of wheat, oats, and
rye, fifteen acres of growing wheat, and—the most substantial
item—eight oxen, valued at £15 6s. 8d., a team which would
probably plough the 200 acres of arable.

From the price at which tithes changed hands in the Middle
Ages the land seems to have been fertile, and the Lilburnes of
Thickley, though in the lower ranks of the landowning gentry,
would, in good times, have led a reasonable though not
extravagant gentleman's existence; in the poor conditions pre-
vailing at the beginning of the seventeenth century life would
not have been easy for a widower with four young children.

The household goods and furnishings given in Bartholomew
Lilburne's inventory had almost certainly been added to by
the time his great-grandson grew up at Thickley half a century
later.   But the boy doubtless knew the two feather-beds with
their gear, the four chests, the brass, pewter, and copper ware,
as well as the armour and accoutrements used by the warrior
of the Field of the Cloth of Gold.[27]

Little distinguished Thickley Punchardon from the country
around.   Several small collieries producing probably not more

than 5000 tons of coal a year were a few miles away, and one—
Carterthorne—produced considerably more.[28] But Richard
Lilburne's family appeared to have no interest in these: coal
and trade were part of their background, but no more, and
they are not likely to have achieved the high standard of living
enjoyed by their Newcastle and Sunderland relations.

Apart from its mines and the trade of Newcastle and Sunderland, County Durham in the early seventeenth century was in
bad condition. These northern lands had never been so prosperous as those of the South. Durham was sufficiently near
the border to feel the effects of centuries of frontier strife, and,
more recently, repeated epidemics of plague and a series of bad
harvests had run down the husbandry of the country and reduced much land to waste. A reporter at the end of Elizabeth's
reign had estimated that of 8000 acres formerly in tillage not
eight score were then being tilled, and that thousands of people
were homeless and starving.[29] This may partly have accounted
for the long absence at Court of Richard Lilburne, an eldest
son and heir.

There was considerable discontent in the North. The union
of the Crowns of England and Scotland in the person of James I
had reduced border warfare, but James had done little to im-
prove the condition of the county. On the contrary, he dis-
regarded the immunity from taxation traditionally granted to the
border lands, and in 1610 the inhabitants were charged with a
subsidy. The retort of the inhabitants of Durham was to request
the representation in Parliament which they had not previously
sought. A Bill in 1623 was brought forward to that effect, but
James refused to ratify it, and in 1627 they petitioned his son,
again vainly, that they might either be called to Parliament or
else enjoy their former immunity. The County Palatine of
Durham returned no Members to Parliament until 1654, and
then two Lilburnes shared the honour of being its first representatives—George Lilburne, uncle of John, and Robert Lilburne, John's elder brother. Two years later Thomas Lilburne,
son of George and cousin of John, and James Clavering of
Axwell were the two county Members returned to Cromwell's
Parliament of 1656.[30] Such confidence in the Lilburnes was a
striking testimony of the esteem in which the family was held.

The religious heritage of the county was mixed. It was

near enough to Scotland to hear the blast of Knox's trumpet, and the influence of the Bishop of Durham was naturally of importance. Bishop Pilkington, who held the see from 1560 to 1576, was a known Puritan sympathizer, and his Dean, William Whittingham, was a friend and supporter of Calvin, a defacer of church monuments, and the chief translator of the Geneva Bible. Thomas Lever, who was appointed Prebendary in 1564, was a member of the reformed Church. He was joined for a year by John Foxe, when several of the clergy were reported to have refused the apparel, and there was considerable Puritan zeal in the county. On the other hand, the rebellion of the Catholic earls at the end of 1569—in the lifetime of John Lilburne's grandfather—cannot have failed to leave a mark on most Durham families both because of the strength of the Roman Catholic religion then revealed and because of the severity of the repression when the whole district was under martial law. Though Romanism was less in evidence after the suppression, there was undoubtedly a considerable amount of underground papistry, and recusant lists were regularly drawn up. Towards the end of the century Jesuit priests were influential in the area, and Sir William Bowes complained in 1595 that " False and disloyall religion " was taking deep root, not only through the number and diligence of the seminaries, but because " scant three able preachers " were to be found in the whole county to preach true religion.[31] Severity following the Gunpowder Plot of 1605 had little effect in suppressing the Roman religion, and in 1616, shortly before the Lilburnes returned to Thickley Punchardon, it was reported that " throughout the bishopric of Durham popery prevails, so that at the ports, Hartlepool, Sunderland, etc., the recusants can import and export as they will." [32]

A year after this Bishop Neile, the friend and patron of William Laud, became Bishop of Durham, and introduced the ceremonial and the doctrinal changes associated with Arminianism. He was also closely in touch with the King, supporting him on his use of the prerogative. Robert Hutton, rector of Houghton-le-Spring, not far from Thickley Punchardon, was one of those strongly opposed to Neile, and he preached against his practices in 1621. More resounding, though not quite on Lilburne home territory, was Peter Smart's famous sermon preached in Durham Cathedral on July 27, 1628, to the text: " I hate them that hold of superstitious vanities." He called the altar " a damnable idol," those who bowed to it " spiritual fornicators," and the bishops " Rome's bastardly brood still doating upon their mother, the painted harlot of the Church of Rome." Smart's sermon caused a " great noise . . . and tongues began to walk at large," and it is unlikely that John Lilburne, then an impressionable schoolboy of ten or twelve, could have failed to hear of it and have been stirred in one way or another by its language. Smart was brought before a hastily constituted Court of High Commission at 2 P.M. on the day the sermon was preached. He was deposed, degraded, and fined £500—in lieu of which he chose to go to prison, where he remained for nearly twelve years, until released by the Long Parliament.[33] His was, perhaps, the first example of suffering for the Puritan cause of which John Lilburne consciously took note.

All over the country, meantime, the main lines of the struggle whose beginnings Richard Lilburne had watched from Greenwich were being drawn with an incisiveness that could not be eradicated and a breadth that comprehended all aspects of social life. Forces that had been building up below ground for centuries destroyed existing contours, and the fissures they created were spreading throughout the social structure, cracking existing relationships in religious and economic, political and constitutional affairs. The Elizabethan compromise in religion had arrested the quarrel between High Churchman and Puritan; the charm of Elizabeth, aided by booty from the Spanish treasure-ships, had obscured the fact that the monarchy was in debt; her strength and wisdom in dealing with both Parliament and people had postponed constitutional tensions and checked economic rivalry. With weaker people at the helm—monarchs with less wisdom but stronger fixed beliefs— the underlying strain was bound to show. With a monarchy favouring Roman Catholicism and restoring High Church practices, sermons like Peter Smart's were bound to be commended. Already, in the September after the Lilburnes left London, the *Mayflower* had sailed with her Puritan emigrants

to the New World, and while the Lilburnes were settling in
to their first winter in the bleak North the Pilgrim Fathers
were facing a still bleaker existence beyond the Atlantic as
they sought to establish the freedom of worship they were
denied at home.

A month after the *Mayflower* sailed James's son-in-law, the
Elector Palatine, who had accepted the crown of Bohemia for
the Protestant faith, was defeated at the battle of the White
Mountain, to the embarrassment of his father-in-law, who was
negotiating a Spanish marriage for his son, the indignation
of English Protestants, and the tears of all who remembered
the Queen of Hearts.   When the following year James called
his third Parliament it readily voted money to help the Palatine,
but turned immediately to its own grievances, discussing
monopolies and impeaching the Lord High Chancellor, Francis
Bacon, for taking bribes.   When it turned again to religion
and foreign affairs it was to affirm its belief in war against the
Catholic League and against Spain in particular, and its desire
for a Protestant marriage for the Prince of Wales.   James's
response was the accusation that " fiery and popular spirits "
in Parliament were debating questions beyond their reach and
deserved imprisonment.   After more exchanges the Commons
drew up their Protestation of December 18, 1621, denying the
King's right to imprison a Member of Parliament, claiming
the right to discuss all affairs of State, and asserting that their
lives and privileges were " the ancient and undoubted birth-
right and inheritance of the subjects of England."   James
punished the leading Members by imprisonment and house
confinement, but their words were in due course heard all over
England, and would be repeated in future years by those
who, like John Lilburne, were too young to understand them
at the time.

Two years after the Commons' Protestation Prince Charles
and Buckingham went to Spain to explore for themselves the
possibilities of a Spanish match, but the rejoicings at their
return, empty-handed, were so great that the impetus launched
an expeditionary force to aid the Palatine.   When James died
in 1625 he bequeathed to his son the failure of this expedition,
a desultory pro-Protestant war, a spendthrift favourite, and a
belief in the Divine Right of Kings.   He did not leave any

recipe for dealing with his Parliaments, nor intimate any satisfactory method of raising money without them.

Two months later Charles married the fifteen-year-old Henrietta Maria, sister of the King of France, thus abandoning the Spanish match, but accepting, almost equally obviously, a Roman Catholic affiliation. It soon became clear that Charles would not come to terms with Parliament or people on any of the outstanding issues, and in 1628 Parliament drew up the famous statement which acquired the proud title Petition of Right. The following year Charles dissolved Parliament and began his eleven years' personal rule. About a year after this began, John Lilburne, then fourteen or fifteen years old, was brought by his father to London and bound apprentice to Thomas Hewson, a wholesale clothier of Londonstone.

How much of the events of the previous ten years would have been known at Thickley Punchardon? Two hundred and fifty miles from Westminster, in a quiet manor-house, in a county unrepresented in Parliament, at a time when news-sheets, even in the South, were only beginning to circulate, news would not have come quickly to the family. Moreover, Richard Lilburne was attending to his manor and rearing his children. But his life at Greenwich had attuned his ear to stories of the Court and of Westminster, and merchant connexions at Newcastle and Sunderland were closely concerned with questions of taxation and loans. And what better purveyors of news—even though a fortnight old—than the three hundred Tyne colliers?

It is unlikely that John Lilburne, as he grew up in Thickley Punchardon, Bishop Auckland, and Newcastle in the years between the sailing of the *Mayflower* and the Petition of Right, would have been unaware of the main issues between King and Parliament. He has left no impression in his writings of these years, no memories of talk between his father and uncles, but the family was remarkably unanimous in its Parliamentarian affiliations. They were all, John Lilburne said in one of his rare references to this period, educated in the Puritan tradition. He is similarly reticent about his schooling. He learnt Latin and a little Greek, and was not one of the " dronnesest " boys at school, yet one gathers that his education did not proceed far, and in after-life he frequently protested that he was no scholar and knew little Latin. His boast that he not only knew, but was known by, the most influential men of Newcastle probably indicates that the family circle was wide and his family popular.[34]

Nor did the background of Newcastle coal—the three hundred colliers plying up and down the coast, the mining activity, the miners themselves, savage, dirty, living a life apart —make any apparent impression on him. He appears to have accepted the merchant connexions of his family and taken for granted his own apprenticeship to a trade, although he was never tired of airing his pride in the fact that his family were gentlemen. It is not clear why he did not stay in the North and share the prosperity of his Newcastle and Sunderland relations. Perhaps a desire to place his son near his wife's people had something to do with the choice; perhaps the pleasant memories of his own early life in Greenwich persuaded Richard Lilburne to give his second son a similar opportunity.

There is an unauthenticated story that John Lilburne ran away from an original apprenticeship in the North.[35] Perhaps it was his own restless spirit yearning for something beyond the commercialism of Newcastle or Sunderland that urged him to seek opportunity and adventure in the capital.

CHAPTER THREE

The London Apprentice

. . . his conscience was soon awakened upon his Master's call.
Englands weeping Spectacle, June 29, 1648

THE LONDON IN WHICH JOHN LILBURNE WAS APPRENTICED WAS
a city of about a quarter of a million people, stretching for
five miles along the north bank of the Thames, three miles
along the south. The river was still a great highway for goods
and passengers, business and pleasure, and the coal-heavers
and the Thames watermen vied with each other in the extent
and variety of their invective. London Bridge was the only
foot- and carriage-way over the river, the usual way of crossing
being by one of the ferries which plied continuously from side
to side, or by a hired wherry from one of the river steps. More
than 2000 small craft, over 3000 watermen, were employed in
one way or another on the river.[1] Busy enough above the
Bridge, below, the shipping clustered so that it seemed " a
very wood of trees disbranched to make glades and let in light." [2]
To the south of the river the line of buildings was thin, and
open country and the Surrey heights came close in to the town.
But the district was becoming more crowded, and in Southwark
particularly the number of workers employed in the small but
expanding capitalist industries was growing. On Bankside the
theatres and bear garden of Shakespeare's time were still popular.

To the north of the Thames the City and Westminster now
formed a continuous line. Eastward from the City the
straggling suburbs reached to Whitechapel and beyond, en-
croaching upon the fields. But it was to the west that the main
development had taken place. Charing Cross, until recently a
separate village, now linked City and Westminster, and from
one to the other an unbroken line of buildings, mostly great
houses and palaces, fronted the river. The building-line was
deeper than to the south, and north and west of the Strand

and Whitehall many new buildings began to balance the older growth of the City. There were new houses in Cannon Row by Westminster, and behind the Strand the Convent garden of Westminster was being developed by Inigo Jones into a residential piazza in the Italian style, with a porticoed church at the west end. Jones had already completed a new banqueting-hall in Whitehall for James I, but his schemes for redesigning the Palace itself were not being carried out, chiefly through lack of money, and Whitehall Palace remained a collection of rambling buildings on both sides of the Charing Cross to Westminster road, connected by a great gateway, the Holbein Gate. Both the Palace and its gardens fronted the river, while on the other side of the road were St James's Park with the Cockpit, much used as a theatre, several minor buildings, the royal mews near Charing Cross, and Spring Gardens behind them. Where the Palace precincts ended another great gateway, the King's Gate, spanned the road. Beyond it, and connected to it by King Street, lay Westminster.

The Palace of Westminster itself had been destroyed by fire in 1512, but the Abbey and St Margaret's Church were preserved, the Painted Chamber was still used for meetings, and in the chapel of St Stephen's the Commons met. The great timbered Hall of Westminster—the finest of its kind in Europe—was still used for State trials, and many of the courts of law—Common Pleas, King's Bench, the Exchequer Court, and Chancery—sat in various parts of the Hall, with only temporary and low partitions separating them from each other and from the courtiers, politicians, and citizens, who wandered at will. A prisoner had only to raise his voice to make himself audible to his supporters, and any popular figure could be certain that his friends would rally to hear him. A few ramshackle shops defaced one of the outer walls of the Hall; booths within filled up space not occupied by the courts of law, and sold not only legal books and perquisites, but a variety of knick-knacks and drapery. Hawkers roamed without and within, both they and the more respectable booksellers with stalls within the Hall stocking news-sheets and popular pamphlets. A large number of them were certain to keep prohibited as well as licensed books as part of their stock-in-trade.

Adjoining the Hall, the Court of Wards and the Court of

Requests were also busy with the comings and goings of citizens and officers, and alive with gossip. At right-angles to it, and parallel to the river, stood the six-gabled building in which met the Court of Star Chamber. Star Chamber, Hall, and various other courts and offices formed three sides of an enclosure, the fourth and northern side comprising the famous clock-tower, whose great bell struck every hour to inform the judges of the passage of time, and the houses of cloth merchants, whose market stood behind. The area thus enclosed was known as New Palace Yard and was the scene of Star Chamber punishment by pillory and mutilation.

West and north of Westminster, lanes led through Tothill Fields and the park to open country. Farther east the churches of St Martin's and St Giles' still stood in the fields. Finsbury Fields, Moorfields, Spitalfields, Goodman's Fields, and many more green spaces lay round the Strand and the City, and footpaths led to the higher open country of Harrow and Highgate and Hampstead. The Strand was still in some sense a ' strand,' with the houses of the wealthy running down to Thames-side, but smaller buildings stood between them and the street. The northern side of the Strand was still not entirely built up, and, as well as the open hills beyond, fields showed between the buildings. Running straight through Temple Bar and into Fleet Street, it was one of the main thoroughfares into the City. At the upper end of Fleet Street the Fleet ditch— dirty, pestilential, almost an open sewer—emptied into the river, and a little to the north of the street stood the Fleet prison. Beyond the Fleet river the road ran up into Ludgate Hill, on top of which old St Paul's was beginning to show a new face in the form of a classical portico which Inigo Jones was building at the west end. Round the churchyard were already the bookshops and stalls whose numbers would multiply in the next few years, and to the north-east stood Paul's Cross, scene of public oratory and exhortation rather than of homely sermons.

Beyond St Paul's spread the City, a narrow huddle of streets, busy with trade and commerce, wealthy and self-contained. It was still a medieval city, and outside the main thoroughfares the streets were unfit for the passage of carriages, and very unpleasant for walkers. They were mostly unmade, there were few paved footways, down the centre of all but the most important streets ran the kennel which took all waste water and refuse. Sewage disposal was elementary, and often the City's defensive ditch, just outside the City walls, was the dumping-place for refuse of all kinds. Insanitary, evil-smelling, plague-ridden—the coronation ceremonies of both James and Charles had been interrupted by plague—it was nevertheless a city of enormous vitality and great wealth, its population growing, its merchants becoming richer. In spite of the movement westward, it was still the home of many men of substance, the hub of trade and commerce, the centre of printing, publishing, preaching, of talk and discussion, and, when necessary, of decisive action. Its citizens were vitally alive, conducting their business in Gresham's Exchange in Threadneedle Street, gossiping in Paul's Cathedral, thronging the innumerable churches whose spires were the most striking feature of any view of the town, clustering round Paul's Cross, rushing down the Strand for a spectacle at Charing Cross or Westminster.

Londonstone, where Lilburne lived with his master, was in Candlewright Street, or Candlewick Street, sometimes already called Cannon Street, right in the centre of the City—north of the Thames, south of the Exchange, east of St Paul's. The origin of the ancient stone was forgotten, but its size, strength, and danger to vehicles were well-known. The street itself was named from the chandlers or candle-makers who used to live there, and referred either to their trade or to the cotton or yarn wick used by them. More recently, the street had been the home of weavers brought over by Edward III, and then of rich drapers and other dealers in woollen cloth, of whom Thomas Hewson was one. He was apparently the agent of one or more of the big clothiers who sent up their bales of cloth to be sold at Blackwell Hall to merchants trading with Turkey and the East. Lilburne, the only apprentice, had a responsible position, handling money as well as stock,[3] a trust that was most likely due not only to the character of the boy himself, but to knowledge of the Lilburne or Hixon family, perhaps dating to Richard Lilburne's Greenwich days. It may even be that Hewson was a Hixon, and that the carelessness of spelling so common in the seventeenth century had resulted in the change of letters. Thomas Hewson was a Puritan, and this strengthens the supposition that the Lilburnes were already of a similar way of thinking.

The impact of London on a boy of fourteen, fresh from a country district more than two hundred miles away, must have been tremendous. When John Lilburne was left by his father with Thomas Hewson he was an eager young man noticeably North Country in speech, somewhat " rough-hewen," in manners, unused to the refinements which the sons of southern squires—even small ones—would accept. He knew neither how to doff his cap politely nor how to " make a legge with grace." [4] But he was quick to learn, high-spirited, something of a leader, and already certain of his own importance: " I had then as much mettle, life and spirit as most young men in London." [5]

Apprenticed to a Puritan master, conditioned by temperament and upbringing to the Puritan way of life, he found himself in London in the fourth decade of the seventeenth century in a veritable hotbed of Puritanism. Eighty years had passed since Elizabeth succeeded her Roman Catholic sister and the Protestant exiles came hastening back from Geneva and Holland. In that time disappointment at the failure of the Elizabethan Church settlement to adopt the reforms of Calvin had transformed the extreme wing of English Protestantism into a zealous reforming group which had been called Puritan. Definitions of the word varied from the pure in heart seeking purity in religion to a nickname indicating pious hypocrisy. It would soon cover all the extremer sects which disorder brought into existence. When Lilburne first mixed with them in London the Puritans were followers of Calvin, believing in the doctrine of Predestination, the cult of the elect, and an individual interpretation of the Scriptures. They took the Communion bread and wine as symbolic, and denied the apostolic succession of the bishops. Individualistic in doctrine, they sought to bring the individual close to God without the intervention of ceremony and ritual. In the Millenary Petition of 1603 they had asked for the abolition of the ring in marriage and of the cross in baptism. Since then they had become more insistent on simplicity of worship, condemning kneeling, bowing, crossing, the wearing of surplices, pictures, and ornament as " Roman " or " Popish," and placing their altar as a table in the body of the church.

They already differed among themselves on questions of

church organization. The Presbyterians, finding a model in the magisterial system of the Old Testament, vested authority in the presbytery, a group of ruling elders and ministers. Their churches were not autonomous, but were subject to a hierarchical control by district and national presbyteries. Their goal was the establishment of an all-embracing national Church —a Church-state like Calvin's at Geneva—in which the civil magistrate, who would be a faithful member of the Church, would punish ecclesiastical transgression in the light of the ruling of the Church elders. Until then they denied the right of the magistrate to interfere with them.

The position of the Independents was fundamentally different. Mainly followers of Robert Browne, they believed that any group of believers constituted a Church " without tarrying for any." Their Church was a congregation of believers, each one of whom had covenanted individually both with the Lord and with the rest of the congregation. ". . . a covenant was made and their mutual consent was given to hold together," wrote Robert Browne, describing the formation of his Church at Norwich. It followed that each congregation was autonomous, recognizing no synodal authority, but only the headship of Christ. There was no separate priesthood, ministers and officers being elected from the whole congregation. Over this democratic Independent Church Robert Browne had laid it down expressly that the magistrate should have no authority.

This insistence upon the removal of ecclesiastical matters from the sphere of the civil magistrate carried with it the inference either of total separation of Church and State or, where that was not practicable, of toleration to practices outside those of the Established Church. Though Browne had urged the former, the latter came to be generally held, especially after 1643, when Independents disclaimed the title of separatists.

A form of worship so lacking in rigidity as the Independent was open to the constant reception of new ideas, as expressed by the Independent pastor Henry Robinson in his parting words to the *Mayflower*: " If God reveal anything to you by other instruments of His, be as ready to receive it as ever you were to receive truth through me." By the thirties London was already alive with sects of various kinds, with individual seekers

after truth, and with many simple souls like John Lilburne,
open to receive the revelation which God would make.

Fundamental as were the differences between Presbyterians,
Independents, and the sects, while they were all fighting the
Anglican Church they maintained a loose kind of unity under
the term ' Puritan.' With the accession of the Stuarts they were
driven to close their ranks and present a temporarily united
front to King and Church.

While the foreign policy of Elizabeth had left no doubt of
her anti-Spanish and anti-Roman intentions, the uncertainties
of James's had left his attitude to Spain, to the Papacy, and
even to his daughter and her Protestant husband, in considerable
doubt. Charles I, by marrying a Roman Catholic, by permitting
Roman Catholic priests to officiate, and by showing favour to
his Roman Catholic subjects, strengthened the fear of the Roman
Church at home at a time when the victories of the counter-
Reformation in Europe, the misery of the Thirty Years War in
Germany, and the persecution of Huguenots in France were
visible evidence of the results of victorious Romanism abroad.
The Established Church of England—underpaid, pluralist,
absentee, inefficient where not corrupt—produced too few protests, too little effort at reform. Inevitably, English Puritanism
became more militant, won more recruits. It was strengthened
by the Bible, the pulpit, and the press.

It is difficult to exaggerate the importance of the Bible in
English. Printing made a reasonably cheap translation readily
available at a time when the English language was particularly
full and flexible. It reproduced the idiom of Hebrew and Greek
in rich, resounding phrases and strange, stirring images that
came to the people with the authority of the Church. English
translations had begun towards the end of the fourteenth
century with the work of Wycliffe, and a century and a half
later the Great Bible of 1539 was ordered to be chained in
every church for all to see or read. The Protestant exiles during
Mary's reign worked in Geneva at a further translation from
the original Hebrew and Greek. While in church it was most
likely the Great Bible that men heard, the Geneva Bible, of
excellent scholarship, handy in size, conveniently divided into
verses, encouraging thought and questionings by its copious

notes, became the private man's Bible, and it was most likely
on this that John Lilburne was brought up in his home in the
North.

The need for unification led the Puritan Dr John Reynolds
to suggest a new translation to the Hampton Court Conference.
The resulting Authorized Version, published in 1611, was the
joint work of a group of Puritan and Anglican divines. It
gradually came into use in churches, rather more slowly, one
supposes, in private families, although the abundance of
Bibles of all sizes printed after about 1616 indicates that many
more families than formerly acquired their own copies. Fewer
Geneva Bibles were printed after the publication of the
Authorized Version. Lilburne, when he was starting to write
pamphlets and, after the fashion of the time, prefacing his
works and interlarding his pages with Biblical texts, was using
the Authorized Version, and no Puritan at this stage seems to
have made any objection to its use or clamoured for the
Geneva Bible. With an English Bible in his hand, it was
natural for a man to believe that he could find God himself
with few auxiliary aids, and easy for him to give a personal
interpretation to every passage. More than any other single
thing, the Bible in the vernacular contributed to the growth of
religious independence.

But if the language and ideas of the English Bible were
intoxicating in print they lost nothing of their emotional
significance when thundered from the pulpit. Preaching had a
heritage which reached to the Middle Ages and earlier. Equally
important, people were accustomed to listening to miracle
plays and, more recently, to the plays of Marlowe and
Shakespeare and Jonson. The generation which thronged the
Globe Theatre flocked around the pulpits of London. The
language they heard in both places was young, vigorous,
elastic, ready to make current new words, phrases, and images
culled from the Bible, from geographical exploration, from
scientific investigation. In particular, invective borrowed from
Hebrew translated into English was most telling when both
sides knew the allusion: whore of Babylon, Bull of Bashan,
Mark of the Beast, were familiar descriptions.

Elizabeth, through a genuine spirit of toleration or the
principle of the safety-valve, allowed considerable freedom to

preachers of the beliefs whose principles she would not in-
corporate into her religious settlement. Edward Dering in
1570 told her to her face that the incumbents of her Church
were " Ruffians," " Hawkers and Hunters," " Dicers and
Carders," " Morrowmasse Priests," " blind guides, and can
not see . . . dumb dogs and will not bark." They contended
" The Parson against the Vicar, the Vicar against the Parson,
the Parish against both, and one against another, and all for
the belly." [6] Sixty more years of this had accustomed the
young men of Lilburne's generation to very strong meat. They
got it in London. Earnest apprentices heard William Gouge
at Blackfriars, Richard Sibbes at Gray's Inn, John Davenport
at St Stephen's in Coleman Street, and later John Goodwin,
who was remembered as " very profitable " years later by
John Lilburne's friend William Kiffin.[7] Across the river
could be heard Henry Jacob, who had led his congregation of
separatists back from Holland to settle in Southwark, and at
St Swithin's by Londonstone, close to Hewson's house, Lewis
du Moulin, son of the French Reformer who had been
appointed Professor at Cambridge, was accustomed to preach.

Congregations were so anxious to hear the Word that,
besides regular ministers, lecturers without cure of souls were
often attached to their churches for the sole purpose of
preaching. But even this did not satisfy a population hungry
to hear and themselves to make known the truth as they
understood it. Increasing numbers of laymen found courage
to interpret the Scriptures for themselves and to communicate
their spiritual experiences to large audiences. John Trendall,
the stonemason, preached in his own house. Samuel How,
the cobbler, preached to show " the sufficiency of the spirits
teaching without human learning," and was refused church
burial, being interred instead in Finsbury Fields in 1640.[8]
Praise-God Barebone, the leather-seller, preached in his shop
in Fetter Lane, in the City. Later John Bunyan, the tinker,
would take up the same story. Meanwhile other London
preachers were working up their audiences to a frenzy of
devotion. " God hath measured our glasse and time even
to a moment," thundered Sibbes at Paul's Cross, " and as
our Saviour Christ . . . saith, *My time is not yet come*: . . .
so let us know that till our houre comes, all the Devils in hell

cannot hurt one haire of our head: And this is a wondrous
ground of confidence, that we should cary our selves above
all threatnings, and above all feares what soever. *Thou canst
doe nothing except it were given thee*, saith Christ to bragging
Pilate, who boasted of his power: alas, what can all the
enemies of Gods people doe, except God permit them ? " [9]
Thus exhorted, what would not the Puritan listener dare !

To the Bible and the pulpit were added the influence of
printed pamphlets and books. Of the increasing number
of printed books which technical developments were making
possible, a growing proportion were religious or moral.
Between 1600 and 1640 nearly one-half of the books printed,
in some years far more, were of this nature.[10] This proportion
includes a large number of purely devotional and seemingly
non-controversial works. Two best-sellers were the books
which John Bunyan's wife brought him as her sole marriage
dowry—Arthur Dent's *The Plaine Man's Path-way to Heaven*,
which ran to twenty-five editions between 1601 and 1640,
" wherein every man may clearly see whether hee shall bee
saved or damned," and Lewis Bayly's *The Practice of Pietie*,
describing " How to read the Bible with profit and ease once
over every yeere," which reached thirty-six editions or more
between 1612 and 1636. Just after Lilburne came to London,
in the half-year ending May 1631, 3000 copies of Dent's
sermons alone were printed in London by William Turner and
Michael Sparke.[11] Though essentially there is nothing revolutionary or even Puritan in such works of devotion, yet
undoubtedly the majority of them, with their ceaseless
questioning, bolstered the spirit of non-conformity.

The Puritan works proper fell into three categories—
doctrinal works, like those of Calvin and Bèza; hortatory
works, mostly sermons, making great play with the glory of
salvation and the dread of damnation; and the martyrology,
of which Foxe's *Book* was the most complete example, but
which was being added to throughout the century.

From Calvin the reader learned that we are regenerate by
faith, that prayer is the chief exercise of faith, that it is the duty
of the faithful to yield their bodies to God, " a living holy
and acceptable sacrifice unto him." He read of " the eternall
election, whereby God hath predestinate some to salvation,

some other to destruction," of foreknowledge, of Predestination, " the eternal decree of God," of our knowledge of election, " to be searched not in the bosome of God but in our selves according to that light which he hath given us in his word." [12]

Following William Perkins, he would try to discover " how a man may know whether he be the child of God, or no." He would search for the " Graine of Mustard-seed, or, the least measure of grace, that is, or can be effectuall to salvation." [13] He sought to reply to the catechism of Thomas Cartwright: " What are the properties of God ? " ; " What is his infiniteness in time or eternitie ? " ; " What is the will of God ? " ; " What is the charge of Householders ? " ; " What is the Magistrate's part ? " [14] From Bèza he learned to distinguish " the true and visible markes of the Catholique Churche." [15]

From Foxe he not only gained inspiration, but found practical examples upon which to model his own conduct. Richard Woodman in 1557, to give one instance from many, might have been John Lilburne a century later. Having been denied a sight of the warrant for his arrest, " I will not go with you," he told the constables, " unless you will carry me by force; and if you will, do so, at your own adventures." [16]

Puritan works were subject to the general control of the press, operative since the incorporation of the Stationers' Company in 1557 gave to ninety-seven London stationers the monopoly of printing books. Two years later a licensing law made control more stringent, and in 1586, by decree of Star Chamber, the right to license a book was vested in the Archbishop of Canterbury or the Bishop of London. Thereafter it was necessary for a book first to be licensed and then registered with the Stationers' Company before being printed. The Company could search for and seize any book printed against its privilege, offenders being brought before the Court of Star Chamber, which was especially concerned with sedition or contempt of authority. The stationers, for their own advantage and backed by the law, acted as efficient instruments in ferreting out the printers and authors of unlicensed books.

In spite of this an increasing number of illegal books were printed. In 1632 *Histriomastix*, the work of the Presbyterian lawyer William Prynne, appeared. Prynne was devout and sincere, but rigid, narrow, and crabbed. He, if any, deserved the more opprobrious meanings attached to the term Puritan. He was strictly Sabbatarian, and the titles of some of his other tracts—*The Unlovelinesse of Love-Lockes* and *Healthes Sicknesse. A Compendious . . . Discourse ; proving, the drinking of healthes, to be sinfull*—both published in 1628, indicate his outlook on life. Prynne found Latin and the law highly suited to his ponderous, condemnatory style of writing. *Histriomastix*, in spite of its title, was in English, but compensated for this by being very long, crammed with marginal notes, and prefaced by texts, with two alternative titles and a very long sub-title which made clear the tract's intentions—*The Players' Scourge*, or *The Actor's Tragedie*—purporting to show " That popular Stage-plays (the very Pompes of the Divell which we renounce in Baptisme, if we beleeve the Fathers) are sinfull, heathenish, lewde, ungodly Spectacles, and most pernicious Corruptions." Women players, in particular, were stigmatized as " notorious whores."

Since not only the populace but the Court, and in particular the Queen, were fond of plays, and the Queen had been known to take part, Prynne's tract was not unnaturally regarded as an outrage, and Prynne was brought before Star Chamber on the charge of libel against the State, the King, and the people. The germ of truth in his work was not likely to be perceived by his judges, and he was sentenced to lose his academical degrees, to be fined, to stand in the pillory and have his ears cropped, and then to be imprisoned for life. All copies of *Histriomastix* were to be burnt. It can hardly be said that John Lilburne, almost certainly mingling with the crowds round the pillory in 1634, was witnessing a Puritan martyrdom, but he at least saw what happened to men who flouted the printing laws.

In the previous year William Laud, then Bishop of London, had been appointed Archbishop of Canterbury on the death of George Abbot. Abbot had inclined to the Puritan viewpoint. Laud was a man of different outlook. Reform the Church he certainly would, but, whereas the Puritans stressed the individual, personal nature of regeneration, Laud was equally concerned that the world should be aware of the reform: whereas the Puritan would find a church anywhere where one or two believers were gathered together, Laud could see one universal Church of which the English Church was part. In practice this meant that Laud enhanced the power of his bishops, who gave continuity with the first Christian Church, and called for the ritual that gave outward piety and visible uniformity to Christian worship. Not only was his sincerity greater than his opponents would credit, but there was a measure of common sense in his own statement of his beliefs that sought a way between the " unnecessary " and " superstitious " ceremonies of Rome and their complete abandonment.

" It is true," he wrote, " the inward worship of the heart is the great service of God, and no service acceptable without it; but the external worship of God in His Church is the great witness to the world, that our heart stands right in that service of God. Take this away, or bring it into contempt, and what light is there left to ' shine before men, that they may see our devotion, and glorify our Father which is in Heaven? ' . . . scarce anything hath hurt religion more in these broken times than an opinion in too many men, that because Rome hath thrust some unnecessary and many superstitious ceremonies upon the Church, therefore the Reformation must have none at all; not considering therewhile, that ceremonies are the hedge that fence the substance of religion from all the indignities which profaneness and sacrilege too commonly put upon it. And a great weakness it is, not to see the strength which ceremonies—things weak enough in themselves, God knows,—add even to religion itself." [17]

The Laudian conception of the Church was very much the counterpart of the Stuart conception of the State. Each wanted order, each implied authority reaching downward, each intended reform from above. An English Church part of a universal Church in all respects except allegiance to the Pope, preserving beauty in symbolism and ritual, spreading its ordered blessings to every corner of the land through prelacy and the Prayer Book—this was a concept held alike by Laud and Charles, and counterpoised by the idea of an integrated State watched over by a benevolent sovereign who would correct abuses and spread prosperity.

Laud and Charles never had any doubt of the value of their

partnership. If ever the late King's aphorism—" no bishop no king "—had any meaning it had it now. Church services became more elaborate, altar tables were removed from the body of the church to the east end and enclosed by rails, the authority of bishops was built up until it could be lucidly argued that their power was *jure divino*. As Puritan pulpit and Puritan pamphlet took up the opposition to the Archbishop, Church and Crown responded by enforcing the licensing laws, punishing offenders, and putting up their own preachers to cry up the prerogative of Archbishop and King.

The State side of the partnership consisted largely in keeping the King supplied with money without having to summon another Parliament: " . . . all the wheels of the prerogative were set in motion to provide money," as Bulstrode Whitelocke, Keeper of the Great Seal, recorded. Tonnage and poundage came in, though somewhat grudgingly; knighthood fines and forest fees were paid, though unwillingly; the monarch's profits from wardship were counted even more outrageous; the income supplied by monopolies drew sharper censure; forced loans and taxation met with growing asperity. The writs of ship-money caused at first little stir, though London in 1634 objected to the charge that was nominally to protect her ships from " thieves, pirates, and robbers of the sea, as well Turks, enemies of the Christian name, as others." Fines imposed on enclosing landlords, on rack-renters, on clothiers who turned their people off work without justification, did, on the whole, more good to the poor, who were thus protected, than to the privy purse. All told, the grist was insufficient and the spirit which might have augmented it was lacking.

In London the citizens were well aware of each issue— religious, economic, and constitutional—their own City constitution, the ancient tradition of their guilds, their own trained bands recruited from their own ranks, encouraging their independent outlook. To John Lilburne and to many of his friends, however, it was still at this time the religious issue which excited them most. Encouraged in his Puritan outlook by his master and by the minister Edmund Rosier, who was a familiar figure in the Hewson house, and not being over-worked, Lilburne found time, as he recounts, for reading the Bible, the *Book of Martyrs*, the works of Luther, Calvin,

Bèza, Cartwright, William Perkins, Henry Burton, Richard Rogers, and Pierre du Moulin, father of the man who preached at St Swithin's by Londonstone.[18] He could not have failed to go round the City churches and hear Sibbes and Gouge, Davenport, Norton, John Goodwin and du Moulin, and the outdoor preachers at Paul's Cross and elsewhere. With William Kiffin and other apprentices he rose early on Sunday mornings to discuss the Scriptures before sermon-time. With them he " diligently attended on the meanes of grace." Exchanging experiences and offering prayer, he battled with the storm in his soul and sought peace from the Bible and from the pulpit.[19]

But Lilburne had already a spirit attuned to earthly injustice. Within a few years of his arrival in London he was suing his master before the Lord Chamberlain on account of the abuse which Hewson sometimes showered on him. Hewson took the unusual behaviour in good part, and the affair was amicably settled, but it serves as an example of the kind of practical democracy which Puritanism engendered. With Lilburne it was more than that. It was a characteristic forecast of his future life. " I challenge you before the High Chamberlain! " was merely Lilburne's first version of the many challenges to authority which sounded throughout his life.

In 1636 the promising young man was taken by Hewson and Rosier to visit Dr John Bastwick, a Presbyterian who was imprisoned in the Gatehouse prison at Westminster for printing scandalous publications in Latin against the bishops. The rigours of normal imprisonment did not match the barbarity of physical punishment, and Bastwick's wife and children lived with him and cooked his meals, while he received his visitors and wrote his books. His chief complaint was that they were able to afford roast meat only once a week.

Among the visitors who came to Bastwick was old John Wharton, eighty-two years of age, a bookseller of Bow Lane, an implacable enemy of the bishops, a dealer in illegal books who several times had been before Star Chamber and been punished by fine and the seizure of his stock. Still a fighter, he begged Bastwick to write something in English that the people could understand. Asked to name a subject, he promptly suggested bishops. Looking at the cheerful, merry old man,

Bastwick began his *Letany*, which, he said, made Wharton laugh " as if he had bin tickled, so that I never saw a man more pleasant at a peece of grillery." " . . . from plague, pestilence, and famine, from bishops, priests, and deacons, good Lord deliver us " was a typical sentence. Even more telling was the description of Laud's progress through the streets of London, reminiscent of the proud Wolsey—the multitude standing bare where he passed, servants " tumbling downe and thrusting aside the little children a playing there." Some of his fun Wharton got from the straight vulgarity of parts of the pamphlet, but, in spite of its pathos, he was tickled at the picture of the prelate's retainers " flinging and tossing the poore coster-mongers and souce-wives fruit and puddings, baskets and all into the Thames," their cries of " Room! room! " mingling with the " wayling mournings and Lamentation the women make crying out save my puddings, save my codlings for the Lords sake, the poore tripes and apples in the meane tyme swimming like frogs about the Thames making way for his Grace to go home again."

The following day more people came to hear the *Letany*. Delighted, they treated Bastwick to a good dinner (roast meat?) and gave him money for more. They sent others to the Gate-house, copies of the *Letany* were surreptitiously circulated, and so Bastwick's fame spread, and among his visitors were Hewson, Rosier, John Lilburne, and some other young men " towardly and fearing God," who, wrote Bastwick, " took pleasure in my society, and I was as glad of theirs." Lilburne several times returned to the Gatehouse, conceiving an ardent admiration for Bastwick, " for whose service," he afterwards wrote, " I could have laid down my life." Bastwick, for his part, formed a high opinion of Lilburne, regarding him " as an honest hopefull and godly youth." " I gave him," he said, " as good councell, as I could give to any, and loved and esteemed of him." He found Lilburne's enthusiasm for the Puritan cause not equalled by his knowledge, and instructed him in many points of doctrinal controversy. He also helped to polish his manners and refine his speech, making him " fit for all Gentlemans and Noble-men's society."

Lilburne spoke of himself to Bastwick, telling him that he was almost out of his time, but that his stock was very small and he had little capital to set himself up with. He thought of going to the Low Countries to find work, and conceived the idea of taking a copy of the *Letany* with him and getting it printed there and smuggled into England—a frequent way of circumventing the printing bans. Bastwick at first demurred, partly in consideration of Lilburne's youth, warning him of the dangers involved and the ruin that discovery would spell to his hopes in life. But Lilburne argued not only the glory of serving the cause, but the possible financial benefits that might accrue, and Bastwick agreed to his plan.

When Lilburne came again to the Gatehouse it was to tell Bastwick that all was ready, and he brought with him John Chilliburne, a servant or assistant to John Wharton, who would receive and distribute the pamphlets in England. Bastwick disliked Chilliburne at sight, and warned Lilburne against him, telling him again and again that he would prove a false friend, for he looked like a knave. But Lilburne was confident and obstinate. Open-hearted and careless, he proceeded with the enterprise that was to mark both the beginning of his personal misfortunes and his first blow for the liberty he was already beginning to value above all things.[20]

Before 1637 was half over, several thousand copies of the *Letany* reached England, a large number were seized at the ports, Chilliburne was arrested, though subsequently released —for a purpose, as it afterwards proved—and Bastwick was tried before Star Chamber. With him were William Prynne, imprisoned in 1633 for the publication of *Histriomastix*, and Dr Henry Burton. Prynne's imprisonment, like Bastwick's, had not deprived him of the visits of friends or the use of pen and ink, and he wrote and published in 1636, by a secret press which was never discovered, *News from Ipswich*. Crammed with marginal notes, prefaced by Biblical texts, it reserved some of its strongest vituperation for the bishops: ". . . devouring wolves and tyrannizing Lordly Prelats raised from the dunghill."

About the same time Dr Henry Burton (some of whose works were already known to Lilburne) preached at Friday Street in his own parish church, laying open the innovations in doctrine, worship, and ceremonies which had lately crept into the church, and calling the bishops, among other things, " anti-Christian mushromes," " fat prebends," " not pastors but Traytors."

While officers of Star Chamber thundered at his door he completed copies of his sermon for the printer, and smuggled them out.[21] Dr Burton was sent to the Fleet prison and brought for trial with Bastwick and Prynne before Star Chamber on June 4, 1637. All three were found guilty and condemned to the pillory in New Palace Yard, to lose their ears, to be fined £5000 each, and to perpetual imprisonment. Prynne, in addition to the second hacking of his ears, was to be branded in the cheeks with the letters S and L for " seditious libeller."

On June 30, 1637, sentence was carried out. The great yard was thronged close with people. The three prisoners arrived, each aware of the part he was about to play. They embraced. Bastwick went first to the pillory, " and his Wife immediately following came up to him, and like a loving Spouse saluted each Eare with a kisse, and then his mouth; whose tender love, boldnes, and chearfullnese so wrought upon the peoples affections, that they gave a marveilous great shout, for joy to behold it." " Had I as many lives as I have haires on my head, or drops of blood in my veynes," announced Bastwick, " I would give them up all for this Cause."

Prynne's speech was restrained. " Had we respected our Liberties," he said, " we had not stood here at this time: it was for the generall good and Liberties of you all that we have now thus farre ingaged our owne Liberties in this Cause. For did you know, how deeply they have entrenched on your Liberties in point of Law, and upon our established Religion in point of Popery; If you knew but into what times you are cast, it would make you look about you: And if you did but see what changes and revolutions of Laws, Religions, and Ceremonies have been made of late by one man, you would more narrowly looke into your Priviledges, and see how farre your Liberty did lawfully extend, and so maintaine it."

Burton, regarding the three pillories, had not failed to remark, " Me thinks I see Mount Calvary where the three Crosses . . . were pitched." Turning to his wife, " I would not have thee to dishonour the day, or to darken the glory of it, by shedding one teare, or fetching one sigh . . . never was my Wedding day so wellcome, and joyfull a day, as this day is." Burton had a nosegay in his hand as he stood in the pillory, and " a Bee came and pitched on the Nosegay, and began to sucke the

Flowers very savourly." " Doe ye not see this poore Bee? "
Burton asked the crowd. " She hath found out this very place
to suck sweetnesse from these Flowers; And cannot I suck
sweetnesse in this very place from Christ? "

Thus the three learned men, martyrs of the Puritan cause,
stood and talked to the people, their necks clamped by the
pillory. The crowds pressed close to hear every word; those
whose printing presses would reproduce the scene in thousands
of pamphlets which would circulate first in London and then
over the whole country, in spite of the printing laws, scribbled
as they stood. Every detail would be reproduced, including the
cutting of the ears, the flowing of the blood, the calls for the
surgeon, and Prynne crying exultantly, " Come seere me, seere.
Burn me, cut me, I fear not ! " In the mounting hysteria only
Burton had time for the young man deathly pale at the foot of
the pillory: " Sonne, Sonne, what is the matter you looke so
pale? " [22]

CHAPTER FOUR

Star Chamber Victim

I feare neither the Devill nor his Agents the Prelates, in this
cause of my God.

JOHN LILBURNE, *Come out of her my people*, 1639

*B*ASTWICK HAD BEEN RIGHT IN HIS MISTRUST OF CHILLIBURNE.
Lilburne's enterprise had been betrayed, and it was probably
through him that the books were seized as they were being
smuggled into England from Holland. Lilburne himself
returned to London in December with his suspicions only
partly aroused. He arranged to meet Chilliburne outside the
Royal Exchange, and noted that he was carefully observed by
agents of the Stationers' Company as he waited fruitlessly for
two hours. Still not certain of his accomplice's perfidy, and
wishing to make contact with John Wharton, he allowed
Chilliburne to arrange a meeting. It was on December 11 or
12, 1637, that Chilliburne gave him word that the way was clear,
and Lilburne followed him down narrow City streets, his hand
on his sword. In Soper Lane he was set on by two pursuivants
of the Stationers' Company, who seized him from behind,
shouting out in the King's name for help and crying that they
had taken the rogue Wharton's man. Lilburne's suspicions
were confirmed when Chilliburne joined in the struggle to
secure him. Though he fought savagely, Lilburne had little
chance. His arms were pinioned by the straps of his cloak, so
that his half-drawn sword was useless. Two or three others
had responded to the shouts of the Stationers' men, and
Lilburne was forced backward into a shop and, a sugar-chest
being in the way, thrown violently over it and relieved of his
sword, " which if I had, and got my back against the wall, I
doe not doubt but I should have made them be willing to let
me alone; for though they had fast hold of me, they quacked
and trembled for feare; and though they were five or six, yet

they cried for more helpe to assist them," Lilburne later recounted with characteristic bravado.

Shouting in triumph that they "had taken one of the notoriousest dispersers of scandalous bookes that was in the kingdom," his captors took Lilburne to the Polehead tavern [1] near St Paul's, where they called freely for wine to make themselves merry, "thinking they had got a great prize." The Archbishop's chief pursuivant came hurrying along to gloat over the capture. "Mr Lilburne," he said, "I am glad with all my heart that wee are met, for you are the man that I have much desired for a long time to see." He too called for wine, to celebrate the arrest, but Lilburne steadfastly refused the proffered sack, and, if his captors thought he might talk and incriminate his friends, they were disappointed.

Lilburne spent that night in custody at the house of the pursuivant Flamstead. About noon the following day, December 12 or 13, without any examination, he was committed to the Gatehouse for importing "factious" and "scandalous" books from Holland. Any consolation he may have found in the fact that his prison had housed also his spiritual teacher, Dr Bastwick, was short-lived, for three days later, by warrant of the Privy Council, he was sent to the Fleet prison. From here Lilburne petitioned the Council for liberty, and as a result was brought to the office of the Attorney-General on January 14, 1638, a little over a month after his capture.

The prisoner was at first treated with the kindness and consideration which his youth and inexperience commanded, and answered, apparently guilelessly, the questions of the Chief Clerk. His story was that, his master being about to retire, he had obtained quittance before his time, and went into the country to obtain the approval of his friends before going to Holland to use his £50 or £60 capital in the cloth trade, to which he had been apprenticed. The questions then became sharper.

" Where were you there? "

" At Rotterdam."

" And from thence you went to Amsterdam? "

" Yes, I was at Amsterdam."

" What Bookes did you see in Holland? "

" Great store of Bookes, for in every Booksellers shop as I came in, there were great stores of Bookes."

He was then asked if he had seen Bastwick's *Letany* and *Answer to Sir John Bankes.*

" Yes, I saw them there, and if you please to goe thither, you may buy an hundred of them at the Booksellers, if you have a minde to them."

" Who printed all those Bookes? "

" I doe not know."

" Who was at the charges of printing them? "

" Of that I am ignorant."

" But did you not send over some of these Bookes? "

" I sent not any of them over."

" Doe you know one Hargust there? "

" Yes, I did see such a man."

" Where did you see him? "

" I met with him one day accidentally at Amsterdam."

" How oft did you see him there? "

" Twice upon one day."

" But did not he send over Bookes? "

" If he did, it is nothing to me, for his doings is unknowne to me."

" But he wrote a Letter over by your directions, did he not? "

" What he writ, I know no more than you."

" But did you see him no where else there? "

" Yes, I saw him at Rotterdam."

" What conference had you with him? "

At this point Lilburne, clearly not wanting either to implicate himself or his friends, nor to tell a lie, lost patience. " Very little," he replied. " But why doe you aske me all these questions? I pray come to the thing for which I am accused."

The Chief Clerk then produced his trump card, the deposition of Edmund Chillington, a button-seller, of Abchurch Lane, off Cannon Street—a near neighbour of both Lilburne and Wharton—who was alleged to have received copies of the *Letany* from Holland. But before telling Lilburne its substance he asked if Lilburne had known Chillington and for how long? Only a little before he went away, was Lilburne's reply. Then Lilburne made his first mistake in denying that he also knew John Wharton—perhaps he was

wishing to protect the old man—but was forced on being
pressed to admit that he did, although he refused to say for
how long. When asked to say what contacts he had with
Chillington since his return, " I am not bound to tell you,"
he exclaimed. " Why doe you aske me all these questions ?
. . . I am not imprisoned for knowing and talking with such
and such men: But for sending over Bookes. . . if you will
aske me of that . . . I am cleare, for I sent none. And of any
other matter that you have to accuse me of, I know it is
warrantable by the Law of God, and I thinke by the Law of
the Land, that I may stand upon my just defence, and not
answer to your intergatorie; and that my accusers ought to
be brought face to face, to justifie what they accuse me of."

It is apparent that here Lilburne is feeling his way, and it is
interesting that he is certain of the law of God, though still
not quite sure of the law of the land. The immediate result
was to arouse the anger of his interlocutor, who reminded the
prisoner that he could be made to answer. Lilburne then,
in a mixture of simplicity and guile, assured his examiner:
" I doe not refuse to answer out of any contempt but onely
because I am ignorant what belongs to an examination, for
this is the first time that ever I was examined." He repeated:
" I have answered punctually to the thing for which I am
imprisoned, and more I am not bound to answer, and for my
liberty, I must waite God's time."

As he could get nothing else out of the prisoner, the Chief
Clerk proceeded to Chillington's accusation—that Lilburne had
printed ten or twelve thousand books in Holland, that he had
a room at Mr John Foote's at Delft, where the books were
probably kept, and that he had made some £80 out of the
enterprise. All these statements, asserted Lilburne, were lies.
He was then asked: " You received money of Mr Wharton
since you came to Towne, did you not ? "

All Lilburne could say was: " What if I did ? "

" It was for Bookes? "

" I doe not say so."

" For what sorts of bookes was it? "

" I doe not say it was for any."

" We have power to send you back to the place from whence
you came," threatened the Chief Clerk.

" You may doe your pleasure," responded the prisoner.

The recalcitrant youth was then sent down to the Attorney-General himself, Sir John Bankes, and there refused to sign the Clerk's account of the interview which had just taken place until he was sure that it correctly embodied his replies. He repeated his assertion that he did not send over any books, and his request that he should be brought face to face with his accusers. He offered to write and sign his own statement, but got no further than " the answer of me, John Lilburne, is . . ." before the pen was snatched from him and he was dismissed, and remanded back to the Fleet.

At this point Lilburne was handed over to Star Chamber, which usually dealt with offences against the printing laws, and ten or twelve days after his first examination he was brought to the Star Chamber office and requested to make payment to enter an appearance. " To what ?" asked Lilburne. " I was never served with any subpoena; neither was there any Bill preferred against me." Lilburne believed they would found a Bill upon his own words, but God, he felt, would help him so that they could not in the least entangle him, although he was ignorant of their proceedings.

To the demand for money he answered that he " was but a young man, and a prisoner, and money was not very plentiful " with him. The whole office was intrigued by the youth who contrived so simply yet so boldly to circumvent their rulings, and " the whole company of the Clarkes in the office began to look and gaze " at him. The next procedure was the taking of the oath. The Bible was proffered, which Lilburne at first pretended not to see. Then the master of the office bade him pull off his glove and lay his hand upon the book.

" What to do Sir? "

" You must sweare."

" To what? "

" That you shall make true answer to all things that is asked you."

" Must I so Sir ? But before I sweare, I will know to what I must swear."

" As soon as you have sworne, you shall."

" Sir, I am but a young man, and doe not well know what

belongs to the nature of an Oath, and therefore before I sweare, I will be better advised."

It was pointed out that he would merely be swearing upon the Bible he knew so well, and some of the clerks began to reason with him and point out that other men had taken the oath, and would he be wiser than other men? Lilburne was firm that he would not take an oath the lawfulness of which he doubted, and that it made no difference whether other men had sworn or not; he would be better advised first. At this there was much amazement, for the Star Chamber oath had never before been refused.[2] It had, however, been common practice for Puritans, brought before High Commission on religious charges, to refuse to take the similar High Commission oath. When Lilburne came before Star Chamber he was already, through his reading and his Puritan connexions, well primed both in the procedure of this court and in the attitude of Puritans before it. He knew that in Star Chamber he would be put through a similar procedure—the oath *ex officio*, the questioning upon interrogatories, the writing down of the prisoner's answers, the largely private trial before the public hearing. In refusing to take the *ex officio* oath, and so rendering the continuation of the trial impossible, Lilburne was applying to proceedings in Star Chamber the conduct of generations of Puritans before High Commission. He has the distinction of being the first to do this, but behind him stretch a long line of Puritan objectors to the oath as presented by High Commission.

The history of the oath *ex officio* remains obscure. It was so called because it was tendered by the Judge of the Court in virtue of his office—*ex officio suo*. It had been in use during the Middle Ages, and by the time of the Reformation was a regular part of the procedure of ecclesiastical courts. Queen Mary in 1557 expressly empowered High Commission to use it " for a severer way of proceding against heretics." The court was directed " to examine and compel to answer, and swear, upon the holy evangelists, to declare the truth in all such things whereof they or any of them shall be examined." [3] Efforts were made to secure from the monarch, the Privy Council, or from Parliament a pronouncement that the oath was illegal, but it still stood both in High Commission and Star Chamber.

Puritan opposition to it became systematic and unanimous towards the end of the sixteenth century, when plans for the establishment of Presbyterianism, as embodied in their Book of Discipline, were under consideration. It was clear that Puritan dissenters brought before the court could not answer truthfully to questions without disclosing their plan. They were consequently faced with the alternative of answering untruthfully or of not answering at all. While some deemed it according to conscience deliberately to mislead the Commission, most refused to take the oath or to answer any questions put to them.[4]

In 1586 Henry Barrowe, John Greenwood, and John Penrie refused to take the oath, were imprisoned, and finally executed, but not before they had written an account of their examination, which was published the following year. In 1591 and '92 Cartwright and other Puritans were tried before High Commission for attempting to practise the Book of Discipline, and stoutly refused the oath *ex officio*, blocking every step the court attempted to take.[5] The oath was discussed at the Hampton Court Conference, and in 1607 there was published a little book which Lilburne knew—*The Argument of Master Nicholas Fuller, in the Case of Thomas Lad, and Richard Maunsell, his Clients. Wherein it is plainely proved that the Ecclesiasticall Commissioners have no power, by vertue of their Commission, to Imprison, to put to the Oath Ex Officio, or to fine any of his Majesties Subjects.*

Nicholas Fuller was a barrister of Gray's Inn, living from 1543 to 1620. His clients in the two cases he cites in the *Argument* were brought before High Commission, the one, a merchant, for being at a conventicle, the other, a preacher, for being concerned in a petition presented to the House of Commons. Both refused the oath. Fuller's thirty-two-page pamphlet, describing their stand and arguing the case against the *ex officio* oath, contains much of the germ of Lilburne's early law. For this all the credit should not go to Coke, whose first *Institute* (the commentary on Littleton), published in 1628, was rather obscure for the youthful Lilburne, and whose second *Institute* (the text and commentary on Magna Carta and other statutes) was not published until 1642. It is significant that Lilburne had been interested enough to use the book

before his own trial by Star Chamber and before he mentions
Coke: the ten or twelve days between his two examinations
would have given his friends ample time to bring him the book
if he had not seen it already.

But, apart from theory and the tradition which was current
among all Puritans in London, enough trials had occurred
since Lilburne's arrival in the capital to teach him how to
answer in similar circumstances.

A group of people taken at a conventicle at the house of one
Barnett, a brewer's clerk, at Blackfriars, for example, consistently refused to take the oath both for religious and for
legal reasons. Samuel How explained on May 8, 1632: " I am
a young man and doe not know what this oath is." John
Woodwyne refused because he desired to know what he should
swear to and what was the end of the oath. Elizabeth Sargeant
knew " she must not sweare but when she is before a Magistrate." Ralph Grafton, an upholsterer dwelling in Cornhill
and one of the leaders of the conventicle, averred that an oath
should not be taken rashly, and " I dare not therefore take
this oath." In all, about thirty people on this particular
occasion refused the oath for like reasons.

On a similar occasion, dealing with a group of conventiclers
taken in a wood near Newington, in Surrey, Laud, in despera-
tion, called to one prisoner: " Come, thou lookest like a good
fellow, that wilt take thy oath," but met with the same reply:
" I am in deed and good earnest, I dare not take this oath.
An oath is for the ending of a controversie, but this is made to
be but the beginninge of the controversie." [6] More recently,
Bastwick himself had refused the High Commission oath before
his imprisonment in the Gatehouse.

The succession of humble people declaring simply " I dare
not take this oath " or " I must swear only before a magistrate,"
suffering imprisonment or other punishment, yet giving away
no secrets, involving no one else, and—above all—by their
refusal blocking proceedings so that the trial was unable to
continue, had taught Lilburne what to say when he himself
was proffered the oath.

It was on February 9 that he was called before Star Chamber
itself. He had no time to make worldly preparation for the
ordeal, but " the Lord according to his promise was pleased to

be present with me by his speciall assistance, that I was inabled without any dantednesse of spirit, to speake unto that great and noble Assembly, as though they had beene but my equalls." Arraigned with him was John Wharton.   The Attorney-General preferred information against both of them for the unlawful printing and publishing of libellous and seditious books, including Bastwick's *Letany* and Prynne's *News from Ipswich*.   Bankes also laid the verbal charge that Lilburne had refused to enter an appearance, and had refused the Star Chamber oath.

Lilburne immediately obtained leave to speak.   The affidavit he declared to be " a most false lie and untruth."   But at first the Lords of Star Chamber were more concerned with his attitude to their court.   Why did he refuse the Star Chamber oath? asked the Lord Keeper.   In replying Lilburne made use of all the current Puritan arguments.

It was the *ex officio* oath, one and the same with the High Commission oath, and was therefore not lawful according to the law of the land, which allowed no man to accuse himself; nor according to the law of God, which would not allow a man to undo himself, nor with the law of Nature, which expected every man to preserve himself.   Moreover, an oath ought to be the end of all controversies and strife, whereas this oath would merely begin them.   If an oath were taken at all it should be before a magistrate.   If a man were tried he must be told of what he was accused and his accusers brought face to face with him.   If asked to accuse himself his answer should be, like that of Jesus Christ, " Why ask ye me?   Go to them that heard me."   And if recent history were needed to support the case against the oath, had not the Petition of Right itself claimed that none should be tried or imprisoned except by the laws and statutes of the realm?   Lilburne claimed, in short, all the protection which, as a free-born Englishman, the laws of the land and the holy writ provided him.   " Upon these grounds," he said, " I did, and doe still refuse the Oath."

The Archbishop of Canterbury brusquely bade him " pull off his glove and lay his hand on the book."

" Most Honourable and Noble Lords," repeated Lilburne, " with all reverence and submission unto your Honours . . . yet must I refuse the Oath."

" With all reverence and submission he refuseth the Oath !
My Lords, doe you heare him ! " exclaimed the Archbishop.

" Submit yourself unto the Court ! " commanded the Lord
Keeper.

" Most Noble Lords," persisted Lilburne, " with all willing-
nesse I submit my body unto your Honours' pleasure."

" My Lords," asserted Lord Dorset, " this is one of their
private spirits. Doe you heare him, how he stands in his own
justification ? "

" This fellow," cried the Archbishop, " hath been one of the
notoriousest dispersers of Libellous Bookes that is in the
Kingdome; and that is the Father of them all "—and he
pointed to old Wharton.

On Monday the 12th the prisoners resisted further attempts
to make them swear, and Wharton declared he would rather
go in the cart to Tyburn than be guilty of such apostacy from
his principles. On the following day, Tuesday, February 13,
at 7 A.M., they were consequently again brought to the Star
Chamber bar, where, after about two hours' waiting, the
Attorney-General arrived to charge them once more with " the
unlawful Printing and Publishing of Libellous and Seditious
Books," the number of which had been added to by a further
deposition from Chillington, and this time the name of James
Ouldam (?Oldham), a turner in Westminster Hall, was given
as a disperser of some of them. With the accusation of illegal
printing was coupled the prisoners' " insufferable disobedience
and contempt." Lilburne still maintained his opposition to the
oath for the same reasons, and Wharton " began to thunder it
out against the Bishops, and told them they required three
Oaths of the King's Subjects; namely, the Oath of Church-
wardenship, and the Oath of Canonical Obedience, and the
Oath *Ex Officio*; which, said he, are all against the Law of
the Land, and by which they deceive and perjure thousands
of the King's Subjects in a year."

The Lords, wondering to hear the old man begin to talk
after this manner, commanded him to hold his peace, and to
answer them whether he would take the oath or no. To which
he replied he desired them to let him talk a little, and he would
tell them by and by. At which all the court burst out laughing;
but they would not let him continue.

This light relief did not help the prisoners. Unanimously then the court declared Lilburne and Wharton " guilty of a very high contempt and offence of dangerous consequence, and evil example," remanded them to the Fleet, there to remain until they conformed, fined them £500 each, and to the end that others might be the more deterred from daring to offend in the like kind thereafter John Lilburne was to be whipped through the streets from the Fleet to the pillory, and both he and Wharton pilloried and then returned to the Fleet to remain until they did conform.[7]

The two prisoners were accordingly sent back to prison. They had the liberty of the Fleet for a few days, until the old man was moved to make to the Warden the oration against bishops he had intended for Star Chamber, after which they were kept in close confinement.

It is evident from the pursuivants' shouts when they captured Lilburne, from the tenor of his examination, as well as from the outbursts of Dorset and Laud, that he was considered to be deeply implicated in illegal printing. The authorities knew the names of some of the other people concerned, and had a good idea where the offprints were kept in Holland. The press or presses used and the name of the prime mover seem, however, to have been unknown. Edmund Chillington, the button-seller, their chief witness against Lilburne, had already been apprehended, and—so Lilburne claimed—was by threats, persuasion, and starvation induced to witness against him. After the trial he was released. John Chilliburne was believed by both Wharton and Lilburne—unfortunately after the event —to have been a spy and *agent provocateur* deliberately placed at Wharton's. His conduct was certainly suspicious, and he was never brought to trial for any share in illegal printing.

Lilburne's rôle was far from clear. It is obvious that, while he was able to deny specific charges, such as sending certain books over on a certain ship, he never unreservedly denied all knowledge of printing in Holland. He was at the house where the books were known to be stored, he knew the mysterious " Hargust " who was thought to be concerned on the other side, he had met Wharton several times with Bastwick in the Gatehouse, he had taken a copy of the *Letany* with the avowed purpose of getting it printed, he was (as he himself admits) trying to make contact with Wharton when he was apprehended. His reasons for going into Holland were never satisfactory: he was going to set up in trade, being out of his time; his master had retired and Lilburne claimed his freedom; he was being watched by the Archbishop's men because of his visits to Bastwick in the Gatehouse. His story of going to friends in the country to get their approval for his journey does not ring true. What friends? His family in Durham were too far away; if to Hixons at Greenwich or Eltham, he would surely have mentioned them somewhere. More likely he left to receive instructions about the printing. He later boasted that he had spent his time in Holland " not like a drone, but for the welfare of England." [8] It is unlikely that he was deep in the counsels of the Puritan printers, but his actual function will probably never be known. The excitement which the case aroused centred not around the question of whether Lilburne and Wharton printed the *Letany* and other books, but around their attitude to their Star Chamber accusers.

The staunch defiance of the old man and the young to this hated court elated the hearts of the London citizens. The news that John Lilburne had stood on his rights as a " free-born Englishman " to refuse the Star Chamber oath spread like wildfire through the City, and " Free-born John," as he was promptly named,[9] immediately secured that place high in the citizens' affections which, in all the many crises of his life, brought them flocking to his assistance.

CHAPTER FIVE

The Puritan Martyr

... and being called ... he chused rather to suffer affliction in
pursuance of a just cause then to injoy the pleasure of sin for a
season.

Englands weeping Spectacle, June 29, 1648

EASTER TERM FALLING ON APRIL 18, 1638, THE SENTENCE ON
Lilburne was " executed with the utmost rigour," and he was
" smartly whipt from the Fleet to Westminster." This was on
a Wednesday, four months after his arrest. The day was un-
usually hot and sunny. Having prepared themselves by prayer
and meditation for the ordeal of the pillory, Lilburne and
Wharton awaited the call of the gaoler. When it came Lilburne
took the old man by the hand and led him down to the prison
yard and the gate. There Lilburne was detained, and John
Hawes, the porter, came to him.

" Mr Lilburne," he said, " I am sorry for the punishment you
are to undergo, but you must strip yourself and be whipped from
here to Westminster." Lilburne had not known the full extent
of his punishment, but he was able to say, " The will of my God
be done " as he was led to the Fleet bridge, where the cart was
waiting. There he stripped to the waist, and as his hands were
being tied to the back of the cart cried out, " Welcome be the
cross of Christ ! " Friends were there to encourage him to
" put on a Couragious resolution to suffer cheerfully," and as
the cart started forward and the executioner drew out his whip
John turned to him. " Well, my friend, doe thy office," he said.
To which the executioner replied, " I have whipped many a
Rogue before, but now I shall whip an honest man."

The horse and cart, the prisoner walking behind, made its
way slowly down Fleet street, through Temple Bar, and into
the Strand, the three-thonged corded whip, with knots upon it,
falling regularly, every three or four paces, upon the victim's

bare back as he recited lines of scripture and cried out, " Halle-lujah, Hallelujah, Glory, Honour and Praise be given to thee O Lord for ever ! "

The crowds that thronged the way spoke words of comfort and exhortation to the young man. Friends asked him how he fared, one came forward and bade him speak with boldness, others bore him company on his two-mile pilgrimage. At Charing Cross he was told by many to be of good cheer, in Whitehall the crowds pressed closer, and as he went through the King's Gate John heard people ask what was the matter, at which he raised his voice and told them:

" My Brethren, against the Law of God, against the Law of the Land, against the King or State have I not committed the least offence that deserves this punishment, but only I suffer as an object of the Prelates' cruelty and malice."

One of the prison officers attempting to silence him, John bade him " meddle with his own businesse," for he would speak come what would, for his cause was good. In King Street many besought the Lord to bless and strengthen the sufferer, and so at last the little procession reached New Palace Yard, where the pillory had been placed between Westminster Hall Gate and Star Chamber. Five hundred blows, three times five hundred stripes, fell upon the prisoner in the progress, according to the estimate of Thomas Smith, a merchant who followed the route.[1]

The dust of the unmade streets had much troubled him, the cart had gone slowly to prolong his punishment, and though the sun had burned fiercely, he had not been allowed to wear his hat.

At Palace Yard the crowd of well-wishers flocked so close to him that Lilburne, feeling faint, was allowed to withdraw a while before facing the further ordeal of the pillory. He was not allowed to rest quietly, however, for there came to him a messenger from Star Chamber to worry him in his pain and weakness into an acknowledgment of error. This failing, re-mission of the pillory ordeal was offered, but to no avail. So, with the sun streaming on his head, his painful weals undressed, his shoulders " swelled almost as big as a penny loafe with the bruses of the knotted Cords," [2] suffering additional discomfort from stooping, because the pillory was too small for him, John Lilburne stood for two hours in Palace Yard.

Born propagandist as he was, and with the examples of
Prynne, Burton, and Bastwick fresh in his mind, he knew that
the pillory, though uncomfortable and undignified, was yet not
a platform to be despised. To speak as he came through the
streets " would have been but as water spilt on the ground, in
regard of the noyse and presse of people." Here there were
people enough, but waiting attentively for what he would say.
So, bowing in the direction of Star Chamber—a defiance typical
of his whole career—John Lilburne stooped and put his head
in the pillory and began to tell the story of his arrest, and his
reasons for refusing the *ex officio* oath. Then he proceeded to
a discourse upon bishops, which soon developed into a violent
attack upon the derivation of their authority and their misuse
of it. Bishops, declared Lilburne, derived their authority from
the Pope, who was the Beast of Revelation, who was Anti-
Christ or the Devil, and he challenged them to deny it. The
crowd was delighted. But when he had been speaking about
half an hour there came " a fat lawyer " bidding the prisoner
stop talking. Free-born John, however, was not likely to lose
such an opportunity and refused, defiantly adding that he would
rather be hanged at Tyburn ! The response was rapid and
decided. Lilburne was gagged so roughly that the blood spurted
from his mouth[3] before, as he later complained, he had reached
" the maine thing and strength " of his argument.[4] But his
resourcefulness was not at an end. He thrust his hands into
his pockets and drew out pamphlets, which he threw among
the crowds, and then continued stamping with his feet until his
punishment had ended.[5]

Great and enthusiastic crowds escorted Lilburne back to the
Fleet prison. There at last he was allowed a surgeon to dress
his back, " which was one of the miserablest," said the surgeon,
" that ever he did see; for the wales in his back, made by his
cruel whipping, were bigger than Tobacco-pipes." [6] Feverish
and exhausted, Lilburne was left unattended and without food.
But the Lords of Star Chamber called for a full account of his
demeanour and speeches during his whipping and his standing
in the pillory, and for the names of the pamphlets he had
flung to the crowd. A public appeal for their surrender led to
the identification of only one of them, so the Warden of the
Fleet himself came to question Lilburne. They were three of

Bastwick's books, Lilburne told him. But how had he obtained them? Did he bring them with him? Were they brought to him by visitors? The Warden was worried: Puritan prisoners were too easily smuggling writing materials and pamphlets in and out of their prisons. But he received no help from Lilburne. The Court of Star Chamber was left to prevent such ill-use of the pillory in future by an order that all prisoners' pockets were to be searched and their hands tied.[7]

After Lilburne's room and clothes had been ransacked he was left alone. Physically weak, overwrought, and spiritually exalted, his emotions found vent in verse:

I Doe not feare the face nor power of any mortall man,
Though he against me rise, to doe the worst he can,
Because my trust, my hope my strength, my confidence and aide
Is in the Lord Jehovahs power, both now and ever staide.

Therefore my soule shall never cease, Triumphantly to sing,
Thou art my Fort, my sure defence, my Saviour and my King,
For in my strayts and trials all, thou well with me hast delt,
Thy mercies and upbearing hand, most sweetly I have felt.[8]

The next day he was brought news of the Star Chamber order which his conduct in the the pillory had evoked: he was to be removed from his private room to the common gaol of the Fleet, there to be kept close prisoner with irons on hands and feet, with none allowed to visit him or send him money.[9]

So Lilburne was taken, ill as he was, to the common gaol, where he lay in a 'hold' in the recesses of the Fleet prison with double chains on his feet and hands, very ill, " in fury and anguish of pain." [10] In his weakness, being unable to help himself or walk alone, he was allowed the services of an old woman, Katherine Hadley, but his surgeon was refused admission.[11] Food and linen sent into him were withheld. Efforts of friends to bribe prisoners to convey food to Lilburne and to arrange that a prisoner in an adjoining cell should pass food to him through a hole in the floor were discovered.[12] Visitors who attempted to gain access to Lilburne were mal-treated, Thomas Hawes being " beaten by the gaolers to the danger of his life." [13] Fellow-prisoners were afraid to show kindness to him. Robert Ellis declared that Lilburne " was used very barbarously and like to have been slain or murdered." When Ellis helped Lilburne he was deprived of his own bed, transferred to a dungeon for five weeks, and afterwards removed to the King's Bench prison, " that they might the more easily have their wills of Mr Lilburne." [14]

So Lilburne lay " in a tormenting condition, full of ex-treamitie and bodilie paine," and could " neither get ease sitting nor lying." Frequently he lay all night in his clothes, that he might keep the irons from pressing into his flesh. When his illness became so acute that the loss of his reason was feared Dr Hubbard, a physician and Justice of the Peace, gained entrance and found Lilburne in an extreme violent fever, lying in irons on both hands and legs to the extreme hazard of his life.[15]

Without means of sustenance, without visitors, Lilburne feared he was being left to die, and he begged leave to petition the Privy Council. The Warden sent word that a petition would be delivered only if Lilburne would recant. Even in his miserable state the spirit of the young man shone through: " unless the Bishops," he said, " by the law of the land, and the word of God, will show me my offence, I will never submit, nor recant, in the least, while breath is in my body." [16]

On May 17, a month after his punishment, Lilburne was brought before the Attorney-General and the Solicitor-General, not for the alleviation of his condition, but for further questioning on his speech in the pillory and the pamphlets he there flung down. Lilburne freely confirmed all he had said against the bishops, admitted that he had scattered Bastwick's works—and named them—but still, after a month of suffering, steadfastly refused to say how he had obtained the pamphlets. He " was unwilling to tell it," he maintained, and signed a statement to that effect.[17] Still baffled, the Privy Council could do nothing but confirm his solitary confinement in iron chains.[18] It would seem to have been simple enough to tighten up the prison system sufficiently to keep prisoners from outside contacts. Yet not only was the source of these pamphlets never discovered, but Lilburne himself obtained writing materials, wrote tracts, and sent his manuscripts to the press when he was allegedly in close and solitary confinement.

Lying in his cell, shackled and alone, his thoughts soared with the ecstasy of the martyr. He was in the line of the blessed saints; he felt neither the lash nor the cruel irons because God was with him. He was suffering even as Peter, and even as his Lord had done. ". . . for my shackled condition that I am in, it is most sweete and pleasant to me," he averred, " in which I am as merry, yea more chearefull, then ever I was in any condition in my life, and can sleepe as soundly in my Boots and Irons, as Peter did betweene the two Souldiers, when he was in prison." [19]

Yet when the ecstasy passed it left but an ordinary young man, suffering pain, afraid he was being left to die, indignant and rebellious. This was the young man who, with the assistance of the old woman Katherine Hadley, who alone was officially allowed access to him, carried on a ceaseless war with the Warden of the Fleet, demanding to petition the Privy Council and the House of Lords, challenging and threatening. This was the young man who managed to write the pamphlets which were smuggled to the outside world, taken to Holland to print, and smuggled back to be widely distributed in England, thus effecting the very enterprise for which he lay convicted.

The first of Lilburne's pamphlets was *The Christian Mans Triall*, written from the Fleet prison on March 12, 1638— before his punishment—and giving a detailed account of his arrest and examination. Very shortly afterwards appeared *A Worke of the Beast*, written immediately after his punishment, containing a shorter account of his trial and with the full story of his whipping and his speech in the pillory. In August was written *Come out of her my people*, which he wrote, said Lilburne, " lying day and night in Fetters of Iron, both hands and legges." [20] It was addressed to a gentlewoman, a citizen's wife and member of the Church of England, to explain the necessity to Puritans of separation from the Establishment. But though Lilburne urged God's people to withdraw their spiritual obedience from the bishops, he would not, at this stage, allow of opposition other than spiritual. Even in cases of civil or temporal oppression " I doe hold it unlawful," he wrote, " for any of God's people, in their greatest oppression by the Majestrate to rebell or to take up any Temporal armes against them." Lilburne, like many more of his countrymen, was soon to change his mind on this issue. With thousands of others, he was compelled to abandon the attempt to maintain spiritual non-conformity without resorting to physical op-position. He was already studying to fit himself to make good his challenge to the bishops, facing the probability of being " hewen in peeces " when he had done. Men of Lilburne's calibre could not long face persecution, whether for spiritual or for civil nonconformity, with spiritual weapons merely. Civil disobedience, including active physical opposition, was already inherent in the defiance spoken in *Come out of her my people*: " I will, come life, come death; speake my minde freely and courageously."

In November of this same year Lilburne wrote a letter which was published as the *Coppy of a Letter to one of his special friends*. It was apparently written to a woman who had visited him immediately after his whipping and before he was put in chains. Lilburne had known her only by sight before she paid this visit to him, though he had heard that she was one who might " enjoy all outward things that heart can desire." She had written to him and prayed for him " whole dayes together," her cheeks " bedewed with teares of Joy in remembrance " of his " meeknesse, patience and smiling merrinesse " in his sufferings.[21] At her inspiration all his spiritual experience poured out in words, and he saw his sufferings under the bishops as the climax to his soul-searchings with William Kiffin and the other apprentices. They showed not only that God had signalled him out for a great work, but that he could enjoy direct communion with the Lord. This feeling of election and direct communication never left Lilburne, and in all his campaigns he would henceforth turn naturally to the Lord for guidance and aid, waiting for the " incomings " of His spirit. Up to this time he had not seen clearly to which of the Puritan churches he belonged. Now he knew that no rigid church organization could hold him, and that only in the Separatist congregations whose autonomy gave freedom to the individual conscience would his spirit have the play it needed.

Some time in the same year, 1638, Lilburne wrote a further tract in favour of Separation, which was in refutation of nine arguments brought forward by a certain T.B. and reported to him by a woman friend, who might have been either of the two women addressed in his other tracts, or a certain Mary Dorman, who also visited him.[22]   On December 20 he painfully concluded a petition to the Privy Council for help.   Straining his eyes in his dim cell, hungry, ill, he was troubled with night-mare fears of murder in the dark on the orders of the Archbishop and the Warden.   Not knowing whether his petition would be delivered, yet hoping for its publication, he launched also into an appeal to the people, begging them to come daily to the prison to ask after him, so that his enemies would know he could not quietly be killed "in a hole and corner."   *The Poore Mans Cry*, containing the appeal and the petition, was published in May the following year, bearing the imprimatur of " a backe-friend of the English Popish Prelates."

The first three of these pamphlets were certainly published while Lilburne was close prisoner in the Fleet.   How did he write them, ill and shackled, or smuggle them out when visitors, even his physician, were theoretically denied?   *The Christian Mans Triall* can be accounted for, as it was written and published before his punishment, when visitors came freely to him. Immediately after his whipping, and before he was laid in irons, there came the mysterious gentlewoman whom Lilburne knew only by sight.   Quite likely the manuscript of *A Worke of the Beast* was near enough ready for her to take away with her.   *Come out of her my people*, also published in 1639, must have been conveyed to the printer by one of the people who had access to Lilburne—his gaoler, Katherine Hadley, Mrs Mary Dorman, the two mysterious women, or fellow-prisoners, several of whom were sympathetic to Lilburne and themselves had visitors.   It is possible that Mrs Bastwick saw him before he was kept ' close '—or even after, for according to her husband she often visited Lilburne.[23]

The *Coppy of a Letter* and the *Answer to nine Arguments* were not published until years afterwards—which might mean that the prisoner failed to get his manuscript out of the Fleet, that his friends failed to get it printed, or that, if they did, copies were seized and destroyed.   Much, if not all, of this earlier writing was printed in Holland; *Come out of her my people* was printed at Amsterdam, Lilburne stated later.   He spoke also of more than 2000 books which had been seized as they came in from the Low Countries, and boasted to the Warden of the Fleet that so long as there existed a printing press in Holland he would get his works published.[24] Undoubtedly the machinery already in existence was put in operation to help the latest propagandist to the Puritan cause, and Lilburne himself would have made contacts when he was in the Low Countries with the *Letany*.

In the absence of any conciliatory attitude in the prisoner himself better prison conditions would be granted him only on the surety for his good behaviour in the Fleet of two Aldermen of £2000 each. Not surprisingly, this was not forthcoming.[25] It is more surprising that his family gave him little help. His sister Elizabeth married Robert Chambers of Cleadon on February 4, in the midst of his troubles. His father and brothers were estranged by John's widely publicized opposition to the bishops—not because they thought he was wrong, but because they feared the outcome of a lawsuit on which his father was engaged. This lawsuit began several years previously, when a Claxton, whose family had married into the Lilburnes' three generations earlier, laid claim to part of the estate at Thickley Punchardon. The contest lacked none of the excitement of border warfare, the Claxtons on one occasion attacking the Lilburne home and maintaining possession of it for six weeks, and on another severely damaging it by fire. It is a pity that John was in London and lost the opportunity of exercising his pugnacity upon his family enemies. The old fighting spirit of the Lilburnes of the border was not lacking, however, in his father, and Richard Lilburne of Thickley Punchardon has the distinction of being the last recorded example of an attempt to settle by combat a dispute concerning real estate. Unfortunately for the record he engaged a champion for the purpose: perhaps his second son would have appeared for him had he been at home.

Three times the champions of Lilburne and Claxton appeared in the lists, but after the third adjournment trial by combat was forbidden. Nevertheless, on September 22, 1636, Ralph Claxton was petitioning the King that Richard Lilburne " will assent to no trial but that of battle, which his Majesty had prohibited, the judges having certified that there is another way more ordinary in these days and as legal." Four days later Richard Lilburne was brought prisoner to London. His son seems to have been more concerned with " following the means of grace " than with the troubles of his father. He has nothing to say concerning this episode of family history. Though Richard Lilburne was probably quite soon released, the issue was still undecided in 1638, when John was in the Fleet. When, about this time, the case came up anew Laud was said by Richard Lilburne to have warned the judges against him on account of his son's behaviour. It was then that he virtually disowned John, writing to his youngest son, Henry, advising him to beware of John and not to follow in his footsteps, for he was " the greatest griefe " to his father. Richard Lilburne, however, retained his lands and the family was reunited, all the members except Henry, who perhaps followed his father's advice too closely, standing firmly by the Parliament and by John in his later trials.[26]

When Lilburne had been in prison for some time it happened that a fire broke out in the Fleet. The street was only a few yards from the prison door, and the alarm of the prisoners was shared by the inhabitants without. Such was Lilburne's reputation that all thoughts flew at once to him, and it was believed that, being desperate, he had set the prison on fire, regardless of consequences to himself. Thereupon the populace outside and the prisoners within all cried, " Release Lilburne, or we shall all be burnt ! " and ran headlong to the Warden, who was compelled to remove Lilburne from his hold.[27]

If they were responsible for the fire or the frenzy of the crowd, neither Lilburne nor his friends gave any sign, but once out of solitary confinement Lilburne's youth speeded his recovery, and he entered fully into all the excitements of seventeenth-century prison life. The prisoners lived as in a large, badly organized hostelry. They were of all types, imprisoned for various offences. They moved freely within the prison, the kind of room and the quality of food depending upon how much they paid for it. Small comforts, writing-paper, extra food, the ease with which their visitors came and went, depended entirely upon the attitude of their gaolers and the amount they could devote to bribery. A great deal also depended upon their relationship—pecuniary and otherwise—with the warden of the prison. The system was managed almost entirely by private enterprise, the prison officers rarely being paid for their work, but, on the contrary, sometimes even themselves paying for the privilege of holding one of these unremunerated posts: the office of Warden of the Fleet passed at the beginning of the eighteenth century for £5000.[28]

John Lilburne was not by nature likely to curry favour with the prison staff, and there were many prisoners kept for crimes of violence with whom he would have little sympathy. It was characteristic that he found himself spectacularly embroiled with a gang of hooligans, and typical that he immediately accused the Warden of setting them upon him. He never lost the fear of murder that was generated during his solitary confinement, and for days on end would barricade himself in his room. With prisoners of all types retaining their arms and using them on the slightest provocation, such fears were not entirely groundless, and Lilburne was, indeed, on one occasion severely wounded in the arm.[29] There is something macabre about this brawling within the dim and sordid confines of the Fleet prison, while outside its walls events were moving towards the climax of civil war.

CHAPTER SIX

The Parliamentarian

My thoughts have been so high of them [Parliament] that if I had had ten thousand lives at the beginning of this war, I should have ventured them all for them.

JOHN LILBURNE, *Copy of a Letter from Lieutenant Colonell John Lilburne to a friend*, July 25, 1645.

*W*HEN LILBURNE WAS SENTENCED BY STAR CHAMBER IN 1638 Charles I had been ruling for nine years without a Parliament, and throughout Lilburne's imprisonment the burdens and exactions of arbitrary rule continued. While he was before Star Chamber the judges in the Exchequer Chamber were deciding against Hampden in the ship-money dispute. The King proceeded to collect ship-money, and it was typical of his policy that, although a fair case could be argued for collecting ship-money for national protection from all parts of the country, he both failed to get the money and aroused the resentment of all those sections of the community, reaching down to all but the very poorest, upon whom the tax fell. In Lilburne's native Palatine his father and his uncle both resisted the payment.[1] Did anyone tell him, while he was in prison, how the coal-owners also refused to pay their assessments, daring the officers to distrain their coals—" a difficult business," as the sheriff of the county sadly confessed, as he did not know what to do with the coal if he did seize it? [2]

Forest fines continued. The forest of Rockingham was being enlarged in 1637, and the six miles of its circumference became sixty. Fines imposed on landlords held to have infringed these limits were outrageous, ranging from Sir Christopher Hatton's £12,000 to the Earl of Salisbury's £20,000, and were never paid, the money that came in to the Exchequer being insufficient to compensate for the trouble caused. Monopolies continued, restricting trade and raising prices.

Even such a laudable project as the attempt to manufacture salt at Shields, in the Tyne lowlands near the Lilburne home, and so to break the monopoly of the imported Biscay salt, was ruined by the setting up of a counter-monopoly which would pay the Exchequer 10*s.* a wey. Other projects, desirable in themselves, through mismanagement or mixed motives led only to trouble without compensating gain to the Exchequer. Such was the scheme for draining the Great Fen in Lincoln-shire, the natives of that dismal waste falling foul of the Dutch workmen brought over to reclaim the land. In social matters measures for checking enclosure or setting people on work were accompanied by fines which caused the resentment of classes more articulate than those who may have benefited.

None of these hardships as yet came within Lilburne's personal experience, but he could appreciate such cases as that of John Trendall, the stonemason of Dover, who in 1639 was brought before High Commission for expounding scripture in his own house and refused the oath *ex officio*. And, when the issue between King and Parliament finally came to a head, it was an issue which Lilburne could fully comprehend which sparked the fuse.

In Scotland a Presbyterian form of worship had actually been established. Underestimating the sincerity of his fellow-countrymen, James had nevertheless tried to establish bishops in order to bring his two kingdoms into accord, and Charles and Laud pursued a similar policy. While Lilburne had been busy in the Netherlands in 1637 the King had attempted to introduce the English Prayer Book into Scotland, not realizing that neither the bishops appointed by his father nor his own Government had sufficient authority in the northern kingdom to make acceptable the English liturgy. The scene in St Giles's Cathedral in Edinburgh in July 1637, when the English Prayer Book was used for the first time and a woman hurled a stool at the minister while another shouted " The mass is come amongst us ! " was not paralleled by any Puritan opposition in England. While English Puritans like Lilburne were suffering singly for their views, the Scottish National Covenant, a religious manifesto attacking the system of Laud, was signed by the majority of the Scottish nation. At the end of 1638, while Lilburne was recovering from his illness and had just been

released from his shackles, a Scottish Assembly meeting at
Glasgow abolished episcopacy in Scotland, and early in the
following year Charles's attempt to coerce his Scottish subjects
ended in a Scottish call to arms.   The King, noting that the
religious issue was embracing also the constitutional—" The
question is not now whether a Service Book is to be received or
not, nor whether episcopal government shall be continued or
presbyterial admitted, but whether we are their King or not " [3]
—also prepared for war.   But the trained bands of the northern
English counties, although accustomed to meeting attacks on
the border, were neither well armed, well trained, nor well led,
and were no match for the Scots, who prepared for war with a
fanaticism—preaching, praying, and drilling—which gave the
English no chance of success.

Lilburne, while the conflict was developing, had passed out
of the ecstatic religious experience which followed his punishment and accompanied his illness.   Encouraged by developments outside the prison walls, his thoughts turned to his
release and to the earthly agents who would compass it.   He
had already petitioned the Privy Council for his liberty.   Now
he began to bombard all kinds of people with petitions—a
technique he would always find profitable.   He wrote to the
magistrates, to the Mayor and Aldermen of London, he wrote
" multitudes " of humble petitions to the King and nobles, he
wrote to friends at The Hague to beg the Queen of Bohemia to
intercede with her brother, the King of England, on his behalf.[4]
He wrote several times to the Wardens of the Fleet themselves,
taunting them with their inability to stop his writing and
printing, and—to make good his boast—a large number of
these letters and petitions actually appeared in print.[5]

In May 1639, with the Scottish army on the English frontier,
he added to the considerable unrest in the capital by appealing
direct " To all the brave, courageous, and valiant Apprentices
of the honourable City of London, but especially those that
appertain to the worshipfull Company of Cloth workers (of
which company, if I live I hope to be a Free man)."   This
letter was secretly printed, and at Whitsuntide, June 4, 1639,
Katherine Hadley took copies of it, and of another pamphlet
called *A Cry for Justice*, and threw them among apprentices
and others holidaying in Moorfields.   The action caused

considerable stir. She was immediately arrested, and the City
authorities confiscated what pamphlets they could. But not
before the apprentices had acted upon the instructions of
Free-born John and flocked " by hundreds of thousands " to
Lambeth Palace, where they not only did as Lilburne requested,
and " in a faire and peaceable way " importuned Laud without
rest that Lilburne be released from prison, but also initiated a
considerable riot. Indeed, wrote Lilburne exultantly ten years
later, this was like to have saved the hangman a job so far as
the Archbishop was concerned ! [6]   The pamphlets, as Laud
noted in his diary, were both " very Seditious Papers," and the
Letter calculated " to excite the Apprentices." [7]   The adventure
lost Lilburne the services of Katherine Hadley, who was sent
to the Poultry Counter, where she was kept without trial for
seven months, and then, still without examination, transferred
to Bridewell, where she was made to pay twelve pence a week
for her lodging and was " churlishly used by the matron, and
put among the common sluts," whose society was " a hell
upon earth to one that fears the Lord." [8]

But a fortnight after she so courageously did her work for
Lilburne the Treaty of Berwick ended the first Bishops' War
and gave the Scots the religious independence they sought.
While their Assembly then formally abolished episcopacy and
the Prayer Book, and ordered that every Scot should sign the
Covenant, there were indications that they would also throw off
the English yoke in matters political. Charles, seeking to re-
establish his authority in both spheres, could no longer evade
the constitutional issue in England. On the advice of Thomas
Wentworth, the Lord Deputy of Ireland, whom Charles created
Earl of Strafford on January 12, 1640, the first Parliament for
eleven years was summoned to Westminster for the following
April.

Eagerly Lilburne and the prisoners for conscience' sake
listened for news of the knights and burgesses who rode up
from the shires and boroughs all over England and Wales with
the petitions of the freeholders and citizens they represented.
The younger Members had never seen a Parliament before:
many of their constituents had never previously voted—a
pamphlet was hurriedly published explaining *The Priviledges
and Practice of Parliaments in England,* describing the method

of election, the electorate, and what purported to be the origin of Parliament.[9] All were in grim mood as Member after Member stood up and read his petition—the honour of being first fell to Harbottle Grimston, Member for Colchester—against ship-money, projects, monopolies, loans and taxation, Star Chamber, High Commission, innovations in religion, tonnage and poundage, knighthood fines, the enlargement of forests and forest fines, the breaches of Parliamentary privilege.[10] Those outside waited for news, not least expectantly John Lilburne in the Fleet prison. The speeches were not immediately published: " . . . it was not then in fashion to print Speeches of Parliament," [11] the presses were only beginning their work, reporters were not allowed in the House, and the news-writers had not learned how to gather news of Parliamentary proceedings. The Members themselves were only just becoming conscious of the propaganda value of their speeches. Several sent letters to their friends and families, a few kept day-to-day diaries, but no one endeavoured immediate publication. The exception was the two-hour speech of John Pym, cataloguing the grievances which " lay heavy upon the Commonwealth." " A good oration ! " cried Members as he finished, and heads of the speech were immediately printed and circulated, being " with great greedinesse taken by Gentlemen and others throughout the Kingdom." [12] There is no doubt, therefore, that Lilburne would have read or heard how Pym had summed up the country's grievances as concerning the liberties and privileges of Parliament, innovations in religion, and " the proprieties of our goods," bluntly announcing that these were the grievances which had disabled them from granting any supply, and would still disable them, until they were redressed.[13] The King was unwilling to resolve the deadlock, and on May 5, within three weeks of its assembly, this Parliament, like its predecessors, was dissolved.

It is likely that even more damage than this hasty dissolution was done to the King's cause by the promulgation of seventeen new Canons by the House of Convocation, unprecedently kept in session after Parliament was dissolved. These repeated in some detail the forms of worship which had caused most offence to all but extreme Arminians, laid down the subjects for preaching at various times, and endeavoured to prevent any change in doctrine or church government by imposing an oath not on churchmen only, but on lawyers, medical doctors, and schoolmasters. Even more important was the insistence that every clergyman should read aloud, once every quarter at morning prayer, a statement expressing in extreme form the Divine Right of Kings: " The most high and sacred order of kings is of divine right, being the ordinance of God himself, founded in the prime laws of nature, and clearly established by express texts both of the Old and New Testaments. . . . For subjects to bear arms against their kings, offensive or defensive . . . is at least to resist the powers which are ordained of God; and . . . they shall receive to themselves damnation." [14]

Coming at a time when many in England were openly supporting the Scottish Covenant, and even the soldiers raised to fight the Scots deemed that the rebels had been " the redeemers of their religion and liberty," [15] this statement seemed a deliberate provocation alike to the Scots and to English Puritans, and marked the King's determination to take the offensive against both. His efforts to raise money, the City's alarm over this and Puritan fears at the threat to their religion, formed the background to the excitements of the spring and summer of 1640. Throughout those months the prisoners in the Fleet were aware of the repeated rush of feet as apprentices streamed down Ludgate Hill and into Fleet Street to swarm into Whitehall and Westminster. Trying desperately to get the money the Parliament had refused, the King on May 7 summoned the Lord Mayor and several Aldermen of London to the Council, but even in face of Strafford's burst of anger—" Unless you hang up some of them, you will do no good with them " [16]—they refused to comply, and four of them were imprisoned. Who can doubt but that Alderman Soames's words reached Lilburne in the Fleet: " I was held an honest man whilst I was a commoner, and I would continue to be so now I am an alderman." [17]

Lilburne's own scheme of the previous year of scattering pamphlets among the apprentices, urging them to seize the Archbishop's palace, was paralleled by the " libels . . . continually set up in all places of note in the City " of which Laud complained.[18] On May 9, 1640, one of these, posted on the

Old Exchange in London, caused the trained bands of Southwark to be called out fully armed in St George's Fields two
days later. The Archbishop fortified his house with cannon
and resisted the five hundred persons " of the Rascal Routous
multitude " who swarmed round it at midnight on the 11th.[19]
The sounds of the riot would doubtless have been heard in the
Fleet. So would—with rising hopes—the noises ten days later,
when rioters broke into Newgate prison to release those
imprisoned for the attack on Laud's house. Attack threatened
also on the apartments of the Queen Mother, the unpopular
Roman Catholic Marie de' Medici, who was assigned the rôle
of evil genius behind the throne. She had sought asylum
in England when her power had been overthrown in France,
and her influence over her daughter was believed to be strong.
Insulting placards against the Queen, an announcement that
the King's palace was to let, appeared overnight. The Lord
Mayor, acceding to the King's request and trying to collect
ship-money, found only one person willing to pay. The City
still refused a loan. Individuals and farmers of the customs
helped a little, but not enough. On July 5 Charles seized the
bullion in the Tower valued at £130,000. His promise of
repayment in six months did not stop the protests of the City,
led by the Merchant Adventurers, who finally lent him £40,000
on the security of the farmers of the customs. Six days later
Charles ordered the debasement of the coinage, but in face of
merchants' threats to raise the price of commodities was
forced to withdraw. The pressed men he was raising south
of the Humber to reinforce the trained bands of the border
counties were openly mutinous. It was noted that these
" Common Souldiers would not be satisfied, questioning in a
mutinous manner, Whether their Captains were Papists or
not . . . laying violent hands on divers of their Commanders,
and killing some, uttering in bold speeches their distaste to the
Cause, to the astonishment of many, that common people
should be sensible of publike Interest and Religion. . . ." [20]
Here was the beginning of that interest which common soldiers
would shortly take on a far larger scale.

While Englishmen were questioning the cause for which
they were impressed, the Scots, " with a sword in one hand, and
a Petition in the other," [21] crossed the Tweed. Lilburne would

have heard of their subsequent progress with more than
common interest—how the English attempted to hold the
lower southern bank of the river Tyne he knew so well, dispersing before the Scots, who forded it at Newburn on August
28. On the same day a petition was presented to the King
signed by twelve peers, but drawn up by a wider group, including Pym, which again summarized the country's grievances
and called for a Parliament. It is noteworthy that this petition
was immediately printed and widely circulated.[22]

The King had little alternative but to agree to the Treaty
of Ripon, which confirmed the presence of the Scots in
Northumberland and Durham with maintenance amounting
to £850 a day until a permanent settlement was reached.[23]
The Scots were orderly; they guaranteed the dispatch of Tyne
coal to London. Even the rumours that they intended to
make every one sign the Covenant were not badly received.
As Vane wrote to Windebank, on September 7, it was a
suggestion which the population, especially the tenants of the
Church, being disgusted with the clergy there, who had held
too hard a hand upon them, might be but too apt to embrace.
It had been well, he added, these things had been foreseen.[24]

While Lilburne's imagination was lively enough to picture
the Scottish army living at the expense of his friends in Newcastle and County Durham, he heard from his prison time and
again the excited cries of the London mob. On October 22
they dashed into the High Commission Court while it was
sitting and tore down benches and threw furniture into the
street; on the following Sunday they rushed into St Paul's
and destroyed quantities of papers they found in an office,
believing them to be records of High Commission.[25] The
King, having failed to raise money, with the Scots quartered on
English soil, riots in the capital, and a steadily increasing cry
for a Parliament, had no alternative but to yield. On November
3, 1640, Members were again gathered at Westminster for the
Parliament which was to outlive the King who summoned it.
As in the previous April, nearly all the Members were armed,
by petition or otherwise, with their constituents' grievances.

Hyde from the North spoke against the Council of the North,
Digby from the West of ship-money, impressment, monopolies,
subsidies. Culpepper rose to speak for Kent: " I stand not

up with the Petition in my hand as others have done before me, I have it in my Mouth . . ." and he spoke of the old grievances against Papists, new ceremonies in religion, of ship-money, military charges incurred by the Scottish wars, of monopolists —" they sup in our Cup, they dip in our Dish." Waller spoke against corrupt judges, against ship-money; Falkland spoke of religion: ". . . it hath been more dangerous for men to go to some Neighbours Parish, when they had no Sermon in their own, than to be obstinate and perpetual Recusants; while Masses have been said in security, a Conventicle hath been a crime, and which is yet more, the conforming to Ceremonies hath been more exacted, than the conforming to Christianity."

But even more than the presentation of grievances the opening of the Long Parliament was notable for the way in which these grievances were being crystallized into a demand for frequent Parliaments: all other issues were becoming comprised in the constitutional. As Harbottle Grimston put it, of the three main matters with which they were concerned—privileges of Parliament, matters of religion, and the property of goods and estates —it was the first, " as the great Ark " in which the other two were comprised. The cause of the troubles, said Digby, was above all " the want of Parliaments, the primary and the efficient cause. Ill Ministers have made ill times, but that Sir hath made ill Ministers." From every point of view triennial Parliaments were necessary. How could the King otherwise raise money? " Projects and Monopolies are but leaking Conduit-pipes " said Sir Benjamin Rudyerd. " The Exchequer it self at the fullest, is but a Cistern, and now a broaken one; frequent Parliaments only are the Fountain." It was left for Lord Digby to expound the constitutional issue without a shadow of doubt. " The People of England," he said, " cannot open their ears, their hearts, their mouths, nor their purses to his Majesty, but in Parliament." [26]

But before a Triennial Act could be passed, amid rumours of foreign troops to support the King, of the " Irish army " to be brought over by Strafford, and the King's intention to secure the Tower, on November 9, six days after the meeting of Parliament, there arose in the House of Commons to present a petition for release from John Lilburne " a gentleman . . . very ordinarily apparelled " in " a plain cloth-suit, which seemed to have been made by an ill country tailor "; with linen " plain, and not very clean " and " a speck or two of blood upon his little band, which was not much larger than his collar." It was one of the Members for Cambridge, making his first contribution to the debates of the Long Parliament. In a " voice sharp and untuneable " Cromwell " aggravated the imprisonment of this man by the council table unto that height, that one would have believed the very government itself had been in great danger by it." Of such effect was the " eloquence full of fervour " with which Cromwell spoke on Lilburne's behalf,[27] allied with the natural feelings of a large section of the Long Parliament, that Lilburne's case was immediately referred to a committee.[28] On the same day monopolists were excluded from the House. Two days later, behind locked doors, the Commons agreed to the impeachment of Strafford and his immediate imprisonment. On November 13 Lilburne and other prisoners were liberated in order to present their cases to Parliament. With what ceremonial were the doors of the Fleet opened to Lilburne? It is strange that he never said. But " he was exceedingly beloved and pitied throughout the land," [29] and his portrait was engraved by George Glover. A fortnight later, when Prynne and Burton reached London from their more remote prisons, they were accorded a triumphal reception, escorted by a hundred coaches, two thousand horsemen, and a great crowd on foot, of whom Lilburne was surely one, wearing in their hats rosemary and bay in token of joy and triumph.[30] A week later Bastwick was given a similar welcome. A week after this, on December 11, a petition said to bear 15,000 signatures was brought to the House by a great crowd demanding the extirpation of bishops "root and branch." On December 18 Laud was accused of high treason: he was " the root and ground of all our miseries," as Harbottle Grimston said in the Commons. In the same month Katherine Hadley was released from prison, and shortly afterwards Lilburne, taking up her case, obtained £10 for her as reparation for her imprisonment.[31]

Throughout 1641 the struggle continued. The City delayed its loan to the King because Strafford's trial was not proceeding sufficiently rapidly. On March 1 Laud was committed to the Tower on a unanimous vote for attempting to alter religion and the fundamental laws of the realm. As he passed through the

City streets the mob rushed at his carriage to pull him out. What would Lilburne's thoughts have been as he watched? Three years had brought this reversal in fortune—the prelate so low, the Puritan apprentice so full of hope. So God had proved Himself. Well might Lilburne recall Sibbes at Paul's Cross: ". . . till our houre comes, all the Devils in hell cannot hurt one haire of our head. . . . what can all the enemies of Gods people do, except God permit them?"

CHAPTER SEVEN

Captain John Lilburne

Well then into the Wars I went . . . an honest, active and stout
Commander . . . as ready and willing to adventure my life as
any man I marched along with.

JOHN LILBURNE, *Innocency and Truth Justified*

LILBURNE HAD MATURED DURING HIS TWO AND A HALF YEARS'
imprisonment. He went in as Hewson's apprentice. He emerged
as a Puritan pamphleteer and campaigner of standing, with the
added lustre of owing his release to the Parliament and to the
good offices of Oliver Cromwell. In prison he had widened his
reading, deepened his thinking, and sharpened the edge of his
naturally antagonistic nature against the injustices of prison life.
He left the Fleet to find all the questions—and more—which
had been at issue when he went in, under discussion by the
Parliament which had freed him. As always, ready to implement
his beliefs with action, he was frequently at Westminster Hall
with his old friends of the City to get the latest news and put in
a word or more for the Puritan cause. He was there towards
the end of March to watch the preparations for the trial of
Strafford. He listened to most of the trial itself, and on May 3,
1641, took part in the demonstration against Strafford in which
merchants and shopkeepers joined with apprentices and the mob
to clamour for a speedy sentence and execution that would end
the uncertainty that was crippling trade. Being asked by an
acquaintance why so many people were there, Lilburne cried
that they came for justice ! Their numbers would grow, he
said, to forty or fifty thousand by the following day, and
although they came now with their cloaks, they would come
then with their swords by their sides ! If they could not have
justice against Strafford, he asserted, they would pull the King
out of Whitehall ! [1] His words were carried to the King, and
the next day Lilburne found himself again in custody, being

brought before the House of Lords on a charge of high treason. It was the very day that the Commons, having heard the report of their Committee, pronounced void the Star Chamber sentence against him as " bloody, wicked, cruel, barbarous, and tyrannical," and voted him reparations,[2] though without naming a sum. Happily for him, the witnesses against him on the new charge failed to agree, and the Lords willingly dismissed it, so that Lilburne found himself unconditionally free, and without stigma.[3]

Six days later an Act against perpetual Parliaments reinforced the Triennial Act of February 16. Two days after that Strafford was beheaded, Archbishop Laud blessing him from his cell in the Tower of London as he passed to execution. Lilburne was among the 200,000 persons on Tower Hill who watched him die.[4] Perhaps it was then that he seized the occasion of so large a concourse to address the crowd on Parliament's behalf. When constables approached to break up the meeting Lilburne exhorted his hearers to stand fast and resist, drawing his own sword on the constables and finally being taken into temporary custody [5]: already he was showing a tendency to oppose all who attempted to check him—friends and foes alike.

In the hectic summer of 1641 the framework of Parliamentary supremacy was completed. Extra-Parliamentary sources of taxation were sealed up : tonnage and poundage and impositions were to be levied only with the consent of Parliament, ship-money was pronounced illegal, the boundaries of forests were limited, and Lilburne had the satisfaction of seeing the Courts of Star Chamber and High Commission formally abolished on July 5, while the Councils of the North and of the Marches of Wales, resting on no positive statute, automatically ceased to function.

But the bare bones of constitutional government do not feed and clothe a man, however young and ardent, and Lilburne had to find work. Hewson had retired; his own capital was negligible. Friends were urging him to go abroad as a factor when Parliament's vote of indemnity in May encouraged him to stay in the capital in the hope of a speedy settlement, a decision which was confirmed when his uncle George came to his assistance about the same time. This was that George Lilburne of Newcastle and Sunderland who was described as

no saint, a man who " might pretend to Tybourn as well as
Religion," whose trades were infinite—chaundler, grocer,
mercer, linen-draper, keelman, freighter to ships, farmer of
collieries, farmer of land.[6] In this case he became with his
nephew a brewer, sinking £1000 in a London brewery, which
he and his nephew controlled jointly.[7] Presumably he supplied
the capital, but left the actual management to John, he himself
remaining in Sunderland near the pulse of his other enterprises.

Lilburne knew nothing of brewing, but it was an industry
which amply repaid the sinking of a little capital, as the growing
number of breweries in London indicated, and which George
Lilburne's business acumen perceived. The decayed brewery
they took over responded rapidly to the injection of capital,
and business prospered. But its ties were not sufficient to keep
Lilburne within doors, and he again played his part in the riots
of Christmas and the New Year of 1641–42. When the usual
City elections were held on December 21 a predominantly
Puritan Common Council was returned, which could be expected to side with the House of Commons as the Aldermen
sided with Charles and the peers.[8] The King, feeling it prudent
in consequence to secure the Tower and its garrison to his own
cause, on December 21 dismissed the Parliamentarian Lieutenant
and appointed Thomas Lunsford, known as a swaggering bully
and suspected of papacy. No more unwise choice could have
been made. The Lord Mayor told Charles that unless Lunsford
was removed he could not answer for the peace of the City.
The atmosphere was charged with suspicion and apprehension.
On Christmas Eve a Frenchman, examined by the watch, admitted he had been at Mass at Somerset House, and bystanders
alleged he added that he had been about such a plot as they
would hear of later ! He was committed. So were two French-
men coming to London by water. They spoke to each other
in French, but their waterman was convinced they spoke of a
plot, saying " that Monday and Tuesday would be the bloodiest
dayes and nights in the City of London." He said nothing
until he had taken his fare and tied up his boat, when he followed
the two men and called for their arrest.[9] By the evening of the
26th Lunsford had been dismissed, but on the following day
uncertainty brought citizens and apprentices streaming once
more to Westminster Hall. As the Members assembled the

crowd cried out against bishops and " Popish Lords." The situation was already ugly when Lunsford with some thirty or forty friends passed through the Hall. Inevitably a skirmish started, and, the news of the affray spreading, hundreds more citizens and apprentices, Lilburne among them, came pouring in from the City armed with staves, swords, and brickbats, forcing their way into Westminster Abbey, damaging some of the monuments, surging around Whitehall Palace. The rioters were ordered home and the trained bands summoned, but as these troops were for the most part the Puritan masters of these very apprentices,the rioters had no fear of serious punishment, and the tumult continued all night. Lunsford escaped by water, some of the rioters were locked into the Abbey, and the following day when the Lord Mayor, accompanied by Lilburne and others, came to inquire after them shots were fired in which both the Lord Mayor and Lilburne were slightly wounded.[10] The tension continued. Only two bishops took their places in the House of Lords; Charles directed that all gentlemen of the Court wear swords and that a guard be posted at Whitehall Gate (the Holbein Gate). The absentee bishops protested that no resolutions passed in their absence were valid. Twelve of them were promptly impeached, and the House of Commons asked for a guard.

Lilburne has left no account of his actions in the subsequent period of rising climax that finally brought the country to open war—the King's attempt to impeach the Five Members, accusing them, in terms that had been applied to Strafford, of traitorously endeavouring to subvert the fundamental laws and government; the strange delay that caused him to arrive at the House of Commons on January 4, when they had already slipped away by water to the safety of the City; the King's pursuit the next day through crowded streets to the Guildhall, where he vainly summoned the Five Members amid cries of " God bless the King ! " and " Privileges of Parliament ! "; the adjournment of the House of Commons and its meeting as a committee at the Guildhall; the departure of the King and Queen for Hampton Court on the 10th and the triumphal return of the Members to Westminster on the 11th, carried by the Thames watermen, escorted by barges and boats and the Southwark trained bands, accompanied by thousands of citizens, apprentices and others, while four thousand of Hampden's Buckinghamshire men came riding in with a petition on his behalf; the King's departure for Yorkshire, his attempts to secure the arms left at Hull after the Scottish war, the raising of troops by both sides.

Lilburne's unprecedented absence from the scene at this time is accounted for by the fact that, having been at liberty for just over twelve months and with his brewery flourishing, he felt free to marry. " I confesse I partly know it by experience," he wrote in later life, chiding a newly married friend, " that divers moneths after marriage are most commonly a time of dotage." He has recorded little of his courtship, save that his wife, Elizabeth Dewell, was " an object deare in my affections severall yeares before from me she knew anything of it." [11] She had honoured and comforted him before she became his wife, even " when he was more like Job upon the dunghill by his sufferings . . . than a man at that time [fit] for her society." [12] This must have been during his imprisonment in the Fleet. Was she perhaps the mysterious woman who visited him immediately after his whipping whom he had known previously only by sight? She became " dearer to him then himself, as she well deserved," [13] and she in her turn was devoted to her husband, serving him and helping him with love and loyalty through all the crises of their stormy married life. Her husband treated her always with the utmost tenderness, quite different from the challenging bravado with which he faced the world. Yet the cause he served came always first. Love her he certainly did, but his was a dedicated soul, and nothing could interfere with the fulfilment of its mission. Never again would Elizabeth Lilburne know the peace of the first few months of her marriage, as she and her husband set up home in London, ran the brewery, and let the outside world go by.

It was a world in which the final alignments in the Civil War were being made. Most of the constitutional and economic changes regarded as fundamental by the Long Parliament had been achieved by the autumn of 1641: assuming the Members were typical of the 40s. freeholders and upward and the mostly comfortably-off citizens who had sent them to Parliament with their lengthy and eloquent petitions, it would seem that the time had come to end strife. Far from this being the case, however, there developed a rift in Parliament and a growth of a King's party sufficient to muster two-fifths of the Commons on a Parliamentary division at the beginning of 1642, against merely one-tenth a year earlier, and, by August 1642,[14] a fighting force not far inferior to that of Parliament.

Lilburne, perhaps, would have explained these facts in terms of religion. Not only had no ecclesiastical settlement been reached, but whenever the House discussed religion a serious division in its ranks was revealed. By the end of 1641 no substantial religious changes had been made in spite of the imprisonment of Laud and the abolition of the Court of High Commission. The Root and Branch Bill never passed the House of Commons. The Grand Remonstrance was passed by a narrow majority only, the clauses which roused most objection being those which referred to religion. At a crucial moment one section of the opposition to the Laudian Church found itself more inclined to reform the Church from within than to tamper with it from without, the reason for this being a double-edged fear both of the inherent intolerance of Presbyterianism and of religious unorthodoxy.

The first was expressed as early as 1641 by some petitioners from Cheshire who were fearful of " the mere arbitrary government of a numerous Presbytery, who, together with their ruling elders, will arise to near 40,000 Church governors." [15] The second was expressed in the many pamphlets which derided the sectaries and their preachers—cobblers, tinkers, pedlars, weavers, chimney-sweeps, and manual workers of all kinds who made " such a giddinesse in the profession of Religion " that almost every one was led by his own opinion. This, in turn, led to fear of social disorder, which was given substance by the fact that almost any preacher at any time was likely to arouse resentment that led to disturbance. At St Olave's, Old Jewry, as the Bishop of Chichester in his lawn sleeves mounted the pulpit, there were cries of " A Pope, a Pope! " In St Paul's sectaries struck the preacher and defaced the organ; others tried to pull down the cross in Cheapside, breaking the arms and legs of the Christ. On December 9, 1641, a crowd of opposite views gathered outside the house of Praise-God Barebone, the leather-seller, who was preaching loudly to a congregation of the elect. They stormed his house, unhooked its sign, and were about to hang up the preacher himself when the constables arrived. The same day some of the congregation at St Sepulchre's dragged off the preacher, Prophet Hunt, who had announced Divine Vengeance on an evil generation.[16]

Such incidents underlined the real meaning of the partnership of Church and State which James and Charles had both realized, and caused many to look again to the bishops as bulwarks of social order. Sir John Strangeways, in the course of the debate on the Root and Branch petition, had already sensed the danger: " If we make a parity in the Church we must come to a parity in the Commonwealth." [17]

While a Royalist party was thus gaining from religious uncertainty, Puritans themselves, of all beliefs, remained in the uneasy alliance which would take them into the Civil War, but split their ranks later on: the very name ' Puritan ' had already become a misleading cover for all who opposed the King or the Church of England.

Economic issues were also confused at the moment of the split into civil war. A predatory Parliament could arouse as much alarm as a predatory king. When the City delayed a loan in 1641 because of the slowness of Strafford's trial and Pym proposed " that in respect of the great necessitie of the publike " they " might compell the Londoners to lend," there was an immediate clamour. It " conduced to the violation of the liberties and proprieties of the subject," as Simonds D'Ewes said. " For certainlie, if the least feare of this should grow that men should bee compelled to lend, all men will conceale ther readie moneie, and lend nothing to us voluntarilie." [18]

At the same time, while many petitions blamed the King for taxation, for stopping money at the Mint, for trade and business stagnation, many could imply support for either side. There were also numerous petitions from the poor, some not even concerned with the issues then at stake, many strikingly resembling the manifestos which would later become so common. The various reasons given for distress were con-fused, including taxation, aliens, popish lords, economic high-handedness, uncertainty. In all these pamphlets is the feeling of real social distress, real poverty, whether of unemployment and low wages or of overcrowded alleys in London and Westminster where foreigners crowd in upon existing accommodation, taking work from the natives and increasing the dangers of plague. There is the desperately baulked feeling of not knowing what to do or where to turn: they have no leaders, they cannot " wage law " (what bitter experience is behind such a telling phrase?). This is the wretchedness and helplessness that, once given the lead, will make a social revolution. At each successive settlement that would be made in the struggle to come this residue would still be left.[19]

The recurring threat to social stability inherent in the situation in 1642 was realized by some who, for that reason, decided to fight on the King's side. John Hotham, for example, deserting from Parliament even after the fighting had started, gave as one of his reasons that he feared that " the necessitous people of the whole kingdome will presently rise in mighty numbers, and whosoever they pretend for att first, within a while they will sett up for themselves to the utter ruine of all the Nobility and Gentry of the kingdome." [20]

If religious and economic uncertainty helped to determine men's allegiance in the Civil War, their personal assessment of the situation also counted—whether the settlement reached by the end of 1641 would be honoured by the King; his ability to break it if he wished; the strength of the Queen's influence; the possibility of foreign aid for the King.

While each side was consolidating its forces, it was at the same time stating its case in print.

The importance of print in the struggle was perhaps first realized when the heads of Pym's speech to the Short Parliament were printed and " greedily taken up " by gentlemen all over the country. The King rapidly published his reasons for dissolving the Short Parliament.[21] Pym, in August 1640, ordered the publication of the Petition of the Peers to the King. The Grand Remonstrance was published, though not without opposition from Members who feared that its wide dispersal would be a threat to social order.[22] In June 1641 a collection of speeches and passages in Parliament from the opening of the Long Parliament to June 1641 was published,[23] and by the end of the year no major speech or resolution failed to find its publisher. A newspaper appeared at the end of

December—*Diurnall Occurrences*. Its appearance was spasmodic, but by the following year there were 167 different ones,
and a growing pamphlet literature reproduced *Declarations*
from each side, petitions and reports from various parts of the
country.[24]   Some one even saw fit to explain the course of
passing Bills in Parliament,[25] just as a year earlier some one had
explained the procedure of election.   At the same time the
spokesmen on either side were appealing to wider principles
of political and moral obligation, seeking precedents in real
or imagined history, quite consciously regarding their work as
part of a regular campaign.

Before the end of 1642 there had appeared several of Henry
Parker's pamphlets, including the *Case of Shipmony* and the
Divine Right of Episcopacie, Sir Robert Cotton's *Discourse
concerning the Power of the Parliament*, reprints of Raleigh's
Maxims of State, of John Ponnet's *Short Treatise of Politique
Power*, of Nicholas Fuller's *Case of Tho. Lad and Rich. Mansell*,
of Lilburne's *Christian Mans Triall*; Bishop Hall had defended
episcopacy, and the replies of Smectymnuus and John Milton
been made.   Robert, Lord Brooke, had written his fine plea
for toleration—*A Discourse opening the Nature of that Episcopacie which is exercised in England*—there had been lives of
Luther, of Jack Straw and Wat Tyler, and of Richard II.   A
new name also appeared in January 1642, that of Richard
Overton, who published a broadly humorous pamphlet entitled
Articles of High Treason exhibited against Cheap-side Crosse.

The rate of growth of the pamphlet literature can be judged
by the collection of the London bookseller, George Thomason,
who, in the year the Parliament met, began to collect one copy
of each of the tracts, broadsides, and news-sheets which came
his way.   For London his collection is virtually complete,
though he may have failed to procure some of the provincial
publications.   He collected 24 in 1640, 721 the following year,
and 2134 in 1642.[26]

This was the very stuff to feed Lilburne's ardour, and there
is no doubt that he was familiar with the pamphlet literature
of these months.   To the abuses known to him personally
were thus added the economic, social, and constitutional
issues which had as yet formed no part of his experience.   In
the same way the religious speculation with which he was

familiar prepared him for the political, philosophical, and historical argument he now encountered. It must have been about this time that he proceeded from Fuller to Coke and became more closely aware of Magna Carta. Soon " fundamental law," " the law of nature," the " compact between King and people," became current with Lilburne, as with all the Parliamentarian controversialists.

When the actual fighting started 43 per cent. of the Members of the Long Parliament, most of them from the West, the South-west, and the North, joined the King. Fifty-five per cent., mostly from the East, the South-east, and the Midlands, fought for Parliament. Many of these may have wished they could have stayed with the 2 per cent. who remained uncommitted. On both sides were large and small landowners, old landed families and new, merchants, industrialists, and lawyers, rising gentry and falling gentry.[27] For the country as a whole it is impossible to generalize, save that the majorities of the West, South-west, and North followed their M.P.'s in being Royalist, while the majorities of the East, South-east, and Midlands followed theirs in being Parliamentarian. In all parts of the country traditional loyalty was important, and any family powerful through land or trade, ancient or *parvenu*, could command support. In some parts a strong tradition— like the non-conformity of East Anglia—decided the issue. Monopolists who had been deprived by Parliament naturally supported the King.

With individuals personal issues frequently turned the scale, and those who were in the King's personal service, like Sir Edmund Verney, never swerved from their support, although perhaps their principles were engaged with the other side. Intense suffering was often caused by such a conflict, the deep uncertainty of Falkland, for example, leading him to seek an early death in battle on the side of the King, whose policy he had—until the Grand Remonstrance—consistently opposed in Parliament.

Nor is it possible to do more than guess at the difference between the rank and file of either side. Agricultural labourers, whom the war passed by, except when a battle or a troop of horse swept over the fields they worked, the riff-raff of the towns ready to tag on to a passing phase of the war, the pressed

men—notorious on both sides for deserting to their homes at
the slightest provocation—the ' clubmen ' who stood for an
organized neutrality, lend support to the view that a great
many people either cared little or merely wished that great ones
would set their house in order without bloodshed.   But there
were parts of the country—for example, the clothing districts
of Somerset—where, as Lord Clarendon noted, the common
people, who had benefited from his social policy, were generally
for the King,[28] while all over the country increasing numbers of
petitions from the poor indicated support for Parliament.   On
both sides it was clear that somewhere in the fighting—even at
the beginning of the war—were soldiers who were merely
fighting for a better standard of living.

The Lilburne family was wholeheartedly Parliamentarian, in
spite of the fact that the county was firmly held by the Royalists
and Newcastle was a Royalist stronghold.   In Sunderland
George Lilburne by this time held a position of commanding
importance, possessing a far greater share both of property and
wealth than any other private family within the borough.   A
man of immense vitality, he married twice and had fourteen
children.   In 1634, when Bishop Morton granted a Charter of
Incorporation to Sunderland, George Lilburne was one of its
twelve Aldermen.   He was certainly ' rising gentry,' a second
son of a landowner of small or middling estate, going early
into trade, flourishing through his own astuteness and his
ability to keep going a variety of concerns, letting money make
money in all of them, selling out at the right time, establishing
his sons as merchants and barristers in London as well as the
North, marrying two daughters to London merchants and
another into the powerful Ellison family of Merchant Adventurers, of older standing commercially than the Lilburnes, but
surely also ' rising.'   During the whole of the Civil Wars
George Lilburne acted as the only magistrate within the
borough, he sat on the Committee of Sequestrations for
County Durham, and did well for himself out of the office.
He himself would sit in Cromwell's Parliament of 1654 as
Knight of the Shire; his son would join Cromwell's Parliament
of 1656, and, like his father, would acquire delinquents' lands.
A family connexion, meanwhile, Robert Ellison, would join
the Long Parliament as ' recruiter ' for Newcastle, but be

secluded at Pride's Purge. George Lilburne's influence was sufficient to bring to Parliament's support an overwhelming majority of the borough of Sunderland, whose voters, like himself, consisted of newly risen or rising middling gentry leavened and encouraged by a number of Scottish settlers. Outside the borough " ancient and opulent " families of gentry more immediately connected with the nobility, and attached to the Crown from hereditary principle, complete this copybook example of Civil War allegiance by being consistently Royalist.[29]

Lilburne's own father and brothers, not themselves connected with trade, but small landowners making a somewhat precarious living, already by some quirk that was probably entirely personal being of a Puritan inclination, followed Parliament in spite of Richard Lilburne's Court associations. The youngest son, Henry, changed his allegiance during the wars, but the rest remained staunch. Richard was early associated with the Parliamentarian Vanes, and was one of the first in County Durham to declare against ship-money. He sat on the Committee of Sequestrations for his county, and did well out of delinquents' lands, though not so well as George. Robert, by marrying Margaret Beke, of Haddenham, in Buckinghamshire, forged another link in the Puritan associations of his family. Margaret was the granddaughter of Richard Beke and Coluberry Lovelace, sister of Lord Lovelace. Coluberry married, as her second husband, Simon Mayne, and their son was Simon Mayne, the regicide. Bekes and Maynes were friends and neighbours of the Hampdens and other Buckinghamshire Puritans. Robert Lilburne distinguished himself as a soldier, particularly during the second Civil War and Cromwell's Scottish campaign. He rose from a captain in Manchester's army to Colonel of Foot in the New Model, and became Governor of Newcastle, receiving two silver flagons from the corporation in appreciation of his services. Like his wife's kinsman, he signed the King's death warrant, and he was returned to Parliament in 1654 for the County of Durham and in 1656 for the East Riding of Yorkshire. When Lambert became Major-General of the five northern counties in 1655 Robert Lilburne acted as his deputy in Yorkshire and Durham.[30]

John Lilburne himself, the second son of a small landowner, apprenticed to a trade, later starting his own business with a small capital and good prospects, would appear to be the typical case of the small man who would benefit from the economic freedom promised by Parliament, and, quite apart from his previous religious experience, his support of Parliament could be expected. He was spared the anguish of a Falkland or a Verney and the sad perplexity of Sergeant-Major Kirle, who could never understand the fiction that to fight the King's irregular government meant shooting at him in the field. Having, as he said, read the Parliament's most excellent Declarations, and having himself sufficiently smarted under the King's irregular government, and believing the King to have violated the compact he made with his people in his Coronation oath, and believing the Parliament would be as good as its word and " secure the Peoples' lawes and liberties " to them, Lilburne gathered together all the friends he could and enlisted as captain in the troop of foot which Robert, Lord Brooke, was raising in the City of London in the summer and autumn of 1642.[31] His brewery, whose stock he valued at £1500, he let to a man called Binman, and his wife came with him and lived in quarters. " Well then into the Wars I went," remarked Lilburne gaily.[32] It was to be war almost to the end of his life. He never went back to his brewery, never resumed his normal life in London. For two and a half years he would be at the wars; well over half of the rest of his life would be spent in prison and exile.

CHAPTER EIGHT

Lieutenant-Colonel John Lilburne

> I scorned to be so base as to sit down in a whole skin ... while
> the liberties and freedomes of the kingdome was in danger.
>
> JOHN LILBURNE, *A Whip for the present House of Lords*

*W*HEN LILBURNE ENLISTED HE WAS A GOOD-LOOKING YOUNG
man with considerable personal charm, vigorous in mind and
body, argumentative to the point of rashness, with the principles
and practice of his future career already laid down. Glover's
portrait of 1641 with which William Larner prefaced the second
edition of *The Christian Mans Triall* showed an aristocratic
and sensitive face, the sweetness, almost gentleness, of the eyes
and mouth and the unassertive set of the head belying his
known physical and intellectual vigour, which, however, was
indicated by the strong nose and high forehead. The deep,
white, lace-edged collar to his doublet was elegant, his hair
was curled up over his ears, a thin line of hair showed on his
upper lip. One would have placed him in the study rather than
the field of action, armed him with the pen rather than the
sword, and expected literary effusions rather than political
polemics.

In the manœuvring and skirmishing of the first months of
the Civil War he moved with Lord General Essex's army to
Northampton, and on September 19, 1642, marched west while
the King's forces occupied Worcester. Rumour of a battle
before the city stirred the Parliament's troops to great eagerness
—" To Worcester ! To Worcester ! " they cried, pressing on
—and Lilburne can easily be imagined in the van. Nothing
happened, however, except that Rupert's men, coming on a
group of Parliamentarian horse led by Colonel Fiennes near
Powick Bridge, sent them scattering away, pursuing them as
far as Essex's bodyguard at Pershore, which also turned and
fled. Lilburne's activities are not recorded. Yet something

of what he saw rankled and was remembered in after-years. What he saw at Worcester and Edgehill, he said in 1648, gave him " cause to doubt, that there was no intention of a speedy end to the war, or of liberty to the people." [1]

When, a month after Powick Bridge, the King's army came down from the high ground of Edgehill on the morning of October 23 they were faced with a Parliamentarian army in which the London foot regiments of Holles and Brooke were prominent. Lilburne was about to be tested for a different kind of valour from that he had shown already. No details of his part in the engagement are known, but " he kept the Field all Night " [2] and won the confidence of Lord Brooke and the praise of the London citizens. When Rupert's horse cut through the Parliamentarian left and swept on to Kineton, where the baggage trains were, and where Elizabeth Lilburne was probably quartered with the women, Lilburne was plundered with the rest. When, after the indecisive battle, the King moved to Banbury and Oxford, which he entered in triumph on October 29, Lilburne fell back with the Parliamentarian army on Warwick and Northampton, and was then entrusted by Brooke with messages to London.

In the capital several of Lilburne's friends urged him to apply for a troop of horse in the new army of 16,000 men, which, amalgamated with the City trained bands, was to serve under the Earl of Warwick. His friends would provide the horse, and Lilburne easily obtained on November 11 the certificate of merit required by Warwick: " that Captain John Lilburne is a man both faithfull, able, and fit to be Captaine of a Troop of Horse (having shewed his valour at the batell of Kenton) [i.e., Kineton or Edgehill]." But Brooke, who had arrived in London, had news that the King was threatening the capital. " Lilburne," said the gentle commander, using the familiar speech, " I intreat thee doe not leave me, and my Regiment now, for I hope we shall beat him, and the wars will be at an end before thou canst get a troop of horse raised, and therefore if thou leavest me now, I shall thinke thou art either turned covetous, and therefore would have a troop of horse for a little more pay, or else thou art turned coward, and therefore would leave thy foot company, now when we are going to fight, and I doe beleeve shall doe it tomorrow."

Nothing could be more calculated to make Lilburne stay. " My Lord," he answered immediately, " it is not fit for me to make comparisons with you, but this give me leave to tell your honour, that because you shall know that I am as free from covetousnesse or cowardlinesse as your selfe, I will take my horse (for all it is so late) and post away to Branford to your Regiment and fight as resolutely tomorrow, as your Lordship shall." He was as good as his word, and reached Brentford at 9 P.M. that evening. The following morning, November 12, Rupert burst on the town out of the mist which heavily shrouded the river. Holles's regiment, which lay in front of the town, received the initial impetus and suffered heavy loss. Fighting bravely, they fell back on the town, where Brooke's regiment was quartered. Lilburne knew the importance of holding Rupert's men while the train of artillery was withdrawn. When Brooke's regiment turned to retreat towards London he therefore, being the senior officer present, galloped after them, seized their colours, and, bidding all whose hearts failed them to march back to London, called on those who had the spirits of men and the gallantry of soldiers and were willing resolutely to spend their blood for the good of their country, to follow him, promising never to leave them as long as he was able to fight.

Not for nothing had he learned how to talk to men. The soldiers turned about to a man and followed him back to Brentford. Being without match, powder, or bullet, they ransacked the shops and houses for any ammunition they could get, and, together with the remnant of Holles's men, disputed the ground bravely for five or six hours. Attacked with cannon and musket on front and flank, with neither breastwork nor trench, but only a small brick house and two or three hedges to give them shelter, the little force of not above 700 men fought desperately against several times their number. Many were driven into the river, some swimming to safety, others drowned. Many more were slain, others taken prisoner. But the train of artillery reached safety. Lilburne himself, escaping drowning several times, was at last taken prisoner and carried to Oxford.[3]

Imprisoned in Oxford Castle, he resisted attempts to bribe him to change sides by offers of Court advancement, and

was then put in irons, kept close prisoner, and compelled to
march into Oxford several times in his irons to appear before
Judge Heath on the charge of high treason. Lilburne amazed
the court by the vehemence and versatility of his defence.
First, he objected to being named in the indictment as
" yeoman," saying " that he would not plead to that Indictment, as it was drawn, for he would not admit any thing on
Record so much to the prejudice of his Family (who were
Gentlemen, and had continued ever since William the
Conqueror in the Bishoprick of Durham) as to answer to the
Name of Yeoman, since he was descended of the chief House
(now in being) of that Family."   Judge Heath ordered the
record to be mended,[4] but Lilburne then objected to being
charged " as he had been a Felon and not a Souldier," and
demanded a sword to fight any one or two of them single-
handed.   Though he protested still " that he honoured his
Majesty as much as any there present," Clarendon declared
" he behaved with so much impudence that it was manifest
he ambitioned martyrdom for his cause." [5]   On one occasion
the court tried to argue with him.   The Earl of Northampton
asked if his conscience had yet convicted him of that crime
for which he stood condemned by law.   Lilburne replied by
asking whether the abuses of the law had convicted their
consciences.   Prince Rupert even intervened to ask if it were
honourable to shed innocent blood by offensive arm.   Was it
lawful, Lilburne retorted, " to shed innocent blood by abuse
of the law? "   He again issued his challenge to combat, Rupert
being added to his list of opponents, his respect for the Prince
being demonstrated by the fact that, whereas he would take on
any two of the rest of them, Rupert he merely offered to fight
single-handed.   Unable to make anything of him, the court
rose, saying " the fellow is mad," and sent him back to prison.[6]

On December 13 Lilburne, through Mrs Primrose, the wife
of a prisoner who was visiting her husband, smuggled a letter
out of Oxford to Elizabeth.   He enclosed also letters to Sir
Henry Vane the younger and to the Speaker of the House of
Commons, containing the news that he and three other prisoners
were to be tried for high treason on the following Tuesday,
December 20.   It was Friday the 16th before the letter to the
Speaker was read in the House, and since the prisoners were

certain to be found guilty and sentenced to death, time was short. The House immediately prepared an announcement of *lex talionis*—a threat of retaliation in like manner on Royalist prisoners—and this was published on the Saturday. This left only two clear days before the trial in which to convey the threat through the enemy lines to Oxford. Elizabeth Lilburne had been frantically petitioning the House of Commons to help her husband, daily and hourly presenting herself at their bar, and she now, although with child, herself set out on the difficult and dangerous journey with a letter from the Speaker to Judge Heath containing the terms of the announcement. After " so many sad and difficult accidents, to a woman in her condition, as would force tears from the hardest heart," she brought her letter to the Royalist headquarters just in time. Her " wisdome, patience, diligence," as her husband fondly wrote, had saved Lilburne's life.[7]

Though reprieved, Lilburne was not released, and suffered considerable privations in Oxford Castle. His money went in buying food to keep him alive. The gaoler was brutal, Lilburne was open to the constant gibes of the Cavaliers, who called him " Roundhead," " Parliament dog," and the like, doubtless finding entertainment in his quickness to resist an insult.[8] Among the other prisoners in Oxford Castle was Edmund Chillington, who came in at the beginning of 1643. Wanting money, he was likely to starve, but Lilburne, burying his resentment, lent him money, and afterwards used his influence with the Earl of Manchester to secure him a commission as officer of horse in Whalley's regiment.[9]

In his captivity Lilburne again took up the pen and wrote a letter to the outside world. He had made contact with Robinson, a Parliament spy in the Royalist camp, and with his help the pamphlet was smuggled out of Oxford and appeared in print in January 1643—one of Lilburne's few legally printed pamphlets. The Cavaliers were entirely undisciplined, and the King, reported Lilburne, a virtual prisoner in the hands of his army. Thus, after four months' actual fighting, Lilburne, like many more of his fellow soldiers, maintained the fiction of a good, but weak, King in the hands of lawless and unprincipled advisers. Parliament was still " that strength of this Kingdome, and champion of true Religion, the Honourable the High

Court of Parliament." [10]   The prisoners later smuggled out
of the castle another letter, addressed to the House of Commons,
which revealed the miserable conditions of their captivity and
the deaths of several of their number.   The letter, dated April
29, took some time to reach its destination, and was not
produced in the House until May 11.[11]   The Commons were
then shocked into taking rapid action, and at last arranged an
exchange of prisoners in which Lilburne was exchanged " very
honourably " and " high above " his " quality and condition "
for Sir John Smith, knighted in the field by the King for regain-
ing the royal standard lost at Edgehill.   Lilburne was received
on his return to London, said Clarendon, " with public joy,
as a champion that had defied the King in his own court."
" I was not a little praysed, and made much of," recounted
Lilburne more modestly, " and proferred the choice of divers
places." [12]   Captain Lilburne had added another facet to his
lustre as popular champion.

His business had suffered during his absence.   Binman had
let the brewery decay and finally absconded, owing nearly a
year's rent.   When he returned from Oxford Lilburne sold
the place for £120 to an armourer named Wright in Bishopsgate Street, reckoning his losses at £700.[13]   His wife, however,
was not worrying, for she had secured for him the offer of a
" place of honour and profit," estimated to be worth about
£1000 a year.   She did not yet realize that Free-born John
would never sit still while others acted.   " I scorned to be so
base as to sit down in a whole skin, to make myselfe rich," he
afterwards said, " while the liberties and freedomes of the
kingdome was in danger." [14]   To her " extraordinary grief "
he therefore refused the post, saying he would prefer to fight
for 8d. a day to secure the liberties and peace of England.[15]
He accepted, however, a gift of £300 from General Essex, for
whom he was full of praise, in return for services and sufferings.
But this he spent largely on his men.   For he immediately
enlisted again, this time—upon Cromwell's invitation—in the
Eastern Association.[16]

By this time the war had assumed a definite pattern.   After
the battle of Brentford the London trained bands had streamed
westward to defend their homes, John Milton in Aldersgate

Street writing his wryly humorous sonnet begging protection for the poet's house. The King, finding 24,000 men facing him at Turnham Green, as well as a variety of onlookers come to see the spectacle of London defending itself against a monarch, fell back on Reading, and, while Lilburne was imprisoned in its castle, Oxford became the Royalist headquarters.

The King held most of the West and South-west, Bristol surrendering to him on July 26. The Earl of Newcastle held the North for him, with the exception of the clothing towns, foraging and quartering his troops on the countryside and plundering those that held out against him with the disastrous effects experienced by Richard Lilburne at Thickley Punchardon. " Son," he wrote to John, " thou knowest our Country was betrayed by those that should have preserved it, and for my affection to the publique, I lost all that ever the enemy could finger of mine, namely, all my stock, my corne, and household goods, and the rents of my lands, all the time that the Earl of Newcastle had the North." [17] London and the South-east held for the Parliament, but the Midlands and the eastern counties were in a sense debatable land, important to the King if he was going to effect a pincer movement on London from the west and the north, and vital to the Parliamentarians in the defence of the capital. Everywhere the general pattern was broken by isolated pockets of resistance in towns and country houses, and sieges and small forays were as much part of the first two years of the war as pitched battles, and took a heavy count.

Lord Brooke, laying siege to Lichfield Cathedral, which had been fortified by Royalists, was killed in the streets of the town on March 2, 1643. On June 18, in the small engagement at Chalgrove Field fought against Rupert, who had issued from Oxford on a foray, John Hampden received his mortal wound. Sir Bevil Grenville, beloved of Cornishmen, met his death at Lansdowne on July 5. The Duke of Devonshire's second son, aged twenty-three, was slain by a " thrust under the short-ribs " in a quagmire near Gainsborough in the same month. On September 20 the London trained bands, returning after a most remarkable sortie under Essex which had raised the siege of Gloucester, found their way barred by Royalist troops at Newbury. There Falkland, throwing himself into the most dangerous part of the fight, met the death he sought. John Pym died on December 8. So the year 1643 took toll of the best on either side, as well as of countless men whose names are not remembered and who, perhaps, supported the side on which they died as reluctantly as the Royalist dying after Winceby fight on October 11, who murmured, "The Commission of Array brought us hither full sore against our wills; we were as true servants to the Parliament, to our religion and liberties, as any in England. . . . We die as true friends to the Parliament as any." [18]

Both sides were hard pressed for men and money. The King raised men by Commission of Array and by impressment. Money he procured from Denmark and Holland, from private gifts, college and other plate, and by enforcing monthly contributions wherever his armies had the upper hand. Parliament raised men by Militia Ordinance and impressment, the latter being regularized by the Ordinance of August 10, 1643. Money it raised by a variety of expedients which became steadily more objectionable. On February 24, 1643, an Ordinance imposed weekly payments upon every county in England, naming Commissioners who were to assess the owners of property at their discretion. On March 27 an Ordinance sequestered the estates of all who gave assistance to the King. When the following day Pym proposed also an excise the revulsion of the House at this encroachment upon property rights was expressed by the Member who was astonished "that he who pretended to stand so much for the liberty of the subject should propose such an unjust, scandalous, and destructive project." [19] It was rejected at this time, but was imposed later.

When Lilburne returned to action the Parliament on the whole had done badly; its troops were mutinous for want of pay, General Essex, though kindly, was lukewarm, a peace party was growing that expressed itself in questions like the one which asked, "Can the plough go when there are no men to hold?" [20] In an effort to speed victory the Scots, on July 19, 1643, were requested to send help to their fellow Puritans, as they had already been asked, on July 1, to send representatives to the Assembly of Divines which was to meet at Westminster to settle religion. Part of the condition of military aid from the Scots was the taking of a Covenant by the English to preserve the Scottish religion and to remodel the English " according to the word of God "—an ambiguous phrase inserted by the English Independents as a safeguard, which yet left no real doubt that the Scots expected the price of their aid to be the strengthening, if not the establishment, of Presbyterianism in England.

Meanwhile Parliament was tightening its own organization by associating the counties favourable to it into groups. By far the most important from every point of view was the Eastern Association, put under the command of the Earl of Manchester in August 1643. Here, also, Oliver Cromwell was operating. The service he had already seen had shown him, among the King's supporters, an enthusiasm for a cause which he failed to find among his own followers. Yet that spirit existed. He felt it in himself. He had seen it in Puritan martyrs like Lilburne. He knew it in the sturdy Independents of East Anglia among whom he lived. These were those " men of a spirit " who would go as far—and beyond—the achievements of the Cavaliers, about whom he had already talked to his cousin, Hampden. Recruiting by cajoling, interesting, bullying, inspiring, Cromwell collected in the Eastern Association Independents of single and uncompromising religious views like himself, whose conscience would brook control from neither Anglican bishop, Presbyterian Synod, nor civil court. So long as they had this spirit, he excluded neither the unorthodox nor those of low degree. His own regiment was filled with men who had " sene vissions and had revellations . . ." and officered by " common men, pore and of meane parentage," " such as have filld dung carts both before they were captaines and sinc." Using such men, he pursued a conscious policy of infiltration. " When any new English man or some new upstart Independent did appeare ther must be a way mayd for them. . . ." In most of the regiments of the Eastern Association he " crammed in one company or other that they or ther officers must be Independents." [21] In this way Cromwell was already forging on behalf of the Independents—though he was not as yet fully conscious of its purpose—the weapon which would answer the challenge thrown down by the Presbyterians when they accepted Scottish aid at the price of the Covenant.

Naturally, when Lilburne was released from Oxford, Cromwell recruited the young man for whom he had spoken in the opening days of the Long Parliament. Lilburne believed that at that time Cromwell " had a spirit for freedom . . . very suitable " to his own, and such a friendship developed that Lilburne could speak of Cromwell as " my then most intimate and familiar bosome friend." On Cromwell's invitation Lilburne posted to Lincoln, where Royalists were besieged, arriving just in time to join in one of the skirmishes round the Castle. It was unfortunate for him that, when he was commissioned Major of Foot on October 7, 1643, it should have been in the regiment of Colonel King, a firm Presbyterian.[22] It was doubtless to provide some leavening that Cromwell had arranged this. Lilburne certainly believed and acted as if it was in order to watch King that he had been appointed. Four days later, on October 11, 1643, occurred Cromwell's successful cavalry action at Winceby; on the 12th the siege of Hull was raised; on the 20th Lincoln was taken by Manchester, Major Lilburne doubtless joining in the attack. By the end of the year Newcastle had been driven back from the mouth of the Wash to Flamborough Head, leaving only small pockets of Royalist resistance.

His wife and child again accompanied Lilburne and lived in quarters at Boston. In December 1643, after a visit to London, Lilburne returned to find that King had imprisoned several officers and townspeople, including some of Cromwell's own troopers, who had assembled at a conventicle in the town. Feeling ran high. Cromwell was about to leave Lincolnshire, and took no action. But from this time on the relations of King and Lilburne deteriorated. Lilburne fell foul of the two regimental chaplains, who were strongly Presbyterian; King became increasingly autocratic in military and financial matters, finally, as Lilburne and others believed, appropriating to his own use wool, horses, and money intended for public purposes. The Committee of Lincoln and Lord Willoughby, the Lord Lieutenant of the county, prepared charges against Colonel King on these and other counts. Lilburne meanwhile was in Newark when Rupert relieved the town on March 21–22, losing in the struggle all his personal belongings, including papers which implicated King and the very clothes he had laid aside while he slept. His escape over eight miles of hedges and ditches remained a painful memory. In April he appeared briefly in Suffolk, where he worked for a time with his brother, Captain Robert, but his general dissatisfaction with Colonel King caused his resignation shortly afterwards while the charges against King were pending in both Houses. He was then appointed to Manchester's own regiment, becoming Lieutenant-Colonel of Dragoons on May 16, 1644.[23]

The dragoons were, in effect, mounted infantry, and rode small horses or cobs. They wore short red coats and no armour, their weapons being sword and carbine or occasionally fowling-piece, their main function to cover the approaches to a position and watch the flanks, which they frequently did by lining convenient hedges and ditches. They generally worked dismounted, a small number being detailed as horseholders to the rest.[24]

While the case against King was being heard in the Lords it was perhaps significant that on May 30 there appeared in his defence to allege that since the case was pending in the Commons it could not be answered in the Lords the arch-Presbyterian, William Prynne. King was nevertheless found guilty in the House of Lords on June 3 on all the counts against him. His case was then referred to the Grand Committee of Privileges, and dragged on for several months. Not until July 3 was King discharged by the Speaker of the House of Commons,[25] though the charges still stood against him in the House of Lords, to be a running sore both to King and to Lieutenant-Colonel Lilburne, who was not the man to leave alone anything that smacked of injustice, as King's Army record certainly did.

Lilburne by this time, following his duties under Manchester, had been shot through the arm on June 3, 1644, at Walton Hall, near Wakefield. But he was not happy with the dilatory Manchester—the " sweet, meek man " who married five times and was never at ease in taking a Royalist stronghold or attacking a Royalist force, believing that if the King were defeated ninety-nine times he would be king still. However, Lilburne took an " eminent " share in the victory of Marston Moor on July 2, 1644, probably being with his dragoons under Okey on the extreme left wing, to the left of Cromwell's troopers, making the preliminary action at a " running march " which cleared the opposing musketeers from the ditch they were holding, and thus opened the way for the cavalry.[26]

It was about a week later, marching from York with four troops of dragoons, that Lilburne received orders from Lieutenant-General Cromwell to quarter in Tickhill, Yorkshire. Tickhill Castle was then held by the Cavaliers, but they sent word to Lieutenant-Colonel Lilburne that they would yield it up upon easy conditions, and that if his men made an assault they would put up nothing but a token resistance. Lilburne immediately rode off to Manchester, who was then at Doncaster, four miles away, for permission to summon the castle. Manchester gave a variety of unconvincing reasons for not doing so: it " was only a little hole," " he valued ten men more than the castle," if it were summoned it might break up his whole army. On Lilburne's expostulation he was dismissed as " a mad fellow." Not deterred, perhaps regarding his dismissal without a positive negative as favourable, Lilburne consulted with Quartermaster-General Ireton, and, assured of his approval for the project, rode back and summoned the castle. Upon the first summons the Governor sent out two Commissioners with articles of surrender which Lilburne, feeling he had been justified and no doubt with a certain pride, hastened to submit to his General. At Headquarters, however, he was received with scorn, and publicly reviled as a " base fellow." The castle, notwithstanding, was yielded up with eighty horses, 120 muskets, some barrels of gunpowder, and a great deal of provender to the value of about £1000, Manchester smugly reporting its capture to the House of Commons as his own achievement, without mentioning Lilburne's name. But he had, declared Lilburne, " in a manner spoyled a souldier of me." Only his overwhelming gratitude to Cromwell kept him in the Army. Otherwise he would have deserted and betaken himself to his travels, away from the baseness and treachery he found among the officers. He told Cromwell as much, but Cromwell was emphatic that his duty was to stay. So, feeling that this was all the return he could make for Cromwell's kindness, he stayed on, trying to do him " faithful service " in maintaining his " honour " and his " just interest." [27]

Manchester's whole conduct after Marston Moor was, indeed, so dilatory that Cromwell himself swung into action, and on

November 25, 1644, laid before the House of Commons a series of charges against him, including neglect and incompetence, calling witnesses who included Ireton, Waller, Haselrigg, Harrington, Hammond, and Lilburne, who on November 30, 1644, gave his account of the summoning of Tickhill Castle.[28]

Cromwell, Lilburne believed, was at this time sent off on a variety of military expeditions so that he was unable to pursue the charge through to its conclusion. In any case, Cromwell became more concerned to play his part in the formation of the New Model Army, which was instituted by the Ordinance of February 15, 1645, while the Self-denying Ordinance of April 3 brought about the resignation of Manchester. By this time every soldier was primarily concerned with the new Army, and every Independent was asking whether it accorded with his conscience to take the Covenant which the Scots had demanded as the price of their aid to the English Parliamentarians. Cromwell had hesitated, but finally agreed. Lilburne, embittered by his experience with King and Manchester, could not find it according to his conscience to do so, and resisted Cromwell's persuasions. It was not only that he felt no confidence in the nebulous promise to reform the Church " according to the word of God," but, as he told Cromwell, he had served the Parliament faithfully out of a principle of conscience, which to him was a greater tie than all the Covenants in the world. If, after his years of service, they still did not trust him he would serve in their armies no longer.[29]

When Lilburne consequently left the Army on April 30, 1645, nine months after Marston Moor and two months before Naseby, he ran into a sea of trouble whither his own uncompromising nature had steered him.

CHAPTER NINE

" *The Darling of the Sectaries* "

[The] crowds and multitudes that run after him . . . look upon
him as their Champion, applauding all his actions.

JOHN BASTWICK, *A Just Defence*, 1645

*T*HE YEAR 1645 WAS OF THE UTMOST IMPORTANCE, BOTH
decisive and divisional.   It was the year of the New Model, of
Parliamentarian victories at Naseby and elsewhere, of the
ascendancy of the Presbyterians in the House of Commons, of
the growing importance of Oliver Cromwell—an Independent
—of the formation of a Leveller party; also of a growing rift
in the ranks of the victors—religious, political, social, and
economic.   John Lilburne not only left the Army, but was so
far in opposition to Parliament that he was imprisoned by it.
Prynne and Bastwick, his heroes of earlier years, were now in
the field against him.   Burton, though not actually with Lilburne,
had taken up the cudgels against the harsh Presbyterianism of
Bastwick and Prynne, and the comrades of 1637 were deeply
divided.   Lilburne's old friend William Kiffin, now become a
keen Baptist, came into the controversy in July to put the case
for separation.[1]

Quietly at work in the City, the elusive but powerful influence
of William Walwyn was hidden under the anonymity of several
pamphlets notable for their reasonableness.   Walwyn was a
Merchant Adventurer from Worcestershire, a comfortably-off
family man of forty-five, brought into the controversy by no
material interest, but through a lively and sceptical mind that
enjoyed the company of Independents and sectaries of all
kinds.   Never happy in the limelight, his influence was recognized by both friends and enemies.   To his mild and tolerant
disposition strife was repugnant, and he was more concerned
with winning individuals to his point of view than in a public
crusade.   Nothing but strong intellectual conviction brought

him to play his part publicly with Lilburne. " All the war I
have made," he once said, " hath been to get victory on the
understandings of men." [2]

About the same time the pseudonym of Martin Marpriest—
pleading for toleration—hid the lively personality of Richard
Overton. Nothing is known of his family and upbringing, but
he was the complete rationalist, entirely lacking the mysticism of
Walwyn or the religious emotion of Lilburne. He joined them,
not because he was aware of individual or personal suffering, but
because the reforms they advocated were consonant with reason.[3]

There continued, meantime, the same superstition, credulity,
cruelty, poverty, which existed before the wars. Witches were
executed, stories circulated of strange apparitions and monstrous
births,[4] the poor begged Parliament to help them support their
" insupportable miseries." [5] On April 23 appeared a tract
against the monopoly of the Merchant Adventurers which
Lilburne found highly commendable,[6] the Clubmen of Dorset
and Wiltshire issued their " Desires and Resolutions " on
May 25,[7] and in September rose in Sussex to defend themselves
against all comers.

It was at the beginning of the same year—on January 10—
that Lilburne's old opponent, William Laud, who had been
in prison for nearly four years and whose trial had dragged
on throughout the previous spring and summer, was brought
to the block, finding comfort at the last that he had laboured
" to keep an uniformity in the external service of God according
to the doctrine and discipline of the Church." [8] Many may
have wondered whether the intolerance for which he was
punished was different in kind from the practice of his execu-
tioners, who were busy creating the background for a uniform
Presbyterian Church.

Since July 1643 the Westminster Assembly had been discussing the establishment of Presbyterianism, while the obstacles
to it were being steadily removed. On March 29, 1644, the
House of Commons had prepared an Ordinance " for suppressing the unlawful assembling and meeting together of Antinom-
ians and Anabaptists." On August 9 Roger Williams' plea for
toleration—*The Bloudy Tenent of Persecution*—was ordered
to be burnt. A resolution of the House of Commons of
November 15, 1644, that no layman be permitted to preach

was confirmed by Ordinance five months later. In January 1645 the House of Commons approved a scheme for the establishment of Presbyterianism, with no allowance for toleration.[9]   On January 2, reinforcing the discussions then taking place in the Commons, William Prynne published *Truth Triumphing*, a demand for rigid ecclesiastical discipline and for the suppression of Independency.

Such an attempt to enforce religious conformity was inevitably accompanied by a strict control of the press, and a Presbyterian Parliament faced with Independent and Royalist opposition took up the very weapons it had proscribed when Star Chamber and High Commission were abolished. It worked through its Committee of Examinations, which, on March 9, 1643, was given power to appoint searchers for presses engaged in " scandalous " printing, to demolish such presses, and to commit to prison printers, vendors, and others concerned. Wide powers of search, and of arrest in case of resistance, were given to the Committee's agents, and Justices of the Peace, officers, and constables were ordered to assist them where required.[10]   An Ordinance of June 14, 1643, appointed a special licenser, repeating that no book was to be printed without license and unless entered in the Register of the Stationers' Company.[11]   The Stationers themselves remained the Government's most willing agent in ferreting out illicit presses, instructions for doing so generally being received from the House of Lords or the Committee of Examinations.

While Milton published *Areopagitica*, his plea for freedom of the press, on November 24, 1644, the practical reply to the Ordinances, as to the Decrees of Star Chamber, was unlicensed printing from presses which carried on their work in secret. Throughout 1643, while Lilburne was in prison in Oxford, they were at work, being, as the Stationers complained in April, operated in " divers obscure Corners of City and Suburbs " by " drapers, carmen and others." [12]   In 1644, while Lilburne was serving in the Eastern Association and posting about on Army business and Cromwell's business, and probably his own business as well, the press or presses continued their work, and it would be a not unlikely assumption that he had a shrewd knowledge of their whereabouts. At all events he could turn them to his own use.

When Prynne's *Truth Triumphing* appeared on January 2 Lilburne, still in the Army, troubled over his broils with King and Manchester, worried over the question of the Covenant, valiantly took up the cudgels against the veteran of invective. He was warned there was as great a disproportion between them as between a tall cedar and a little shrub. But Lilburne had become aware of his power of words: "having received a talent from the Lord," he conceived himself bound in conscience to employ it and lay it out for his Master's best advantage. So he replied, "Goe you and tell the tall Cedar, the little Shrub will have a bout with him." As good as his word, he wrote to Prynne five days later, putting the case both for freedom of conscience and freedom of the press. Though couched in fiery language, the letter was reasonable enough. He complained of the bitter language of Prynne's pamphlets and of the muzzling of the press by the Presbyterian faction. But, he boasted, though the Independents could not print so fast as their opponents, yet they could "speake and lay downe as strong Arguments," to prove which he flung out once more a challenge to debate. He stated his own case for freedom of conscience quite clearly: he had no objection to an Established Church so long as there was complete freedom outside it for those of other beliefs. "First . . . I am not against the Parliaments setting up a State-Government for such a Church as they shall think fit, to make the generality of the Land members of, for I for my part leave them to themselves, to doe what they shall thinke good, so that they leave my Conscience free to the Law and Will of my Lord and King." [13]

Ralph Wharton took the letter to Prynne.[a] When, after three or four days, no answer had been received Lilburne proceeded to publish it without license from one of the illegal presses, and it appeared in print on January 15. Two days later the Committee of Examinations was sending to the Stationers "to know of them by whose fault it happens that such scurrilous, libellous, and seditious pamphlets are every day Printed and published. . . ." [14] The Stationers, who had been busy tracking other unlicensed pamphlets, had that very day "found out a Person, who had in his House divers scandalous Books and Pamphlets, and a Letter for Printing." The

[a] Perhaps the son of old John Wharton?

person in question was Nicholas Tew, a stationer of Coleman Street. Upon his refusal to speak before the Committee, Tew was committed close prisoner to the Fleet and ordered to be examined by two Justices of the Peace.[15] In the afternoon the Justices extracted from him the confession that a printing press had been brought to his house in Coleman Street, and there used by Robert (? Richard) Overton, who lodged there, and others whom he did not know. The letter of Lilburne to Prynne and another book of Lilburne's—possibly the *Answer to nine Arguments*, which was reprinted at this time [16]—had been printed there, but Tew either would not or could not tell from whom he received the manuscripts for printing, and he was sent back to the Fleet.[17]

On the same day Lilburne was also summoned before the Committee of Examinations, and for this reason came up to London from the Army. Walking in Moorfields, however, he met with a painful accident, when a pike was run into his eye, endangering both his sight and his life, and causing his case to be held over until his recovery. He never fully regained his sight, having thereafter to use spectacles, and his face remained slightly disfigured. John Vicars, the Presbyterian minister, gave glory to God for a just punishment on the author of the *Letter to Prynne*.[18]

By the time his case came forward again, on May 14, Lilburne had left the Army and returned with his family to live in Halfemoone Alley, Petty France, in Westminster. All he saw in the capital confirmed his fears. Religious persecution was so bitter that " all sorts of conscientious people " were " altogether discountenanced and discouraged; and the City . . . fill'd with daily relations of strange and very hard usage towards them in all quarters." [19] In May considerable alarm was also felt at the fall of Leicester to the King's army and the advance of his troops towards Cambridge. In both cases the citizens turned to Lilburne. He was one of a committee of sixteen elected at a popular meeting at the Windmill Tavern on May 31 to decide on action against the King.[20] His leadership of a group of Independents became more decided. He had access to a printing press; he became increasingly intimate with Walwyn and with sectaries in the City. He was associated with Overton. Prynne asserted that he had already, during his Army service, been spreading Independent literature throughout Lincoln-shire, and that others, notably William Larner the printer, had on his instructions been doing the same in Kent.[21] In fact, so easily did he slip into a position of leadership among the discontented elements of the City, and so soon did Prynne and Bastwick, his friends of earlier days, enter the lists against him, that it would seem highly probable that during his Army service he had been in close touch with malcontents in London, and that a loose kind of organization already existed to welcome him as leader.

On May 14, being sufficiently recovered from his accident, Lilburne, together with the printers Henry Robinson and Jane Coe, was summoned before the Committee of Examinations on the charge of printing the *Letter to Prynne*. Coe and Robinson were dismissed, but three days later Lilburne was once more being questioned. He answered boldly with a vigorous denunciation of the intolerance of the Parliament, but his outspokenness was allowed to pass, and the following day he was released with permission to send in a written answer to the Committee. But to speak his mind to so small an audience was not enough for Lilburne. Shortly afterwards the illegal press was again at work, and there appeared the *Reasons of Lieu. Col. Lilbournes sending his Letter to Mr Prin*. The persecution he found in London, declared Lilburne, was the result of provoking language in pulpit and press, and the man chiefly responsible was Prynne, who wanted the Independents cut off by the sword, and who divided " the affections of those that formerly were one until such bitter dividing spirits as his kindled a blazing fire of discord and dissension amongst " them. While Prynne was guilty of these " bloody, unchristian and dividing practices," the Independents, avowed Lilburne, remained loyal to the Parliament, and he again challenged Prynne to settle the issue by free debate.[22]

Not free debate, but arrest, followed this fresh audacity, and on June 18 Lilburne was again before the Committee of Examinations on the charge of printing and publishing this pamphlet. Again, however, he was dismissed, the Committee showing itself not unduly harsh in face of Lilburne's strong language.

Troubled over the public situation, Lilburne nevertheless

had to support his wife and family. When he left the Army
his thoughts naturally turned to the trade to which he had been
apprenticed. He had a little capital put by, and he considered
the possibility of trading in cloth. Here he was brought up
against another restriction, for the Merchant Adventurers,
presumably because of their loans to Parliament, retained their
monopoly of the cloth export trade. The right of the Merchant
Adventurers to their monopoly, wrote Lilburne in anger, was
based merely on prerogative, and not on law made by common
consent in Parliament.[23] He read, as he always contrived to
do, the books pertinent to him at the moment, and highly
praised the *Discourse for Free Trade*, published on April 23,
1645, whose author proved to Lilburne's satisfaction that the
Merchant Adventurers were acting against the known law of
the land.

By this time Lilburne and his father were on better terms,
but Lilburne's hopes of receiving his younger son's portion
were dashed by the depleted condition in which the family
lands had been left after Newcastle's depredations. There
still remained the reparations which had been voted him five
years previously, but which he had never received, and the
arrears for his Army service. He petitioned Parliament, but
his petition was not read. He importuned the Speaker to no
avail. He then spent, so he claimed, £100 on printing the
petition, and himself distributed 150 copies at the door of the
House, but to no effect.[24]

So Lilburne rode off westward in July to get assistance from
Cromwell where he lay with the army which was following the
defeated Royalists after Naseby. Cromwell's stock was high.
On June 10 he had been appointed Lieutenant-General. On
the 14th Naseby brought a Parliamentary victory nearer than
it had ever been, and Cromwell, reporting to the House of
Commons, pleaded for liberty of conscience: " He that
ventures his life for the liberty of his country, I wish he trust
God for the liberty of his conscience, and you for the liberty
he fights for." [25]   In this mood he was the more willing to accede
to Lilburne's request when that stickler for freedom came to
him near Langport. While there, Lilburne witnessed the battle,
probably from the hill overlooking the valley where both
Cromwell and Richard Baxter were watching. How much of

the soldier in him regretted that he was not able to help the dragoons lining the hedges and covering the advance of the Parliamentary cavalry? At least, he was able to bring back to the House of Commons an early and detailed account of yet another Parliamentarian victory—to which he could not resist making an addendum, based on his own experience, for improving the condition of the Parliamentarian soldiers. Give them shoes and socks, he said, give them encouragement, and go on recruiting ! [26] He brought back also a letter from Cromwell on his behalf, and with this, and as a bearer of good news, he may well have hoped for a favourable response. Far from this being the case, he found himself caught up on the charge of writing and printing the Marpriest pamphlets, their attribution to him probably meaning—unless the authorities were very wide the mark—that Lilburne and Overton were already connected.

Tew's imprisonment had ended the activity of the illegal press at Coleman Street, but illicit printing was continuing, and Prynne declared the Marpriest pamphlets to have been printed by Henry Robinson at a private press with printers from Amsterdam.[27] He also averred that he recognized them as being from the same press as the illegal pamphlets for which Tew had been arrested—the *Letter to Prynne* among others [28] —which would indicate that the secret press had been moved from one place to the other. After Prynne's statement nothing further seems to have come from it, the assumption being that Prynne's accusation was sufficiently accurate for it to be again removed.

The charge against Lilburne of printing the Marpriest pamphlets was not pressed, for, waiting in Westminster Hall on July 19 to be called by the Committee, he met William Walwyn and some other City friends who were come to give evidence before the Committee of Examinations against the Speaker, William Lenthall, and his brother, whom they accused of correspondence with the Royalists and sending money to the King. Never prudent, full of zeal to right another injustice, without waiting for proof, and regardless of possible injury to his own case, Lilburne immediately busied himself with the affair. He spoke of it in the Court of Requests to a friend called Hawkins and to Henry Ireton. He rushed to get the Scoutmaster-General of the City to speak to Walwyn.

Within a few hours Lilburne's interference came to the ears of John Bastwick, too good a Presbyterian still to regard with favour his young friend of earlier years, and of Colonel King, with a score to pay off against Lilburne. Bastwick and King jointly informed the Speaker that Lilburne was libelling him. On the strength of this Lilburne was on the same day—July 19, 1645—taken into custody, and on the 24th was brought before the Committee of Examinations on the charge of uttering slander against the Speaker.[29]

The man who was brought before this Committee was the Free-born John who had resisted Star Chamber tyranny, and, having been before them twice already, he knew what to expect. He knew also that it was a Parliamentary Committee, and not, therefore, legally constituted as a court. In practice, too, it acted illegally. When Lilburne asked the cause of his commitment he was not told. He then demanded that the Petition of Right, which condemned the similar Star Chamber offence of imprisonment and examination without cause shown, might be read. When the Committee asked him whether he had accused Lenthall he refused to reply until he was told the reason of his commitment. In demanding this " I build upon the Grand Charter of England," he said. " I have as true a right to all the priviledges that doe belong to a freeman, as the greatest man in England." Upon saying this he produced " his birthright," Magna Carta, and proceeded to read therefrom.[30] The Committee remained unimpressed, merely asking Lilburne if he would express his opinions by way of petition. This he declined to do. But he would, he said, write his defence and sign his name at the bottom if they would give him pen and ink. " Gentlemen," he said with earnestness, " I speake not the words of rashnesse or inconsideratenesse, but of deliberation, having something pondred upon them before I came to you, neither doe I speake the words of lightnesse, as though I would say a thing this houre, and fall from it the next, but I speake that which I will stand to, and live and dye by, humbly submitting my body to your pleasure." [31]

As he was being taken away Lilburne talked to the sergeant-at-arms, asking if he knew why Strafford and Laud had lost their heads.

" I doe not know."

"I will tell you . . . it was because they troad Magna Carta under their feet, and indeavored to rule by their own wills." And lest the sergeant should not realize the full import of his words, Lilburne proceeded to read Magna Carta to him, and finally requested that he would warn the Speaker that a fate similar to that of Strafford awaited him and all the Commons if they did not abide by the Charter.[32]

The following day, July 25, there appeared in print—evidence of the continued existence of the illegal press—the *Copy of a Letter from Lieutenant-Colonel John Lilburne to a friend*, which gave an account of his treatment by the Committee and his own defence, which developed, as might have been expected, into a vigorous indictment of the Parliament. Not only were Members of Parliament persecutors of religion other than their own, not only did they set up arbitrary and illegal courts, not only had they induced people to fight in the name of freedom for what was merely tyranny in a new guise, but throughout they lived in pomp, superfluity, and bravery when thousands who had spent all they had in the world and done the kingdom good service had not a bit of bread to put into their mouths, and many poor widows and fatherless children who had lost their husbands and fathers in the public service cried "Bread, bread" at their door. There was "no remedy left for redresse," concluded Lilburne, "but the little ones to be eaten up of the great ones."[33] This pamphlet, declared Prynne, produced by "a private Unlicensed Presse (alwaies ready at his command)," was the most seditious pamphlet yet penned.[34] It was continued proof of the efficiency of an organization which could command a press and print so rapidly without discovery, of the increasing fluency of Lilburne's pen, and of the growing social content of his teaching. His eyes were now open to inequalities of wealth and privilege, as they had already been to religious inequality. The man who, growing up in the Palatinate, had never once in his works spoken of the barbaric state of the coal-miners, was now fully conscious of the hardship and want resulting from three years of civil war.

On August 9 the House of Commons gave an order for the finding of the author of the *Letter . . . to a friend*, the sergeant-at-arms being sent to fetch Lilburne. The latter refused to go

until he had seen the warrant.   It was his right so to do, and
" I will not," he said, in words which still ring as typical of
Free-born John, " abate you, nor the greatest man in England
the breadth of one haire, of what I know to be my previledge." [35]
He went, finally, but told the Committee he would answer
in his own way or not at all.   A crowd accompanied him to the
Committee-room door—worthy followers, for they demanded
justice according to Magna Carta and threatened to bring up
the whole City.   Nevertheless, Lilburne was committed to
Newgate, and two days later, on August 11, 1645, the House
of Commons confirmed the order.[36]

Lilburne's position was unenviable.   His energy, his youth,
his enthusiasm, had gone to the Parliament's cause.   Now
he was imprisoned by Parliament as surely as he had been
by the bishops.   His Army arrears were still owing, his indemnity unpaid, his trade closed to him by the Merchant
Adventurers' monopoly, his religious freedom threatened by a
Presbyterian Establishment.   " And after I see I was rob'd
of my trade," wrote Lilburne, " and in greater bondage by my
fighting for justice, liberty, and freedome, then I was before:
I was at a mighty stand with myselfe what to do to provide
for my selfe and family." [37] His writings reiterate the question
which, in various forms, would soon be on every one's lips:
" What have we fought for all this time? "

His wife was again expecting a child, and, according to
custom, was permitted to reside with her husband in Newgate.
Thus prison was added to the home life which hitherto had
consisted largely of Army quarters.   In the few months in
Halfe-moone Alley she had prepared her childbed linen,
leaving it carefully packed away in her drawers.   But she had
not counted on the Stationers' agents, who in the family's
absence ransacked the house in their search for ' dangerous '
books and seditious manuscripts.   Terrifying the old woman
in charge, they even ran up to the bedrooms and, bursting open
closets and drawers, made off with baby linen and other goods.[38]

But his friends rallied to Lilburne's assistance with a petition,
which they presented to the House of Commons on August
26, signed by two or three thousand citizens " of good qualitie
in London," which demanded Lilburne's release and the
payment of his arrears and reparations.   Parliament was in

a difficult position. Should they bring him to trial and so give him a wide platform for airing his views? To keep him in prison without charging him smacked a little too much of the tyranny they had denounced, besides arousing the hostility of the active group which supported him. So, perhaps not yet fully comprehending the revolutionary doctrine implicit in Lilburne's teaching, and being much occupied with military affairs, the plea of the Recorder of the City of London that Lilburne be released on the grounds that no charge had been laid against him was admitted by the House on October 14, 1645,[39] and Lilburne was set at liberty.

The troubles of 1645, which brought Lilburne face to face with the veterans of the Presbyterian movement, completed what was begun seven years earlier, when he stood in the pillory in New Palace Yard and bowed defiantly to Star Chamber. He was now a mature man with imprisonment and Army service behind him, with close experience of various religious factions, and with a family man's responsibility. As captain, major, and lieutenant-colonel he had deepened his knowledge of men and learned how to talk to people of all kinds. His preaching among the soldiery was already notorious. He had more than his share of a personal charm which made him attractive alike to men and to women—" a very gallant fellow," " John " to all the ladies, as Bastwick wrote.[40] Crowds accompanied him wherever he went. A petition presented to the House of Commons on his behalf could raise many thousand signatures. " O Lord, bring thy servant Lilburne out of prison, and honour him Lord, for he hath honoured thee," prayed Mr Knowles, the Independent minister at St Helens in August.[41]

He and his group had access to a printing press which, in spite of the Committee of Examinations and the Stationers' Company, continued to turn out " seditious libels " which were scattered abroad by agents and even offered for sale in defiance of the ban of the authorities, and which did " extraordinary hurt " and " much incensed . . . the brethren of the Separation." [42] Outside London there is no doubt that in Lincolnshire and other parts of the Eastern Association and among the soldiers themselves the influence of Lilburne lived after his departure from the Army. It may be guessed that in Kent,

Hertfordshire, and Buckinghamshire his name was not unknown. His opponents made no secret of the influence of Lilburne's tongue and pen. "Behold how great combustions and tumults have they kindled among the Ignorant Vulgar, who adore him as the onely Oracle of Truth, when as he is a meere Legend of Lyes," wrote Prynne. His writings "kindled a publike dangerous flame, disaffected divers of his Seditious Faction, and set their tongues nay hearts against the Parliament." In "sundry private Conventicles" Lilburne's "Seditious Faction" sat "brewing mischiefe" and "ripening publike Mutinies"; [43] they not only sent out emissaries to preach their doctrines, but distributed tickets announcing the times and places of their meetings.[44] Many of these took place at the Windmill tavern, where Lilburne was "a great stickler," speaking "strange things" and inserting "strange clauses" into many petitions to Parliament, as the Presbyterian minister Thomas Edwards reported.[45] The "crowds and multitudes that run after him," recounted Bastwick, "look upon him as their Champion, applauding all his actions"; for "the poore people" were "all deluded by his false information" into thinking "his imprisonment, and the proceedings of the honourable Committee of Examinations, to be against the liberty of the Subject, and against Magna Charta, and the Petition of Right. . . ." [46]

Lilburne himself not only spread abroad his pamphlets and made speeches to the Committees who interrogated him, but made even of prison a platform from which to disseminate his views. Not only was he tireless in practising propaganda on the prison staff, but "This upstart monstrous Lawyer," as Prynne in fury termed him, actually sat in Newgate with the Book of Statutes lying open before him, reading and interpreting law to the crowds who came to visit him, telling them that in a few days he would make them understand the laws and statutes of the realm as exactly as any lawyer in the kingdom.[47] This opening of the mystery of his craft to the vulgar infuriated Prynne almost past endurance. He attempted to counter Lilburne's influence in *The Lyar Confounded*, but this had little discernible effect other than spreading abroad information of Lilburne's activities—for which Lilburne's friends must have been as grateful as a curious posterity.

Neither Prynne nor Bastwick could stop the crowds who accompanied him to every Committee-room door. The prim Bastwick, injudiciously mixing with the " Rabbel rout, tagragge and bobtaile " that followed Lilburne in his troubles, received short shrift. He was very high, they told him, but they had known him low enough. Not long since he had lived on their alms, and they had kept him from hanging, but now he was turned apostate and a persecutor of the saints. If, said Bastwick, describing the scene, ". . . if ever you had seen the picture of Hel . . . in York-house, where all the postures of the damned creatures, with their grisly lookes are described, and had also taken notice, what ghastly, ugly sower [sour] and musteds [? mustard], faces out of dolour, paine and anguish they made, and had been amongst the company, and had seen what grisly looks they out of malice, rancor and envy to the Presbyterian-party, and especially to my selfe had made, and had withall heard their confused hiddious noyses, calling for the liberties of the Subjects, and for the benefit of Magna Charta, and the Petition of Right, and for a publike hearing, you would have thought your selfe in the very Suburbs of Hel . . . the complexion also of many of them being like the bellie of a Toad."

To add to the ludicrous picture of Lilburne's supporters Bastwick gave a splendid description of William Walwyn, who seems, contrary to custom, to have been prominent on several such occasions—a man with " a great white and browne basket-hilted beard, and with a set of teeth in his head, much like a Pot-fish, all staring and standing some distance one from another, as if they had not been good friends; it may be conjectured, he picks them twice a day with a bed-staffe, they looke so white and cleane. . . ."

Bastwick concluded his pamphlet weightily, leaving Lilburne " to his A.B.C., which is a great deale better imployment for him then the grave and weighty matters of State, and the study of politicks, and the great Mysteries of Divinity." [48] But John Lilburne could not be dismissed as easily as that, both because he was not that kind of man and, more importantly, because he was becoming the spokesman of a group whose ideals and hopes, like his own, the war had failed to satisfy.

CHAPTER TEN

England's Physician

> I ... with my poor one Talent ... have used my best endeavours
> ... to shew the maladies and remedies of this sick, swouning,
> bleeding, and dying Nation.
>
> JOHN LILBURNE, *Englands Birth-right justified*, October
> 1645, Preamble

*I*N SPITE OF ALL THEY KNEW ABOUT LILBURNE, THE AUTHORITIES
had not taken the elementary precaution either of refusing
access to his friends or of depriving him of pen and ink while
he lay in Newgate. The two pamphlets which were written
and printed by the secret press during the two months of his
imprisonment were of the utmost importance.

The first, *Englands Miserie and Remedie*, announced on the
title-page that it was " a judicious letter from an Utter Barrister
to his special friend concerning Lieutenant Col. Lilburn's
Imprisonment in Newgate." Thomason wrote " Lilburne's
own " on his copy. The style and approach, however, is unlike
Lilburne. Lilburne knew and used a little Latin, but this
pamphlet is written by some one better versed in the language.
Since, however, the testimony of a man who knew not only the
pamphlet itself but the gossip of the City cannot be brushed
aside, it may be assumed that this is a joint work, that Lilburne
and one of his visitors—possibly Walwyn—drafted it jointly,
that Lilburne supplied the autobiographical matter and his
collaborator wrote round it and took it to the press.

Englands Birth-right justified is a different matter. On this
Thomason has written " supposed to be Lilburne's or some
friends of his." It is written anonymously " By a well-wisher
to the just cause for which Lieutenant Col. John Lilburne is
unjustly imprisoned in Newgate." There is possible collaboration here also, but far more essential Lilburne. It is a fifty-
page pamphlet of close printing, with numbered points under

headings and sub-headings which tend to lose themselves as the writer's enthusiasm runs away with him. But the form matters less than the content; the most important paragraphs stand by themselves, and in thought and expression show a clear advance over the earlier pamphlets. To the intensely personal experience of the Puritan martyr has been added an appreciation of social and economic, political and constitutional issues. The preamble, addressed to all the free-born people of England, states the general position that those who have fought for the Parliament find themselves in a worse plight than formerly, their lives, their estates, their precious time spent, their lives, laws, and liberties endangered. Nevertheless, ". . . neither Petitions can be easily accepted, justice truly administered, the Presses equally opened, the cryes of the poor heard, the teares of the oppressed considered, the sighes of the prisoners regarded, the miseries of the widow and Fatherless pittyed, nor scarcely any that are in distresse relieved."

The pamphlet itself plunges straight into the overall remedy —the observance of the rule of law. Lilburne is obviously familiar with Parliament's published collections of *Remonstrances* and *Declarations*, with the works of Henry Parker, and with the way in which Parliamentarian spokesmen, in opposing the King, had built up the supremacy of law. By this time, also, the *Institutes* of Sir Edward Coke have become second only to the Bible in Lilburne's esteem, and, following Coke, it seems to be the common law, reinforced by such statutes as Magna Carta and the Petition of Right, which Lilburne regards as binding alike on King, Parliament, and subjects. But he recognizes that Parliament has power to " annull a Law, and to make a new Law, and to declare a Law," and therefore other statute law takes its place beside the Charter and the Petition of Right. But it must be " declared." " For where there is no Law declared, there can be no transgression." Law locked up in the breasts of Members of Parliament is no law at all, and no man can be judged or tried except by the known laws of the land.

It is natural that Lilburne should seize on law, declared and secure, as his lifeline: the Parliament of which his thoughts had been so high had failed him, and his first reaction was to find firmer ground beyond it in the laws. So he now avers that it is the " declared, unrepealed Law " which is the people's protection against both anarchy and tyranny. " It is the greatest hazard that can be run into, to disart the onely known and declared Rule; the laying aside whereof brings in nothing but Will and Power, lust and strength." But how should the layman know these laws? ". . . all the binding Lawes in England " should " be in English . . . that so every Free-man may reade it as well as Lawyers." The Bible had been translated, so ought the laws to be translated from the Latin and old French in which so many of them were hid—merely for the lawyers' advantage, who " juggle, and put false glosses upon the Law . . . for their own ends." A legal trial, Lilburne avers, returning to his old contention, should consist in a charge laid openly in English in accordance with known and declared laws, adversaries brought face to face, and the accused at liberty to make his defence; no man should answer to interrogatories or be called upon to incriminate himself. To this the Parliament had pledged itself in its Act abolishing Star Chamber. Its failure to carry out its pledge was but one of many examples of talking in one way and acting in another.[1]

Monopolies were another example. Monopolists were thrown out of the House four years previously. Why, then, did the monopolies of preaching, of the Merchant Adventurers, and of printing remain? The " Spirit of God doth command every man that hath received a gift, to minister the same one to another," yet the Parliament had engrossed the preaching of the Word only to such men as " weare Black and rough garments to deceive." As for the Merchant Adventurers—" a company of private men . . . who have ingrossed into their hands the sole trade of all woollen Commodities that are to be sent into the Netherlands "—they are acting " contrary to the law of Nature, the law of Nations, and the lawes of this Kingdome." Wool is the staple commodity of the kingdom, to trade in it " so essentiall a Priviledge to all the Commons of England, that whosoever gives it from them, and by any pretended Patent or Authority whatsoever, assumes it to themselves, are as culpable of the greatest of punishments whatsoever, as those that are guilty of Robbing the Free-men of England, of their birthright and Inheritance." He takes the opportunity of boosting the *Discourse for Free Trade*, announcing the forth-coming publication of a second part.

" The third Monopoly, is that insufferable, unjust and tyran-nical Monopoly of Printing," carried on by Parliamentary Ordinance as it was in Canterbury's time, and still by the Stationers' Company, " the very same Malignant fellows who turning with every winde, doe endeavour by all possible means, as well now as then, to sell and betray the Kingdome for their own gaine." When book-selling " should be like a cryed Faire, and each one free to make the best use of their Ware," by Parliamentary Ordinance the Stationers " suppresse every thing which hath any true Declaration of the just Rights and Liberties of the free-borne people of this Nation," and " under pretence of searching for scandalous Books " call smiths and constables, even the trained bands, to help them break open and rifle houses, chests, trunks, and drawers, to rob and steal from law-abiding citizens, and to carry them before Committees of Examination and even to prison. The next monopoly to be feared will be upon bread and beer ! [2]

He finds that Parliament, having taken the Solemn League and Covenant—which itself has proved an " unhappy make-baite " breeding " constant heart-burnings "—has yet not ob-served its clauses. Having vowed to endeavour the extirpation of popery and prelacy, it has made an Ordinance for the strict payment of tithes, which Lilburne regards as the mainstay of popery, the taking away of which would be the most direct way to uproot papists, " for the Clergy are such greedy dogges . . . that they can never have enough." Besides, tithes are " an unjust and unequall thing in a Civill sense," in that priests, who form not more than a thousandth part of the population, take a tenth, or even a seventh, part of the products of a man's labour, for which they have not laboured with their hands or with the sweat of their brows.[3] He speaks of petitions in pre-paration in the City and in " many Shires in the Country." A few months later petitions were, in fact, presented to the House from London, Buckinghamshire, and Hertfordshire com-plaining of tithes, some, at least, emphasizing the civil and economic side which Lilburne stressed: there seems no reason to doubt that he, or his organization, had some hand in their preparation.

Tithes are not the only burden which, unjustly, fall heaviest upon the poor. Lilburne turns to the excise. In its search for fresh sources of income Parliament had reluctantly passed an Excise Ordinance in 1643. A direct tax upon articles of consumption is always unpopular, and as its scope was extended it became a very real hardship. Lilburne speaks of the hatters, working early and late " with heavy and hot labour," compelled to pay excise on all their materials, even the fire they use, the bread they eat, the liquor they drink, and the clothes they wear; and then an excise is finally levied on the finished article ! Such a method of taxation " layes the burden heavily upon the poore, and men of middle quality or condition, without all discretion, and scarcely maketh the rich touch it with one of their fingers." [4] Let taxation, says Lilburne, be as it used to be, by subsidy, " which is the most just, equitable, and reasonable way of all, for it sets every tub on its owne bottome, it layes the burthen upon the strong shoulders of the rich, who onely are able to beare it, but spareth and freeth the weake shoulders of the poore."

In spite of the country's great distress, Members of Parliament hamper or refuse petitions, they turn out of office better men than themselves, and install instead neuters " that are neither hot nor cold, nor have any other principle whereby to walke, but base pecuniary principles and self-Interrests," and they leave unpunished enemies to the public good like Manchester, King, and Vane. In this way the kingdom will be destroyed. " Meanwhile, though many conscientious men have laid out their witts, their time, their paines, their purses, their blood; yea, and all that in this world is most precious to them for the preservation of the Publique, yet they must not sit in Parliament, though never so fit and able, unless they will take this make-bate persecuting, soul-destroying, Englands-dividing, and undoing Covenant." [5]

The way is now clear for Lilburne's immediate suggestions for reform: the enforcement of the Self-denying Ordinance and annual Parliaments. The Self-denying Ordinance, which had passed the House of Lords on April 3, 1645, required any Member of either House to resign any office or post conferred upon him by the existing Parliament. Lilburne complains that many place-holders are still left; but he would also go further and have all Members " lay aside all places of profit in the Common-wealth " which had come to them. He had learned already that the possession of office " breeds nothing but factions and base cowardlinesse, yea and sowing up of mens lips, that they dare not speak freely for the Common-wealth, nor displease such and such a faction, for feare of being Voted, and thrust out of their unfit to be enjoyed Offices." This would mean calling Cromwell home from the field of battle to the House, but the service he would do in Parliament would outdo his achievement in the Army, " for he is sound at the heart, and not rotten cored, hates particular and safe Interests, and dares freely speake his minde." [6]

Lilburne went further in advocating the payment of Members of Parliament who were poor, or had lost their estates. They would be paid their " master's wages," and so would have no excuse for competing for places of profit. Finally, he demanded annual Parliaments. " Ought not the Free-men of England, who have laboured in these destroying times, both to preserve the Parliament, and their owne native Freedoms and Birth-rights," have the right once a year to inquire after the behaviour and carriage of those they had chosen? [7]

In guiding people in their choice of candidates Lilburne makes use of a new name, that of Major George Wither, who wrote several political treatises and poems, one of which had been published only a month previously—further evidence of Lilburne's continued reading—and from which he quoted: " Some men give their voices to their friends, some to their Landlords, some to the richest . . . men's merits are measured by the aker, weighed by the pound." [8] But, above all, says Lilburne, beware of sending to the House lawyers who grind the faces of the poor and are " as little use . . . in the House of Commons, as . . . a Plague or Pestilence, or . . . Bishops and Popish Lords in the Honourable House of Peers." [9]

Englands Birth-right justified covered all that the sects, the small farmers and tradesmen, the artisans, the poor, the im-prisoned, and those with any feeling of injustice in city or country could demand. It asked for a general protection of " declared " and, presumably, written law in English, for the abolition of monopoly, freedom of speech and of the press, toleration (would this include papists?), for the abolition of the excise and of tithes, for the calling to account and punishment where necessary of all office-holders, and particularly those who had charge of public moneys, for the instant trial and punishment of all suspected of treason against the Commonwealth. It asked for the reform of City government, with the translation and publication of its Charters, and, to show he was not neglectful of the military situation, Lilburne urged the beleaguering of the King's garrisons in the North of England. As a first step to all this, he asked for the strict application of the Self-denying Ordinance, to be followed by annual Parliaments and the payment of Members where necessary.

It was a far-reaching programme, beyond the means of any party, and Lilburne's suggestions for immediate action inevitably seem plain and homespun beside its rosy plans. He urged his followers by petition and " all other lawfull wayes and addresses " to make their grievances known. Petitioning was, indeed, a technique he himself had already tried, and under his influence it was to become one of the chief ways of embarrassing, if not of influencing, the Parliament. And—though proposed action remained weak and fragmentary when compared with the indictment—yet the exhortations which accompanied them made " lawful ways and addresses " into such a Crusade that to petition might seem equivalent to unseating a dynasty or overthrowing a social order !

" Oh Englishmen ! " exclaimed Lilburne, " where is your Freedoms? and what is become of your Liberties and Priviledges that you have been fighting for all this while, to the large expence of your Bloods and Estates, which was hoped would have procured your liberties and freedomes? but rather, as some great ones Order it, ties you faster in bondage and slavery, then before; therefore look about you betimes, before it is too late, and give not occasion to your Children yet unborne to curse you, for making them slaves by your covetousnesse, cowardly basenesse, and faint-heartednesse; therefore up as one man, and in a just and legall way call those to account, that endeavour to destroy you, and betray your Liberties and Freedomes." [10]

There was, moreover, at times something of the spirit of class warfare in Lilburne's words. " Well," he remarked,

" these are brave times for the wicked, who are advanced by
the ruine of the godly, the allowed thiefe permitted to rob and
destroy the honest man, the rich to rob, plunder and sequestrate
the poore, untill they can get no more, but when they have
gotten all, and done with all what they please, it rests only
that the poore also, in their turne, render them the like measure,
and finde out their Riches for the States service, which all
this heavy time they have saved, whiles poore mens estates
have been exceedingly destroyed." [11]

In shrewdness and breadth of observation, in its frequent
pungent expression, as well as in its proposals for reform,
Englands Birth-right is a marked advance on Lilburne's previous
writings, yet the years between had been spent largely in the
Army. How and when had he managed to equip himself to
write like this? Long evenings in quarters, rests after the day's
march, could be only part of the answer. Doubtless he talked
with other soldiers—with Henry Ireton, perhaps with Cromwell, with visitors to the Army, with Cromwell's troopers
gathering at their conventicles in Boston. His collection of
books—kept probably where his wife lived in Boston—included Parliament's *Declarations*, Parker's *Observations*, Coke's
Institutes, his old friend Fuller's *Argument*, with many religious
treatises and sermons augmented after each visit to London
by fresh literature. It is noteworthy, for example, that the
pamphlet on free trade was seen by Lilburne almost immediately upon publication.

On his visits to London he met the leaders of the City
Independents, finding old friends, perhaps, in John Goodwin's
congregation, sharing the general disquiet at the deliberations
in the Assembly, seeing the war from the angle of the discontented workmen of the capital, chafing at the inadequacy
of Parliament, making contact with his friend William Larner
and other publishers. He was open to influences so diverse as
those of Richard Overton and William Walwyn, both of the
utmost importance at this formative period of his career. He
perhaps joined the gatherings in the library of Walwyn's house
at Moorfields, enjoying the talk of a man of wide and humane
learning. One can only guess at the books Walwyn would have
lent to Lilburne, of the fresh vistas he opened. It is even possible
that Walwyn, himself averse from publicity, was deliberately

grooming the young man for the spectacular rôle of party leader. At all events, Lilburne galloping back to Boston after a day or two in the capital, with his holster full of fresh literature, his head full of fresh ideas, had plenty of material to occupy the long evenings in quarters, to mature him and to fit him for the part he would play on his return to civilian life.

Englands Birth-right justified made it clear that he could play this rôle. It was the first manifesto of a party in the making. Expressing grievances, naming reforms, suggesting action, working his readers up to a pitch of excitement, keeping his own name and case always in the picture, Lilburne in this pamphlet gave substance to the group which had formed round him. No one had yet named it, and it was a group rather than a party. But from the autumn of 1645 it was coherent and purposeful, its members recognizable as those who were afterwards called Levellers, and it acknowledged John Lilburne as its leader.

CHAPTER ELEVEN

"The Pearl in a Dunghill"

Thou do'st well, O England, to give up this thy first-born, Lilburne, the son of thy strength, and high Resolution, for Freedom.

A Pearle in a Dounghill, June 1646

WHEN MR KNOWLES'S PRAYER WAS GRANTED IN OCTOBER 1645 and Lilburne was released from Newgate he returned with his family to Petty France. One of his first actions was to petition the House of Commons for payment of his arrears for Army service and for the promised reparations for his sufferings in the Fleet. On November 10 the House of Commons discharged him from his Star Chamber fine. The Lords concurred, and on February 12, 1646, having assigned him Mr John Bradshaw and Mr John Cook as counsel, heard his case anew. Counsel marshalled the facts admirably, and the Lords ordered the obliteration of the Star Chamber sentence " as illegal, and most unjust, against the liberty of the Subject, and the Law of the Land, and Magna Charta." Not to lose the publicity value of this retelling of his punishment, Lilburne had the proceedings published the same day. The Lords also set in motion the machinery for granting him reparations, and on April 27 an Ordinance was read a third time to raise for Lilburne £2000 from the estates of Lord Cottington, Sir Francis Windebanke, and the Warden of the Fleet.[1]

But while the old antagonisms were being formally obliterated the new were piling up. In particular the presses, some secret, some open, were producing a spate of pamphlets marked by a growing bitterness between Presbyterians and sectaries. On February 26 Thomas Edwards set out in the first part of *Gangræna* to catalogue all the heresies of the sectaries, and Walwyn came in for so much abuse that he abandoned his anonymity, and a pamphlet duel between the two continued

throughout the year, Walwyn countering Edwards' vilification
with a sardonic irony that left him master of the field. These
pamphlets were licensed, but the secret press was again at work
in spite of the fact that Joseph Hunscott, the Stationer, had
tracked down and confiscated the press which had printed
Lilburne's *Letter to a Friend* and *Englands Birth-right*. It had
been found in an old farmhouse in Goodman's Fields, just
outside the City near Aldgate. While the Stationers were
breaking in at the front the printers had escaped by a rope
from a back window, but had left their press behind.[2] It was
with some surprise, therefore, that on March 20 the Stationers
were faced with the anonymous and unlicensed *Last Warning
to all the Inhabitants of London*, a bold plea for toleration.
Two days later they appeared at the sign of the Blackamoor
in Bishopsgate Street, and without showing warrant arrested
William Larner and searched his house and shop, finding
fourteen copies of the pamphlet.

Larner had already been connected with Lilburne. He was
a Gloucestershire man, a bookseller and printer, and a member
of the Merchant Taylors' Company. In December 1641 he
published a second edition of *The Christian Mans Triall* with
Glover's portrait. He served in the Parliamentarian Army
in Lord Robartes' regiment—or was it that of Robert Greville,
Lord Brooke?—was invalided home with arrears amounting to
£46, and resumed his trade of bookseller at the sign of the
Blackamoor. Besides printing unlicensed pamphlets from this
press, he was associated with the illegal presses at Coleman
Street and Goodman's Fields,[3] was named by Prynne in 1645
as one who distributed Lilburne's pamphlets, linked by the
soldiers in 1647 with Overton and Lilburne, and accused by
the *Moderate Intelligencer* in 1649 as being one " who had in
designe to divide the Army." [4]

When the Stationers arrested Larner in March 1646 they
needed the assistance of the constable to get him before the
Lord Mayor at the Guildhall, where the procedure made familiar
by Lilburne's examinations was carried through. Larner on
every point proved an apt disciple. " I desire," he said, " the
liberty of a Free-man of England not to answer to any interrogatories." He refused to pay the fee demanded, and when,
on April 3, he was brought before the House of Lords and

accused of being the author, printer, and publisher of the *Last Warning*, and a Mr Smith witnessed that Larner had given him money to buy a press for the purpose, Larner did not deny the charge, but, as Hunscott put it, he " had learned so much of Lilburne's language " that he appealed to the Commons.[5]

The imprisonment of Larner, so far from solving any problems for the Lords or the Stationers, had merely served as another focal point for Leveller activity. When Larner's brother and Jane Hale, both in Larner's employ, were brought to the Lords' bar they stoutly refused to be sworn or to answer questions, and were promptly committed to the Fleet. On April 20, when Hunscott and others searched Larner's person and room in prison, they found the manuscript of a pamphlet which, in spite of all they could do, was published twelve days later as *A true Relation of all the illegall Proceedings against William Larner*. On the same day the same secret source produced *Every Man's Case ; or, a brotherly support to Mr Larner*. To add to the Lords' chagrin, they were produced by the same press which had printed the *Last Warning* ![6]

By this time Lilburne himself was preparing to swing again into action. The obliteration of his Star Chamber sentence had brought neither the promised reparations nor the payment of his Army arrears, and to add to his financial difficulties Colonel King was demanding £2000 damages from him for slander. On this count Lilburne was apprehended on April 14, 1646, by order of the House of Commons. His defence was that the Committee of Lincoln had already brought a charge of high treason in the House of Lords against King for the betrayal of Crowland and the negligent loss and delivery of Grantham to the enemy, that the charge was still pending, and that Lilburne, as a witness, could meanwhile not be summoned by an inferior court.

Perhaps partly to emphasize his defiance, he showed himself in Westminster Hall on May 26, when he distributed copies of Walwyn's *Word in Season*, a warning to " well minded people " against a City Presbyterian *Remonstrance* which was then before the House. He also wrote to Justice Reeve, officer in the Court of Common Pleas, not to deny that he had called King a traitor, but to prove that his accusation was true. As usual, writing a letter was but an excuse for publication, and on June 6 the letter

appeared in print under the title *The Just Mans Justification*.
Not content with reiterating his charges against King, Lilburne
also accused Manchester of complicity. The House of Lords
immediately took up the case on behalf of its Member, and four
days after publication summoned Lilburne to its bar.

The warrant for Lilburne's arrest was delivered at 6 A.M. on
June 11, when Lilburne was still in bed at his house in Halfe-
moon Alley. He refused to obey the Lords' warrant, saying
he would defend himself in his own house against twenty such,
because they had no authority to make him, a commoner, dance
attendance upon them or appear before them in any criminal
case. This statement, however, he promised to make himself
as his plea at their bar.

He was as good as his word, and, walking through the streets
towards Westminster, meditated upon the exact nature of his
protestation, desiring God, " according to His wonted manner,"
to direct him, and awaiting the " In-comes of His Spirit." When
it began to take shape in his mind he stepped into a friend's
lodging near by to draft and copy it. Going then to a member
of the Upper House, Lilburne showed him a copy of his
Protestation, asking him to get the Lords to consider it. If the
Lords, added Lilburne fiercely, meddled with him and so
trampled Magna Carta underfoot he would draw his sword
against them as willingly as he had done against the King !
Lilburne continued his way to the House of Lords by water,
and was called to their bar about one o'clock. He was shown
the letter to Reeve and asked if he knew it. " Is there any
charge against me ? " he countered. " May I see and read it ? "
His interrogators paused, but Lord Stamford pressed the Speaker
to hold the prisoner to the question. " Then," said Lilburne,
" I have my reply here." And he handed to the Clerk of the
House the *Protestation, Plea, and Defence of Lieutenant-Colonel
John Lilburne*.[7]

It was typical of Free-born John. ". . . to be robbed of my
life, or give way to be made a slave to any whomsoever, either
by a voluntary giving up, or in silent suffering to be taken from
me, my native, naturall, just, legall and hereditary freedomes
and liberties, I am resolved rather to undergo all extremities,
hazards, miseries, and deaths, which possibly the wit of man
can devise, or his power and tirany inflict." From defence it

passed to an attack on the peers. "You . . . Peeres as you are called," exclaimed Lilburne, "merely made by prerogative, and never intrusted or impowred by the Commons of England . . . Magna Charta hath justly, rationally, and well provided that your Lordships shall not sit in judgment, or passe sentence in Criminall causes, upon any Commoner of England either for life, limbe, liberty or estate." Lilburne appealed, therefore, from the Lords to the Commons, his " competent, proper and legall triers and Judges." [8]

Lilburne presented this document to the Lords, they refused to receive it, he refused to take it back, and so, when he was commanded to withdraw, it was thrown after him, and he found himself once again in Newgate, charged with delivery at the bar of the House of Lords of " a scandalous and contemptuous paper."

For twelve days Lilburne was kept close prisoner in Newgate, not even his wife being allowed to visit or so much as speak with him from the yard. She resorted to the expedient of going to a friend's house a short distance away, through the window of which she conversed with her husband at a distance of forty yards. The authorities stopped this, however, by threatening to board up both Lilburne's window and his friend's. [9]

A diversion which the prisoner failed to appreciate was offered when John White, chief warder of the Tower, but sometime clothier in Reading, who had known Lilburne as an apprentice and whose son served in the Parliament's Army, visited him in prison. If White regarded Lilburne as a young man who would defer to the advice of age he reckoned without the fiery temper which met any attempt to deprive him of what he deemed his " just rights." White's exhortation to Lilburne, " for the glory of God, to carry himselfe humbly," was a tactless pricking of the caged lion, which met with what those who knew Lilburne might have expected. After abruptly asking if that were all he came for, the prisoner seized White by the coat, saying that if he had not been an old man he would have thrown him downstairs. The " rough speeches " and " sturdy gestures " of Lilburne indicated to White that discretion was the better part of valour. But, once safely down the stairs, he sent up a parting shot to the effect that spiritual pride would be Lilburne's overthrow, and fled as the infuriated prisoner bounded down the stairs after him.[10]

When White entered he found Lilburne writing a letter, with some one standing by to receive it. This may have been the appeal which Lilburne sent to the House of Commons, as the result of which a committee was appointed to examine his case under the chairmanship of Henry Marten. This pleased Lilburne, for he thought highly of Marten, the eccentric and wealthy Member for Berkshire, son of Sir Henry Marten, an opponent of monarchy, an Independent if not a free-thinker, and the Member of Parliament with most sympathy for Lilburne's group. A copy of Lilburne's *Appeal* reached his printer, and, together with the *Protestation* he had made to the Lords and a full account of his arrest and imprisonment, was illegally published on June 16 in *The Freemans Freedome vindicated*, which would seem designed to perpetuate his imprisonment: the Earl of Manchester, he remarked, was " so closely glu'd in Interest " to the Cavalier party that he had protected Colonel King from justice. " His Lordship's Head hath stood, it seemes, too long upon his shoulders," concluded Lilburne.

These pamphlets were not only being printed, they were being sold clandestinely by respectable booksellers, hawked about the streets by a variety of people, and included in the stock of most of the vendors of news-sheets and other ephemeral literature, like the book-women of Westminster Hall, whose stalls were more than once searched for Lilburne's works. A bookseller named William Browne and his family were deeply implicated, as Hunscott suspected, but was never able to prove. Browne's daughter was accosted by Hunscott while hawking pamphlets in the street, and was sufficiently unmindful of her loyalties to tell the Stationer that she had her pamphlets of Lilburne in Newgate. Browne's house was promptly raided, where the stationers found many " scandalous books," but Browne himself escaped through the garden, and when subsequently captured escaped again from the constable who had him in charge. Recaptured, he managed to elude examination, threatening to sue Hunscott for false imprisonment and to knock out his brains if ever he came to search Browne's house again ! [11]

Lilburne also enjoyed himself spreading propaganda among the prison staff. With Briscoe, the sheriff of Newgate's clerk, Lilburne spent some time emphasizing the fact that no man could be taken, arrested, attached, imprisoned, but by due process of law. Briscoe, however, could see no further than his immediate duty, which was, he said, to do as the Lords ordered.

On June 23 there arrived an order from that House to bring Lilburne before it at ten o'clock. Lilburne refused to go, on the grounds that " their Lordships sitting by vertue of Prerogative patents and not by Elections or common consent of the People, hath . . . nothing to doe to try me, or any Commoner whatsoever in any criminal case," and also that since his case had been sent to a committee of the House of Commons, the Lords had no right to continue their charge against him. He barricaded himself in his room.[12] The Deputy Keeper and his attendants broke open Lilburne's door and took him by force to Westminster. There, waiting in the Painted Chamber to be called, Lilburne naturally attracted a crowd, and it was not long before the Lords sent out asking Lilburne to be quiet. He sent back word that he would not be quiet until they exceeded the tyranny of their fellow-lords the bishops by cutting out his tongue and sewing up his mouth !

When he was called to the Lords' presence the Keeper of the Black Rod commanded him to kneel. Lilburne refused. " I have," he said, " learnt better religion and manners than to kneel to any human or mortal power, however great, whom I have not offended." [13] For this fresh impudence he was sent back to Newgate under a further order, dated that same day— June 23—for his close imprisonment without pen, ink, or paper, and with none but his keeper to have access to him.[14] When published on July 10 the Lords' indictment against Lilburne occupied two and a half columns of print in their *Journals*: the charges included the utterance of scandals against the Earl of Manchester and the Earl of Stamford, and the delivery, printing, and publication of the *Protestation* and other pamphlets all of which did " falsely, and scandalously, and maliciously, charge the Peers in Parliament with Tyranny, Usurpation, Perjury, Injustice, and Breach of the great Trust in them reposed," were " high Offences against the Laws and Statutes of this Kingdom," and tended " to stir up Differences

between the said Peers and other the Subjects of this Realm."
Lilburne was consequently charged with " High Crimes and
Misdemeanors done and committed by him." [15]

On the 11th Lilburne was again before the Lords to meet this
charge.   Three times he was called, and three times refused to
comply with the requirements of the House.   The first time he
refused to kneel, the second, he put his fingers in his ears to
avoid hearing the charge against him read, saying " he would
not hear it; he having appealed to the House of Commons
from this House, to which he would stand to as long as he had
Life."   The third time he loudly announced that he would stand
by his appeal to the Commons so long as he had any blood in
his body.[16]   Disregarding this, the Lords pronounced Lilburne
guilty of the charges he had refused to hear, and of high contempt to the honour of their House, and sentenced him to a
fine of £2000, imprisonment in the Tower during the pleasure
of the House, and disqualification from office or place, military
or civil, in Church or State.   Care was to be taken that he
" neither contrive, publish, or spread any seditious or libellous
Pamphlets against both or either of the Houses of Parliament,"
that none speak with him save in the presence of the Keeper,
that when he took the air in the Tower the Keeper should
accompany him, and that his wife, if she wished to see him,
should live in prison and not be allowed to go in and out of the
Tower.   These restraints were to be removed when Lilburne
gave satisfactory bail not to contrive, write, or publish any
scandalous, libellous pamphlets against both or either of the
Houses of Parliament.   *The Just Mans Justification* and *The
Freemans Freedome vindicated* were to be publicly burned by
the public hangman the following Monday at the Old Exchange
in London and New Palace, Westminster.[17]

So, after a brief spell of liberty, John Lilburne was securely
locked up in the Tower at the pleasure of the House of Lords,
with the utmost precautions taken against his writing or
publishing any further pamphlets.   The detailed care of the
Lords' orders in this respect showed both the sharpness of
Lilburne's pen and the tenderness of his opponents' skin.
Subsequent events were to demonstrate the impossibility of
depriving him of pen and ink or of moderating his influence.

In the Tower, where he was lodged in Cold-harbour, next the

Traitor's Gate, Lilburne's most severe trial was at first his separation from Elizabeth. ". . . my wife," he wrote, " is all the earthly comfort that now in this world I have left unto me. . . . And truly . . . God hath so knit in affection, the hearts and soules of me and my wife, and made us so willing to help to bear one another's burdens, that I professe, as in the sight of God, I had rather you should immediately beat out my braines, then deprive me of the society of my wife." [18] His request that his wife be allowed access to him was finally granted on September 16.[19]

The general question of prison discipline and organization soon absorbed Lilburne. Directly he arrived at the Tower he demanded to see the warrant by which he was committed. He was angry when accused of walking in a prohibited part of the Tower: " I have as good right to enjoy any priviledge within the Tower, as any prisoner in it." He was incensed when told he could not leave his chamber after candles were lighted: " I am a free-born Englishman . . . and I am not to be subject . . . in the Tower unto any other orders, but what are consonant and agreeable to the fundamental Laws of the Kingdome."

He was reinforced in his skirmishes with the Lieutenant of the Tower by the book *The Mirror of Justices,* supposedly written by Andrew Horn, a citizen of London, in 1289. *The Mirror* had been enthusiastically quoted by Coke in the second *Institute*, had been printed in the original medieval French later in 1642, and appeared in English in 1646, at about the time the Lords sent Lilburne to the Tower. It purported to be a summary of the law as it existed before the Norman usurpation. The legal rights the author asserted were remarkably like those Lilburne claimed for himself; his objections to legal abuses were remarkably like Lilburne's own. His insistence that Magna Carta and other statutes were reassertions of native rights, and his claim that in pre-Conquest law there existed a body of doctrine to which free-born Englishmen could appeal, matched Lilburne's own beliefs. *The Mirror* now took its place in his library of much quoted works.

His faithful followers were not leaving Lilburne in the lurch. On the 23rd of June appeared two anonymous pamphlets referring to Lilburne—*A Pearle in a Dounghill,* an account of Lilburne's career which the title was intended to epitomize,

and *The Just Man in Bonds*. It was fairly clear that Walwyn
had written the second, and that either he or Overton was
responsible for the first.[a] It was certainly Overton who, three
days before the Lords issued their indictment, had published
*A Remonstrance of many Thousand Citizens of England to their
owne House of Commons, occasioned through the illegall
Imprisonment of John Lilburne*. The frontispiece was the
portrait of Lilburne which had appeared in *The Christian Mans
Triall*, but with prison bars superimposed. The Lords were
still worried over this when, on July 31, there appeared *An
Alarum to the House of Lords, against their Usurpation of the
Common Liberties in their tyranicall Attempts against Lieutenant-
Col. John Lilburne, Defender of the Faith*.

About this time the Committee of Examinations took into
its direct employ one Robert Eeles. The exact position of
Eeles and his wife was never clear. The members of the
Stationers' Company regarded Eeles as being " a common
printer and seller of unlicensed books," and on one occasion
seized and searched Mrs Eeles for illegal pamphlets as a
" common disperser of all kinds of dangerous pamphlets." [20]
Eeles was no friend to the Levellers, however, to whom he was
known as " Robin the Devil." [21] Somehow, it is clear, he
became sufficiently acquainted with their secrets to enable
him to track down to Overton's house the press that had
printed the *Alarum*, the *Remonstrance*, the *Last Warning*, and
several of Lilburne's works.[22]

On August 11, 1646, consequently—the day after Lilburne
was securely confined in the Tower at the Lords' pleasure—a
company of musketeers surrounded Overton's house in the
early morning. Robert Eeles and Abraham Eveling broke
into Overton's bedroom and, with sword and pistol drawn,
arrested him as the printer, publisher, and dispenser of Lilburne's
books, and as the author of the Marpriest pamphlets. While
Overton, in true Leveller fashion, was demanding over the
hubbub to see the warrant, his house and clothes were ransacked,
and his printing press discovered and seized. He was finally
dragged away, protesting, and trying to tell the crowd that had
gathered that he was being arrested unlawfully.

At the Committee of Examinations, Overton was asked if he

[a] See bibliography.

were a printer. He refused to reply, whereupon Eeles volunteered the information that Overton " was one of Lilburne's bastards." Overton then declared he would appeal to the Commons. " But this is Lilburne-like ! " exclaimed Lord Hunsdon, and Overton was sent up to the House of Lords, where he still maintained his refusal to answer to interrogatories, and on the same day was committed to Newgate.[23] The unpleasant Eeles received little satisfaction for his work. He was not allowed to keep the press for his own use, and friends of Overton's set on him in the street, dragged him before a Justice, and had him committed to prison for house-breaking.[24]

But although this press was not available to the Levellers, and although Lilburne, Larner, and Overton were all in prison, Lilburne on August 21 published *Liberty vindicated against Slavery*, an indictment of the prison system, and Overton on September 9 published a full account of his arrest under the title *A Defiance against all Arbitrary Usurpations either of the House of Lords or any other upon the Soveraignty of the House of Commons*.

There followed two months' silence—perhaps because the secret press had been worked too hard, perhaps because the prisoners were more closely watched. But in October both Lilburne and Overton were brought before a committee of the House of Commons, and this seemed to be the signal for a fresh outburst of Leveller activity. On October 9 a petition from Overton to the House of Commons was printed, and on the 12th he shot *An Arrow against All Tyrants*. On November 3 he was again before the committee, and, since neither his release was ordered nor a legal warrant for his imprisonment issued, he refused to go back to Newgate of his own free will, but was taken forcibly by water to Blackfriars, and then, because he refused to walk, was dragged, still protesting, through the dirt of the streets, in spite of the expostulations of the crowd he attracted. Back at Newgate, Overton had his copy of Coke's *Institutes* taken from him and was clapped in irons. ". . . me thought," he afterwards said to Henry Marten, in marked contrast to Lilburne's protesting vehemence in like circumstances, " they were the comlyest gingling Spurres that ever I wore in my life." [25]

But Lilburne was too robust to spend all his time in high

seriousness, and a good deal of horse-play developed when he and the Royalist prisoners in the Tower were allowed communication. In the autumn of 1646, for example, occurred the memorable scene involving gaoler White, whom Lilburne had treated so roughly in Newgate. White, described as " an old tall man in black, with a great staffe in his hand," was secured by Lilburne and a group of Royalists and made to sign a " recantation " that Lilburne was not the writer, author, or contriver of *Liberty vindicated against Slavery* or *An Alarum to the House of Lords*, and an expression of regret at the scandalous language he had used against Lilburne in prison. The signatories of this remarkable paper included Christopher Comport, another warder, and the Royalists Sir Lewis Dyve, Sir John Glanville, Sir William Morton, Sir Henry Vaughan, and Sir John Strangeways.[26]

On October 28, and again on November 6, Lilburne was before the committee appointed by the House of Commons to examine him. On November 9, in obedience to order, he handed a written copy of his speech to the Chairman, Colonel Henry Marten. Not to miss the opportunity which being provided with pen and ink afforded, he gave a detailed account of his conduct before the Lords, and made his indictment of them as strong as possible under the vigorous title *An Anatomy of the Lords Tyranny and injustice exercised upon Lieut. Col. John Lilburne, now a Prisoner in the Tower*. Needless to say, a few days later it was published from an unknown press. On the 19th appeared yet another pamphlet—the anonymous *Vox Plebis*—which coupled support for Lilburne with a comprehensive condemnation of the prison system. Some thought it was by Lilburne, but Secretary Nicholas, who described it as " a shrewd piece," declared that more hands than Lilburne's were in it. Perhaps it was by Overton, or even Marten.

But Lilburne had now moved on to fresh fields. He made the somewhat strange request that Marten should not immediately present his report to the House because of other " weighty matters " that Lilburne had in hand. These may have been connected with the City disturbances of the autumn and winter of 1646.

CHAPTER TWELVE

" *Defender of the Faith* "

John Lilburne, Defendour of the Faith and of his Countries
Freedoms, both by his Words, Deeds and Sufferings, against
all Tyrants in the Kingdome.

> RICHARD OVERTON, *An Alarum to the House of Lords*
> July 31, 1646, title-page

*T*HE BACKGROUND AGAINST WHICH LILBURNE AND OVERTON
and the secret printers were playing their parts was one of
growing social and economic distress and continued political
and religious intolerance, in spite of the military ascendancy
of the Parliamentarian troops. The battle of Naseby on
June 14, 1645, had virtually ended the first Civil War. Smaller
engagements and sieges continued into 1646, in May the King
took what seemed to him the better path and gave himself up
to the Scots, while Oxford, his last foothold, surrendered in
June. On July 13 Parliament sent its proposed terms of settlement to the King at Newcastle. The Newcastle Propositions
entailed the taking of the Covenant by the King and all office-
holders, a Presbyterian settlement, and the control of the
militia for twenty years by Parliament. By the end of the year
Charles had sent nothing but a delaying answer, and it was
clear that the terms were also unacceptable to every one not of
the Presbyterian faith.

London had superimposed grievances of its own. The
government of the City was vested in the Common Council,
election of which, by charter of King John, was the right of the
freemen of the City. Nevertheless, the Common Council was
in practice controlled by the Lord Mayor, who was elected
by the Liveries of the City Companies, and the Aldermen,
who were *ex-officio* members of the Common Council. The
Civil War had brought no change for the better. Not only
did the Lord Mayor and Aldermen control the Council to

such an extent that they could refuse to put a question to the vote and could dissolve the court at pleasure, but they even took upon themselves the prerogative of calling a Common Council. The citizens were thus fairly in the hands of an oligarchy of the wealthy and powerful, who, at the same time, were predominantly Presbyterian. National politics were repeating themselves in the City. In Parliament a Presbyterian majority, who had no time to attend to petitions complaining of shortage of food, rising prices, free quarter, poverty, and taxation, had managed to consider an important piece of legislation for the benefit of the gentry and nobility who formed the bulk of its Members, and on February 24 passed the Act which abolished wardship and all burdens connected with feudal tenures. At the same time in the City a Presbyterian-controlled Common Council was governing the City in the interests of a group of merchants and traders often closely connected with their Parliamentary prototypes. Lilburne, Walwyn, and the others, in the City as elsewhere, took up the case of the underprivileged.

In *Englands Birth-right justified* of October 1645 Lilburne had stated the case of the freemen of the City and made specific demands for the reform of City government. Twelve months later, from the Tower, while supposedly without writing materials, he produced two comprehensive pamphlets —*Londons Liberty in Chains* and *The Charters of London*. While he was in prison a number of City radicals—evidently members of Lilburne's group acting upon the advice which Lilburne and others had been giving them—decided to claim their right to vote. Led by Mr Wansie, a watchmaker of Cornhill, on September 29, 1646, they made their way to the Guildhall, but were kept out by force. Wansie then began to read aloud a protest which had obviously been prepared beforehand, and was seized by the marshal and dragged into the building. When questioned concerning the authorship of the *Protestation* he denied knowledge of either the framer or the deliverer of it. John Lilburne, however, printed it in *Londons Liberty*. A day or two after the election, he said, a copy fell into his hands—presumably brought by one of his visitors, possibly his wife, who by that time was allowed access to him—and his spirit was so inflamed with indignation at this fresh betrayal of London's liberties that he went to Mr Colet, Record Keeper of the Tower, and for £3 or £4 obtained copies of those Charters of London most to his purpose. Making further inquiries of "a man versed in antiquity," he found there was in print a book some hundred years old, containing many of the old franchises and liberties of London. Lilburne sent to Duck Lane, and with some difficulty procured a copy of this old book, which, being in Latin, he sent with the copies of the charters to a friend to translate into English. These translations Lilburne used in *The Charters of London.* The translator remains unidentified, but he wrote the opening section to *Londons Liberty*, and, on his own statement, was the author of the citizens' *Protestation.*[a]

The story of the preparation of these two pamphlets reads like that of a man sitting at home in his study, with a secretary to execute his commissions, rather than that of a political prisoner, except that Lilburne had the advantage of having the Tower records to hand and the collaboration of the Record Keeper. He had merely to be a little circumspect in the actual composition, writing bit by bit as occasion offered, hastily slipping his work out of sight when observation seemed likely. At the end of *Londons Liberty* he begged the reader to excuse his mistakes, " by reason I am prohibited to have Pen, Ink, and Paper; I am forced to write a peece, and then a peece, and scarce have time and opportunity seriously to peruse and correct what I write; and in regard I cannot be at the Presse, either to correct, or revise my own lines."

In the opening of *Londons Liberty*, published on November 2, Lilburne's unknown helper demonstrated from Magna Carta that City officers should be elected annually by all freemen. The practice which had crept in of recent years of election or appointment by Aldermen and Common Council was a mere usurpation. The sole power of government had thus become vested in an oligarchy, which not only deprived the citizens of the right to vote, but imposed upon them monopolies and taxation which, in turn, led to decay of trade and impoverishment. In a fine exhortation to the citizens the unknown writer entreated them: ". . . continue the claims of

[a] It may have been he who helped with *Englands Miserie and Remedie* (supra, p. 126).

your right, and with courage and resolution maintain and
preserve your just and undeniable Liberties and Priviledges,
which are thus unjustly extorted, and kept from you by fraud
and force, lest it be said in after ages; . . . These were the men,
who when a free Parliament were sitting, subjected them, and
their Posterity to voluntary slavery. . . . Oh! the unexpressable
misery, and besotted condition possessing this Nation, that
we should be so regardlesse of ourselves and Posterity, as
thus in, and by cowardly silence, to betray ourselves, and to
beget Children, to live and remain (by our meanes) Bond-
men, and Bond-women; yea slaves." The similarity between
this exhortation and those in some of the later Army pamphlets
is striking.[a] Can they be by the same hand? Is this hand
Lilburne's and talk of a friend calculated to mislead? Or is there
another unknown who was able to pen these stirring appeals?
Edward Sexby comes to mind. But was he a Latin scholar?

The campaign for the reform of City government was carried
on more specifically by Lilburne in *The Charters of London*,
published on December 18, in which he maintained that the
Commons of London—the poorest as well as the richest—had
the right of choosing annually the Lord Mayor, two sheriffs,
Aldermen, and other officers. He further urged the citizens to
demand an inquiry into the finances of the City, which he
believed to be too often devoted to " hugger mugger " and
private enrichment rather than public ends.

City government could hardly be considered without reference to the City gilds and companies, whose control, like that
of the City itself, had passed to an oligarchy. To the protests
being raised by the commonalties of many gilds and companies
Lilburne lent his voice. The " Companies, Corporations and
Fraternities " of the City " are so many conspiracies to destroy
and overthrow the lawes and liberties of England, and to
ingrosse, inhance, and destroy the trades and Franchises of
most of the Freemen of London," he wrote in *Londons Liberty*.
The whole government of London and its companies he
designated as that of " prerogative Patentee Citizens," who were
worse than " high-way men, pick-pockets, and house-breakers."

It was, however, the pamphlet entitled *Regall Tyrannie
discovered*, published anonymously early in 1647, which caused

[a] E.g., *infra*, p. 176, letter of the agitators to the soldiers in Wales.

the Stationers to act once more, and on January 5 they made a further raid on Overton's house, authorized to search for, seize, and burn all copies of this very long pamphlet which not only declared all kings from William the Conqueror onward to be tyrants, but called on its readers to root up the pretended power of the House of Lords, and announced that the power of the House of Commons was " merely derivative " and dependent upon those that betrusted it. Loose sheets of this pamphlet, in process of being bound, as well as other " scandalous pamphlets," were actually found in Overton's house. Overton's wife, Mary, and her brother, Thomas Johnson, who was stitching the sheets of *Regall Tyrannie*, were both arrested.

The prisoners were brought before the Lords in the afternoon of January 6. Asked by the Speaker " who brought the scandalous Pamphlets called ' *Regall Tyranny Discovered* ' to her Shop, and of whom she had them," Mary stoutly refused to answer. Thomas Johnson would say no more than that he found them there. Both prisoners continued their refusal to answer to interrogatories or make oath concerning the life, liberty, or goods of Richard Overton or themselves. Johnson was committed to the New Prison in Maiden Lane and ordered to be brought before two Justices the following day.[1] Mary, " with her tender Infant in her armes of halfe a yeares age, was most inhumanely and barbarously dragged headlong upon the stones through all the dirt and the mire in the streets, and by the way was most unjustly reproached and vilified by their Officers, with the scandalous, infamous names of wicked Whore, Strumpet, etc. and in that contemptible, barbarous manner was cast into the most reproachful Goale of Bridewell, where restrained."

Mary Overton must stand with Elizabeth Lilburne in a niche of fame dedicated to those women who not only shared their husbands' ideals and aspirations, but actively participated in the fight to realize them, sacrificing home and family life in order to do so. Mary's baby died while she was in prison, the two children she left at home were taken in by neighbours, and the Overtons' house shut up. In March 1647 Mary unsuccessfully demanded from the House of Commons her release. The petition in which she did so was one of remarkable force and ability, which showed that her high spirit was unimpaired.[2]

A month after the arrest of Mary Overton members of the Stationers' Company were again in a flutter of concern over the publication of further " sedition " in the form of the pamphlet *The Oppressed Mans Oppressions declared*, attributed again to Lilburne. This time it was John Lilburne's house they raided, and directed by one, Whittaker, loaded three porters with Lilburne's papers and other goods, including nearly a thousand copies of *The Charters of London*, which, Lilburne claimed, with copies of the charters themselves, cost nearly £20 to produce. The following day, February 8, at nine o'clock in the morning, there arrived at Lilburne's lodging in the Tower a warrant to take Mrs Lilburne, who was with her husband at the time, into custody for dispersing her husband's books. Lilburne also was to go before the Committee of Examinations at two o'clock.

Lilburne lost no time. First, he gave his wife detailed instructions. He prepared a statement, which she signed, and of which a copy was kept, which she was to hand in to the Committee, to the effect that it had no right to examine her upon interrogatories and that no person ought to be judged but by the laws of the realm. Then he began to prepare his own statement.

By this time Lilburne had grown far more familiar with the Lord than when he first suffered at the horse's tail. So, needing all his power and wits to combat his enemies on the Committee, " I lifted up my soule," he said, " to my old and faithfull Counceller, the Lord Jehovah; and in my ejaculations pressed my Lord, and master, with a great deale of grounded confidence and cleerness of spirit, to declare and manifest his faithfullnesse, in being present with me, to counsell, direct, incourage and stand by me, according to his promise of old (made unto me) in the tenth of Matthew." Jehovah did not fail him. ". . . to his praises and glory I desire to speake it, he presently came into my soule with a mighty power, and raised me high above my selfe, and gave me that present resolution that was able to lead me, with a great deale of assured confidence, to grapple with an whole host of men." So, although he was summoned before he was a quarter through his preparation, Lilburne departed for Westminster with great assurance.

Since the weather was cold Lilburne and his escort walked

by land to Westminster, arriving with time to spare, during which he continued his writing. When called before the Committee Lilburne recognized Whittaker, who had raided his house, and others of the " theevish catch-poule Stationers " and many Members of Parliament. Corbett, the Chairman, took up a copy of *The Oppressed Mans Oppressions*, and asked if Lilburne would own it. The prisoner refused, unless and until given leave to answer in his own way. After some demur this was granted.

If, Lilburne began, the Committee were *not* a court of justice it had no right to try him; if it *were*, he demanded a public hearing; and he refused to continue until the doors of the Committee-room were opened to the public, who could then see and hear Free-born John's stand for liberty. While he was reading his paper he was interrupted by Committee members many times, until his wife in exasperation burst out with a loud voice and said, " I told thee often enough long since, that thou would serve the Parliament, and venter thy life so long for them, till they would hang thee for thy paines, and give thee Tyburn for thy recompence, and I told thee besides, thou shouldst in conclusion find them a company of injust, and unrighteous Judges, that more sought themselves, and their own ends, then the publique good of the kingdome, or any of those that faithfully adventured their lives therefore." Elizabeth was evidently more than a faithful disciple of her husband. On this occasion he desired the Chairman " to passe by what in the bitternesse of her heart being a woman she had said," and her outburst was allowed to pass.

When Lilburne had finished reading his paper he was asked, in accordance with his promise, to say whether he admitted writing *The Oppressed Mans Oppressions*. He replied calmly that he had come with the full intention of doing so, but had intended getting the maximum publicity first ! He offered to correct the printer's errors and sign the book himself, but regretted he could not do so on the spot since he had the use of one eye only, and needed spectacles. He then requested, and obtained, the discharge of his wife, on the grounds that she had been acting under his responsibility, and proceeded to lodge a complaint against Whittaker for breaking into his house. When he withdrew, having called the tune from beginning to end of his examination, the spectators, who had enjoyed themselves hugely and wanted more of this entertainment, were crying out that they would have no more closed committees ! [3]

In spite of Lilburne's stand before the Committee on February 8, the year 1647 was going badly for him. Marten had not yet made Lilburne's report to the House. Although Larner had been released in the previous October, Overton, his wife and brother-in-law, Larner's brother and maid, were all in prison. With Lilburne's wife and Lilburne's house suspect, illegal printing was becoming more difficult, and rigorous searching among street hawkers and the book-women in Westminster Hall and elsewhere curtailed the circulation of Leveller literature. John Goodwin's Independent congregation, who on previous occasions had helped financially and in other ways, and were still supplying some of his prison necessaries, were becoming lukewarm, and even positively hindered Lilburne's cause by obstructing the collection of signatures to petitions on his behalf that were circulating in Buckinghamshire and Hertfordshire. Christopher Feake, an Independent minister living near Hertford, reported that through the interference of Lieutenant-Colonel Sadler and others signatures were collected by the hundred rather than the thousand. On February 13 Lilburne wrote to Goodwin and John Price begging them to visit him in prison.[4]

Nevertheless, when " the honest, man-like, and Saint-like Inhabitants of Bucks and Herts," as Overton and Lilburne called them, arrived at Westminster on February 10 they had about 10,000 signatures to a petition asking for the redress of their own grievances and the release of Lilburne, Overton, and the other Levellers. Being refused access to the House, they left six of their number, primed with detailed instructions, to make a further attempt, again unsuccessfully. These facts Lilburne and Overton, making contact with each other, managed to publish in *The Out-cryes of oppressed Commons* on February 28. They were also again working among their friends in the City.

In March the Leveller group in London was planning a far more comprehensive expression of discontent than any that had yet appeared, and was collecting signatures to a long printed petition. A copy of this, circulating at an Independent meeting conducted by Thomas Lambe, was intercepted by an informer, a Mr Boys, or Boyce, and passed to the House of Commons, who, on March 15, referred it to a committee to find the authors.[5] Parliament had, indeed, cause for alarm. The ' large ' petition, as it was commonly called, after acknowledging the advantages of Parliamentary government and the abolition of Star Chamber and High Commission, proceeded first to a vigorous attack on Parliament and then to enunciate a comprehensive programme of reform.

The petitioners had been " filled with a confident hope, that they should have seen long ere this a compleat removall of all grievances, and the whole people delivered from all oppression over soule or body." Instead of which, " such is our misery, that after the expence of so much precious time, blood, and treasure, and the ruine of so many thousands of honest Families, in recovering our liberty, Wee still find the Nation oppressed with grievances of the same destructive nature as formerly, though under other notions." The House of Lords exercised the power formerly held by the Council Board; though Star Chamber had gone, examination upon interrogatories remained; in place of persecution by the Court of High Commission was persecution by a Presbyterian Parliament. Monopolies, tithes, unequal and unjust punishments, imprisonment for debt, and harsh treatment by gaolers were allowed to continue. It is hard to believe that the indictment was not strongly influenced by Lilburne.

The list of demands was far-reaching. As *Englands Birth-right* can be taken as the Leveller programme of 1645, so can this City Leveller petition be taken as their programme for 1647. Its clauses covered freedom of conscience, of speech, and of the press; law and prison reform; the abolition of all monopolies and of tithes, constitutional reform, and social legislation in the interests of the poor. Again, it is hard to believe that the author of *Englands Birth-right* was not actively concerned.[6]

Among the initiators of the ' large ' petition were the well-known Leveller friends of Lilburne, Nicholas Tew and William Walwyn. The latter, according to habit, remained in the background so far as the actual agitation was concerned, but claimed a wider public by committing details of the affair to paper and publishing them anonymously, through the secret press, on June 14 under the title *Gold tried in the fire*. Tew was a printer and publisher who had been several times already before the Committee of Examinations on account of his interest in the Leveller press. Associated with Tew were Major Tulidah and William Browne, the intrepid Leveller bookseller who caused Hunscott such exasperation by repeatedly escaping arrest. The presence of Major Tulidah has special significance as a soldier who is known to be one of Lilburne's visitors and who played an important part in the Leveller movement in the Army. He was undoubtedly one of the " London Agents " whom the Levellers used to keep contact between City and Army, and of whom Parliament became increasingly suspicious.

Deprived of their petition as a focal point of agitation, the Levellers turned their attention to Colonel Leigh's Committee, which the House had appointed to discover the authors. When Thomas Lambe, at whose congregation the petition was intercepted, was summoned to give evidence he was accompanied by a crowd of supporters, including Nicholas Tew. Finding that their petition was being treated by the Committee as a libel, a group of Levellers drew up a statement avowing it to be " no scandalous or seditious Paper . . . but a reall Petition." In the Court of Requests, Nicholas Tew was reading aloud a copy of this certificate for the approval and signature of those about him, telling them, " If we cannot be allowed to petition we must take some other course," when he was arrested by order of the Committee and sent to Westminster prison.

In the disturbance which followed the Committee ordered its room to be cleared, and Major Tulidah and others who objected were forcibly ejected, Tulidah being committed to prison the following day. A second petition was thereupon prepared, complaining of the Committee's attitude towards the petitioners, desiring an examination of the whole affair, and the recognition of the right of petitioning as essential to freedom. This, together with the original petition and Tew's certificate, was presented to the House two days after the disturbance in the Committee —on March 20.[7]

Major Tulidah was released on bail on March 26, but Tew, refusing to petition the House, was still in prison. The London Levellers prepared and presented, therefore, a third petition, asking for the liberation of Tew, an inquiry into the conduct of the Committee, and the placing of restrictions upon committees' powers to commit. Meanwhile citizens flocked daily to Westminster. On April 30 William Browne was heard loudly declaring " they had waited many days for an answer, and would wait no longer but take another course." For this he was arrested, retorting when asked his name, " The time may come when I may take your name! " On May 20, when he was being questioned by the House of Commons, the Levellers and their friends again gathered at Westminster. The House, alarmed by the concourse of citizens at its doors, was " sensible that it was fit for them to be more than formerly quick upon these occasions." [8] Without more ado, therefore, it voted the third Leveller petition seditious, scandalous, and a high breach of privilege, and that this third petition, as well as the original one, should be burnt by the common hangman.[9] Two days later, on May 22, the petitions were duly burnt at Westminster and the Exchange. " Now we shall have an end of our troubles," remarked a Presbyterian who was standing by. " Noe, this is but the beginning of them, and, I doubt not, but to see that hand, which hath burnt this Petition, to hang some of them who caused it to be burnt," retorted an Independent, who was thereupon arrested and sent to the New Prison.[10]

Lilburne watched from the Tower with a mixture of enthusiasm that his methods of appeal were being so well applied and exasperation that no good was coming of them. His friends at this point gained access to him and sought further advice. He had none to give, except that they should petition again, asking for a declaration from Parliament of the people's rights and privileges and guidance on the method of presenting petitions. In this instance the citizens rejected Lilburne's advice, and instead drew up another petition of their own, which was again rejected. At this they sent word to the House that they would petition no more, but seek redress in other ways.[11]

Lilburne had already come to this conclusion. " I am now in good sober resolved earnest, determined to appeale to the whole Kingdome and Army," he announced in May.[12] This decision was reinforced by the fact that in April the City Presbyterians had, with Parliamentary sanction, remodelled the Militia Committee by ejecting Independents and substituting their own men. This put a force of some 18,000 men under Presbyterian control, and gave both City and Parliament a force upon which it could rely in cases of Leveller disturbance like that occasioned by the 'large' petition, and from which it might even hope for support against the Army. Lilburne immediately realized the seriousness of the move, and in *Plaine Truth without Feare or Flattery* warned his readers against the new men of the Militia Committee: "I could read you a Character of most of them . . . Colonels West and Bellamy, the one an oppressive Gaoler, the other an arrogant Magppye, and Bromfield that ran away at Newberry." Will they defend the peoples' liberties? ". . . the Hawke will as soone defend the Dove, and the Kite the Chickens!" But the people were not bound by the Parliamentary Ordinance which put such men in control, "for we are not bound to obey to our own damage and destruction." "The welfare and safety of the People is the supream Law. . . . People by the Law of Nature have power to preserve and secure themselves." He who makes is greater than that which is made, and therefore the people have power to change that which is "uselesse, hurtfull, or unprofitable."

Thus Lilburne turned Parliament's own arguments against itself. But he was warned that there was also another move on foot. Since the fighting seemed to be over, Parliament was planning to disband the Army, and there would then be no force able to stand against the Parliament backed by the City militia. "And therefore yee free Commons of England," cried Lilburne, "up quickly, and looke about you; consider seriously the snare prepared for you. . . . Be vigilant . . . to keep the Army on foot, for your owne defence, and preservation of your selves, your estates and liberties, Country and posterities, from inextricable vassalage and irrecoverable ruin." [13]

It was not only the citizens of London who were reading these words. Lilburne had vowed to appeal to the whole kingdom and to the Army, and in the Army he found an opportunity for propaganda and organization not possible among citizens. Soldiers could be approached in their occupational unit, they already had a sense of common purpose, a feeling for organization, and their very numbers generated enthusiasm for a common cause and a mass movement. It is not surprising, therefore, that the most detailed Leveller organization was that achieved by the Army.

CHAPTER THIRTEEN

Seducer of the Army

I made a vigorous and strong attempt upon the private Soldiery
. . . and with abundance of study and paines, and the expence
of some scores of pounds, I brought my just, honest, and lawfull intentions, by my agents, instruments and interest to a
good ripeness.

JOHN LILBURNE, *The Juglers discovered*, September 1647

THE BACKBONE OF THE NEW MODEL ARMY WAS THE EASTERN
Association, permeated by the freeholders and freeholders'
sons fighting for conscience' sake who were moulded by
Cromwell and influenced by Lilburne. Sir Thomas Fairfax
replaced Essex as Commander-in-Chief, Colonel Philip Skippon
became Sergeant-Major-General, Oliver Cromwell Lieutenant-
General, Henry Ireton Commissary-General. The Ironsides
themselves—Cromwell's own regiment of the elect, as renowned
for piety as for valour—were divided among several regiments
of the new Army. So, although over half the foot soldiers of
the New Model were pressed men of no fixed belief, there was
leaven enough.[1] The men of firm belief carried their ideas
with them and first influenced and finally dominated those of
no particular creed.

Richard Baxter, a Puritan minister equally opposed to
episcopacy and sectarianism, took a chaplaincy in Colonel
Whalley's regiment, which contained many Ironsides, in order
to minister to the soldiers' spiritual needs and to reclaim those
who were far gone in unorthodoxy. He came down to the
Army after Naseby in June 1645, and in the following months
realized that not only Independency but sectarianism of various
kinds was flourishing, particularly Anabaptistry and Anti-
nomianism. ". . . their most frequent and vehement Disputes,"
wrote Baxter, " were for Liberty of Conscience, as they called
it; that . . . every Man might not only hold, but preach and

do in Matters of Religion what he pleased." Moreover, the doctrine of Independency in religion had become independency in politics, and there was much talk of State democracy as well as of Church democracy.

Baxter believed these sentiments to have been inculcated by a few " seducers." ". . . the greatest part of the common Soldiers, especially of the Foot," he reported, " were ignorant men, of little Religion," and therefore " ready instruments " for " a few fiery, self-conceited men," who " kindled the rest, and made all the noise and bustle and carried about the Army as they pleased." These men were the followers of Lilburne, their sentiments his sentiments, and he himself, though in prison, the chief " seducer," as Baxter realized when he described them as those " that afterwards were called Levellers."

The most dangerous group of all Baxter found in Major Bethel's troop of Whalley's regiment. Not only were Bethel's men fiercely Independent in religion, and fiercely opposed to the King—as their tremendous charge at the battle of Langport had borne witness—but they were vehement against all government but popular, and disputed their case with such intensity that " they drowned all Reason in fierceness, and vehemency, and multitude of words." They had once formed part of Cromwell's Ironsides and were the men with whom Lilburne had been mixing in the Army. His early history, his stand against Colonel King and the Earl of Manchester, his Army record, his propaganda as he posted about on Cromwell's behalf and his own, his distribution of pamphlets—all enhanced the influence which the publicity he received after he left the Army did nothing to dim. Baxter was much perturbed, yet it was hardly surprising, that he found " abundantly dispersed " in the Army the pamphlets of Lilburne and Overton, and that the soldiers took these with them to their quarters to read " when they had none to contradict them." [2] These pamphlets, a mixture of concrete grievances and general principles, their very titles rousing appeals that rolled off the tongue like a verse of Scripture—*Englands Birth-right justified, Innocency and Truth Justified, The Just Mans Justification, The Freemans Freedome vindicated, Londons Liberty in Chains, Regall Tyrannie discovered, The Oppressed Mans Oppressions declared, The Out-cryes of oppressed Commons*—were expressing the very views of which Baxter complained, and found a ready response in the soldiers as citizens. When, at the end of the first Civil War, the Army was involved in matters which touched it closer as soldiers, it turned naturally to Lilburne and found him ready.

Lilburne made no distinction between his own case and that of the soldiers: " Lilburne's Freedom—Soldiers' Rights ! " (to adapt their later slogan) might well have been his own motto. He regarded his own case as not merely his own, but " concerning the essential and fundamentall liberties of . . . all and every individual Commoner in England." [3] So when questions of pay and arrears, of indemnity, and of religion came to a head in the spring of 1647, uniting the Army against the Parliament as formerly they had been united against the King, Lilburne, although imprisoned in the Tower, was their inspiration, guide, and mentor.

Arrears of pay had been growing throughout the war. By March 1647 the foot soldiers were eighteen weeks, the horse and dragoons forty-three weeks, in arrear,[4] and many men had still not received full payment for service in the Army before the creation of the New Model. Next to the pay issue in importance was the question of indemnity for the soldiers for acts done during the war. The men were suffering, they said, at every Assize—dragged to gaols, beaten and abused, even hanged—for acts done under command of their officers and in war conditions. The local magistrate of Royalist sympathy, whose own or whose neighbours' horses or provisions had been requisitioned by the Parliament's troops, was frequently only too ready to make use of his legal power as partial compensation for the failure of his forces in the field. Power in the provinces, it was clear, often remained unaffected by the fortunes of war, and the soldiers were left to make the bitter complaint that in the courts their very enemies were made their judges.[5] Even " neuters," they declared, disliked " none so much as Souldiers looking upon them as their immediate disturbers." [6] The fact that statutes still in force prescribed death for stealing money or goods to the value of 5*s*., or taking a horse, gelding, or mare, lent substance to the Army's fear of reprisals for war-time requisitions, as Lilburne emphasized in *Rash Oaths unwarrantable*, published at the end of May.

The third question concerned religion, the largely Independent and sectarian Army demanding freedom of worship, yet fearing persecution, from the predominantly Presbyterian Parliament. Lilburne, still clamouring for his own arrears of pay and loudly demanding freedom of religion, had for months been speaking with their own voice.

Discontent came to a head when Parliament, without meeting the Army's grievances, proposed to disband part of it and send the rest to Ireland where Royalist and nationalist forces were still in arms, " for it was observed by some," as Whitelocke remarked, " that a Victorious Army, out of imployment, is very inclinable to assume power over their Principals." [7] The soldiers, however, concluded " that they who have beene so badly payd, in England shall be holely neglected if they shall goe into Ireland " [8] or disband to their homes, and refused to do either. Realizing the trouble which a full muster would entail, Parliament then decreed that disbandment should be " Troop after Troop, and Company after Company " in different places and at successive times.[9]

In the Army revolt which followed, the influence of John Lilburne and his friends was decisive, and the Leveller movement came to vigorous life. Groups of Levellers had existed from at least the end of 1645, but the birthplace and cradle of the organized Leveller movement was the Parliamentarian Army in the spring of 1647. It was the product of religious freethinking and material hardship, worked upon by a simple philosophy naturally and immediately applicable to the circumstances. Its nurse, tutor, and guide was John Lilburne, whom the stone walls and iron bars of the Tower could by no means keep from nurturing the charge at whose birth he assisted. His were the very utterances to rouse the soldiers to action. If he was frequently talking about himself this made little difference, because, as he boasted, they were of and comprised in him: " The Commons of England are not a little concerned in me." [10] Parliament would not meet his and their demands, but if, as Lilburne was telling them, Parliament's authority derived from the people, of whom they, the soldiers, were an integral part, then they had every right to coerce or to change the Parliament.

In taking up these ideas the cavalry were more advanced

than the foot soldiers. Supplying their own horse and equip-
ment, they were generally middle-class volunteers of the type
of the Ironsides, literate and intelligent, the first to get the
Leveller literature. Later they would read it aloud round the
camp-fires at night, or repeat by heart some easily remembered
exhortation to those unable to read. These were thickest
among the pressed men of the foot, who came from all walks
of life, and were slower to organize than the horse.

When in March 1647 the horse soldiers were talking of
calling a meeting there is no doubt that Lilburne was helping
them. By the end of 1646 he was allowed such visitors in the
Tower as would give their names and addresses to the warder;
but there were few who would so simply agree to furnish the
Government with a list of Lilburne's supporters. ". . . a
pretty devise, could your Lordships but catch Old Birds with
chaffe ! " scoffed Lilburne.[11] Some angrily expostulated with
the warders, generally being thrown out for their pains, some
simply kept away, others evidently came under assumed
names, or by bribery or some other means escaped the vigilance
of the warders. Lilburne himself, in compounding for a rent
of 15s. a week for his room (finding his own linen), had made
it conditional upon his gaoler using him and the friends that
came to see him " with civilitie and humanitie," [12] According to
John White, who had met with such short shrift at Lilburne's
hands in Newgate and the Tower, only two or three of note
came to see the prisoner, the rest being " men's wives "—
Lilburne was always attractive to women, and the strength of
the women Levellers was notable—and " some straggling
Souldiers." [13] Yet through these Lilburne was supplied with
writing material, conveyed his manuscripts to the press, and,
as the months advanced, directed the Leveller movement both
in City and Army. Among the " straggling soldiers " of whom
White was so scornful was the vigorous Edward Sexby, the
chief intermediary between Lilburne and the Army, whose
visits the Government was to have good cause to rue. Sexby
kept copies of Lilburne's pamphlets, and was the chief medium
for their distribution among the soldiers.[14] Major Tulidah,
later a participant in Army Council debates, who spent part
of his time in Leveller activity among the London citizens,
would certainly have come too. Special messengers from the

Army were constantly riding in to Lilburne to keep him informed of developments and ask his advice. Independent ministers constituted an intelligence service: there was Christopher Feake, for example, who had obtained the sequestered vicarage of All Saints, Hertford, in January 1646. He had been a great preacher in London in 1645, was already on the borderline of sectarianism, and would become a Fifth Monarchy man. The known support for the Leveller leaders from Buckinghamshire and Hertfordshire makes it certain that, with the Army closing in on the capital from the eastern counties, a constant intelligence would be simple. Sir Lewis Dyve, a Royalist imprisoned in the Tower at the same time as Lilburne, declared that Lilburne's intelligence was very accurate.

Lilburne himself used various messengers—Sexby, probably Tulidah, a certain Tim Trevers, or Travers, Captain John White, perhaps the son of gaoler White, who had a son in the Army. Elizabeth was used by her husband on more than one known occasion to take letters and messages to Cromwell and the Army; the secret journeys of this intrepid woman, who was bearing her husband's children as uncomplainingly as she ran his messages, can be readily guessed. Whether it was due to their own stupidity, or corruption, or a complete inability within the framework of the prison system to isolate even a dangerous political prisoner, the authorities were never able to keep Lilburne from his contacts.

On March 11 Parliament received word that the Army was on the march towards London. Shortly afterwards the officers of Fairfax's regiment were circulating a petition for signature, but withdrew it after Parliamentary pressure. The rank and file then stepped in and circulated a petition of their own, to which, after securing some amendments, the officers gave their support. This petition, with its five simple demands covering indemnity, security for pay and arrears, relief to widows, orphans, and the maimed, and guarantees to cover volunteers for the Irish service, should not have caused alarm; [15] the fact that the petitioners were approaching the House with arms in their hands, that at the very same time the London Levellers were actively pursuing their ' large ' petition, and that agents of both City and Army were in contact with Lilburne spelt danger.

Cromwell had the difficult rôle of satisfying his soldiers and appeasing the House of Commons. On March 24 an agent of the Army came post-haste to the Tower to report to Lilburne that Cromwell was like to " dash in pieces " the hopes of the country's " outward preservation," because he had promised the House that the Army would not petition until it had laid down its arms. Under stress of alarm another agent appeared the following day.[16] But Lilburne was already writing to Cromwell, for whom he had maintained both a youthful hero-worship and a deep feeling of gratitude, sending off the letter in haste by the nearest messenger to hand—his wife, " the gravest, wisest, and fittest messenger I could think of, and though a Feminine, yet of a gallant and true masculine spirit." [17] Again he acknowledged to Cromwell the old debt, spoke of his warm service on Cromwell's behalf, of intimate meetings in London and elsewhere where he and his wife received favour and friendship from Cromwell, acknowledged gratefully a further " large token of friendship " made since Lilburne's imprisonment, and finally appealed to him, as he had done before, to turn from his evil advisers—" O Cromwell thou art led by the nose by two unworthy covetous earthworms, Vane and St John "—to return to the way of the saints and rely on the Army.

The earnest sincerity of this letter is beyond doubt. ". . . If the Army doe disband before they petition," he urged, " I and all such as I am, must truly lay the whole blame upon you, and truly declare the House of Commons bribe Cromwell to betray the liberties of England into their tyrannical fingers. Sir, is it not the General's Commission to preserve the lawes and liberties of England? And how can he and those with him, without being esteemed by all men . . . the basest of men, to lay downe their Armes upon any conditions in the world, before they see the lawes and universall well known liberties of England fairly settled." If " tyranny be resistable," he urges, " then it is resistable in a Parliament as well as a King." There is an air both of resignation and of conscious power about this letter, for all its obvious haste. He has given up worrying about his own earthly affairs: " Sir, I have but a life to lose . . . being now sufficiently able to trust God with my Wife and Children." This is partly, perhaps, because of the tremendous forces which, in the Army, he is now about to conjure with, and which have swept personal considerations aside. " Sir, I am not mad," he says, " nor out of my wits, but full of appre-hensions of slavish consequences, reason and zeale, and should bee glad it could speedily and justly be cooled by you, before it flame too high, which you will further understand I have grounded cause to make it." [18]

With the ' large ' petition of the London Levellers confiscated and their subsequent agitation crushed, with Goodwin's congregation turning from him, with many of his faithful friends imprisoned, Lilburne had turned to the Army. Now his old friend Cromwell was cutting that prop from under his feet. If he did so Lilburne felt that he, and all comprised in him, would perish. An Army without its arms would be as rotten timber to the tread, as ineffective as the London citizens with their paper petitions. So Lilburne threw all into the Army campaign, building upon his existing influence, reiterating the oneness of his and the Army's cause. He was half fearful of the forces that he would unleash, and made his last appeal to Cromwell to act for him. But Cromwell sent nothing but a non-committal verbal reply, and Lilburne acted.

A letter to Fairfax of July 22 makes it quite clear that he consciously turned to the Army at this particular time. He had, he said, worked first among his friends in the City and country: " I underhand in City and Country applyed my selfe vigorously to my friends and fellow Commons, strongly to petition to the House of Commons." But some of the petitions were slighted, others burnt, some of the petitioners imprisoned. Consequently he next " made a vigorous and strong attempt upon the private Soldiery . . . and with abundance of study and paines, and the expence of some scores of pounds, I brought my just, honest, and lawfull intentions, by my agents, instruments, and interest to a good ripenesse." [19]

In a further letter to Cromwell he was even more explicit: " And when by much industry and with much opposition from yourself and others of your fellow Grandees in the Army, I had been instrumentall with the expence of a great deale of money, and with all the interest and industry I had in the world; acted both night and day to settle the Souldiers in a compleat and just posture, by their faithfull agitators chosen out by common consent from amongst themselves, as resolute, fit, and just instruments to effect my Liberty, to give a checke to tyranny, and settle the peace and justice of the Kingdome, not looking for any good at all from yourselfe." [20] He had acted when he realized, after his letter of March 25, that he could hope for nothing from Cromwell—" no longer looking for any good . . . from yourselfe."

In neither letter does he say precisely what he did. How could he, writing so near the event, give away the secrets of his party? The spending of money, the reference to his " interest," imply that his organization was behind him; the " agents " would have been the " straggling soldiers " and others who made their way to him in the Tower. The whole tenor of the passages implies that Lilburne was working consciously to an end—that of " settling " the soldiers—and that agitators, or representatives, had been decided upon as the means.[a] The objects of the agitators' activities, and the order in which Lilburne gave them, throw into sharp relief his motives: they were to effect his liberty, check tyranny, and settle the kingdom.

Parliament meantime was sufficiently aware of the unrest in the Army to declare on March 30 its " high dislike " of the " dangerous " petition which the soldiers were circulating, naming its promoters " Enemies to the State, and Disturbers of the Public Peace." [21] This merely inflamed the men and hastened their organization. On April 20 came the first hint of success by Lilburne and his associates. " They now speake it openly," wrote a correspondent from Suffolk to the House, referring to the soldiers' petition, " that they will send it upp, with two out of every troope." [22] By April 28 eight regiments of horse had chosen such representatives, or agitators, who issued and signed a joint letter which each regiment then presented to its officer.[23]

On April 30 the House was thrown into consternation when Major-General Skippon produced a copy of the agitators' letter. Three of the signatories—Edward Sexby, William Allen, and Thomas Shepherd—were sent for. The House was anxious to know whether the officers were concerned, or whether it was a purely rank-and-file affair. The troopers replied they thought few of the officers knew or took notice

[a] ' Agitator ' was then used in the sense of ' agent ' or ' representative.'

of it. When it was attempted to draw them on the interpretation of certain clauses in the letter they answered stoutly " That
the Letter being a joynt Act of those several Regiments, they
could not give a punctual Answer, they being only Agents;
but if they might have the Queries in Writing, they should send
or carry them to the several Regiments, and return their own
Answers together with and comprized in the rest." [24]

The issue and presentation of this letter, signed by the
elected representatives of eight regiments of horse, marks the
beginning of organization among the rank and file of the Army.
The letter itself not only put the position of the soldiers and
their grievances with great clarity, but was couched in the
splendid and moving language which characterized all the
agitators' and other Leveller manifestos. " Wee who . . .
have often seen the devouring Sword of a raging Enemy drawne
forth against us, threatning destruction to us, and now see
them vanquished, and ourselves seemingly settled in peace and
safety, are yet sensible of another more dangerous storme
hanging over our heads." " Can we be satisfied with a Comple-
ment," they ask, " when our fellow Souldiers suffer at every
Assize for acts meerly relating to the Warre? " " Hath anything been desired by us that hath not beene promised, or then
we have just cause to expect? " Since the Army had been
victorious, they said, they " hoped to put an end to all Tyranny
and Oppressions, so that Justice and Equitie, according to the
Law of the Land, should have been done to the People, and
that the meanest subject should fully enjoy his right, libertie,
and proprieties in all things; . . . Upon this ground of hope,
wee have gone through all difficulties and dangers, that we
might purchase to the people of this Land, with our selves,
a plentifull Crop and Harvest of Libertie and Peace; but
instead of it, to the great greife and sadding of our hearts, wee
see that oppression is as great as ever, if not greater." [25]

From this time on the men set the pace. The next step was
the organization of the foot regiments a month later. This was
presaged in a letter from London of May 5—probably from
Sexby.[26] It spoke of a meeting of horse and foot, declaring
that ". . . all our friends doe hope the Army will be well united
by this meeting." [27] The letter was written from London,
" our friends " being presumably Lilburne and the London

Levellers. The meeting was successful. The foot soldiers followed the example of the horse and chose committees for every troop and company, representatives of whom they sent to confer with the agitators of horse at Bury St Edmunds. Each foot soldier contributed 4d. towards the expenses of the meeting.[28] The rank and file, both horse and foot, had thus by the middle of May their own elected representatives. Nevertheless, in spite of such plain omens, Cromwell continued to assure the House that the Army would disband, and the House, ignoring letters of warning from the Army,[29] persisted with its plans. In the Army the initiative passed more definitely to the agitators. Urgent communications sped backward and forward between them and their friends in London. Lilburne urged disbandment at no price. Judge David Jenkins, a Royalist imprisoned in the Tower and in touch with Lilburne, argued that only an Act of Oblivion, a general pardon, full payment of arrears, and provision for liberty of conscience would suffice.[30] Fearing that Parliament would try to get control of the train of artillery at Oxford, the agitators sent orders to Colonel Rainsborough's regiment in Hampshire to march to Oxford to guard against the seizure. They put pressure on the officers at a general council of war at Bury St Edmunds on May 29 to carry a vote resisting disbandment and calling the whole Army to a general rendezvous.[31] War between Parliament and Army was open when Fairfax, on May 31, in accordance with this vote, announced that the regiments would not be drawn out for disbandment at the time appointed.[32] On the same day Lilburne published a letter to Henry Marten under the title *Rash Oaths unwarrantable*, in which he aptly and arrogantly mixed his own, the country's, and the soldiers' cause, and inflamed to white heat the Army's resistance to Parliament: " King Charles his seventeen years mis-government before this Parliament . . . was but a flea-biting, or as a mouldhill to a mountain, in comparison of what this everlasting Parliament already is . . . the Commons of England may bid adieu to their Lawes, Liberties, Freedomes, Trades and Properties, unless they speedily take a course for the electing of a new Parliament." Thus inflamed, the agitators were ready when Parliament defied the Army's vote and attempted disbandment, starting with Fairfax's regiment.

When Parliamentary Commissioners arrived at Chelmsford on May 31 they found no regiment to disband. Two hours earlier Major Goodge's company had violently broken open the room of the lieutenant of the regiment, set a musket at his breast, possessed themselves of the colours, and marched towards Newmarket, where they said a general rendezvous of the foot would be held. When asked by whose order they were removing their quarters they answered that they had received orders from the agitators to do so.[33] Colonel Jackson and two others, who rode after the mutineers, were greeted by about a thousand of them at Braintree with cries of " Here come our enemies ! " When he read them the votes of Parliament which the Commissioners had brought with them some one shouted out, " What doe you bringing your twopenny pamphlets to us? " The men, together with the other companies of Fairfax's regiment, then marched off towards Newmarket and the rest of the Army, taking with them wagons with ammunition and surgeons' chests. Captain White, one of Lilburne's messengers, was said to be most active in this mutiny, issuing orders " as if he were the Lieutenant Colonel." [34]

The Commissioners were helpless, and two days later were recalled by Parliament. Two days after that Cromwell joined the Army at Newmarket,[a] having decided to control the movement of the Army which he could not and, perhaps up to this point, did not wish to stem. Earlier in the day of his arrival, Friday, June 4, the Army had its promised rendezvous on Kentford Heath, about four miles from Newmarket, where seven regiments of foot and six of horse were drawn up. When Fairfax arrived, going from regiment to regiment and saying a few words to each " of judgment and moderation," he was greeted with cheering and acclamation.[35] The agitators presented him with *An Humble Representation of the Dissatisfaction of the Army*, which was then unanimously agreed upon and subscribed by the officers and soldiers of the various regiments. The following day, Saturday, June 5, the Army was once more drawn up on Kentford Heath. Some of the

---

[a] He had been attending the House of Commons as Member of Parliament. He had resigned his Army post after the passage of the Self-denying Ordinance, but immediately been reappointed by the House of Commons with the rank of Lieutenant-General.

soldiers called out that officers who had not stood by them should be cashiered, and Colonel Robert Lilburne's men actually drove some off the field.[36] Afterwards the soldiers unanimously agreed upon and subscribed *The Solemne Engagement of the Armie*, pledging themselves not to disband until its provisions were granted. Both documents justified the organization of the rank and file, and dismissed Parliament's concessions as inadequate. The *Solemne Engagement* further stipulated that the governing body of the Army should no longer be the Council of War, a gathering of officers, but a Council of the Army, on which two commissioned officers and two private soldiers elected from each regiment would serve with those general officers who stood by the *Engagement*. To this Council of the Army all offers of security or satisfaction had to be submitted, and ". . . without such satisfaction and security . . . we shall not willingly disband, nor divide, nor suffer to be disbanded or divided."

The Council of the Army functioned for the first time on the following Thursday, June 10. Once again the greater part of the Army was drawn up, this time at Triploe Heath, near Royston, to hear the latest concessions of Parliament. Before the Commissioners arrived the agitators issued their instructions, the first being that while the Commissioners were on the heath the soldiers were " to be very silent and civill." Major-General Skippon, in the name of the Commissioners, addressed Fairfax's regiment, reading the latest Parliamentary votes and urging their acceptance and the Army's disbandment. Then, apparently according to plan, an officer stepped forward and replied that the motion of the regiment was that the proposition should be referred to the newly elected Council of the Army. The Commissioners asked if this were the wish of the whole regiment. " All, All, All! " cried the soldiers, and amid cries of " Justice, Justice! " the Commissioners withdrew.[37]

CHAPTER FOURTEEN

Agitator-in-Chief

An Agitator is a late spurious Monster of John Lilburne's
generation . . . begotten of Lilburne with Overton's helpe.

The Character of an Agitator, November 11, 1647

AN ANONYMOUS CONTEMPORARY OF LILBURNE'S GAVE IT AS
his opinion that an agitator was " a late spurious Monster of
John Lilburne's generation." [1]   Lilburne himself, without
decrying his own influence, paid tribute to the work of the
soldiers who, " to their eternall praises be it spoken, did the
worke to their hands, . . . like prudent and resolved men." [2]
The organization they achieved was remarkable.

The agitators were elected on the basis of companies and
troops.   From each troop and company several men were
elected, small groups which probably functioned severally as
committees for each troop or company, and jointly as a
committee for the whole regiment.   From their number the
regimental committee chose two or more agitators to represent
the regiment on a Council of Agitators.[3]

Here the agitators seemed " to acknowledge no officer but
to rule and dispose of all things " as they thought good.
" They take into consideration," wrote Denzil Holles, " what
is fit to be done, what not, and give their orders accordingly,
examine and censure the Orders and Votes of the Parliament,
receive all complaints, give the redress, send out their Warrants
and Commands, write their letters, exercise a general power
over all, set-up a new form of government in the Army." [4]   There
was a constant correspondence between the agitators and the
various regiments of the Army, the issuing of advice, instructions, information.   On May 4, for example, was published
the remarkable *Advertisements for the managing of the Councells
of the Army*, in which the men were advised to appoint a
council, to get in touch with soldiers and sympathizers in the

provinces, and to persuade the officers to stand firm with the men. They were advised as to the lines their propaganda should take, and warned not to delay action too long " least Resolution languish and courage grow cold." [5] Their desires for the " redresse of all arbitrary and exorbitant proceedings throughout the Kingdom, and . . . for publique justice and due punishment . . . upon all offenders whomsoever," " Reformation in civill justice," " the Subjects libertie confirmed, the Kingdome settled, delinquents detected and punished, the Soldiers and Sufferers satisfied and rewarded," [6] were in accord with other Leveller manifestos. Their advice to " keepe a partie of able pennmen at Oxford and the Army, where their presses be imployed to satisfie and undeceive the people," [7] is interesting not only because of the importance they attached to printing and the fact that the instruction was carried out, but in its reference to Oxford. With the main Army in the Eastern Counties, why should their penmen be at Oxford, as well as with the Army? Was there, in fact, a Leveller press at Oxford? Hunscott and his friends had had no success in tracking the secret press since the beginning of the year, although Leveller pamphlets continued to appear, and it is not impossible that a band of workmen at Oxford were carrying out the work farther away from the vigilance of the Stationers.

Much importance naturally attached to prompt information from London concerning the activities of Army sympathizers and the movements of their opponents. In this respect Leveller agents seem to have been very efficient. The Army was kept closely informed of the events of March to May, when the City Levellers were preparing and presenting to Parliament their series of petitions. In this civilian agitation the Army's own man, Major Tulidah, was so active that he was imprisoned. The printer of the petitions (presumably the London petitions of March onward) was " taken and undone," reported a correspondent to the Army on May 18, who raised again the question of the Army's having its own press and printers, for ". . . if it be not thought on to have a Presse in the Army wee are undone." [8]

The note of urgency in this letter took effect. Numerous pamphlets were published both by the Army in general and by

the agitators in particular.   Holles described the Army as
" countenancing and publishing seditious pamphlets, (for which
they had a press which followed the army)," [9] and Baxter noted
that the Council of Agitators had its own printer and published
" abundance of wild pamphlets." [10]   The printer of the general
Army pamphlets was a certain John Harris, who himself wrote
under the name of " Sirrahniho."   It is likely that the printers
to the agitators were a different group of men, associated with
the Levellers, and Baxter's statement that the Council of
Agitators had its own printer bears this out by implying that
there were, in fact, two presses.

Frequent reports came to the agitators from London.   There
were many meetings in the capital, and plans were prepared in
case the Parliament proved stubborn.   A correspondent of
May 18 reported that Parliament still intended " to disband the
Foote first, and then the Horse, and that by Regiments, and
they to be 40 miles assunder."   The agitators must therefore
not slacken their efforts: " Believe itt my deare fellowes, wee
must now be very active to send to all our severall Regiments
of Horse and Foote and [let them] knowe that nothing but
destruction is threatened . . . and, Sirs, you must be sure to
send to the Foote, and . . . be sure they doe not turne.   Loving
freinds, be active, for all lies at the stake.   This is the stratagem
that was spoken on the other night." [11]

Much of this correspondence backward and forward to
London was carried on in code.   From London on May 25
came a further report to the agitators, written partly in cipher,
from one who said he had ridden hard to London for the
purpose.   The House had ordered the Army to disband regiment
by regiment.   On a note of urgency—" Pray, Gentlemen, ride
night and day "—they are advised what to do: frame a petition
in the name of all the soldiers to be presented to the General
by the agitators;   try to get rid of hostile or unhelpful officers
—Skippon of the higher command and Jackson and Gooday,
the last two to be fetched away by thirty or forty horse, care
having been taken to secure their men;   call the whole Army
to a rendezvous;   and stir up the counties to petition for their
rights and appeal to the Army for help.   These far-reaching
plans are given by the correspondent who signs himself " 102 "
on the authority of " 59 " and " 89." [12]   Most of them were

carried into effect. The agitators framed their petitions, several unsympathetic officers were removed by their agitators—Colonel Sheffield's men dismounted their dissenting officers and seized their horses and arms [13]—they insisted upon, and obtained, two meetings of the entire Army, and they stirred up the counties to such good effect that petitions came pouring into the Army as it approached London.

The soldiers must literally have carried out the exhortation of their London correspondent—" Pray, Gentlemen, ride night and day "—by the use of travelling agitators, who rode to the other divisions of the Army and to other counties distributing literature and spreading propaganda. About May 20, for example, a detailed letter, describing the election of agitators in the southern Army and urging the northern forces to do likewise, was dispatched to Yorkshire in the care of three agitators of horse—Richard Kingdom of Cromwell's regiment, Thomas Diggel of Harrison's, and John Caseby of Fleetwood's. These gentlemen, explained the letter, would help the organization of the northern forces, and the southern Army as a whole would assist to the utmost of its power. By June 15 this work had borne fruit, and John Hodgson, a surgeon, and Henry Lilburne, brother to John, led Colonel Copley's troop through the streets of Leeds to a rendezvous on the moors, where they were met by other troops. Here the surgeon and Henry Lilburne read them some papers and explained the attitude of the southern Army and its desire for the co-operation of the northern troops. One hundred and fifty soldiers agreed to stand together, and they appointed a further rendezvous for the following day, when twice that number appeared and recorded their names in writing. When they returned to quarters they were wearing in their hats Fairfax's blue-and-white colours to signify their unity with the southern Army. They chose agitators, demanded a general rendezvous, and when their commander, Sydenham Poyntz, arrested the delegates of the southern Army and hanged a soldier they took Poyntz himself prisoner and brought him under guard to Fairfax's quarters at Reading.[14]

A letter from Buckinghamshire in June described how the Army " post up and down the Countrey their Agents, with Letters and Instructions." [15] They planned, with Lilburne's connivance, to employ fifty such emissaries, one into every county, with instructions to incite the people to agitate for a dissolution of Parliament.[16]   A letter from Lancashire of July 3 described how two of these agents set to work.   On arrival they distributed copies of *The Declaration of the Armie* to the inhabitants and the soldiers stationed there, and one remained dispersing more literature to the Anabaptists and other sectaries who came flocking in, while the other set off for a neighbouring county.[17]   The petitions from the counties and the suburbs which poured in to the Army as it approached London indicate that their propaganda fell on good ground.   That the soldiers stationed at Newcastle supported, almost to a man, the southern Army was, no doubt, also due to the influence of some of these special messengers from the South.   Of a regiment between 1200 and 1400 strong not only none of the men, but, with the exception of a captain and a lieutenant, none of the officers, supported Parliament against the Army.[18]   The agitators also made a special point of winning over the garrison who were guarding the King at Holmby—a success of the greatest importance to them.

On June 18 the agitators sent to the Navy, explaining the Army's reasons for refusing to disband, and appealing to the sailors for support [19]; on July 12 they sent an eloquent letter to the third division of the Army in Wales.   When, after " the expence of so much blood and treasure . . . we were expecting to see and reap the fruit of all our weary travails," they said, we are told " we should never reap any of them, but that we who had fought to sett our Selves and a Kingdom free should now in the issue be more compleatly slaves than ever."   They wrote in order that the Welsh soldiers might have the opportunity of defending the nation's freedom and liberty at a time when others were endeavouring to suppress it.   Such a defence, they concluded in a magnificent peroration, would " sett a badge of honour upon such a people to posterity, that you should have your part in redeeming the kingdom of England and Dominion of Wales from oppression and slavery, and your children yet unborn shall bless God for you; which if not, consider what a blott of infamy will lye on you and us to after ages, if we shall sitt still in such a time as this, when it shall be said by them lying under oppression, ' our predecessors had a prize in their hands, and an opportunity offered to have freed us from it and have made us happy, but woe to us, through their neglects they have lett it slip, and left us in misery.' " [20]

Leader of the agitators was Edward Sexby, one of the three troopers called before Parliament in March 1647 in connexion with the first petition of the agitators, and one of the few to retain the confidence of his regiment when new agitators were elected. He was a Suffolk man, entered Cromwell's regiment of horse about 1643, and was one of those transferred to Fairfax's troop on the formation of the New Model. He was in constant touch with Lilburne in the Tower, kept copies of the leader's pamphlets, was almost certainly one of those who supplied Lilburne with writing materials, carried his manuscripts to the press, and brought him news from the Army, and was probably responsible for much of the detailed propaganda and organization of the agitators. His later history reveals a man of great tenacity, a convinced Republican, an able writer, and one who would stick at nothing to achieve his ends.[21]

Who the penmen of the Army were can only be guessed. Perhaps a preliminary draft by Lilburne was given definite shape by Sexby, having first been considered by the Council of Agitators. Perhaps Sexby, or one of the Army men, outlined the points of a new *Declaration*, and Lilburne wrote round them one of his exhortations. Perhaps Wildman, who was active in Army affairs in the autumn of 1647, and who wrote at least part of *The Case of the Armie* and the later vigorous *Putney Projects*, had a hand in other manifestos as well. This may, however, be doing less than justice to Sexby. If he wrote, or partly wrote, *Killing No Murder* in 1657 [22] he could also have written the earlier Army declarations without help from Lilburne or Wildman. But whoever wrote them, these pamphlets remain among the most noble and stirring appeals for justice in the English language, and of an intellectual quality sufficiently high to suppose intelligent and politically conscious readers.

From the example of the foot, who subscribed 4*d*. a piece towards defraying the expenses of the first meeting of their representatives with those of the horse, it seems probable that the men contrived in part to finance themselves, although it is unlikely that payments so large as 4*d*.—half a day's wages —could have been made frequently by privates. It is probable that in the first place, when the Army was united, some of the officers helped the agitators with money. Sexby, for example, wrote to the agitators on May 17, 1647: " There wants nothing but money, therefore tell the Officers they must disburse the money." [23]   Lilburne, when he spoke of his work among the soldiers, mentioned on at least two occasions the use of money to further his ends, and implied that the civilian Leveller movement was helping the Army.

By October 1647 the agitators, following a similar progression to Lilburne's, had appealed to the Parliament, the Army Council, and were now about to appeal to the people. A Royalist letter of intelligence put the position neatly: " The King . . . raysd a Parliament he could not rule, the Parliament raysd an Army it could not rule, the Army made Agitators they cannot rule, and the Agitators are setting up the people whom they will be as little able to rule! " [24]

CHAPTER FIFTEEN

King's Advocate

... let Caesar have his due, and us the free Commons ours.
JOHN LILBURNE, *Plaine Truth without Feare or Flattery*,
April/May 1647

WHILE ONE ACT OF THE DRAMA WAS BEING PLAYED ON THE heathlands of the eastern counties, and another in the capital, yet another was being enacted in the gentler air of the Midlands, whither to Holmby House, in Northamptonshire, some thirty-five miles from Oxford, the King had been brought when the Scots, tired of waiting for a settlement, had handed him over to Parliament and returned home.

The fact that he was still one of the chief actors in the play had not been forgotten, and, while attempting to disband the Army, Parliament was also negotiating with the King, its Commissioners actually being at Holmby House, together with the contingent of dragoons under Colonel Graves who were guarding the King, while the soldiers were electing their agitators and drawing up their manifestos. The Army was already afraid of a one-sided settlement between Presbyterians and King. As early as April 20 a letter from Suffolk had said that the " soldiers both in Norfolke and Suffolke sing one note, namely, that they have fought all this time to bring the King to London; and to London they will bring the King." With the statement the writer linked the name of Lilburne. " Sum of the soldiers do not sticke to call the parliament men tyrants. Lilborne's bookes are quoted by them as statute law." [1] A fortnight later it was reported from Saffron Walden that " some of the Foote about Cambridgeshire give out that they will goe for Holdenby and fetch the King." [2] Ireton's men were said to be forward in this talk, and it was even rumoured that Ireton himself had approached the King with an invitation to take refuge with the Army. [3] But it was when the Army learned of Parliament's secret negotiations with the Scots and the French that it became really alarmed, fearing both the loss of the ends for which it had been fighting and the unspeakable evil of a new war.

Lilburne's writings had for long been warning soldiers how near they were to losing all they had fought for, and he now—some time between the end of April and the end of May—wrote *Plaine Truth without Feare or Flattery*, a scorching indictment of Parliament, containing some of his most stirring exhortations to the Commons of England. In it he began to link the King with the free peoples of England against Parliament. Addressing Parliament, he told them: " You keep the King under restraint . . . yee will neither admit the King to do justice, and redresse our grievances, nor will yee your selves: yee have made no other use of the King's power and name, then to deceive, oppresse, and abuse the People." ". . . let Caesar have his due," he said, " and us the free Commons ours. . . . If the King be King let him raigne: if he have otherwise deserved, why proceed ye not legally against him, that the World may see and judge, and ye be cleared of all calumny and aspersion? " Lilburne was, in fact, asking for the King what he consistently demanded for himself.

And who was it, he asked, who kept the King under the restraint of such a man as " wicked Colonel Graves," a " debauched," " lewd shamelesse man," " as if they were afraid to intrust any of the honest Commanders about him "? It was the leaders of the Presbyterian party—Manchester, Holles, Stapleton, and others—" who are absolutely the chiefe instrumentall causes of all the evils, wee have lately suffered, and doe still sustaine, and some of which have received vast summes of monies, whereof they know themselves unable to give any good account." While the Army was on foot, " whose integrity and zeale for justice they feare (and therefore onely would disband them) they cannot impose such particular peculiar conditions upon the King, as will fully secure them, and conduce to their Presbyterian designe." So the Army was to be disbanded and the King kept safe by the Presbyterians until they could impose their will on him. ". . . this I doe beleeve," said Lilburne, " is the summe of all." Put in this way, the cause of the Army and of the King had much in common. Lilburne made it seem closer still: " But must the King and his People be still divided, the breach lye open, and the differences uncomposed, the Kingdome unsetled, the People's peace and happinesse still delayed, and our miseries still prolonged and continued, to satisfie the unjust desires of a company of matchlesse Machiavilian traytors, who to save themselves, have endeavoured by all meanes to destroy us? . . . Wee the free Commons of England, the reall and essentiall body politicke, or any part of us, may order and dispose of our owne Armes and strength, for our own preservation and safety; and the Army in particular . . . may lawfully retaine, order and dispose of their armes and strength to and for the preservation and safety of the King and Kingdome, the principall end for which they were raised."

When, in the same pamphlet, Lilburne quoted Solomon— " Take away the wicked from the King and his Throne shall be established in righteousnesse "—it might reasonably be accepted as advice to take away the King from the wicked, or to remove him from Parliamentarian and Scots influence.[4] Who knows what the Army messengers and the London agents were carrying backward and forward between the Tower and the Army? Lilburne and the agitators were in close council, and it would be surprising indeed if the plan to remove the King from Holmby owed nothing to Lilburne.

At the end of May information leaked out that Parliament was negotiating both with the Scots and the French with the intention of carrying off the King—perhaps to Scotland—and bringing in another Scottish Army to use against the recalcitrant regiments in England. The London militia was being re-organized under Presbyterian control; it was believed that Parliament was trying to get control of the Army's train of artillery, most of which was held at Oxford; a Scottish invasion would be the end. Already the Independents had been fighting the new Militia Ordinance. Now the agitators took steps to secure the artillery at Oxford and laid their plans for securing the King against Presbyterian abduction.

The fifth instruction of the *Advertisements for the managing of the Councells of the Army* warned the agitators to " prevent the removal or surprisal of the King's person." On May 28 a letter, probably from Sexby, spoke obscurely of some design which, it seems, would follow directly the artillery at Oxford was secure, and of some counter-scheme they needed to outwit: " Let two horsemen go presently to Colonel Rainsborough to Oxford, and be very careful you be not overwitted. Now break the neck of this design, and you will do it well." After this— *i.e.*, having secured the artillery and countered the hostile scheme—they were " not to dally," but were to take " a good party of horse of 1,000, and . . . have spies with them before to bring . . . intelligence." They were to quarter their horse overnight, and to march in the night.[5]

It seems that the agitators had something to do at Oxford besides securing the artillery. Colonel Rainsborough was there, and a printing press was there. It is not unlikely that their plans included something connected with the press, and that Rainsborough, an officer of known sympathies with the Levellers, would help them. No publication that might be attributed to the agitators appeared at this time, but the other part of their scheme was carried out, for by the following day they were satisfied that the artillery was safe. " Oxford, where our magazine is, we have well secured," they reported in a letter of the 29th. But, the writer continued, " I wish things at Holmby were as secure." [6] The agitators had, however, won over the garrison there, who supported them almost to a man.[7]

On May 31 Cromwell had a meeting with several people at his house in Drury Lane. He was still trying to reconcile Parliament and Army, and had not yet thrown in his lot whole-heartedly with the soldiers. He clearly knew of the plans for bringing in a Scottish Army and of the importance to these plans of the King's person. At this meeting was Cornet Joyce, the man chosen by the agitators for the difficult task of managing affairs at Oxford and Holmby. What Cromwell said to Joyce is not known. It is certain that he knew un-officially of Joyce's assignment, and that he did not forbid the enterprise. It seems likely that he and those with him gave a general approval to the mission of securing the King from Presbyterian attack, but no more.[8] It is also likely that Joyce did not care so very much what Cromwell said, his orders having come from the agitators.

It was, however, on this very day that Fairfax had at last informed Parliament that the Army would *not* disband, and Lilburne had published *Rash Oaths unwarrantable*, which, besides announcing that the evils of the King's government were " as a flea biting " compared with those of Parliament, solemnly declared that, having read and weighed nearly all that had been written on the subject, he was convinced that the King had not by *will* imposed monopolies, ship-money, and other burdens, but was made to believe it was right to do so by his judges and counsel at law. They were back in some respects where they had started, with rescue operations afoot to save the King from evil counsellors !

Joyce proceeded to Oxford, and, finding the artillery strongly secured in good hands, continued towards Holmby on June 2 with 500 men. He arrived in the evening, Colonel Graves fled, and the two bands of soldiers fraternized. Joyce's statement to the Parliamentary Commissioners confirmed that he was acting " with the authority of the soldiers " to protect the King from being used as a tool in furtherance of a new war.[9] He wrote a letter next morning to an unnamed person : " Sir,— Wee have secured the King. . . . You must hasten an answere to us, and lett us knowe what we shall doe. We are resolved to obey noe orders but the Generall's." [10] It is thought, on the evidence of Holles, that Joyce wrote a letter from Holmby at this time to Cromwell.[11] If this is, in fact, the letter it would seem that Joyce, having proceeded so far, felt in need of outside support from some one who had approved his enterprise up to that point, and that both he and Cromwell were putting themselves in the hands of Fairfax. This assumption is not at all probable. The phrasing of the letter is sufficiently ambiguous to make it far more likely that Joyce was writing to some one who had more directly primed him in the enterprise, and that he was speaking, not of a person, the General, but of the general good, the generality—in the sense that the General Council of the Army was not a meeting of Generals, but of the general body of the Army, in rather the same way as ' the public ' was, and still is, used to signify the general body of the population. Several examples of current usage support this view. It might even be, indeed, that by " General " Joyce was referring to the General Council of the

Army, though it is extremely unlikely that so large and public a body would have sanctioned plans for the King's removal. If the word was used in this way it is more likely that he was referring to the General Council of the Agitators, and that Joyce was determined to obey no orders but theirs.

At all events, during the following day Joyce and his men became suspicious that some new plot was hatching to seize the King from under their very eyes, and this apparently decided him—and here he was acting purely as the instrument of the agitators—to remove the King then and there; and the only place of real safety was the Army. Joyce thought first of Oxford, where the troops were loyal and the agitators strong, and this may have been the agitators' original plan; but, the King desiring Newmarket, this seemed no worse choice, for here the main Army would take charge.

When the King stepped on to the lawn of Holmby House in the early morning of the 4th and asked Joyce by whose commission he was being removed the Cornet's reply was unequivocal: "The Soldiery of the Army; or else I should not have dared to have done what I have." His reasons also were straightforward and convincing. It was because "being informed his Majesty was to be conveyed away, which, if not prevented, might have caused another war, and involved the whole Kingdom in Blood again." [12] In answering in this way Joyce was using the expressions of the soldiers and agitators in obeying instructions from the Council of the Agitators and the Council of the Army. In dismounting their officers, in riding to rendezvous, in seizing stores or ammunition, the troops were constantly saying, "We did it because the agitators ordered it, because the soldiers ordered it; we did it in the name of the army." This was no new conception, and Joyce did not need the explicit authority of a higher officer to make it seem to him that he was acting for the whole Army.

His subsequent actions make it equally clear that the agitators were the prime movers in taking the King from Holmby. The first thing Joyce did as they rode away was to send a letter by an agitator to a person unknown to say: "Lett the Agitators know once more wee have done nothing in our owne name, but what wee have done hath been in the name of the whole Army, and wee should not have dared to

have done what wee have, if wee had not been sure that you
and my best old friend had consented hereunto, and knew that
I speak nothing but truth." [13]   Whoever " you " or " my best
old friend " might be, the emphasis on the agitators is emphatic,
and Joyce's assertion that " wee have done nothing in our
owne name, but what wee have done hath been in the name of
the whole Army " supports the belief that when he wrote of
" the General " he was thinking of the whole of the Army
or their representatives.[14]

On June 4, the day when Cromwell abandoned his attempts
at compromise and joined the Army and the soldiers subscribed
their *Humble Representation* on Kentford Heath, the King
left Holmby. The following day, with the King on his way to
the Army, the *Solemne Engagement* was unanimously agreed
to by the soldiers. On the 8th the King reached Newmarket,
and two days afterwards the gathering on Triploe Heath confirmed the creation of the Council of the Army. It was indeed
a good week's work !

CHAPTER SIXTEEN

Lilburne's Freedom—Soldiers' Rights!

I resolved ... to make my complaint to the Commons of England, and to see what the private Soldiers of his Excellencies Army, and the Hobnayles, and the clouted Shooes will doe for me, and all themselves concerned in me.

JOHN LILBURNE, *Letter to Marten*, September 15, 1647

CONTEMPORARY OPINION IS AGREED ON THE POWER OF THE Army and of the agitators in the spring and summer of 1647. " The Army now did all," wrote Denzil Holles, " the Parliament was but a Cypher, and only cried Amen " to what the Council of the Army had determined.[1] Sir Thomas Fairfax, who ought to have known, confirmed the power of the agitators. " The power ... I once had," he wrote, " was usurped by the Agitators." [2] Sir John Berkeley, the Royalist, who was often with the Army conducting negotiations on behalf of the King, added the interesting observation that on the Council of the Army, though Cromwell and Ireton and their faction were strong, yet the agitators were even more powerful.[3] A correspondent of Hyde gave it as his opinion in the autumn that though the Army ruled all, yet the agitators ruled the Army.[4] He might have added, with only slight exaggeration, that John Lilburne ruled the agitators !

For the history of these months is of Lilburne spurring the agitators, the agitators, needing very little encouragement, pushing the Council of the Army, and the Army, in its turn, exerting pressure against the Parliament. The grandees were not happy at their rôle of buffer between agitators and Parliament. Discussions at Council meetings showed the grandees not only slower to move than the ranks, but anxious to control the more extreme elements, uneasy at the active participation of privates in what had always been officers' discussions, yet deeming their presence unavoidable. Something of the truth of the situation was conveyed in a letter from the Army of July 17—probably from Rushworth, the secretary to the Council of War. He spoke of the " Agitators, who now in prudence we admit to debate; and . . . it is the singularest part of wisdom in the General and the Officers so to carry themselves . . . as to be unanimous in Councills, including the new persons into their number. It keeps a good accord, and obtains ready obedience." [5] When " ready obedience " was not obtained the officers tried to intimidate the agitators or to bribe them with promise of promotion; when this did not work they ' packed ' the Council with their own nominees.[6]

Before June was out the agitators were sending to Lilburne in the Tower complaining that Cromwell and Ireton would break the Engagement of Triploe Heath.[7] This was serious for the soldiery, since it was becoming increasingly clear that the repeated presentation of a lengthening list of demands to a hostile House of Commons would settle no problems; it was personally serious for Lilburne, since his agents were telling him that, while the agitators, " his true friends," were supporting his case on the Council of the Army, Ireton was his chief opponent.[8] Fostered by Lilburne, there grew among the soldiers the conviction that Parliament's dilatoriness could be countered by nothing short of physical coercion.[9] As one of the soldiers' manifestos expressed it: " If the effects be but removed, and the cause still remaining, that cause will beget the like or worse effects for the future." [10] The immediate cause was the presence of the eleven Presbyterian Members of Parliament most hostile to the Army.

Spurred on by the agitators, the Army, on June 15, delivered its formal charge against the Eleven Members, together with its demand for their suspension; Parliament, faced with the alternatives of surrendering the Members or attempting force, prepared for the latter, promising pay and arrears to all who would desert the Army, encouraging old soldiers to support Parliament by promising arrears, planning to use the City militia. Lilburne wrote at once to Cromwell at St Albans on June 22, begging him " as for my life " to march at once to the City, where his friends would be able to help him sequester the Eleven Members.[11] Was Lilburne speaking merely of

Cromwell's friends, or was he referring to Levellers who would come to the assistance of the Army?

But a charge against eleven Members of Parliament was one thing, a march on the capital another, and the Army Council hesitated to go further. On July 1, with the Army only as far as Wycombe and the Eleven Members still in their places, Lilburne wrote again to Cromwell. He could see the work of the agitators being undone and he himself as far from freedom as ever. ". . . you have rob'd," he wrote, " by your unjust subtiltie, and shifting trickes the honest and gallant agitators, of all their power and authority, and solely placed it in a thing called a Counsell of Warre, or rather a Cabinet Junto of seven or eight proud selfe ended fellowes, that so you can without controule make up your owne ends." His agents, he said, had repeatedly warned him—" my often intelligence told me againe and againe "—of the perfidy of certain counsellors, presumably the younger Vane, St John, Dr Stanes, Muster-master Watson, Scout-master Nathaniel Rich. He had already tried by writing to prevent their betrayal, but to no avail, and now makes one further appeal. " Unlesse," he said " you . . . take some speedy course, that I face to face may speake my mind to your selfe of which I desire a positive and satisfactory answer within foure dayes at the farthest . . . looke to your selves as well as you can, for the uttermost of my strength and interest shall speedily be amongst you publiquely." This may be a threat to break prison, as the agitators had repeatedly begged him, and to lead their revolt in person.[12] He pondered this during the summer, and —characteristic bravado—" had I come, and could have got so many to have followed me . . . I should have made no more scruple of conscience with my own hands to have destroyed them [i.e., Parliament]." But, he says—and here is one of his characteristic, but fleeting, moods of humility—" I hoped the great worke of the Kingdome would speedily be done by more abler and wiser instruments than I judged myselfe to be." [13] In this moment of insight he realized that dissolving Parliament was not enough. Men of maturity and experience would be needed to establish a settled government.

So Lilburne stayed in prison, but encouraged the agitators to send emissaries into the counties to incite the people to support their demand for a dissolution of the House of

Commons. This they were doing in July. On the 16th, at a meeting of the Army Council, they reinforced their appeal by a *Representation* asking " out of their deep sence of the sad and heavy pressures, great distractions, continual fears, and eminent dangers, under which this poor and bleeding Kingdom groans " for an immediate march on London, so that the Army could force the Parliament to establish " the Kingdom's ease and preservation." They linked themselves openly with the Levellers by asking for release and reparation for Lilburne, Tew, the Overtons, and other London Levellers then in prison, and Lieutenant Scotton, in the course of the debates, said that Lilburne's imprisonment lay heavily upon their spirits.[14]

Cromwell and Ireton opposed immediate marching on the grounds that a negotiated treaty was more durable.[15] Lilburne, on the very day of the debate, gathered together his letters to Cromwell, adding a final exhortation to the private soldiers and their " honest " officers to the effect that they were now dissolved from all obedience to Parliament and could positively disobey it " as unjust, tyrannicall, and unrighteous," and that they were " dissolved into the originall law of Nature " and held " their swords in their hands for their own preservation and safety." [16] On the following day Overton from Newgate warned them not to be " demurred, protracted and delayed, by the old, beaten, subtile Foxes of Westminster." [17] Five days later Lilburne wrote to Fairfax urging his own case—" I am confident you have not a business of greater weight and consequence than mine "—and threatening to appeal again to all the Commons of England and the private soldiers.[18] But before the letter was published not only had the Eleven Members departed from the House of Commons, but the Army, having yielded to the agitators, was again on the march.

In spite of the Presbyterian majority in the Houses, a Presbyterian party of considerable size in the City, and a great deal of mob violence on both sides, the welcome given to the approaching Army was hearty and spectacular. Lilburne in the Tower missed nothing of the drama as there approached the Army that had defeated the King, partly purged the House, and that he expected would set him free, headed by the man who had twice rescued him—from the Fleet and now, as he hoped, from the Tower. Southwark, its population of recently displaced small masters always opposed to the big-business Presbyterian interests of the City, announced its support of the Army; the gentry of Hertfordshire sent to Fairfax to say that two regiments of trained bands of 1300 men each and two troops of horse were ready to attend him. Independent Members of both Houses—about fourteen of the Lords, the Speaker, and some hundred Members of the Commons—rode out to meet the Army at Hounslow. On August 2 the Army was drawn up, some 20,000 strong, on Hounslow Heath. Arranged in battalions, it was a mile and half long. Along the whole length rode the General, the Lords, and the Commons, amid great shouting and cheering, the men throwing their hats in the air and crying out for " Lords and Commons and a free Parliament." On the 5th the Army was at Hammersmith, whence Fairfax wrote a letter to the City, informing it that he had been compelled to advance for the security of Lords and Commons. On the 6th the Army entered Westminster—a triumphant procession, escorting the Independent M.P.s, and each soldier wearing a laurel-leaf in his hat.[19] On the 7th it gave an exhibition of its strength by marching through the City; Lilburne from the Tower listened for the tramp of their feet and the ring of their horses' hooves as years before he had listened from the Fleet for the hoofbeats of the assembling Parliament. Release must have seemed very near when Fairfax himself entered the Tower and, calling for Magna Carta, declared, " This is that which we have fought for, and by God's help we must maintain." [20]   Still, however, the Presbyterian majority in the Houses remained, and on the 9th a resolution of approbation of the Army's proceedings was lost in the Commons.[21]   The need, therefore, of a more thorough purging of the House was apparent.

Once again the agitators took the lead. On the 5th, when the Army was at Hammersmith, they had proposed purging the House. On the 14th they renewed the proposal.[22] On the 18th a majority of the Army Council supported them.[23] On the 20th Cromwell, giving effect to this decision, had a regiment of cavalry drawn up in Hyde Park and himself, with those other officers who were also Members of Parliament, went to the House. The threat of force proved sufficient, and the most prominent Presbyterians left the House, leaving the majority to the Independents.

It would have been a fitting climax to Lilburne's career if the gates of the Tower had been flung open and he had been received into the arms of the victorious Army. It was what the news-sheets and gossip-writers expected. On the 6th, when the Army was at Westminster, on the 7th, when it marched through the City, on the 20th, when Cromwell purged the House—any one of these days would have been appropriate for the release of the Leveller leader. But as the days and weeks passed he, as well as the Overtons and other Levellers, was still in captivity. Their continued imprisonment emphasized the rift which was growing between the Levellers, represented by the agitators, and the grandees.

Lilburne's wife had for some time been haunting Army Headquarters, both at St Albans and at Kingston, to press for her husband's release. He himself had written again to Cromwell on the 13th at Kingston, begging for a meeting.[24] His anger against Cromwell on personal grounds was growing. He had, at Cromwell's request, reported on the conduct of Colonel King of the Eastern Association, and so become involved in the quarrel between Cromwell and Manchester which indirectly led to his present imprisonment. As he had written to Cromwell on July 1: " . . . you pluckt your head out of the coller, and I was catched in the bryers." [25] On the 13th he also sent by his messenger, Captain John White, a paper in which he showed the influential positions in the Army of all Cromwell's relatives and friends; thus, according to Lilburne, Cromwell had engineered his own advancement while leaving true patriots like Lilburne to languish in captivity. He threatened to publish the paper with his comments. He also sent a note to Fairfax on August 26 begging that he might state his case before a committee chosen by Cromwell and himself, with Fairfax as umpire—a slightly new version of the famous challenge to debate.[26] On the same day Lilburne's Leveller friends presented a petition on his behalf to the House of Commons, which, purged of the chief Presbyterians, might have been expected to show some sympathy. But the petition was referred to Marten's Committee, which was asked to report on September 7. The delays, excuses, protractions, and postponements which had deferred the report of this Committee, appointed nearly twelve months earlier, would have driven distracted men of steadier temperament than Lilburne. Now, with Cromwell still making no sign, Lilburne on the following day implemented the threat to stir up fresh trouble among the private soldiers by a further publication.

The agitators were perturbed at the various turns of events which always flung them away from their goal, and bewildered by the attitude of their officers to the King. The importance of the King as a bargaining factor was, indeed, self-evident, and there had been no need for Tim Trevers to ride to Cromwell at St Albans on June 22 primed with a letter and many arguments from Lilburne [27] to get Cromwell and Ireton constitution-making with the King. Not the negotiations, but their nature, appeared to the agitators to be starkly treasonable.

Ireton drew up the heads of a scheme which was laid before the Council of the Army on July 17, when a committee of twelve officers and twelve agitators was appointed to consider them. But before this committee had reported Ireton and Cromwell were in frequent consultation with the King and his advisers, and so carried away by hopes of a settlement that, without consulting the Army Council or the committee, they altered some of the articles of the original scheme " in most material points. [28] When this was disclosed to a subsequent meeting Rainsborough was so disgusted that he immediately left and gave an account of the affair to John Lilburne. Soon Lilburne was writing indignantly of the familiarity of Cromwell and Ireton with the King, and of the constant presence of the King's agents, Berkeley and Ashburnham, at Army Head-quarters. The soldiers took up the reproach. Having fought the King for five years, why did the officers now make an " idoll of the King "? " Why permit they so many of his deceiptfull Clergy to continue about him? Why doe themselves kneele, and kisse, and fawne upon him? ... Oh shame of men ! Oh sin against God ! What, to doe thus to a man of blood; over head and eares in the blood of your dearest friends and fellow Commoners? " [29] It was not at all what they had intended when he was first brought among them by Cornet Joyce, and reinforced their determination to ask Lilburne's advice.

On August 21 in response to their request, this advice was ready; on the 27th Lilburne published it in a special soldiers' edition of *The Just Mans Justification*, one of the pamphlets

cited in 1646 as a cause of his imprisonment; he repeated it in
The Juglers discovered on September 28. Clinched, as Lilburne
well knew how, with telling phrase and apt metaphor, the
advice constituted a new programme, more far-reaching than
the immediate issue, to stand beside *England's Birth-right* and
the ' large ' petition. For the Army his advice was simple.
The soldiers must contest to the death the preservation of the
Engagement of June 5, they must require an immediate report
from their agitators and change them frequently, " for standing
waters though never so pure at first, in time putrifies." The
House of Commons, in spite of its mild purging, still showed
itself unready to free Lilburne and his friends, and therefore
the soldiers must press for a further purge. The reforms to
follow this action were the abolition of monopolies and tithes,
the translation of the law into English, " free and equal justice,"
the abolition of free quarter, and the dealing with all public
money through the Exchequer. As a final piece of advice
Lilburne threw in the caveat to " trust your great officers . . .
no farther than you can throw an Oxe ! " Here, as early as
August 21, Lilburne is speaking of changing the agitators.

With Lilburne's new appeal spreading widely, with his case
due to be reported in the House on September 7, Cromwell on
the 6th made the visit for which Lilburne had so long asked in
vain.

It was a month after the occupation of London by the Army,
ten days after Lilburne's latest ' Advice ' to the soldiers, that
Cromwell, ostensibly come to inspect the ordnance, visited
Lilburne in the Tower. Sir Lewis Dyve, the Royalist, watched
the friendly and courteous greetings which passed between the
two men, confident that, ere nightfall, he would know what
passed between the leaders of the two factions whose difference
he hoped would let his master in again.

When alone, Cromwell spoke fairly to Lilburne, asking him
how it had come that he had fallen out with his best friends
and become such an enemy to Parliament. He urged patience
and moderation, and begged Lilburne not to speak with so
much bitterness of the Parliament, but rather to suspend judgment and Parliament would speedily proceed with those things
that would render the kingdom happy. Lilburne denied that
he had fallen out with his old friends, but accused them of

falling off from him and their first principles by allowing the
House of Lords to cast him into prison to the utter undoing
of himself, his wife and children, whereas all he asked was a
fair and legal trial. He went on to say that the greatest crimes
objected to in the King's time were, in comparison with Parliament's actions, both glorious and righteous.

Cromwell replied patiently that the King's reign was a *habit*
of oppression and tyranny, whereas those things in Parliament
which seemed to swerve from the right rules of justice were by
way of accident and necessity, which would speedily be reformed
as soon as those necessities were removed. He believed
Lilburne's fears to be " the infusions of some subtill cavaleres
with whom he conversed." But Lilburne swore " he was the
selfe-same man as when he had the honour first to be knowne
to him." And, he added pugnaciously, he would, by all the
ways he could possibly invent, labour to destroy the Parliament
as he had formerly done the bishops, rather than that they
should destroy him, his wife and children, by keeping him longer
in prison.

Cromwell let Lilburne understand that his release was
delayed because it was feared that he would go down to the
Army and " make new hurley-burleys there " : Lilburne's
latest diatribes were obviously in Cromwell's mind. If he
would be quiet he would be set free. No, replied Lilburne,
he would not promise, unless he could get satisfaction for his
losses, wrongs, and injuries. It would all be done, urged
Cromwell, if he would but have patience. Meantime, honourable employment would be given him in the Army. This
brought out all Lilburne's bellicosity. As the case now stood,
he said, and according to those principles by which he perceived
they now steered their course, he would not be engaged in
either the Parliament's or the Army's service for all the gold in
the world.

" Well," said Cromwell, " though you have given me little
encouragement, yet such is the affection I beare you, as you
shall see I will not be wanting in my best endeavours to procure
your liberty of the Parliament, whereof I hope you shall find
the effects in a very short time."

Lilburne, always amenable to kindness and a straight discussion of his affairs, was touched and softened by Cromwell's

visit. Arguing that he could follow no employment in England, for oaths stood in the way of industry and tithes in the way of agriculture, he offered to go abroad for twelve months if released, on condition that he were paid the £2000 awarded as his Star Chamber reparations and half his Army arrears, and that the House of Commons would unequivocally deny the jurisdiction of the House of Lords over a commoner. Lilburne drew up a document to this effect, with which Cromwell appeared well pleased.

The two men went to dine with the Lieutenant of the Tower. Never a man to let slip a favourable moment, Lilburne at table spoke of the hard usage of the prisoners in the Tower, and Cromwell, with ready sympathy, spoke with several of them after the meal.[30] But when he left, Lilburne was no better off than before. No report on his case was made the following day: it is conceivable that Cromwell needed time to ponder the implications of Lilburne's attitude. It was ordered for first business on the 8th, but there was then no time, and it was deferred until the 9th, when it was again postponed and ordered to take first place at the next sitting of the House. Not until then, September 14, did it come before the Members. But the Report was immediately recommitted, on Cromwell's motion, in order that search could be made for precedents concerning the Lords' jurisdiction over commoners![31]

It was then that Lilburne roused himself for the greatest effort of all. He had been deceived by Cromwell's fair speeches in the Tower, put in a false position in order to make offers that would bring him into disrepute. He would have no more truck with men of place or office, but would go straight over their heads. " I . . . am resolved," he wrote the following day to Marten, " to make my complaint to the Commons of England and to see what the private Soldiers of his Excellencies Army, and the Hobnayles, and the clouted Shooes will do for me, and all themselves concerned in me." The private soldiers were his first objective; the " Hobnayles and the clouted Shooes," though subject all the time to Leveller propaganda, were the object of a separate campaign a few months later. Cromwell's design, he now declared, was " to keep the poore people everlastingly . . . in bondage and slaverie, with a rotten and putrified Parliament." Law had no longer any meaning;

" there is now no power executed in England, but a power of
force, a just and moral act done by a troop of Horse, being as
good law as now I can see executed by any Judge in England."
If the law had not rescued him, then the soldiers must, and he
called upon Gideon's army to risk all in battle against the Lords,
the lawyers, the clergy, and " the present new upstarts."

Since the agitators elected to execute the soldiers' will were
no longer trustworthy, there was only one thing to do.   It
" behoves the gallant Soldiers, in every Regiment to call home
their respective Adjutators, and require an account of their
Stewardship, or Adjutatorship at their hands, and without
more adoe to send new ones, and fresh ones to the Head
quarters, in the roome of all those, that cannot give a satisfactory and just account how they have managed the trust
they reposed in them." [32]

The earliest evidence of the effect of this advice comes from
the Royalist, Dyve, who was in a good position to know
what Lilburne was doing. Apart from telling Charles that
six regiments had cashiered their old agitators and chosen
new,[a] on October 5 he wrote to say that they had been
meeting " every day constantly."   Lilburne told Dyve that
their object was to purge the House and suppress Cromwell's
faction, and Dyve had no doubt about his influence. " Mr
Lilborne," he told the King, " set this business first on foot
and hath a great influence upon their counsells." [33] He was
certainly influential enough for Rainsborough to think it
necessary to consult him on October 31, when the *Agreement
of the People* and the Ware rendezvous [b] must have been in
their minds, and to stay with him for two hours.

The new agitators were the leaders of the second phase of
the Leveller movement in the Army, in which the agitators
were not only in open and constant hostility to the grandees,
but, worked on by Lilburne, were talking in terms of ' the
people,' and a new Parliament, and were in constant touch
with the hobnails and clouted shoes to whom the other half of
Lilburne's appeal was addressed.

　　　[a] *Infra*, p. 199.　　　　　　[b] *Infra*, pp. 205, 214 *ff.*

CHAPTER SEVENTEEN

Royalist Intriguer

... as things stand ... you must apply to the King ... [I] doe
confidently believe hee will grant anything that is rationall,
that you or the Kingdome can desire at his hands.

JOHN LILBURNE, *Jonah's Cry*, letter of June 22, 1647

*I*T IS DOUBTFUL WHETHER THE SOLDIERS WHO HAD WALKED
so faithfully with Lilburne until now would have approved of
his conduct at this time. For Lilburne himself, while straining
to get his case heard and stirring up the common soldiers to
make a stand against the Army command, was being driven
into closer contact with the Royalists in the Tower with whom
he was imprisoned.

Chief of these were Judge David Jenkins and Sir Lewis
Dyve. From September 8, 1647, there was also Sir John
Maynard, one of the eleven sequestered Presbyterian Members,
who after the occupation of London by the Army was charged
with levying armed force within the City, arrested by general
warrant under the Speaker's hand, and committed to the
Tower during the pleasure of Parliament. How far he took, or
needed, advice from Lilburne is impossible to say, yet the
conduct of this Presbyterian and near-Royalist was most
Lilburne-like. Being impeached of high treason, Maynard
wrote to the Speaker of the House of Lords on February 4,
1648, refusing to make any defence, claiming to be tried by
jury, and citing Magna Carta and the Petition of Right. He
repeated this at the Lords' bar the following day, refusing to
kneel or recognize the jurisdiction of the House of Lords over
a commoner. Fined £500 and remanded to the Tower, he
issued several protests to the same effect, and still refused to
kneel to them or acknowledge their authority in his case.[1] The
pursuit of principle makes strange bedfellows ! The friendship
which ripened between the two men produced in Maynard an

admiration for Lilburne and a commiseration with his sufferings that was turned to practical account later.

With Judge Jenkins Lilburne talked law, and later acknowledged he had learnt much from him. The Welsh judge had been brought to the Tower in April 1647 for declaring that the rule of law was inseparable from the rule of the King, and he kept up a written legal battle with Henry Parker until his removal to Newgate and his trial in February 1648, when he still staunchly maintained there was no law without the King and refused to kneel to the House of Commons. As with the Presbyterian, so Lilburne found there was much with which he could agree in the Royalist—the security of person and property based upon law, the veneration of Magna Carta and the Petition of Right, and the refusal to acknowledge an authority not considered in accordance with these. The stout-hearted judge, for his part, reinforced Lilburne's pleas to the soldiers with his own legal advice.[2]

With Sir Lewis Dyve Lilburne talked of his friends, his plans, and of the King. Dyve, then forty-eight years old, had been in prison since his capture after the taking of Sherborne Castle by Fairfax in August 1645. Since at least November 1646 he had been in communication with the King, keeping a copy of each letter he sent. A voluble companion like Lilburne was a godsend to any weary prisoner, especially one with an axe to grind; and Lilburne's grindstone was well suited to the plans which Dyve intended to shape.

By June 1647 Lilburne and the Royalist prisoners were in frequent communication, and Lilburne made no secret of his views that a settlement with the King would be as acceptable as any other so long as it safeguarded the rights and freedoms of all the Lilburnes of the nation. Gullible as when he brought Chilliburne to see Bastwick in the Gatehouse, he apparently never suspected that Dyve's only desire was to sow discord among the King's enemies, and that every conversation with Lilburne was faithfully reported to Charles. He even introduced Dyve to the Levellers and agitators who came to visit him. Dyve knew as early as July 6 of the discontent of the soldiers with their officers and their determination " to reinvest the agitators into their former power." On September 29 he reported to the King that six [a] regiments had cashiered their old agitators and chosen new, who had " a sollemne meeting " on the 28th with Levellers of the City. In the same letter he hinted at some attempt " which will shake both the power of their Grandees and of the Houses "—probably a first broaching of another rendezvous. He knew the agitators' mind pretty well—their antagonism to their officers during the summer, their design to overthrow Cromwell's faction and dissolve the House of Commons, their daily meetings in London, their propaganda and use of emissaries or travelling agitators. He was also in a good position to note Lilburne's visitors—a visit from Rainsborough at the end of October, a gathering of " some that are most intimate in their counsells " in August. He transmitted to the King Lilburne's warning against Scout-master-General Watson and Quartermaster-General Staines. He made use of Lilburne's constant intelligence service, which, he reported, for the most part seldom proved false. He received all the information Lilburne gave him under promise of great secrecy, and immediately passed it on to the King.

Watching Lilburne's every movement, noting each visitor, listening avidly to every remark, counting on making capital for his master from Lilburne's success, Dyve felt assured of Lilburne's confidence. When Cromwell came to the Tower Dyve added a postscript in his letter to the King: " Cromwell is come, ostensibly to review the ordnance, but actually to speak with Lilburne; I am confident that, ere nightfall, I shall know what passed between them." He was right. Lilburne came to Dyve in the evening and made a " long relation " of his conversation with Cromwell, which Dyve remitted in his next letter to the King. One thing only Lilburne omitted, and that was his offer to go abroad if justice were done him.

It is doubtful whether Lilburne gave anything away by this converse with Dyve, highly distasteful though it would have been to many of his followers. He had certainly made no secret in his writings of his recent belief that the King was more likely than the Parliament to give the people satisfaction, and that an agreement with the King that would safeguard the people's " liberties and freedoms " was better than any other

[a] He was probably wrong in saying six rather than five.

agreement that would not. Dyve's hopes that through Lilburne
he would be able to mould the minds of the Levellers to the
King's wishes were unfounded. Lilburne was gullible, but
absolutely incorruptible and stubbornly obstinate where his
and the people's " just freedoms " were concerned.

Nevertheless, a small group of Lilburne's most intimate
friends disagreed with him in his attitude to the King and
needed to be won over. Lilburne had heard that William
Kiffin, the Baptist, had been to speak with the King and had
received such assurances of liberty for the future that he had
been completely satisfied of the King's goodwill. Lilburne
therefore requested Dyve to ask the King if he would see six
or seven of Lilburne's friends of influence in the Army and
give them equal satisfaction. Lilburne named those most in
need of convincing—Captain Reynolds, Major White, Captain
Mitchell, and Sexby. Reynolds, White, and Sexby were the
three he asked to be received first. Captain Paul Hobson of
Fairfax's regiment of foot would act as intermediary. If
the King would satisfy these men Lilburne would pawn his
life, so Dyve reported to Charles on October 5, " that within
a moneth or six weekes at the farthest the wholl army should
be absolutely at your Majestie's devotion to dispose thereof
as you pleased."

Although the visit to the King of the Baptist Kiffin and the
readiness of the fanatic Hobson to act as intermediary indicate
that a sectarian fringe was willing to consider the restoration of the monarchy on their own terms, it was soon made
clear by events that both Dyve and Lilburne had over-estimated
both the power of the Levellers in the Army and their sympathy
for the King. When Dyve's letter-book ends at the beginning
of November it is nevertheless still on the cheerful note that
the King's enemies would " breake each others power, to make
way for His Majestie's to be brought in." [3]

Dyve, indeed, was essentially romantic, and in this respect
had much in common with Lilburne. Both were given to
wishful thinking where their own plans were concerned—as the
King may have realized, for there is no evidence of his direct
encouragement to Dyve, though the information given, and its
source, should have been sufficiently interesting. The delight
in intrigue, the almost schoolboyish sense of conspiracy, which

runs through the *Letter Book* is confirmed by an observation made by John Evelyn when he met Dyve in Paris four years later. " This Knight," he wrote in his diary, " was indeede a valiant gent: but not a little given to romance when he spake of himselfe." [4]

By the time Dyve's *Letter Book* ends, the situation in the Tower had changed. While Marten's Committee was, presumably, still searching for precedents concerning the jurisdiction of the Lords over a commoner, Lilburne came forward with a novel proposition that was simply another version of his challenge to debate. He would argue this same question, he said, before any public assembly against any forty lawyers they cared to nominate, and if any three lawyers gave it under their hand against him he would submit to punishment—provided only that six or ten of his friends could be present to take an account in writing of all that passed at the debate.[5] This *Proposition* was read in the House on October 4, and the following day Marten was ordered to make his report on the next Saturday. When Saturday came it was postponed until Tuesday, then to Friday, October 15. On that day the House was regaled with a re-reading of the judgment given against Lilburne by the House of Lords in July 1646, and decided to refer the case to an open committee, with John Maynard in the chair—not the man who was then in the Tower with Lilburne, but a lawyer of the same name.

Whether or not this cat-and-mouse policy was deliberate, it would have worn down a prisoner less ebullient than Lilburne. He now, unflagging, turned to prepare the *Grand Plea* which he made in person to Maynard's Committee when it opened its hearing on October 20. He claimed the judgment of the House of Commons in his case, repudiated afresh the power of the Lords over a commoner, demanded reparation from the Lords for their tyranny, and requested that he be left to take his own course against gaolers, prison-keepers, and others who had wronged him, that he be given money for maintenance so long as he remained in prison, and that his overdue reparations be settled upon estates able to bear them.[6] But he could not say all he wished. His bodily strength was not equal to that of his spirit. Although he had been allowed £2 a week maintenance by the House of Lords, not a penny had been paid;

many friends, thinking he was provided for, had not helped as they otherwise would, with the result that he was ill-fed and undernourished.[7] Physical exhaustion, combined with the alternate hope and despair of the last months, with the work of organization in the Army and of intrigue with Dyve, and with the final excitement of at last getting his case heard, made him unfit to bear alone the burden of speaking in his own defence, and brought him to a halt. ". . . my present strength and voice," he murmured, " is in a manner quite spent, so that I cannot well go on at present, though I have all my matter ready." Perhaps too willingly the Committee adjourned itself until October 26.[8] On that day it did not meet, and Lilburne took this to be a deliberate shelving of his case. So he sent to Maynard the rest of his plea, which he would have made on the 20th, asking the Committee to consider his case without calling him—a true indication of his utter weariness. But both *Grand Plea* and *Additional Plea* were published by his faithful friends.

Perhaps his physical unfitness had something to do with the fact that on November 9 Lilburne was given liberty on bail during the day to prepare his case and attend the Committee.[9] Freedom during the day revived his spirit and restored his energies. Who spoke for him, or why he was granted this concession, is unrecorded. It is surprising enough that he should be let free at a time of grave unrest in the Army, more surprising that the concession should be granted and received so casually.

Probably Lilburne's efforts to reconcile the agitators and the King slackened as his own case absorbed more of his energies. Possibly he realized he was being over-sanguine in imagining he could effect such a compromise. On the one hand, Cromwell's attitude to the agitators was hardening, as his quarrel with Rainsborough emphasized. On the other, Sexby was being difficult to move in the direction of a visit to the King, even if time had allowed it. A significant meeting of which, unfortunately, no record exists was Rainsborough's visit to Lilburne in the Tower on Sunday, October 31, when Dyve reported they were together for two hours, but of which he received no report from Lilburne, this silence being in itself remarkable. But by November 11 the question of a meeting with the King had become academic, for on that day Charles fled from Hampton Court and made his way to the Isle of Wight.

Various reasons were adduced for the King's flight: an intention to make for France frustrated when the expected vessel failed to appear; the apparent friendliness of Hammond, the Governor of the island; the King's distrust of Rainsborough, the man who was expected to be the leader of the Leveller faction in the Army when Cromwell was overthrown; [10] the King's belief that the agitators were not so powerful as Dyve professed, his doubts whether the Royalists would benefit so much from their ascendancy as Dyve believed. Certainly by the beginning of November events in the Army Council had shown the determination of Cromwell to break the new agitators, and Charles would have realized then, if not before, that Dyve's rosy picture of their ascendancy was coloured by Lilburne.

There is insufficient evidence to say whether directly or indirectly Lilburne played any part in the King's flight. Charles left behind him at Hampton Court a letter to Parliament explaining his departure in terms of his personal safety, which various reports from his agents other than Dyve had convinced him was threatened by the agitators. This was underlined by another letter found at Hampton Court after his departure. Addressed to the King, it was signed by E.R., and stated that the writer's brother had the previous day—i.e., November 8— been at a meeting of eight or nine agitators who had agreed to kill the King. As a final spur to the King's flight the letter fits into place. But a great deal of mystery surrounds it. If " E.R." were genuine initials neither the writer nor his brother has been identified. But the story was current that Henry Lilburne, then a lieutenant-colonel in his elder brother Robert's regiment of foot, was the writer, and that his informant was Free-born John himself. John's known wishes at the time to negotiate with the King do, indeed, make it not unlikely that he would have found this way of warning the King without jeopardizing his own relationship with the agitators, making use of the Royalist sympathies of his brother which became open during the second Civil War, and of which it may be supposed that John already had some inkling. This assumes that the agitators had been correctly reported by John, and that the substance of the report had not been misinterpreted by Henry. It is possible, however, that some more general remarks by John were taken up by Henry, and that the initiative of sending the letter came from the younger brother, and not from the Leveller. But although the story of John Lilburne's implication can be made to sound plausible, the whole theory is somewhat dashed by the fact that he was not at bail until the day following the supposed meeting. Although his visitors to the Tower were many, it is stretching credulity rather far to imagine either that eight or nine agitators actually plotted the murder of the King within its walls or that the Leveller leader could slip out of its precincts for an evening meeting before his bail was operative. Besides, if Lilburne wished to warn Charles, would he not have used Dyve, as he did in the case of Watson and Staines? Or would he have felt this too much like disloyalty to his friends? The leaving behind at Hampton Court of such a letter in itself casts doubt upon its authenticity. For being warned by such a friend, would the King not naturally take the letter with him or destroy it, to preserve the contact for future use? But if the letter were planted after the King's flight the Royalists would have been quick to say so. If they planted it themselves, what could be their object apart from discrediting the agitators—which they could hardly desire, since they hoped to benefit from their success—or veiling by a supposed reason the real reason for the King's flight? The remaining hypothesis, that the letter was a ' plant ' by some one who wished for the removal of the King, but that the Royalists thought it genuine, only makes sense if there was good reason for some one wishing the King away from Hampton Court. The idea that Cromwell resorted to this subterfuge to get the King to Carisbrooke is not convincing. It was, however, given some credence later by Lilburne. The story gained currency that Lilburne had intended to murder the King at Hampton Court; but he was also accused of apostatizing to the Cavaliers. How could both be true, he asked. The second was merely spread abroad to damage him personally; the first was merely a device by the grandees for getting the King into their " mousetrap " in the Isle of Wight. So Lilburne supported the theory that the flight from Hampton Court was intended to lead to the window at Whitehall, and added one more count to his charge of perfidy against Cromwell. The fact that Henry Lilburne had two months previously married Ann Rushworth, sister to the Army's secretary, adds piquancy to the situation.[11]

Yet the only reasonable reasons for the King's flight are the simple ones that he wished to be in a better position to make contact with his friends, that he perhaps thought of Hammond as a lenient gaoler and the Isle of Wight as well placed either for a journey to France or a return to the capital, that recent doubling of his guards caused him to fear for his safety, and, as he said in the letter he left at Hampton Court: " Liberty being that which in all Times hath been, but especially now is, the common Theme and Desire of all Men; Common Reason shews, that Kings less than any should endure Captivity." [12]

Lilburne was at this time less closely in touch with the agitators than at any other. He had seen the new agitators elected. Now he was concentrating upon his Committee, with insufficient energy, possibly, to do more. Yet, while he was struggling with the House of Commons, with Dyve at his elbow, the ten years of his teaching were bearing fruit in another way destined to make a more permanent mark on the understandings of men—in the document which was the banner under which both Army and civilian Levellers would henceforth march—the *Agreement of the People*.

CHAPTER EIGHTEEN

The Agreement of the People

Wee the free Commons of England, the reall and essentiall body politicke.

JOHN LILBURNE, *Plaine Truth without Feare or Flattery*, April/May 1647

BY THE END OF 1647 LILBURNE AND THE LEVELLERS WERE laying increasing stress upon constitutional reform, and, in doing so, elaborated the most original part of their programme. This was not because they abandoned the rest of their demands —their pamphlets are abundant evidence to the contrary—but rather that they attempted to use political reform in the interests of the social and economic ends they sought. Their inability to secure under existing forms of government the ' freedoms ' for which they had fought drove them back to search for a new principle of political obligation.

Lilburne himself epitomized this development. He had by this time, in his own person, opposed bishops and Presbyterians, Army command and City council, King, House of Lords, House of Commons, their committees, and their instruments. In neither spiritual nor civil rulers had he found satisfaction. Neither in his worship nor his work, in his writing nor his speaking, in peace nor war, had he won security or freedom. On the contrary, each step he took trammelled him further. Starting from the demand for freedom of religion, Lilburne had been forced to the demand for freedom of speech and the press. His transgressions in this direction had caused him to be brought before the House of Lords and Committees of the House of Commons. He then repudiated the judicial authority of both these bodies, and launched a campaign for trial by a court of law in accordance with principles he deduced from Magna Carta, Statutes of the Realm, and the works of Coke. The imprisonment which followed his conduct induced, in its

turn, the demand for prison reform. At the same time, knowing that economic and social distress was being aggravated by
the war, he made various demands for its alleviation. Constantly his experience added to his platform: he was kept
from the cloth trade by the monopoly of the Merchant
Adventurers, his arrears of Army pay and reparations were
withheld from him, his house was ransacked by the Stationers
in search of illegal literature, his private life was distorted by
poverty, imprisonment, and his inability to follow a trade.
Lilburne's experiences were not exceptional: it was his ability
to focus attention upon them and give concrete form and substance to grievances deeply felt but confusedly expressed that
gave him his power and his importance.

By every means open to him he attempted to change or
coerce the bodies that denied him satisfaction. Though not
himself a Member of Parliament, he could influence those
who were by individual approach, he could distribute leaflets
to assembling Members, he could organize his followers to
present petitions. He could secure the maximum publicity for
every stand he made against any authority. Above all, he could
write and print. It was his inability—in spite of the uproar he
created—to make any material alteration in his own condition
or to effect any major reform within the existing constitutional
framework that induced him to deny the ultimate superiority of
Parliament and to " ravel back " authority to the people.

This setting up of the people had been implicit in Lilburne's
writings since 1645. Parliament's insistence that the King was
subject to law he turned against themselves; they too were
merely its instruments. Parliament had declared *salus populi
suprema lex*. Lilburne agreed, and used the phrase to make
them responsible to the people. They were, he said, responsible
to the people as ambassador to prince; the people were
obliged to support them only so long as they acted demonstrably for the public good. For who but a madman, he asked,
using a well-known argument, would obey the General who
turned his cannon against his own troops? Having thus
progressed from one authority to another and arrived at the
people, it became necessary to ask how the supremacy of the
people should be expressed.

Lilburne and his associates were deeply imbued with the

spirit of law. Not only the polemics of the controversy with
the King, but also their religious training, had fostered the
Levellers' regard for law. Not only the Old but the New
Testament is soaked in the atmosphere of law. "Think not
that I am come to destroy the law, or the prophets: I am not
come to destroy but to fulfil" were the words of Jesus of
Nazareth, despite the revolutionary nature of his teaching.
Parliament had based its claim against the King on 'fundamental' law. Coke had extolled both the common law and
particular statutes. Pym had told Parliament that the "law is
that which puts a difference betwixt Good and Evil, betwixt
Just and Unjust." Lilburne told Parliament: "You are not
in the least above the laws, but while they are Laws and are
unrepealed, they are as binding unto you, as the meanest men
in England." [1]   "All Magistracy in England," he said, "is
bounded by the known and declared Law of England." [2]   The
law was "the surest Sanctuary that a man can take, and the
strongest fortresse to protect the weakest of all." [3]

While the Levellers' attitude to laws was, on the whole, one
of great respect, their attitude to Law was tinged with reverence. Law, to them, contained an element of the divine or
mystical. The more remote in antiquity the law, the truer this
became. This attitude was particularly marked where Anglo-
Saxon law was concerned. All laws made before the Norman
Conquest appeared to the Levellers as inspired—as applicable
to the seventeenth as to the tenth century. When the Levellers
were specific in their references to law it was the laws of Edward
the Confessor, Anglo-Saxon law in general, Magna Carta, or
the Petition of Right to which they referred. The last two,
being made after the Saxon period, were regarded merely as a
reassertion, or winning back, of liberties lost at the Conquest.
When no specific law could be found to meet the Levellers'
purpose they appealed to 'fundamental' law. Since, however,
there were no specific written laws of the constitution which
could with certainty be claimed as fundamental, 'fundamental
law' meant different things to different people. Coke was
probably alone in the precision with which he related fundamental law to common law. The other parties in the dispute,
the Levellers included, were openly, even if sometimes unconsciously, opportunist in their use of the term. To the

Levellers it appeared to mean either a law so remotely established as to have received the stamp of antiquity (and therefore of authenticity in the Levellers' eyes) or else a law which appeared to them to be in accord with the principles of ' Nature ' or of ' Reason ' or of ' Right.'   Lilburne, in one sentence alone, jumbled together Reason, Custom, Saxon law, Parliament, Natural Law, God, as the necessary sanctions for ' fundamental law.'   ". . . the Fundamentall Law of the Land," he wrote in October 1646, " is the PERFECTION *of Reason, consisting of Lawfull and Reasonable Customes, received and approved of by the people : and of the old Constitutions, and modern Acts of Parliament, made by the Estates of the Kingdome. But such only as are agreeable to the law Eternall and Naturall, and not contrary to the word of God.*" [4]

In this way almost any law could be interpreted by the Levellers as ' fundamental.'   But in practice the law which they venerated consisted of certain laws of the constitution which safeguarded civil liberties, such as Magna Carta, Habeas Corpus, and the Petition of Right.   Such laws were " bucklers of defence "; they muzzled the mouth of violence and enabled the innocent to feed and sleep securely.[5]   Their successive battles with authority taught the Levellers that one of the first replies of a state threatened by attack was the abrogation of the rights granted by these laws, and part of their struggle had always been to maintain them.

But, while appealing to the supremacy of law and requiring the enforcement of some laws, the Levellers were quite consistent in demanding the repeal of others.   For, they said in effect— and here again they were consciously or unconsciously following the Bible—though law was righteous in its *essence*, particular laws could be, and frequently were, bad.   Bad laws were in the nature of an aberration from the true nature of Law, and were due, not to any evil in Law, but to evil in the law-giver.   Like the writer of the 94th psalm, they condemned him who "frameth mischief by a law"—not law itself, but the law-maker.

But if one ' mischief ' can be framed by a law, so can many. Injustice, no less than justice, can be erected into a legal system. This, in fact, was the Levellers' reading of the Norman Conquest in its constitutional aspect.   The ' just laws ' of Saxon England had been replaced by a tyranny legally riveted upon the free-men of England. The laws associated with the Norman Conquest and the feudal system were not ' Law ' to the Levellers in its quasi-mystical or ' fundamental ' sense, but perversions whose evil was due to the iniquity of the Norman law-giver: the abrogation of Norman law was quite in accordance with the Levellers' reverence for Law as a whole.

By and large, therefore, in spite of the conventional vagueness of much of their language, the Levellers' attitude to Law was essentially practical. Laws and institutions were judged in the light of their effect upon civil liberties and individual rights. Talk of fundamental law was merely an attempt to guard against the charge of innovation by an appeal to history and to precedent. While indulging in quite as much of this vague talk as their contemporaries, the Levellers were honest enough to admit to themselves that no such thing as fundamental law existed, and practical enough to attempt to make one.

This attempt to create a fundamental law, in the form of a written constitution, comprises the Levellers' supreme contribution to political science. They alone translated the wordy theorizing of the pamphlet literature into a concrete constitutional programme—*An Agreement of the People*. But it cannot be too strongly emphasized that this constituted only one part of their teaching. The Levellers were not simply constitutional reformers. Possibly very few people are. Constitutional reform was demonstrably the means to the end of social and economic betterment and of civil and religious liberty which the Leveller literature had for years been demanding. The *Agreement of the People* was not the end, but the vehicle which would take them to the end they sought. The continued appearance of Leveller pamphlets urging particular reforms underlines this crucial fact.

The *Agreement of the People* was designed to ensure representative government and to protect the people against oppression from their own representatives. It was intended both to create the legal framework of civil liberty and to preserve it intact from the operation of adverse forces. How far any constitution can be permanently protective; to what extent any written law can protect one section of the community against another; the relationship of majority rule to fundamental law; whether the Levellers could, or whether they would have wished to, hold their fundamental law against the wishes of a majority—in short, the validity of the whole concept of fundamental law—the Levellers never discussed.

Ireton's *Heads of the Proposals* had not been completely at variance with the Levellers' desires, and marked a long step towards religious toleration and the limitation of the power of King and Parliament. They provided for biennial Parliaments and a redistribution of seats, which would make Parliament more amenable to the electors; the repeal of acts interfering with religious freedom, control of the militia by Parliament, the banning from office of delinquents; and for the immediate appointment of a Council of State, which would superintend the militia, conduct foreign negotiations (but without the power of peace or war), and in general carry on functions similar to those of the Privy Council or of the Committee of both Kingdoms. Under such a scheme a king could be made amenable to Parliament, and the measures noted in the *Heads of the Proposals* for immediate action were all in the direction of popular reform—the right to petition, law reform, the repeal of forest laws and of monopolies, the abolition of tithes and the excise, the payment of arrears.[6]

The Levellers objected to the *Heads of the Proposals* not so much in themselves as because they believed that the King would not sincerely consent to them, and that he had, in fact, already prevailed upon Ireton and Cromwell to alter them materially. In deference to the King's wishes, so the Levellers claimed, Ireton reduced both the period during which the militia was to be controlled by Parliament and during which delinquents were to be barred from office. Moreover, they asserted that Ireton's original scheme had abolished episcopacy and confirmed the sale of bishops' lands, and had limited the power of the monarch by providing that two immediately succeeding Parliaments could give effect to a Bill even without the royal assent. The dropping of some clauses, the amending of others, the fact that it provided for no extension of the suffrage, still confining the vote to the 40s. freeholder, reduced both the *Proposals* and the concrete reforms appended to them to so much verbiage. The fact that the grandees were negotiating with the King on these lines seemed to the soldiers to spell perfidy.[7] Although Charles professed to prefer the

Heads of the Proposals to any other scheme that came before him, negotiations were still dragging on in September, to the rising indignation of the Levellers. In the Council of the Army on September 16 Rainsborough was so indignant with Cromwell that he cried that " one of them must not live! " [8] In the House of Commons on the 22nd Harry Marten called upon Members to vote that there should be no more addresses made to the King—a motion which was lost by 84 to 34 votes, with Cromwell acting as teller for the Noes. The exasperation of the rank and file contributed to the election of the new agitators, to whom there fell the task of preparing their own constitutional settlement.

Lilburne's preoccupation with his defence was probably the chief reason why another writer was called in to help to prepare a document to put before the Council of the Army. This was John Wildman, twenty-four years old, known as a major, although his Army service was unspecified. He was educated at Cambridge and studied law in London, was probably a friend of Harry Marten—they both came from Berkshire, took wives from the same county, and held similar Republican views [9]—and it would be surprising if he had not come under the influence of William Walwyn, whose turn of mind would have been most acceptable to Wildman. His friendship with Lilburne seems to have been well established, although he does not earlier figure by name in the Leveller literature. Lilburne neither then nor later expressed any ill-feeling or jealousy that this younger man of superior education, grounded in the law, should be called in to his party's counsels at this critical time. It is probable that Wildman stood in something of the same relationship to the Leveller leader—then a man of thirty-two—as Lilburne himself to Bastwick ten years earlier. Wildman's knowledge of law was probably the decisive reason for his employment by the soldiers in October 1647, for it was common practice to get a legally trained man to prepare documents or ' cases ' of various kinds [10] (the agitators called their document *The Case of the Armie*). Wildman already may have had experience with some of the Army manifestos, and, indeed, may have been one of the Army's penmen at Oxford. Finally, his known republicanism would have commended itself to Rainsborough and to Sexby, and, at this particular time of exasperation with the King, to many other soldiers, and served as an additional reason why he, and not Lilburne, who was at that very time trying to arrange a meeting between the agitators and the King, was their draftsman on this occasion.

It was on October 9 that *The Case of the Armie* was completed. On the 18th the new agitators, attending the Army Council for the first time, presented it to Fairfax, justifying their action by the light of the law of nature and nations which declared the safety of the people to be the supreme law. On the 20th Lilburne presented his *Grand Plea* to the committee which was hearing his case. On the 22nd the Council of the Army appointed a committee of twenty officers and agitators to meet at Ireton's quarters to consider *The Case of the Armie*, their report to be received at the Army Council meeting at Putney on the 28th. On the 27th the new agitators of the five regiments of horse and several civilian Levellers met to consider their plans. It seems clear that the new agitators were guided by the experienced Sexby, who had maintained the trust of his regiment, and by Wildman, and it would have been strange if no contact at all had been made with Lilburne. Two civilians, Wildman and Maximilian Petty, were elected to join the agitators at the following day's meeting. Lilburne, on the day of the debate, was due to go again before his committee. It was something of a personal tragedy for him, and is a frustrating loss for posterity, that the arch-debater was not present at the most stirring debates of the seventeenth century, to cross swords with Cromwell and Ireton. As it was, the burden of the debate fell on Wildman, Sexby, and Rainsborough, with Petty an able second. None of lesser calibre could have stood up to the formidable combination of Cromwell and Ireton in debate— Ireton with his magnificent style, logic, and breadth of knowledge, Cromwell, narrower in sweep, yet forceful and tenacious.

The Case of the Armie was long, covering most of the ills of the nation, asking for the dissolution of Parliament within nine or ten weeks, and biennial Parliaments, announcing that " all power is originally and essentially in the whole body of the people " and " their free choice or consent by their Representors is the only originall or foundation of all just government." [11] But before the Council meeting on the 28th the

Levellers had decided to base their case on a more concise document—*An Agreement of the People*—that would prepare the ground for the reforms mentioned in *The Case of the Armie* and other Leveller pamphlets.   Even in *An Agreement of the People* the particular is mixed with the general, but the document as a whole stands or falls on its general, constitutional proposals. Some of the agitators made this clear in a letter to their officers and other soldiers.   " We desire you may understand," they said, " the reason of our extracting some principles of common freedom out of those many things proposed to you in *The Case Truly Stated*, and drawing them up into the form of an Agreement.   It's chiefly because for these things we first engaged against the King. . . . Therefore these things, in the Agreement, the people are to claim as their native right and price of their blood, which you are obliged absolutely to procure for them. And these being the foundations of freedom, it is necessary that they should be settled unalterably, which can be by no means but this Agreement with the people." [12]

Its title announced it to be *An Agreement of the People for a firme and present Peace upon grounds of common right and freedom*.   There is no indication of authorship.   The preamble reads like many other agitator and Leveller manifestos—splendid in language, austere in sentiment, noble in aim. " Having," it said, " by our late labours and hazards made it appear to the world at how high a rate we value our just freedom, and God having so far owned our case as to deliver the enemies thereof into our hands, we do now hold ourselves bound in mutual duty to each other to take the best care we can for the future to avoid both the danger of returning into a slavish condition and the chargeable remedy of another war."   They had come to the conclusion that the root of their troubles was political and constitutional.   " Since," they concluded, " our former oppressions and scarce-yet-ended troubles have been occasioned, either by want of frequent national meetings in Council, or by rendering those meetings ineffectual, we are fully agreed and resolved to provide that hereafter our representatives be neither left to an uncertainty for the time nor made useless to the ends for which they are intended." [13]

To that end they demanded four reforms.   The first was equal electoral districts, according to the numbers of inhabitants.

When Ireton asked if that implied manhood suffrage the Levellers replied that it did.[14] *The Case of the Armie* had already implied this in more general terms. On November 11 a letter from several agitators to their regiments reporting on subsequent proceedings in the Army Council said that after a long debate it was carried with only three against, " That all soldiers and others, if they be not servants or beggars, ought to have voices in electing those which shall represent them in Parliament, although they have not forty shillings per annum in freehold land." [15] Subsequent versions of the *Agreement*, of December 10, 1648, and May 1, 1649,[16] incorporated clauses to this effect. The Levellers intended a male suffrage, but would not allow that men who worked for others as servants or wage-earners could have an interest not comprised in their masters': their mentality was essentially pre-capitalist, although they professed to speak for the " hobnayles and clouted shooes and leather aprons." It is clear that they thought of those who were small masters still, not those whom a developing capitalism in many industries was driving down to the status of wage-earners. In their demands for manhood suffrage they thought so little of these people—as, indeed, they did of women, in spite of their work for the Cause—that, taking their exclusion for granted, they frequently forgot to specify it. A similar outlook was demonstrated when a Member of Parliament tried to disperse a crowd of petitioning Leveller women led by Mrs Chidley. The House " could not take cognizance of their petition," he told them, " they being women, and many of them wives, so that the Law tooke no notice of them." The logic of the women's reply was not immediately apparent, " for they replyed, that they were not all wives," but they continued to press for the hearing of their petition.[17]

The second and third demands of *An Agreement of the People* were for the dissolution of the existing Parliament and for biennial Parliaments. The fourth consisted in an attempt to preserve the nation from possible tyranny by the Parliament it had elected. This protection was to be given in the form of ' reserving ' certain spheres of action from the power of Parliament. There was one general reserve, that of religion, in which Parliament was precluded from using compulsion of any kind; two more specific reserves which said that a Parliament could neither impress nor question concerning acts done during the war; and, finally, two vague clauses aiming at equality before the law which allowed Parliament to exercise no exception or favouritism in the execution of justice, and stated—high-sounding but vague clause—" That as the laws ought to be equal, so they must be good, and not evidently destructive to the safety and well-being of the people." The *Agreement* was to be signed and accepted by the people, both soldiers and civilians. Its somewhat strange title was intended to convey both this fact and the agreement of soldiers with citizens: many of the soldiers' statements spoke of an agreement *with* the people, emphasizing that only if soldiers and people agreed and stood together would a favourable settlement be reached. " England's Freedom—Soldiers' Rights," which they caused to be printed on each copy of the *Agreement*, stressed their desire for unity.

In general, the principles of the *Agreement of the People* owe much to the religious beliefs of the men who drew it up. The idea of a covenant or contract such as the *Agreement* was a familiar one implicit in the Puritan faith. Its source was the Bible, for had not Jehovah made a covenant with His people? In historical times a contract had actually been made between William the Norman and his feudatories, and each king in his coronation oath renewed the contract between monarch and people. Charles Stuart, said the Levellers in 1647, had by contract and agreement made when he took his coronation oath, received his crown and kingdom.[18] Reference to the contractual origin of civil society appeared almost as a matter of course in the Parliamentarian writings. Parker spoke of the origin of government in compact. Cromwell thought that the King was king by contract, and Ireton argued that private property in land and goods was similarly founded. As immediate examples, the Levellers had the Scots and Parliamentarian Covenants before them when they drafted their *Agreement*.

Manhood suffrage—each man having a voice in matters that concerned him—was again inherent to the Independent congregations and sectarian meetings which the Levellers frequented. As early as July 1647 Lilburne had said that " every individual private Souldier, whether Horse or Foot, ought freely to have

their vote, to chuse the transactors of their affaires, or else in
the sight of God, and all rationall men, are discharged from
obeying, stooping or submitting to what is done by them." [19]
The Levellers' desire to extend the suffrage is not remarkable;
more surprising is their wish to limit it and preclude beggars
and servants and wage-earners, thus shutting out from State
government the very poor whom they would welcome to their
religious congregations.   They had not matched the unique
importance of the individual which their religion taught with
the value of each individual in politics.

Constitutional principles were always accompanied in the
seventeenth century with wide appeals to moral and political
obligation inherited from the French Wars of Religion, the
Reformation, the Middle Ages, and beyond.   Though the
Levellers were essentially practical reformers, they were forced
to vindicate their ' just ' demands at the bar of principle.   By
1645 they were familiar with the Law of Nature and the Law
of Reason, and had imbibed the doctrines of *salus populi*, and
the right of resistance.   None of these principles was new or
peculiar to the Levellers.   What was distinctive was their use
of them to condemn all political institutions not founded upon
the principles of their *Agreement*.

In appealing to the Law of Nature the Levellers were using
a concept which had come down through almost every channel
of tradition, and with which Parliamentarian writings were
saturated.   The pamphlet *Doctor and Student*, by Christopher
Saint Germain, which Lilburne often quoted, and which was
many times reprinted, discussed the question.   Parker in his
Observations, another book frequently mentioned by Lilburne,
linked natural law with *salus populi* as the governing principle
of society.   Prynne drew from it justification of the right to
resistance.   Milton also gave it his authority.   Those who
would reform the state, he said, are " not bound by any statute
of preceding Parliaments but by the law of nature only." [20]
". . . By naturall birth," wrote Overton, " all men are equally
and alike born to like propriety, liberty and freedome . . . from
this fountain or root, all just humain powers take their original;
not immediately from God . . . but mediatly by the hand of
nature." [21]

Apart from ' fundamental ' law and the Law of Nature, the

Levellers' most frequent appeal was to Reason as a criterion of
government. Here again they were following a well-worn track
from the Greeks throughout the Schoolmen, the Reformation,
Renaissance, and the Parliamentarian spokesmen. " Right
Reason is the wise man's precedent," announced John Cook,
the Parliamentarian. " If it be not reason, the pronunciation
of 10,000 judges cannot make it law." [22] ". . . no government
can be just or durable," declared Lilburne, " but what is
founded and established upon the principles of right reason,
common and universal justice, equity and conscience." [23] " All
Formes of Lawes and Governments," wrote Overton, of all the
Levellers the most passionate advocate of Reason, " may fall
and passe away; but right Reason . . . shall and will endure
for ever; it is that by which in all our Actions wee must stand
or fall, be justified or condemned; for neither Morality nor
Divinity amongst Men can or may transgresse the limits of
right reason, for whatsoever is unreasonable cannot be justly
termed Morall or Divine." [24]

From the Laws of Nature and of Reason the Levellers
educed man's natural and inalienable rights. From the individual to the social is a short step, and the good of each or
the rights of each easily become the good of all or the rights
of all. Thus *salus populi suprema lex*, and, in Latin or English,
this concept appears frequently in Leveller writings. The
new agitators reminded Fairfax that " the Safety of the People
is above all Forms and Customs." [25] Overton warned the
Parliament that " the edge of your own arguments against the
King . . . may be turned upon your selves, for if for the safety
of the people, he might in equity be opposed to you . . . even
so may you by the same rule of right reason, be opposed by
the people in generall . . . for the safety of the people is the
Soveraigne Law." [26]

Given *salus populi*, with Reason to act as judge, it is a short
step to the right of resistance, and the Parliamentarian writers
had already followed in the steps of earlier writers when the
Levellers took over from them. Lilburne had used the argument
when telling the Army not to disband. Parliament was told
that its power was " merely derivative and bounded within
this tacit Commission, to act only for the good of those that
betrusted them." The power donated " ought always to be

exercised for the good, benefit, and welfare of the Trustees, and never ought otherwise to be administered: which whensoever it is, it is justly resistable and revokeable. . . . It being against the light of Nature and Reason, and the end wherefore God endowed Man with understanding, for any sort or generation of men to give so much power into the hands of any man or men whatsoever, as to enable them to destroy them, or to suffer such a kind of power to be exercised over them, by any man or men, that shall assume it unto himself, either by the sword, or any other kind of way." [27] So fundamental was the right of resistance that no contract by one generation could bind the next; " for whatever our Fore-fathers were; or whatever they did or suffered, or were enforced to yeeld unto; we are the men of the present age, and ought to be absolutely free from all kinds of exorbitances, molestations or Arbitrary Power." [28] Fundamentally, the right of resistance was based on the necessity of self-preservation. ". . . the souldiery may lawfully hold the hands of the Generall who will turne his Cannon against his Army on purpose to destroy them, the Seamen the hands of that Pilot, who wilfully runs his Ship upon a rock " was the argument used by Parker in his *Observations*, by Fairfax and the Army when opposing Parliament in June 1647, by Rainsborough and Wildman at the Putney debates, by Lilburne in his letters to Cromwell and in his pamphlets.

So far as the actual laws of the land were concerned, Lilburne solved the question of obedience—again like the Parliamentarian theorists—by distinguishing between the letter and the equity of law. This distinction was fundamental to the Leveller position, since it so neatly allowed for the necessary loophole of resistance, even to the known laws of the land. ". . . for the Law taken abstract from its originall reason and end, is made a shell without a kernell, a shadow without a substance, and a body without a soul. It is the execution of Laws according to their equity and reason which . . . is the spirit that gives life to Authority the Letter kills." [29]

Lilburne and the Levellers must not be judged too harshly because, in the end, they were driven back to a subjective determination of the right and occasion of resistance, and failed to find a formula to cover it. Attempts had been made for hundreds of years with little more success, and much of sixteenth- and seventeenth-century thought, notably in the French wars of religion and particularly in the *Vindiciae contra Tyrannos*, published in 1574 and many times reprinted in the sixteenth and seventeenth centuries in England, as well as elsewhere, was an attempt to find an answer. It was left to Theodore Bèza, Calvin's successor at Geneva, to proclaim the necessity of active opposition to the persecuting monarch who broke the contract made between king and people. And the works of Bèza were among those upon which the young Lilburne nurtured himself in the City of London. But even Bèza could not point to a universally applicable formula to cover the situation, which remained in the last resort subjective.

Once given the sovereignty of the people and the right of resistance, it was logical to extend the argument from monarch to Parliament. Again, it was the Levellers who took the argument to its conclusion. With sovereignty of the people and the right to resistance the opponents of the Levellers coupled the incompatible concept of supremacy of Parliament; the Levellers pointed out that if the people remained sovereign they could not have conveyed that sovereignty to any other authority, and that in them, consequently, rested the determination of the necessity of resistance either to monarch or to Parliament.

Sovereignty of the people, based on the Laws of Nature, Reason, and Equity, expressed through a fundamental law and by manhood suffrage, was the Levellers' conception of the state. The assumption underlying the *Agreement of the People* is that this state would be a republic; but there seems no reason to doubt that the Levellers would have accepted a constitutional monarch who kept within the framework of their constitution.

During the debates at Putney on the *Agreement of the People*, which lasted from October 28 to November 11, much of this theoretical superstructure was swept away in the excitement of the argument, and men's basic attitudes came to the surface. Ireton was revealed as the man of property, dreading an anarchy that would interfere with property rights: " All the maine thinge that I speake for is because I would have an eye to propertie," [30] he said. Rainsborough emerged as a generous-hearted humanitarian whose sympathies went naturally to the underdog: " I thinke that the poorest hee that is

in England hath a life to live as the greatest hee; and therefore
. . . I thinke itt's cleare, that every man that is to live under a
Government ought first by his owne consent to putt himself
under that Government." [31]   Sexby was also full of sympathy
for the oppressed, yet combined more bitterness in his attitude:
" Wee have engaged in this Kingdome and ventur'd our lives,
and itt was all for this: to recover our birthrights and priviledges
as Englishmen, and by the arguments urged there is none. . . .
I wonder wee were soe much deceived." [32]   Rainsborough's
was the gentle humanitarianism that comes from a secure
background and a not empty purse; Sexby's the bitter cry for
justice that comes more frequently from the dispossessed.

It was at Putney that the name ' Leveller ' was first publicly
used.   Cromwell christened them Levellers at Putney, said
Lilburne, in order " to render their persons odious in the eyes
of the people of England." [33]   Richard Baxter confirmed this:
it was used by Cromwell, he said, " to make them odious . . .
as if they intended to level Men of all Qualities and Estates." [34]
The Levellers, while accepting the term as a party name,
indignantly repudiated its implications.   " We profess," they
said, " that we never had it in our thoughts to Level mens
estates, it being the utmost of our aime that the Commonwealth be reduced to such a passe that every man may with as
much security as may be enjoy his propriety." [35]

Many contemporaries believed the charge of social levelling,
but there were others who supported the Levellers' own
statement of their position.   Mrs Hutchinson, the wife of the
Parliamentarian colonel, applied the term Leveller to " public-
spirited men " who " stood up in the parliament and the
army " declaring against the factions of Presbytery and
Independency and the ambitions of the grandees of both.
She called them " good-hearted people " who would have
common justice belong equally to the poorest as well as to the
mighty.   " For this and such other honest declarations, they
were nicknamed Levellers." [36]   Clement Walker agreed with
Mrs Hutchinson in describing the Levellers as being miscalled
" only for endeavouring to level the exorbitant usurpations of
the council of state and council of officers." [37]   The Levellers
remained acutely sensitive to the implication of ' social
levelling,' their refusal to admit either servants or wage-earners

to the franchise lending support to their denials. Even Rainsborough, in spite of his championship of " the poorest hee,"
made no special plea for the extension of the vote to these classes.

While discussions continued at Putney the new agitators
were proceeding with their plan for calling a rendezvous like
the already famous gatherings at Newmarket and Triploe
Heaths. Their plans, however, were undermined by Cromwell,
who carried a motion on the Army Council that the meeting
should be in three parts: instead of a mass meeting they would
have to deal with three smaller meetings. Even more important,
Cromwell carried a vote for sending both agitators and
officers back to their regiments—a summary dismissal of the
Council of the Army, thinly veiled by the assertion that it was
for a fortnight only, which deprived the agitators of an official
talking-point.[38]   Still the plans for the rendezvous on November
15 went forward, though the determined opposition of the
higher command caused much misgiving.   Rainsborough, if a
Royalist communication can be trusted, at the last moment
tried to prevent a demonstration as premature, believing his
party would prove too weak.[39]   On November 14 the Army
command violently counter-attacked the Levellers in a *Remonstrance to the House of Lords*,[40] while the new agitators
warned the soldiers not to be discouraged by opposition from
their officers, " and if any Declaration or Propositions about
pay, or Arrears, be offered to you, remember you have been
fed with papers too long, we desire that there may be a generall
Randezvous, and no parting from each other, till we be fully
assured, we shall not returne to burthen the Countrie by
free-quarter, untill our Arrears be actually secured, and the
foundations of our native Freedom, Peace, and security . . .
established." [41]

On November 15, 1647, the first of the three rendezvous
fell to be held at Corkbush Field, between Hertford and Ware,
Hertford being Army headquarters. Drawn up on the field
were four regiments of horse—Fairfax's own, Colonel Fleetwood's, Colonel Rich's, and Colonel Twistleton's—and three
regiments of foot—Fairfax's, Colonel Hammond's, and Colonel
Pride's. When the General came into the field Colonel Eyres,
Major Scot, and others were observed haranguing the soldiers,
seeming to incite them against the General, while others were

distributing papers, found to be the *Agreement of the People*. Eyres was committed immediately into the Marshall's hands, and Scot was taken into custody and sent up to London. Colonel Rainsborough and others, however, approached the General and in the name of the soldiery presented him with a copy of the *Agreement of the People*. Then there appeared marching on the field Colonel Robert Lilburne's and Colonel Harrison's regiments, which had not been summoned to this rendezvous and were therefore guilty of mutiny by their very appearance. They had driven away their officers, pelting some of them with stones, the only man above the rank of lieutenant with them being Captain Lieutenant Bray. Each one of them had stuck in his hat a copy of the *Agreement of the People*, folded so that the words which headed it in bold type, *England's Freedom—Soldiers' Rights*, were prominently displayed. When commanded to cast away the papers from their hats Harrison's regiment complied, but Lilburne's proved more unruly. Under their bold exteriors, however, there was much doubt and wavering. The presence of the General whom they had been accustomed to follow in three years of Army discipline and, above all, of Lieutenant-General Cromwell, whom they had so many times followed to victory, overawed all but the boldest. They permitted Bray to be arrested for having led them to rendezvous contrary to orders, and when Cromwell himself angrily rode among them, tearing the papers from their hats, they seem to have admired his courage rather than resented his action. Several of the more prominent soldiers were seized and tried on the spot for mutiny. Three were sentenced to death, and one, Richard Arnold, shot on the field before the eyes of the assembled regiments. After that there was little trouble, and when Fairfax addressed the men they " received him fairly." Though much had been expected from it and it had caused considerable alarm, the Ware mutiny had failed. John Lilburne himself, taking advantage of his bail, had ridden to Ware to play his part in the proceedings. But he never appeared on the field. There was nothing for him to do but return disconsolately to London.[42]

In the excitement of the summer of 1647—the Army's approach to London, the expulsion of the Eleven Members, the triumph of the Army over Parliament—the civilian Levellers abandoned their own campaign, hoping to see their grievances speedily righted. But, finding themselves still without redress, in closer touch this time with the Army, they renewed their agitation.

In the autumn their campaign centred round the *Agreement of the People*. On November 3 the *Agreement* was published and " by the approbation of the Army offered to the joynt concurrence of the Free Commons of England." On the 9th the House declared it " destructive to the Being of Parliaments, and to the fundamental Government of the Kingdom." [43] On the 23rd the City Levellers, in *The Petition of many free-born People*, begged the Commons to accept the principles of the *Agreement*. ". . . there can be no liberty in any Nation," they said, " where the Law-giving power is not solely in the people or their Representatives." This petition was avowed " seditious and contemptuous," and five of the ringleaders committed to prison.[44] " O yee Commons of England! can you still beare it! " exclaimed their friends. ". . . when will you shew yourselves Englishmen? " [45] On the 25th and the 29th Levellers flocked to the House demanding the release of these five men, and matters looked so ugly that the Lord Mayor offered the City guards to the House. The latter appointed a close committee for examining the business of the ' London Agents,' thus indicating their belief that the London Levellers and the agitators were connected.

The year ended stormily, inconclusively, and unhappily for all concerned. Lilburne, on bail but not at liberty, began to haunt the door of the House of Commons, where he had a brush with Ireton on December 22 concerning the soldiers taken prisoner at Ware; he published nothing after his *New complaint of an old grievance* on November 23. The Levellers had failed to get the *Agreement of the People* accepted; the King, at Carisbrooke, was still confined; the populace, suffering from trade stagnation and the scarcity of food, grew increasingly restless. Cromwell saw mutiny in the Army, Ireton social revolution in the country, Parliament a chaos of conflicting principles on every hand. All three saw a renewed Royalist menace as their own plans for a settlement broke down and the King opened afresh his intrigues with the Scots. The need for unity caused the grandees to deal leniently with the Ware prisoners; though the trials lasted until December 23, the only punishment imposed was that of running the gauntlet. It inspired prayer meetings at Windsor on December 21, 22, and 23, where Cromwell and other officers exhorted the soldiers to unity and " pray'd very fervently and pathetically . . . from Nine in the Morning till Seven at Night," proving from Scripture the necessity of unity and obedience to commands. The King, on December 28, signed a secret agreement with the Scots in which he engaged to establish Presbyterianism for three years and suppress Independency and sectarianism if they would help him to his throne again. John Wildman gave the year its *coup de grâce* with *Putney Projects*, published under the pseudonym of John Lawmind on December 30, which purported " to unfold plainly the mystery of Cromwell's and Ireton's deceipt." This comprised not only their underhand dealings with the King and their betrayal of the soldiers, but their neglect of Free-born John, " that gallant champion for English freedom " whom they permitted still " to consume in prison."

But Lilburne's fire had still not consumed him, and before the year 1648 was far advanced there was proof that in the confused closing of 1647 he was once more organizing his followers, this time with Wildman as his associate.

CHAPTER NINETEEN

Party Leader

I count it my glory and honour among the sons of men that I
have had so great a hand in forwarding of that Petition.

JOHN LILBURNE, *To the House of Commons*, January 19,
1648

*T*HOSE WHO RELEASED LILBURNE ON BAIL COULD HARDLY HAVE
imagined that his liberty would be used for no other purpose
than effecting his own release. Yet when two informers, Robert
Malbon and George Masterson—" the lying shepherd of Shore-
ditch "—appeared at the bar of the House of Lords on January
18, giving " information of dangerous and bloody consequence "
against Lilburne and Wildman, they created a considerable stir.
The Lords sent at once to the Lieutenant of the Tower to know
why Lilburne was at liberty, the Lieutenant could only refer to
the Commons' order for bail, and the Commons were left to
hear the unfolding of plans for Leveller organization more
detailed and more widespread than they had thought possible,
with John Lilburne at its centre.[1]

By this time, more than five years after the outbreak of war,
increased taxation and trade dislocation were being felt by all
classes. About £330,000 was being raised each year from the
excise, which had been levied on goods of almost every description, including food and drink. Assessments raised by
monthly payments from the counties for the support of the
New Model Army amounted to £641,000 in 1647. London
had in addition been subject to direct taxation and the raising
of loans, while the counties had to bear " the intollerable
burden " of free quarter, plunder, damage to crops and other
property. Rents everywhere were falling, and an increasing
number of petitions to Parliament and Army bore witness to
the very real distress felt by all classes. *Vox Populi*, published
on November 1, 1647, was typical of many. It spoke of the

" many great and grievous pressures . . . laid upon us during these miserable times; . . . our estates . . . exhausted, our grounds left unmanured, and growne out of tillage, our Stocks consumed, and those small sums of money which we have laid up for the preferment of our children, spent to the last farthing in those frequent taxes which have been put upon us for the use of the Armies." It spoke also of free quarter and the " many insolencies " of the soldiery, " especially in the houses of poore Countrey people, who neither have the spirit to oppose, nor the wit to perswade, nor any other meanes to hold faire with them, then by permitting all they have to their power and pleasure." The many collections for " poor plundered people " which Whitelocke noted in his diary could do little to stem the discontent. With little money to spare, internal trade languished; in the uncertainties of the situation foreign trade declined, people were put off work, and distress spread among industrial workers.

Tithes still remained, an economic even where not a spiritual burden; the multiplication of committees with executive powers and the growth of a bureaucracy with summary powers of arrest, fine, and imprisonment were further sources of trouble, and there was no redress from " those Dens of Robbery," the courts of law. The " Committee man " was the typical abomination of many writers, who, like the author of *Times Whirligig* of February 9, 1647, regarded him as an " upstart," " new-made " man, or who merely saw that he creamed off for himself moneys that should have gone to public use. The demand that all who handled public funds should be called to account was familiar from Levellers and others. War profiteers, as usual, appeared " swolne great " by their neighbours' losses. They were accused by an anonymous writer of endeavouring in 1647 to embroil the nation in a new war, " finding by experience, that they can fish best in troubled waters, and escape best in the presse." [2] To all this was added a series of exceptionally bad harvests, beginning with 1646. The price of bread had more than doubled, that of oats, rye, and peas rising in proportion, while the price of meat increased by about 50 per cent. between 1645 and 1648.[3]

Discussion of social and economic matters was rife. The rich were asked to forgo one meal's meat a week and give the

corresponding value to help maintain the children of the poor.[4]
One writer advised how to economize in diet and apparel.[5]   A
particularly lurid pamphlet of January 1648 from " many
thousand poor Tradesmen " who were " ready to famish
through decay of Trade " asserted that taxes, customs, and
excise so raised the price of food that there was nothing left
to spend, and tradesmen, already hit through taxation and high
prices, could not sell their goods.

The writers of this pamphlet were acutely class-conscious.
" O you Members of Parliament, and rich men in the City, that
are at ease, and drink Wine in Bowls, and stretch your selves
upon Beds of Down, you that grind our faces, and flay off our
skins, Will no man amongst you regard, will no man behold
our faces black with Sorrow and Famine? . . . What then are
your russling Silks and Velvets, and your glittering Gold and
Silver Laces? are they not the sweat of our brows, and the
wants of our backs and bellies? "

Why, ask the petitioners, does not Parliament use the revenue
from sequestered royalist and bishops' lands to help them?
Why does it not call for an account of public money?   In this
way it could add thousands of pounds to the public exchequer,
taxes could be reduced, trade would revive, and the poor be
saved.[6]

The " poor Tradesmen " who wrote this pamphlet were
Leveller supporters from Wapping and Southwark.   One of the
reasons for Leveller strength in these districts was the location
here of many of the small industries of the capital—brewing,
tanning, glass-making, felt-making and hat-making, sackcloth
and linen-weaving, dyeing, silk-spinning, soap-boiling, and the
manufacture of alum.   All these had been expanding since
Elizabeth's time ; they were attracting capital and were being
reorganized.   In the process the small master was often driven
out of business to become unemployed or a wage-labourer.[7]
An unfulfilled hope that Parliament or Army might reverse the
process had brought many of them into the struggle against the
King.   With Parliament upholding the Merchant Adventurers'
monopoly, increasing taxation, and imposing an excise, and
with their industries caught up in the dislocation of war, their
position was worse than ever.   Lilburne's appeal to the " hobnayles," the " clouted shooes," and the " leather-aprons "

seemed to come direct to all these people, and they rallied to
the Leveller standard.

The London Levellers had for some time been meeting at
the Whalebone, the inn behind the Exchange, at the Mouth in
Aldersgate (the Levellers " two new Houses of Parliament," as
Mercurius Pragmaticus called them), and at the Nag's Head by
Blackwall Hall. " Whaleboneers " became a popular nickname,
and it was when leaving the Mouth on November 10, 1647,
that Tobias Box, agitator and London agent, had been arrested
with incriminating papers about him. The Nag's Head was
the scene of many meetings with Independents at the end of
1648. To elude detection the Levellers also held meetings in
private houses, often outside the City boundaries, where innumerable lanes and turnings, all narrow and badly lit, could—
and did—hide a multitude of plots and crimes. Not far east of
the Tower, East Smithfield [8] joined Ratcliffe Highway, which
ran on to the hamlet of Ratcliffe. To the south of Ratcliffe
Highway lay Wapping, a low-lying district stretching down to
the river, only recently reclaimed from marshland for the rude
dwellings of seafaring families, a few market gardeners, and
the manufacturers of the alum whose stench was the subject
of constant complaint. It was a district eminently suited to
crime and intrigue. Here, at the house of Mr Williams, a
gardener, in a tiny alley called Well Yard, a small Leveller
meeting was held on January 17, 1648, primarily to deal with
the questions and uncertainties or ' scruples ' of various supporters.[9] When George Masterson, a Presbyterian minister,
and a friend entered they were thought to be genuine ' scruplers '
at the fringe of the party who could be won over to the cause.
Lilburne was in the chair and did most of the talking. He still
wore the short red coat of the dragoons, and carried with him
a sheaf of correspondence from the counties. As they listened
the spies realized they were uncovering the most ambitious
project yet broached by the civilian Levellers.

It began, so they learned, in the autumn of 1647 in Southwark.
Lilburne and some of his friends had drawn up a long petition
for presentation to Parliament, several thousand copies of which
they had already printed and paid for. Regular meetings had
for some time been held south of the river, and trustees had

been appointed to promote the petition in every parish. The organization was then extended to London, where sympathizers, meeting at the Whalebone, elected a committee to rouse support in every ward of the City, the outparishes, and the home counties. A central committee was then elected, meeting three times a week, on Mondays, Wednesdays, and Fridays, at the Whalebone, and on three other days of the week at Wapping, Southwark, or other places where the Levellers were strong. Money for printing, agents' and other expenses, it was hoped to collect from sympathizers. For this purpose Thomas Prince and Samuel Chidley—who had both become prominent at the time of the City Levellers' petition in November 1647—were elected treasurers, and collectors were appointed for each district to collect sums ranging from 2*d.* to 2*s.* 6*d.* weekly.

Public meetings to gather support and answer questions were a feature of the campaign on which Lilburne was particularly keen. He was always present at such meetings " to open and unfold the excellency of that Petition and to answer all objections against any particular in it." He appeared to be the secretary of the whole organization, conducting correspondence with the counties and towns in other parts of the kingdom who were being brought into the campaign. These were given details of the organization in the capital, and told how to proceed themselves. They were to arrange meetings in every division of the county, appoint active men in every parish to read and explain the national petition, take subscriptions, obtain signatures, and move as many as possible to come in person to Westminster on the day the petition was to be presented. Agents were meanwhile being sent out all over the country on a preaching crusade which would rouse people to a realization of their wrongs and prepare them for the petition. County groups were asked also to appoint London agents who would keep them in touch with the central organization and supply them with pamphlet literature. Above all, people were to be made to understand the questions at issue. Mere passive signature of the petition was not enough. Men must be prepared to support it in all their actions, in the full realization that they were fighting for their liberties and privileges. Otherwise, said John Lilburne, " I would not give Three pence for Ten thousand hands."

Apart from London and Southwark, the organization in
Kent was the most advanced. Lilburne visited Dartford
personally, and was in touch with Army men in the county.
Remembering, too, the Hertfordshire and Buckinghamshire
men who had petitioned for him and Overton thirteen months
previously, he visited Watford and made a special appeal to
them. A report from the agents in Gravesend, Maidstone, and
other Kentish towns was due on Sunday, January 23, when
four of the central committee, including Lilburne and Wildman,
were to meet the Kentish agents at Dartford.

In addition to the petitions already printed, the ordering
of 3000 more was announced at the meeting at Well Yard, and
also the use of smaller type in order to reduce expense. Distribution of literature was to be helped by soldiers then
stationed at Whitehall, who would also take copies of the
petition and distribute them in the counties. Lazarus Tindall
alone, of Colonel Barkstead's regiment, was ready to take
1000 copies for the soldiers' use. Lilburne estimated they
would get over 100,000 signatures.

As Lilburne emphasized, the main premise of the petition
was that the House of Commons was the supreme representative. The House itself, although professing this, still acknowledged the legislative power of the Lords, contemplated the
return of a monarch with a veto, and allowed various courts
and committees to exercise arbitrary power over the people.
The petition asked that the House of Commons would really
assume to itself the function of supreme authority, and speedily
refer all petitions to a committee instructed to report by a
given date. It contained no hint of treason to the House, but
rather a raising of its prestige. But the Smithfield petition, in
suggesting the reforms it wished the Commons to introduce,
became a new Leveller manifesto, and constituted a particularly
succinct version of the Leveller programme, dealing with law,
prison reform, monopolies, freedom of conscience, electoral
reform on the lines of the *Agreement of the People*, the reform
of the House of Commons by the ejection of lawyers and
insistence upon a quorum, various economic reforms, and the
ending of poverty, " the too long continued shame " of the
nation.

The Wapping meeting was held primarily to deal with those

' scruplers ' who for various reasons scrupled to petition the
House of Commons further, and Lilburne had been specially
asked to attend and bring with him John Wildman, who, after
the Putney debates, had returned to London, where he had an
office in St Martin's Le Grand.[10] Most political organizations
have to face criticisms from right and from left, and the
questions which came from the meeting on this occasion showed
that the Levellers were no exception. How could they continue
to do what the Government had declared unlawful? asked
one man. How could they in conscience and honour continue
to petition so unconstitutional and apostatizing a House?
asked another. Some thought they should not make a disturbance until the House had been given another chance, for
it had recently, on February 11, passed a vote of No More
Addresses to the King. The answer to this was that the petition
was far more fundamental than any such vote, since it struck
at the root of tyranny—the negative voice—whereas the vote
did not. When some one objected that to petition the Commons
at all was a recognition of their authority, who, by their actions,
did not deserve it, Lilburne replied that it was necessary to
own a visible authority for the time being. When it was
argued that most people were as willing to be slaves as any
were to have them so, and that for the Levellers, who were
but a minority, to strive to make it otherwise was but " to
sow the wind," Lilburne's answer came that they were in the
world to do the best they could for their generation, even
though some were unwilling to save themselves.

Lilburne's case was, generally, that they were tied in duty
and conscience, to the uttermost of their power, to preserve
the interest and being of the House of Commons in such a way
that the people were not enslaved; this was, indeed, the purpose
of the petition. When some one spoke of the rumour that he
was being bribed to desist from the petition he told how Lord
Wharton had sent an offer of money which he had declined,
feeling sure it did not come without a proviso. He spoke also
of the rumour that Cromwell had been offered the Earldom
of Essex by the King, and his son and son-in-law other honours,
and how an unnamed Member of Parliament had exclaimed in
his anger that he could be another Felton at such news !

To all these plans and discussions the spies had been listening

and the next day Masterman, " the Divinity-driver of Shore
ditch," " comes with a full careere to the House of Lords, as
if he had been running for a fat benefice," and tells his tale
" with as much confidence as if he had been at least Secretary
to John and his Free-borne Councellors." Without formal
charge the Commons immediately withdrew Lilburne's bail
and sentenced Wildman to imprisonment. Word of the
betrayal flew round. On the 19th Lilburne, still at liberty,
arrived at Westminster about three or four o'clock in the
afternoon to find his friends and supporters already waiting
at the Commons' door. He immediately spoke to them, protesting against his condemnation by the Commons in his
absence, justifying the Wapping meeting, reminding his hearers
of previous unjust convictions and the burning of their petitions.
He promised the Sergeant to appear next morning without the
issue of a warrant if he were allowed to go to his London
lodging that night, instead of surrendering himself up to the
Tower, as the Commons had ordered. This was agreed, and
Lilburne again went home to sleep in his own house—as it
seems he had frequently done, in spite of the fact that his bail
was technically for the daytime only.

The next morning he rose early to prepare himself to meet it.
Several friends came to the house to advise and help, but
Lilburne was in one of the highly spiritual moods in which
he would make no preparation for meeting the Commons,
saying that his refuge was in the tenth Matthew—" But when
they deliver you up, take no thought how or what ye shall
speak: for it shall be given you in that same hour what ye
shall speak. For it is not ye that speak, but the Spirit of your
Father which speaketh in you." " My heart," he wrote afterwards, " was all on fire, and my soul did thirst and long to be
amongst the Parliament-men, that in the might and strength of
my strong God, I might talke to them." Friends urged in vain
that a little more practical preparation was advisable. He
liked well the tenth Matthew, said one, yet for all that he
loved to use means. Lilburne replied that he liked that well
too, but in this case, not knowing what they would say to him,
or lay to his charge, all discourses to him below the tenth
Matthew were to no purpose.

His friends accompanied Lilburne to Westminster, where

many more sympathizers from London and Southwark were waiting to support him. Before the Commons Masterson—"the Judas priest"—repeated his account of the Wapping meeting, contending that the petition was but a blind to destroy both Houses of Parliament. But in his excitement he got parts of the story ludicrously wrong, interpreting, for example, a reference to Fairfax's colour—the blue ribbon—as meaning some "desperate design" for which the wearing of the colour would be a signal, only those who wore it being marked for safety.

Lilburne had been listening to Masterson's story with rising emotion, but a lawyer's mind. It was full of lies and mis-interpretations, yet "in law it was nothing." So he resolved to take no cognizance of it, but instead he recounted, "I fixed my mind very seriously upon the Lord Jehovah, my old experienced refuge, strength and support, and was a wrestling with him for the incomes of his own selfe, that so I might speak freely and boldly, in his might and power." His converse with the Lord did not reduce his sense of the dramatic. The House was full, and while Masterson was speaking Lilburne watched the faces of the Members keenly to mark their reactions. When the priest had finished the Speaker signed to Lilburne to answer. Lilburne took no notice, and forced the Speaker to address him. Then, with a little bow in his direction, and after a suitable pause, Lilburne began.

He was not bound to answer them, he said, since they had failed to put the charges against him in writing. He would, however, proceed if promised liberty to speak his mind freely. After some consultation this was agreed, and Lilburne began his long harangue. Raising his voice in an effort to speak audibly, he admitted his participation in the drafting, printing, and financing of the petition and arrangements for its dispersal, and then proceeded to justify that proceedure.

The theme of his argument was that Parliament had told the people vaguely that they were to fight for their liberties, that the people had no clear conception of those liberties, and had been deliberately confused by Parliament until all that was clear to them was "that their burthens are greater now then ever they were before, and that they have been made fooles, in pretendingly to fight for liberty." Lilburne told the

Members to their faces that the "people are generally . . .
more for the King then for the Parliament, but what's the
reason? but because their burthens are greater now then
before." " Nay Sir, as to the petition," he said, " I dare here
at your Bar with confidence aver it, that there is never a man
in England that dare or can speak against the body or scope
of it, unlesse it be those that have guilty consciences within
them, or those that are of, or allied unto some of those corrupt
interests that are there in struck at." For myself, he said,
". . . I count it one of the most glorious morall actions to
promote that Petition. . . . I count it my glory and honour
among the sons of men, that I have had so great a hand in
forwarding of that Petition as I had." Though much of his
speech was general Leveller propaganda, Lilburne did not
fail to emphasize in his defence that the chief purpose of the
Wapping meeting had been to persuade those present that they
were still tied in duty and conscience to preserve the interest
and being of the House of Commons.

While Lilburne spoke the Commons listened attentively. He
was always more amenable to kindness than to force, and,
touched by their attention, he turned to the Chair. " Mr
Speaker," he said, his voice hoarse with the effort he had made
to be heard in his long speech, " I . . . am overcome . . . that
you have heard me with so much patience speak my minde
so largely. . . . I take it for a greater obligation and ty unto my
spirit, then all the favours that ever I received from this House
from the first day of their sitting."

Wildman was then called to the bar several times. Like
Lilburne, he began his defence with what the *Commons
Journals* laconically described as " a Salvo of his Rights as an
Englishman." The House then went into debate for some
hours. Lilburne and Wildman, waiting in an anteroom,
heard the sentence of commitment—back to the Tower for
Lilburne, to the Fleet for Wildman, on the charge of treasonable
and seditious practices.

To the warrant of commitment the prisoners objected,
since it merely stated they were to be detained " during
pleasure." The hundreds of Leveller supporters, who had
waited throughout the long hearing, took up the cry that
their leaders should not be taken away without a legal warrant,

but, the Speaker having returned home, it could not be
amended, so the prisoners, on promise of return next morning,
were allowed to depart to their lodgings.

That evening was spent by Lilburne in consulting Coke's
Commentaries. When he appeared at the House next morning
it was with Coke's *Institutes* in his hand, and on his tongue
a list of reasons why the warrant against him was illegal,
chief of which was that it gave only a general cause for commitment. The House refused to hear him; the Sergeant prepared
to take him to prison. Free-born John thereupon addressed
himself to the soldiers guarding the House, and "fell of
preaching law and justice" from the *Institutes* in his hand,
telling the soldiers they would be betraying the liberties they
were raised to fight for if they laid hands upon him. The
crowds supporting him, it would have been a bold soldier
indeed who dared to do so! A fresh company under Colonel
Baxter, who had not heard the discourse, was thereupon
brought up, and Lilburne's friends ordered from Westminster
Hall.

Lilburne immediately handed his books, staff, and gloves to
friends, in order to be free to fight, and began to make his way
outside with the crowd: he was determined not to be left
behind to make his stand unobserved. At the top of Westminster Hall steps Baxter laid hands on Lilburne, who, prevented by the density of the crowd from drawing his sword,
cried out instead, "Murder! Murder! Murder!" Several
of Baxter's soldiers rushed at him with drawn swords, but
Elizabeth flung herself between, while several of his friends
who tried to reach him were knocked down with the butt-ends
of muskets. At last, with a strong guard of soldiers, Lilburne
was forced away by water to the Tower, Wildman being conducted to the Fleet.[11] "Now, the next time that John comes
abroad," remarked the news-sheet *Mercurius Pragmaticus*, "it
will be in Print, I warrant you, to wire-draw the whole Story
of the businesse, with all the secrets of the designe." [12]

CHAPTER TWENTY

Release

> ... seeing honest John is got loose, 'twill not be long ere Mr
> Speaker and Noll Cromwell be both brought to the stake.
>
> *Mercurius Pragmaticus*

> ... assure your self that if ever my hand be upon you, it shall
> be when you are in your full glory.
>
> JOHN LILBURNE, *Letter to Cromwell*

*P*ragmaticus WAS RIGHT. *A Whip for the present House of Lords*, published on February 27, gave Lilburne's version of the affair, joined with a rebuttal of the calumnies against him and his party which had been rising since the previous autumn, and which were strongly expressed in an anonymous pamphlet published on February 14 and brought to Lilburne in prison. Called simply *A Declaration of some Proceedings of L. Col. John Lilburne and his Associates*, it was one of the most reasonable and shrewd of the anti-Leveller publications. As Lilburne suspected, it was written by Walter Frost, the secretary to the Committee of Both Houses. The House of Commons had, in fact, taken the Levellers seriously. They knew that both the Smithfield petition and the supporting *Mournfull Cries* had been widely circulated; they had good reason to know, also, the extent of social distress. So on January 20 they ordered the Committee of Both Houses to draw up a refutation of the Levellers for publication to the people, and on February 5 the Committee instructed its secretary to set to work.[1]

Frost was so eminently reasonable in his approach to the Levellers that he appended to his pamphlet copies of the Smithfield petition and the *Mournfull Cries*. As the suppression of the petition had been very thorough, and the Levellers did not reprint it until more than a year later, when it appeared as an appendix to one of Lilburne's pamphlets, Frost was, perhaps, carrying his sense of fair play a little too far. As providing one of the only two known sources of the petition, posterity is grateful.

Anyone who took stock of the Leveller party in 1648 would have found many petitions and pamphlets which expounded its programme. These pamphlets made it clear that the Levellers were not only suffering from intolerable pressures of various kinds—religious, social, economic, constitutional— but that their programme had developed from demands for particular grievances to a more general demand for constitutional reform: the first *Agreement of the People* was not produced until October 1647, while Leveller pamphlets urging the other reforms had been appearing since 1645. Among the most important were *Englands Birth-right justified* of October 1645, the ' large ' City Petition of March 1647, Overton's lesser-known *Articles for the Good of the Common Wealth* of July 1647, the Smithfield petition, and the *Agreement of the People*.[2]

Taken as a whole, the Leveller programme appeared hardly consistent. They asked for freedom from State intervention in some directions, for State action in others. They demanded the rule of the majority where their demands were likely to be those of the majority, as in social legislation, but not in the case of religion, where their particular form of worship was likely to be that of a minority. Their programme finds unity in that it was essentially a programme for the weak. Freedom of conscience is the demand of a minority not sufficiently strong to exercise its beliefs. The demand for the vote comes from a class conscious of certain disabilities. The same applies to demands for freedom of speech and press and person. They are most frequently the reply of a suppressed group to the party in power. The excise, whose reduction the Levellers demanded, hit the poor hardest. The raising of wages was for the benefit of the poor; the State schools and hospitals for which they asked were primarily for the use of the poor; public works were for the unemployed. Where weakness was due to being in a minority the Levellers required toleration: where it was due to State action—as in the case of the monopolist companies—the Levellers demanded *laissez-faire*. Where it was due to poverty or the helplessness of the individual they demanded State aid. Where weakness was due to the disabilities of a class they demanded political democracy.

Its economic demands, in particular, were those of a decaying class. In industry a rapidly developing capitalism in the century preceding the civil wars was squeezing the independent artisan out of his independence and crushing the small trader by the weight of monopolist companies. In two of the districts where the Levellers were strong—London and Southwark, and the South-west—this development was marked. While the South-west was the home of the clothing industry, the varied industries of Southwark—brewing, tanning, glass-making, felt-making, hat-making, soap-boiling, and many more—were among those which showed enormous expansion and great increase of output, and where capitalist enterprise was replacing the small master.[3]

In agriculture a parallel capitalist development was meanwhile being measured both by the progress of enclosure and by the tightening of commercial relations between the small-holder and the landowner, the latter being accentuated by the sweeping changes in land-holding which resulted from sequestration and sale of Royalist estates. In particular, the insecure copyhold tenant was penalized in the interests of the new owners.[4]

Although the Levellers never distinctly repudiated capitalist development in either industry or agriculture, and although it is nowhere explicitly stated, small peasant proprietorship seems to have been their ideal of an agrarian society, and small commercial and manufacturing units their ideal of an industrial society.

In its social demands the Leveller party was more explicit, demanding aid to widows, orphans, and the maimed, the appointment of trustees to determine what stocks, houses, lands, rightly belonged to the poor, the provision of stocks of raw materials to provide work, the provision of hospitals and schools. Nowhere was there an attack on private enterprise as such. Rather, the championship of the small man and the small unit was accompanied by a respect for his property which was part of a deep-seated respect for private property in general.

In some respects—as in their demand for law reform—the

Levellers were in accord with their generation, although they pushed their demands for the translation of the law into English, for the reform of the clumsy and dilatory Court of Chancery, for the reform of the criminal law and of the law of debt, for the reform of procedure and jurisdiction, farther and more vigorously than many of their contemporaries. In other respects—as with prison reform—the Levellers, and Lilburne in particular, were pioneers a century and a half before Howard, in not only exposing the brutality and degradation of prison life, as Luke Hutton and William Fennor had already done, but in propounding a definite programme of reform.

With such a solid backing behind the Levellers, Frost's task of refutation was not easy. His *Declaration*, nevertheless, was dignified and not unimaginative, although he was able to deal with only a small part of the Leveller programme. He pointed out that the " unseasonable seed-time in 1646 and the unkindly Spring following" had caused widespread dearth in other countries as well as in England, and was responsible for much of the hunger of which the Levellers complained. The Levellers worked up the subject for their own ends. Referring to the lurid *Mournfull Cries*, the author asked: " Where are those famishing babes? and where are those pining carkasses? . . . Where are those faces black with sorrow and famine? . . . Let the famishing pined Carkasses, those black faces be seen, the view gives a deeper impression then heare-say." He accused Lilburne and his friends of exaggerating people's wants and preventing their alleviation. They " tell the soldiers of their arrears " and " help them to heighten the sense of their present wants and sufferings " in order to stir up trouble. Frost was probably reflecting Cromwell's own views fairly accurately when he remarked: " The dispute is not now of what is absolutely best if all were new, but of what is perfectly just as things now stand. It is not the Parliament's work to set up an Utopian Common-Wealth . . . but to make them as happy as the present frame will bear."

As for Lilburne himself, " The present temper of his spirit gives some ground to beleeve, that he added much to the weight of his pressures, by his want of meeknesse to bear what Providence had laid him under." Besides, " Let his services be as great as himself, or his friends will have them, yet 'tis

possible for a man to reflect too much upon his own desert."
In any case it was uncertain that Lilburne had retained his
original allegiance. Some thought that " he brought not the
same affections from Oxford, that he was carried prisoner
thither withall." This was repeating a charge that Lilburne
had already denied the previous October—that he had been
fuddled with drink by his Royalist captors, and then won to
their support. But Frost further accused him of consorting
with Royalist prisoners in the Tower, particularly with Judge
Jenkins. It is interesting that Dyve was not mentioned.

Frost also referred to the view, gaining currency since the
Putney debates, that the Levellers wanted all goods in common.
" There hath been a good while a rumour of a pestilence that
walketh in darknesse. . . . And 'tis the Doctrine of Parity or
levelling, bringing all mens Estates to an Equality." This it
was, not the taxation of which the Levellers complained, that
caused the export of estates and hindered the exportation of
goods.

When Frost's authorship was confirmed to Lilburne he
immediately wrote him a long letter, which he sent by hand.
Not receiving an immediate reply, he added the letter to the
account of his arrest which he had already prepared. Un-
deterred by the length of the resulting pamphlet, his Leveller
press had it printed and distributed as *A Whip for the present
House of Lords*.

In his letter to Frost Lilburne gave strong circumstantial
evidence to show that, far from being won over to the Royalists
at Oxford, he had been regarded as such a staunch advocate
of Parliament's cause that the Cavaliers kept him away from
weaker prisoners whom they hoped to convert. Besides, he
asked, how could he be accused both of being a Cavalier and
of plotting to murder the King? He vigorously and indignantly repudiated the charge of social equality, and challenged
Frost to prove that any one of the Leveller leaders showed the
slightest tendency to the destruction of liberty and property or
the setting up of " Levelling by universall Communitie " or
anything in the least like it. The only way in which they were
levellers was that they would " indure tyranny, oppression
and injustice no more in apostatized Cromwell and Ireton,
and their . . . confederates then in the King and his Cavaliers

. . . but desire that all alike may be Levelled to, and bound by the Law."

Lilburne always coupled liberty and property. Freedom to live unrestricted entailed freedom to possess: no passionate defender of the rights of the individual could argue otherwise. It was "liberty and propriety," not "communitie and levelling," for which the Levellers stood. Yet, in refuting the charge of social levelling, Lilburne did not add, as he might have done, that his compassion was wide and that his fierce demand for liberty was refined by a generosity and tempered by a sense of justice that would never endure the existence side by side of great poverty and overweening wealth.

Lilburne's prison pamphlets continued throughout April, May, and June—*The Prisoners Plea for a Habeas Corpus, The Lawes Funerall, Englands weeping Spectacle*—their titles alone tell his story. After vain searching at the beginning of 1647 for further Leveller presses, the Stationers seem to have slackened their efforts, and Leveller pamphlets continued with scant hindrance. This was partly, no doubt, due to the general breakdown of the licensing machinery as the pamphlet literature grew in volume—from under 700 pamphlets in 1645 to over 1400 in 1648. But the position was complicated by the fact that from the spring of 1647 the Army had its own press, and that the agitators had another which may have been separate from the regular Leveller press. One may have been at Oxford, and others could easily have been hidden in the alleys of Southwark or Wapping. Levellers and agitators together produced in 1647 over forty pamphlets, compared with about fourteen in 1645.[5] The type and format of most of these gave no clue that could lead to a secret press. There appeared to be more than one compositor at work, the type used was old and worn, some of it was probably of Dutch origin, though it may have been in England for many years before the Levellers obtained it. But all this was true of hundreds of other pamphlets.[6] A fresh ordinance against unlicensed or scandalous pamphlets of September 30, 1647, imposed stiffer penalties on authors, printers, booksellers, and hawkers, but the Levellers were not intimidated, and their pamphlet literature was hardly reduced in 1648. On the contrary, their propaganda was made more effective by the production of a Leveller newspaper. *The Moderate* suddenly appeared for the week June 22–29, 1648, in paper, type, and format almost indistinguishable from *The Moderate Intelligencer*, which had been running since 1645 and published by John Dillingham. Gilbert Mabbot, the licenser, had suspended *The Moderate Intelligencer* for certain words contained in its previous issue—" Dieu nous donne les Parlyments briefe Rois de vie longue "—and a group of people associated with the Levellers had endeavoured to secure the goodwill of the paper by substituting their own publication, *The Moderate*, saying, " This is the true *Moderate Intelligencer*." The House of Lords, however, reversed Mabbot's decision, and commanded that Dillingham's publication, and no other, be licensed under the name. *The Moderate* then decided to drop all pretence of being a continuation of *The Moderate Intelligencer*, and, changing its day of issue from Thursday to Tuesday and increasing its pages from four to six, started at No. 1 for the week of June 13. It survived all efforts at suppression, and ran without intermission until No. 63, September 18–26, 1649, when, without a word of explanation, it ceased.[7]

The Moderate was the greatest help to Lilburne and the Leveller movement, quoting petitions and pamphlets, closely reporting events of importance, giving detailed accounts of social conditions in various parts of the country, gathering together newsletters and other reports. Towards the end of 1648 these items became more frequent, and the effect of their publication week after week was to produce a lurid picture of the sufferings of the country. None of the other journals paid such attention to local affairs, and *The Moderate* stands as the chief social as well as political news-sheet. By the autumn of 1648 it had also started a series of leading articles some of which may have come from Walwyn's pen. Each week a different topic was dealt with. No. 15 contained a lucid account of the origins of the war. Following issues dealt with law reform, the *Agreement of the People*, the nature of government. One told the reader that " Love, Uprightness, and Integrity, procures Favor with God and Man, and must destroy thine enemy, at least make him ashamed." Another asked the question: " What avails it to overcome the persons of men, and to prosecute, and enslave them, unless you therewith conquer their Reasons and Understandings? "

Lilburne was brought before the Judges of King's Bench in response to his appeal for *habeas corpus* on the morning of May 8. When asked who his counsel was he replied loudly that he wished to plead himself, because that lawyer was not in England that dare, or would, say one-quarter of that for him that he wished to say for himself. So he put on his spectacles, held his plea before him—" as the lawyers do their Briefes," he said, betraying the amateur's desire to appear professional— and stated his case. But Justice Bacon remanded Lilburne back to the Tower, declaring that, since the House of Lords was a superior court, he had no jurisdiction to interfere with its judgment. There had been no advance over the position of twelve months earlier. Lilburne was still in prison on the ruling of the House of Lords, and no court would dispute its jurisdiction over a commoner. ". . . if this be good Law which you declare unto me," cried Lilburne, " then perfect slaves are we indeed ! " [8]

Yet it had been rumoured that Lilburne would fare far worse. " It is thought that shortly he will cast his feathers at Tyburne," *Mercurius Melancholicus* had reported.[9] That the Government was prepared to deal less harshly with him and to try to reason with the public on the Levellers' own ground was due to its need to prevent divisions in its ranks in view of rising Royalist activity. Even Army and Parliament were drawing together. " The Presbyterians and Independents," remarked one of Hyde's correspondents, " are minded rather to submit themselves to the inconveniences of each other's friendship, then by variance to lay themselves open to the Prelatical and Popish party." [10] On April 30 great prayer meetings were held at Windsor, in which the renewed Royalist menace was discussed as an act of God and attributed, after the belief of the Puritans, to some failing on the part of the Army. Major Goffe preached to the text " Turn you at my reproof," and Cromwell urged that they each seek out the cause of such sad rebukes from the Lord. Finally, recounted one who was present, we were " led and helped to a clear agreement amongst ourselves, not any dissenting, that it was

the duty of our day, with the forces we had, to go out and
fight against those potent enemies, which . . . in all places
appeared against us." [11] To this meeting came, on May 1,
news that war had broken out again in Wales, and Cromwell
hastened westward.

The resolve to sink other differences in order to go out and
fight the Royalists was shared by the Levellers. But what of
Lilburne? Sir John Maynard, Lilburne's fellow-prisoner in
the Tower, had been released on June 3. On July 27 he rose
in the House of Commons to plead for Lilburne's liberty.
There were enough people to attribute Maynard's speech to
pure expediency—a Presbyterian desire to enlist Lilburne's
support against Cromwell. But the speech was sincere and
moving, a reflection of the genuine friendship for the Leveller
which had been generated during their prison companionship,
and which probably owed something to the pamphlet which
Wildman, at Lilburne's request, had written in support of
Maynard. " I shall acquaint you," said Maynard in the
House, " what this brave invincible Spirit hath suffered and
done for you "; and he gave a brief account of Lilburne's
sufferings under the bishops and of his military career from the
battle of Edgehill, " where he kept the Field all Night," to the
" famous Battle in Marston-Moor," where he was " an eminent
Actor," his taking of Tickhill Castle, and his help and encouragement to his fellow-prisoners at Oxford.[12]

The occasion of Maynard's speech was a weighty petition
from the Levellers, to which in the space of seven or eight days
they had secured eight or nine thousand signatures. Grateful
as he was to Maynard, his " true friend and faithfull and
couragious fellow-sufferer," Lilburne declared that he was
" chiefly beholding " to this petition for the release voted by
the House of Commons on August 1, and confirmed by the
House of Lords the following day.[13] The fine and sentence of
imprisonment imposed on Lilburne by the House of Lords two
years earlier was then remitted, and he was at last free from
the long controversy which had dogged him since that time.

The release from prison of the Leveller leader on August 2
caused much anxious speculation. Would he abandon his
quarrel with the grandees in order to present an unbroken

front to the King's forces? Was he as inclined to the Royalist interest as some of his enemies asserted? The fact that it was a leading Presbyterian and bitter enemy of the Army grandees who spoke so eloquently on Lilburne's behalf made many believe that his release would be a thorn in the flesh of Cromwell. *Mercurius Pragmaticus*, at least, had hopes that " seeing honest John is got loose, 'twill not be long ere Mr Speaker and Noll Cromwell be both brought to the stake." [14]

This view was reinforced by the appearance before the Lords on the very day they had concurred in Lilburne's release of Major Huntington, who preferred a charge of opportunism and self-aggrandizement against Cromwell on account of his negotiations with the King the previous autumn. Huntington had then been Cromwell's confidant, but, wishing to continue negotiations after Cromwell had rejected them as useless, had resigned his commission. His narrative made it appear, by words attributed to Cromwell, that the Lieutenant-General was willing to use force against all who opposed his will, the Parliament included.[15] Lilburne, exulted *Mercurius Pragmaticus*, would make a brave second to Major Huntington! [16] Lilburne himself recounted that he was " earnestly solicited again and again " to join the impeachment, " and might have had money enough to boot to have done it." [17]

Cromwell's hands were full. His negotiations with the King had failed, and he was faced with the renewed civil war he had striven so hard to avert. He had not settled the Levellers, he left behind him enemies in Parliament and Army, and the causes of discontent witnessed by the Levellers had not abated. After three months the war was not going well. At the end of May the fleet had declared for the King, the Scottish Royalists crossed the border on July 8, while Fairfax was laying siege to Colchester and Cromwell was still in Wales. Prince Charles appeared with the fleet at the end of July, blockading the Thames in an effort to make London declare for the King. Petitions begging for terms with the King and the ending of the war multiplied. Parliament, in spite of its vote of No More Addresses in February, agreed on August 1 to reopen negotiations with the King. On that day the Commons ordered Lilburne's release. On the same day Cromwell, pushing on by forced marches to check the Scots, arrived at Leicester, with his foot soldiers not only weary but in want of shoes and stockings. This was the time when Cromwell's enemies had chosen to strike by producing Major Huntington and releasing Lilburne.

Honest John was not the man to play second to such a tune. He would neither embarrass Cromwell nor help "a Scotch interest." He rounded furiously on Huntington, and the day following his release hastened to write to Cromwell a letter which he sent by Sexby, still his faithful friend, in which he said he scorned to strike Cromwell while he was low. ". . . Assure your self," he said, " that if ever my hand be upon you, it shall be when you are in your full glory, if then you shall decline from the righteous wayes of Truth and Justice: Which, if you will fixedly and impartially prosecute, I am Yours, to the last drop of my heart bloud (for all your late severe hand towards me)." [18] Cromwell had in many ways in the past shown his regard for the man who had in him, after all, the root of the matter that Cromwell so much valued. The receipt of the letter pleased and cheered him. By the end of the month Colchester had surrendered to Fairfax, while Cromwell had defeated the bulk of the Scots Army at the battle of Preston, and himself entered Scotland.

Robert Lilburne distinguished himself in the second civil war, soundly defeating the Northumbrian Cavaliers on July 1.[19] But shortly afterwards the youngest of the three Lilburne brothers met his death. Henry Lilburne was Lieutenant-Governor of Tynemouth Castle when the Royalist leanings, which had been apparent in the rumours surrounding the King's flight to the Isle of Wight, caused him unexpectedly to declare for the King on August 9. It was ironic that it was Haselrig who again acted against a Lilburne and sent a force from Newcastle which regained the Castle for the Parliament in a bitter assault in which Henry Lilburne was killed. His head was displayed on the castle gate; his estate of some £2500 was confiscated. His family mourned their "unfortunate" youngest son, and John, without any evidence, blamed Haselrig for his deflexion.[20]

Later in the year the death of Rainsborough at Doncaster was a heavy blow to the Leveller party, and some people believed his death to be not unwelcome to the grandees, who were glad to be rid of an influential Leveller of the high command. His family brought his body to London, and *The Moderate* called upon " all in whom any sparks of his brave soul " dwelt to meet the hearse and follow it to burial in Wapping Chapel on November 14. Thousands did so, wearing the sea-green emblem which became the Leveller colour, newspapers widely reported his funeral, and many elegies were published in prose and verse.[21]

Lilburne took no part in the second civil war. He found lodgings for himself, with his wife and three children, in Brewer's Yard, Westminster, and wondered how to support his family. As he had emphasized repeatedly, he had not a penny inheritance in the world: the small estate at Thickley Punchardon had suffered too heavily during the war to be able to help him, and he had no trade to turn to. In all these years he had received no allowance for prison maintenance, and not a penny of his promised reparations had been paid. It had been observed the previous autumn that he was emaciated—Lilburne " hath almost bark't himselfe to an Anatomy " [22]—and he was weary of his buffetings from one gaol to another. Of his three children, two had been born to him in prison. Elizabeth had been baptized while he was in Newgate in September 1645; another was named Tower ! The ceaseless activities of his wife—devoted, indefatigable, and at times as fanatical as he himself—may be gauged from the remark of a news-sheet on the rumour of her husband's release: " 'Twill not be long er'e . . . his wife Elizabeth may give over petitioning, and have time to receive Petitions from all Quarters to her high and mightie husband." [23]

In granting him freedom on August 1, the House of Commons also set up a committee to inquire into his reparations. As matters stood, an Ordinance of 1646 had allowed him £2000 from the requisitioned estates of various Royalists; but since these estates had in various ways become entangled Lord Coventry's estate was substituted. Hearing of this, Lord Coventry's heir came posting to London in time to stop the sequestration, helped, Lilburne believed, by the Vanes and Sir Arthur Haselrig. It was then proposed to settle Lilburne's reparations upon the public exchequer. But Lilburne refused to accept anything from the public purse, and also, on September

4, presented yet another petition asking for an increase in his
indemnity, pointing out that Bastwick, whose sufferings had
been no greater, had received £4000. Six days later, as always
mixing the personal with the public, his familiar figure joined
a crowd petitioning the Commons against a personal treaty
with the King.

On September 5 the House ordered Lilburne £300 for immediate subsistence and £3000 from a newly sequestered estate,
that of Sir Henry Gibb in Jarrow, County Durham, being
mentioned. Lilburne favoured an estate in his home county,
where his father and uncle sat on the Committee for sequestrations, but before deciding on Gibb's rode north to get a list
of other delinquents' lands. While in the North he took the
opportunity of observing Cromwell, who was then following
the Scots northward after his victory at Preston on August 18.
He was profoundly dissatisfied, all he heard and saw pointing,
he said, more to self-exalting than to the good of the Commonwealth. But he continued to follow his own affairs, riding into
Scotland to make sure there was really evidence against Gibb
as a delinquent. He was satisfied on this count, but was
nevertheless very uneasy about the transaction. " I had no
stomach to his, or any other Delinquents' Lands," he said.
Gibb had never been summoned to answer to any crimes, he
had never done Lilburne a personal injury, nor was there any
security in the transaction. Still undecided, Lilburne returned
in haste to London, the double journey having taken not more
than five days.[24]

The reason for his haste was to have a hand in a large new
petition which the London Levellers—helped, perhaps, by
Harry Marten, who was being very active at this time—were
preparing to present to Parliament. It was a document of
twenty-seven points, which, although lengthy, stated the complete Leveller programme comparatively succinctly, covering
everything from constitutional reform and religious toleration
to the opening of fenland enclosures. Lilburne claimed that
about 40,000 signatures were obtained, and on September 11
a great crowd brought it to the House of Commons.[25] A week
later the rumoured negotiations between Parliament and King
were known to have begun at Newport, in the Isle of Wight,
and once again a realignment of forces became necessary.

CHAPTER TWENTY-ONE

Disillusion

> . . . They then as a cloke take up the way of an Agreement
> again . . . by this means they . . . beget an acquiescence . . . till
> they . . . so far effect their business as to the introduction of an
> absolute platform of tyrannie, long since hatched by Ireton.
>
> *The Hunting of the Foxes*, March 21, 1649

BY THIS TIME IT SEEMED AS THOUGH EVENTS OF THE SPRING OF
1647 were repeating themselves. The King's forces had been
defeated, and once again a predominantly Presbyterian Parliament attempted to treat with the King. Again petitions poured
into Parliament from the soldiers and from the countryside for
the payment of arrears, the taking off of free quarter, and this
time for justice against the " man of blood " and all who had
brought the country to a new war. Fairfax and some of the
officers were prepared to go along more or less passively with
the Parliament, but it was not necessary for the Levellers to
organize opposition to a treaty, for no less a person than
Commissary-General Ireton actively assumed the leadership.
The Levellers therefore were faced with the alternatives of
making a third grouping in the Army or of supporting Ireton.
With the memories of the Putney debates in their minds, they
were not unaware of the fundamental differences between them
and the Commissary-General. On the other hand, a treaty with
the King was a real and pressing danger. They attempted first
a compromise with Ireton and the more radical officers of the
Army, but were finally driven over once more into independent
Leveller activity.

In November 1648 Lilburne and some friends sent to Cromwell in the North reminding him that their only object in
supporting the war was the securing of a just government.
Cromwell's answer seems to have suggested a meeting between
Independents, soldiers, and Levellers, which took place at the

Nag's Head later in the month, Lilburne, Wildman, and Walwyn
being among those who attended. Wildman opened for the
Levellers, proof of his influence and the confidence of his friends.
Mr Wildman, said Lilburne, " laid open . . . the just ends of
the War . . . as exactly as ever I heard in my life." But the
soldiers present told the Levellers plainly that the thing to do
was " first to cut off the Kings Head . . . and force and
throughly purge, if not dissolve the Parliament." It seemed a
reversal of Lilburne's and the Levellers' previous stand that
they should oppose this. Yet logic was on their side. Though
the King was " an evill man in his actions," said Lilburne, the
Army also " had couzened us the last year, and fallen from all
their Promises and Declarations, and therefore could not
rationally any more be trusted by us without good cautions
and security." There being two tyrants in the country, he said,
it was to the people's interest " to keep up one Tyrant to
balance another, till we certainly knew what that Tyrant that
pretended fairest would give us as our Freedoms." If the King
were beheaded, the Parliament purged, and all government
devolved upon the Army to be executed according to " their
wills and Swords," with no power remaining as a counter-
balance, " our slavery for future . . . might probably be greater
than ever it was in the King's time, and so our last errour
would be greater then our first." Let an *Agreement of the
People* come first, urged Lilburne, and the prevention of tyranny
by King, Army, or Parliament would follow.

This meeting chose four of each group present for a continued
discussion, and Lilburne and his friends were drinking wine
in the shop below, not unpleased with the results of the meeting,
when Walwyn's notorious free-thinking and Lilburne's hot
temper nearly wrecked their plan. For they received a message
from John Price, an Independent attached to John Goodwin's
congregation, to say he could not sit with Walwyn, " for he
had a prejudice against him." Lilburne jumped to his feet
to reply that Walwyn had more honesty and integrity in his
little finger than Price had in his whole body, and if there was
no Walwyn at the meeting there would be no Lilburne either !
In the interests of an agreement he was quietened by his friends,
and both Walwyn and Price agreed to withdraw, leaving a
committee of three a side. Amid rumours of the King's escape

from the Isle of Wight and continued attempts at negotiation by the House of Commons and the Council of Officers, it met on the 15th and drew up a scheme for a new *Agreement of the People* to be drafted by representatives of the Army and the counties and submitted for approval to the country as a whole. But when their messenger reached Army Headquarters at St Albans it was found that Ireton had produced his own plan for a settlement, which he had embodied in a *Remonstrance*. Whereas in 1647 the Levellers' *Agreement* had to compete with Ireton's *Heads of the Proposals*, their new *Agreement* had to compete with his *Remonstrance*, the fundamental difference between *Remonstrance* and *Agreement* being that, whereas Ireton would immediately bring the King to justice, and then establish the new constitution, the Levellers urged that the *Agreement* must be accepted first, and that only within the framework of a new constitution should the King be dealt with. Any other approach, they feared, would open the door to the rule of force.

Their fears were given foundation when the Army, as in 1647, began to move towards the capital, reaching Windsor on November 24. Here Lilburne and his committee met Ireton and other officers at the Garter Inn, when " a large and sharp discourse " ensued, principally about liberty of conscience. At Putney in September 1647 the debates between grandees and Levellers had turned largely upon the question of universal suffrage and the authority of Parliament. Now the sharpest difference concerned Ireton's determination that the State should keep a compulsive power to use when religious freedom became politically dangerous. The Levellers' opposition to anything short of complete religious freedom had been stiffened by the passage of a fresh Act in the previous May against heresy and blasphemy, which had shown them what they might expect from a Parliament whose power over conscience was unrestricted. They were determined that the ' reserve ' of religion in the *Agreement of the People* should stand.

Disappointed at the outcome of the Windsor meetings, the Independents and Levellers resolved to return to London, the Levellers to stir up their interest there. But Colonel Harrison caught Lilburne and his friends at their lodgings on the point of departure. This fanatical sectary was obviously sent as one likely to have influence with Lilburne, and the attempt to placate the committee was a sign of Ireton's uncertainty and need for allies. Harrison was almost apologetic as he made excuses for the breakdown of negotiations. It was necessary for the Army to press on to London. It could not stay long enough at Windsor to perfect an agreement. Parliament and King might at any time come to terms, and then the Army would be disbanded and the Levellers destroyed.

The Levellers agreed willingly enough that they had little cause to trust Parliament. Yet if they deferred the settling of an *Agreement* until the Army had purged the House of all save forty or fifty of its friends this " mock power," with the Army supporting it, could " bid them go shake their ears for an Agreement and go look for it where they could catch it ! " Yet, rather than throw over all their negotiations, the Levellers suggested a further committee of four a side—Levellers, Independents, soldiers; even Presbyterians if they would come in from the beginning. The difference between this and previous committees would be that all concerned would pledge themselves to accept its majority decision. Harrison liked the suggestion, and Lilburne followed him to Ireton's lodging, where he was told that the Commissary-General agreed to the scheme. Seeking out the Independents just as they were taking horse, Lilburne obtained their ready agreement, and, overtaking them later on the road to London, had further talk with them.

In London, at a large meeting, the Levellers chose Lilburne, Wildman, Walwyn, and Petty to represent them, and all concerned, except the Presbyterians, posted back to Windsor, where, in the Council Chamber of the Castle, they had a long discussion with the officers. But the haste of the Army to be off was overriding. It left Windsor on November 30, on the following day it once more seized the King and had him conducted from the Isle of Wight to Hurst Castle, on December 2 it entered London, on the 6th Colonel Pride began to purge from the House all who opposed the Army, and that night Cromwell entered London from the North: again, as when he rode to the Army in June 1647, he arrived to find a *fait accompli*.[1]

Lilburne, for the second time in little over a year, heard the

sounds of an Army marching in the capital. Then he was
waiting for deliverance from prison; now he was waiting for
the establishment of freedom. Then he had been urging its
approach; now he mistrusted it. Then he had been forgotten,
betrayed; would the Army fail him a second time? If it did
its leaders were irrevocably condemned as traitors and apostates.

One of the first things they did was to try to win him to their
side. They needed a persuasive pen to justify their actions,
and, inviting him to their rooms for a friendly talk, Harrison,
Waller, and Constable suggested that they might use their
influence to obtain his reparations if he would engage his pen
for them. As they might have expected, Lilburne flung the
offer back in their teeth. " I would as soon engage for the
Turk as for you," he declared, while you are planning such
things as the breaking of the House and taking off the King's
head ! [2]

Discussions then began again at Whitehall between Ireton,
the Independents, the Levellers, and Marten, the only Member
of Parliament who attended, and " a long and tedious tug we
had," wrote Lilburne, " with Commissary Generall Ireton
only, yea sometimes whole nights together, Principally about
Liberty of Conscience, and the Parliaments punishing where
no law provides, and very angry and Lordly in his debates
many times he was." Finally, " for peace sake," the Levellers
agreed to a compromise expecting, in accordance with their
understanding of the terms upon which the meetings had taken
place, that this majority decision would enable an agreed
document to be circulated among the regiments and the whole
nation for subscription and agreement. Instead it was sent to
the Council of Officers, which met at Whitehall, where the
whole business started over again. The ultimate decision was
to be made, not by the people as a whole, but by an Army
Council which no longer even included representatives of the
ranks. Lilburne and his friends, although they accepted the
invitation to be present at these meetings, were bitterly disappointed and angered at what they deemed the betrayal of
the terms upon which the committee had been meeting.
Lilburne may have been mistaken in Ireton's message at
Windsor; Ireton may not have realized the crucial importance
Lilburne was attaching to his words. The matter was never

thrashed out, and the Levellers laid yet another charge of perfidy against the grandees.

Hard words passed between the officers and the Levellers at the Whitehall debates. Lilburne accused the officers of trickery and challenged them to the field. A fight being about to develop, Sir Hardresse Waller, the acting President, rebuked Lilburne. Thereupon Free-born John threw down his challenge to Waller, and in a rage left the meeting " for a pack of dissembling juggling Knaves," vowing never to enter into consultation with them again, " for there was neither faith, truth, nor common honesty amongst them." Lilburne returned to his party—" those that chose and trusted " him—and gave a detailed account of the way in which the Army leaders had " couzened and deceived " the Levellers. And so, Lilburne said, he " absolutely discharged " himself " for medling or making any more with so perfidious a generation of men as the great ones of the Army were, but especially the cunningest of Machiavilians Commissary Henry Ireton." [3]

Posterity is again denied the record of Lilburne actually in debate with the grandees, for the records of the Army Council debates at Whitehall are far from complete. Lilburne's quarrel and departure from the scene are not mentioned, and only two or three short speeches by him are recorded—too little to show his calibre. It is clear, however, that discussion ranged round the Levellers' attempt to ' reserve ' religion from the civil magistrate. There was general agreement that the magistrate had no power over conscience as distinct from action. " That is a right," said Ireton. " I will agree to that. . . . For if that were the Question, I should be sure to give my *noe* to the allowance of any man to be punished for his conscience." But the questions to be faced were whether they should allow freedom for anything a man cared to call religion—even idolatry or atheism?—and whether they could discriminate between freedom of conscience and " that exhorbitant liberty which those that are nott Religious butt would pretend to bee soe, would take," even to the damage of the civil peace.

To Ireton the supreme purpose of a commonwealth was peace —not liberty. If necessary, the latter must be sacrificed to the former. You cannot, he said, provide that the really conscientious man shall not be persecuted without denying to the

magistrate a power which, in the interests of peace, he ought
to have. Lilburne put liberty first. He never squarely faced
the question of the magistrate's duty in preserving civil order,
but assumed that conscience would lead men to right actions,
and that the only activities to be curbed by the magistrate were
those which were self-evidently political and not religious.[4]

The Whitehall debates led to no conclusion, and Lilburne
resorted to the expedient that came naturally to him: he
published the version of the *Agreement of the People* he believed
to have been agreed upon with a short letter dated December
10.[5] He also prepared a statement of the Levellers' deep dissatisfaction called *A Plea for Common Right and Freedom*,
which, with fifteen others, he delivered into Cromwell's hands
at the Mews on December 28. The documents were connected,
for the *Plea* requested a reorganization of the Army Council
that would prevent the private's interest from being overridden,
as Lilburne conceived it had in the discussions on the *Agreement
of the People*. Although not yet suggesting the reappointment
of agitators, it attempted to guard against control of the Council
by one or two persons, evidently Cromwell and Ireton being
in the petitioners' minds. A minority of the commissioned
officers, it maintained, did not constitute a Council. Members
should sit " in a distinct orderly way, so as they may be observed
by the President when they are inclined to speak," and the
number of times a person could speak to a question should be
limited—this was surely aimed at Ireton ! Finally, the discussions in the Council should be freed of all controls and
checks by superior officers. Instead of agitators, the petitioners
offered to appoint four Levellers to attend and take part in,
though not to vote at, Council meetings: this was, in fact,
what had already been done at the Whitehall debates.

The officers finally published their version of the *Agreement
of the People* and submitted it to the Rump on January 20, 1649.
Although a measure of agreement had been reached between
officers and Levellers, there was a fundamental difference in
the spirit in which the two groups regarded the *Agreement*.
The Levellers would submit theirs direct to the people for
approval. As Lilburne said, he " adjudged it a just and reasonable thing to publish it to the view of the nation, to the end
that all men might have an opportunity to consider the equity

thereof, and offer their reasons against anything therein contained, before it be concluded." [6] The officers submitted theirs
to the Rump with the request that it be taken into consideration
and *so much of it as Parliament thought fit* be circulated among
the people.[7] The Levellers would make of the *Agreement* a
binding written constitution, emanating from the people; the
officers would make of it simply a scheme for constitutional
reform approved by the existing remnant of the Long Parliament. In fairness to the officers it had to be conceded, however, that their deference to Parliament was partly due to their
unwillingness to seem to force a settlement by the Army in
opposition to the civil power.

The same difference in spirit marked the attitude of Levellers
and officers to the new Parliament they proposed to elect. The
Levellers postulated the constant and permanent retention of
power in the people; the officers, for the term of its office,
would transfer power to Parliament. The Levellers claimed
supremacy and binding force for the *Agreement*; the officers
would allow a greater discretion to their representatives.

So far as the clauses of the *Agreement* were concerned, a
common danger had driven the two parties into substantial
accord on electoral matters. Levellers and officers agreed that
the Long Parliament should be dissolved on or before the last
day of April 1649; they agreed to biennial Parliaments, intervals
between Parliaments to be filled by a Council of State; and
they agreed, broadly speaking, to a new distribution of seats
which would redress the weight which had hitherto attached to
the counties at the expense of the boroughs and cities. Even
concerning the franchise a measure of accord had been reached.
It was agreed that electors should be persons of twenty-one and
over not receiving alms, but assessed ordinarily towards the
relief of the poor, who were not servants to or in receipt of
wages from anyone else. The Levellers would have added that
they should also have signed the *Agreement*. The principle of
the ' reserves ' remained in both *Agreements*. Religion, in the
officers' version, was not expressed in the form of a reserve, as
it continued to be in the Levellers' *Agreement*, yet it was to be
above the power of Parliament to alter. There was to be a
public profession of the Christian religion, not popery or prelacy.
Toleration would extend to all religions which did not cause

" the civil injury of others, or . . . actual disturbance of the
public peace," although it did not necessarily extend to popery
or prelacy. The Levellers maintained religion as their first
' reserve ' which would allow the representative at its discretion
to direct the nation in its worship, so long as it was not compulsive or express popery, but would allow of no compulsion
whatever " in or about matters of faith, religion, or God's
worship." Between the two schemes is all the difference
between a limited and a complete toleration, between a toleration which allows discretion to the civil magistrate to act for
the public peace, and one which places religious freedom outside
any interference from earthly authority. The many sectaries
among the Levellers could never feel secure without full freedom
of worship, and the direct action which their programme demanded would have placed the Levellers outside the scope of
the officers' toleration. At the same time, the very sincerity
with which they held their religious creed caused them to
demand, as a principle, the removal of the influence of the
magistrate from the religious sphere. Finally, as Captain Clarke
pointed out in the Whitehall debates, they might wish to reserve
religion from the magistrate at a future time when they had
lost the opportunity. It was necessary for them to act while
they had the chance, and so guard against tyranny in the future.

By the time the officers presented their version of the *Agreement* to Parliament other matters were pressing for priority, and
with Parliament's non-committal acceptance of the document
the matter was shelved. Lilburne, meanwhile, at the end of
December had ridden north on his private affairs. He could
gain nothing by staying in London. The Army now had as
much control over Parliament " as any schoolmaster had over
his boys," [8] and the Levellers had been defeated in their efforts
to mould a settlement. Before Pride's Purge they might have
worked up feeling in the country to act as a balance between
Army and Parliament. Instead their energies had been deflected
to constitution-making. Ireton had played for time and won.
Although the Whitehall debates revealed a man far less rigid
and more willing to meet the Levellers than the man at Putney,
this might have been mere expediency. His haste to reach
London, his postponement of the debates until after Pride's
Purge, the misunderstanding over the terms of the discussions,

while not necessarily making him the " Machiavilian " traitor he appeared in Lilburne's eyes, were at least the opportunism of a man who realized that time was not on his side.

While Lilburne was in the North events marched forward to the trial and execution of the King on January 30, 1649. Lilburne opposed both measures. Yet so little did his opponents understand his fundamental position that they asked him to join his brother on the High Court of Justice which was instituted by special ordinance on January 3. It was a striking testimony to their wish for unity, and perhaps to their feeling of insecurity, that they should seek the co-operation of the Leveller leader, for he had already, in the discussions that had just taken place, made his position clear. His opposition had nothing to do with sentiment, with affection for the King, with veneration for the monarchy, or any lingering influence of Sir Lewis Dyve. Nor did it indicate anything but continued hostility to all that Charles's Government stood for: it was based on a number of premises, sound and statesmanlike, concerning both the desirability of deposing the King *at that time* and the method by which he was to be brought to trial.

At the Nag's Head early in November Lilburne had already intimated that the Levellers were playing for a balance of power. However evil the King, however tyrannous the Parliament, they must be kept as a balance to the Army until the new Government was settled. With the occupation of London and the purging of the House one counterweight was gone. To abandon the King without any security would be to open the door to the rule of force, which Lilburne had feared since the spring of 1647. The people would be left solely to the " wills and swords " of the Army, he said, " by which . . . they might rule over us arbitrarily, without declared Laws, as a conquered people. . . . And besides . . . we would not trust their bare words in generall onely, for they had broke their promise once already, both with us and the Kingdom; and he that would break once, would make no conscience of breaking twice, if it served for his ends." [9] Therefore the establishment of the new Government must come first, the trial of the King afterwards.

But Lilburne also denied that the Army or the purged Parliament had any right to bring the King to trial. The Army clearly had not, for martial law applied only to soldiers. The Parliament had not. Had not Ireton himself argued in 1648 that the Long Parliament was already become a mock power, a pretended Parliament? How much more so was the doubly purged House? With a " mock Parliament," Lilburne argued, there were neither legal judges, nor Justices of the Peace, nor any legal authority in England. This being so, all those that were executed at Tyburn were murdered, and the judges or Justices that sentenced them were liable to be hanged for acting without a just and legal commission either from " true Regall " or " true Parliamentary " power. Lilburne had argued thus with the officers at Windsor. However guilty the King might be, they would be guilty of murder if they took away his life before they had established a legal authority in England. They were charging him with murder, and justice ought to be done for blood, but still it must be done justly. " For in case another man murder me, and a day, a week, or a yeer after my brother or friend that is no legal Magistrate, executes him therefore, yet this is murder in the eye of the Law, because it was done by a hand had no Authority to do it." So Lilburne pressed again and again that the King's trial should be stayed until a new and equal Parliament was elected upon the basis of the *Agreement of the People*. Then he could be tried either by Parliament itself or by judges sitting in the Court of King's Bench.

The officers asking him how a king could ever be tried by the law of the land, Lilburne replied that the law expressly laid down the penalty of death for murder, and made no exception for king, queen, or prince. When it was objected that it could hardly be proved that the King with his own hands killed a man Lilburne replied that the law of England counted the instigator as guilty as the actual perpetrator.

Of the two methods of trying the King, he preferred a trial by established law rather than by special Court set up by Parliament, for this would emphasize the ubiquity of law, making clear that no man was born lawless, and that magistrates as well as people were subject to its penalties. To try the King in an extraordinary way, that had " no reall footsteps nor paths in our Law, would be a thing of extraordinary ill Precedent; for why not twenty . . . as well as one? and why not a thousand as well as twenty? and extraordinary cases are easily made and pretended by those that are uppermost ! " [10]

Lilburne was thus on every count opposed to the High Court of Justice which the House of Commons established on January 6, 1649, to the whole of its hearing, to its verdict, and its sentence, as well as to the execution itself, which took place on January 30, while he was away in the North. It was all the more galling that as he rode home through Boroughbridge the postmaster and others should tell him that the Cavaliers of those parts were hotly incensed against him as being responsible for the murder of the King ! [11] Perhaps the fact that his brother Robert had signed the death warrant had something to do with this.

Lilburne had finally declined the offer of any estate in payment of his reparations, but asked instead for an annual rent to be fixed on delinquents' lands. An ordinance to this effect, entailed on estates in County Durham, had been passed on December 21,[12] shortly after Lilburne had left the Army Council meetings in disgust. In the Palatinate Lilburne found that Sir Arthur Haselrig, Chairman of the Committee for Sequestrations, and Chairman of the Militia Committee, was " Lord Paramount " of the district, a law to himself, even cancelling and amending instructions from London to his own wish. Sir Henry Vane was one of his associates. Both had large interests in the North, and neither family was well disposed to the Lilburnes. Richard Lilburne's expectations of becoming under-sheriff of the county had been dashed by their means, Haselrig asserting in the House of Commons that " there was never an one of the Lilburne family fit or worthy to be a Constable in England." Sir Henry Vane the elder was regarded by John as his " old bloudy enemy " from Star Chamber days, and his son was one of the " covetous earthworms " of whom Lilburne had begged Cromwell to beware. The Lilburnes warned John that Haselrig's position on the Committee for Sequestrations was quite unauthorized, and that he had recently of his own will imposed 4s. a chauldron excise upon coal, netting thereby over £100,000 a year, and that George Lilburne had incurred his displeasure by refusing to follow his example.

Lilburne stood amazed, accusing his brethren of low and

mean spirit to allow such a thing. But they only shrugged their shoulders. Arthur Haselrig was a powerful man in Army and Parliament, with soldiers at his heels; the county was unrepresented in Parliament. They advised John to see nothing and hear nothing, but to look after his own affairs. For once he acquiesced. But the count against Haselrig was stored up for future use. When Haselrig for £400 bought out his interest in some mines which were included in his reparations Lilburne was content, although he was far from satisfied with the first instalment of less than £200, which was all he could collect in rents from the lands assigned him, free quarter and taxes having " ate out the bowels, soul and life " of the estates.[13]

Lilburne returned to London bitterly disillusioned on every count, resolving to devote himself to the wellbeing of his wife and children. " I was in a kinde of deep muse with myself," he wrote, " being like an old weather-beaten ship, that would fain be in some harbour of ease and rest." This was the first time, in all his troubles, that he had spoken of turning aside from his agitation, of wanting rest. He found it now among his supporters in Southwark, where he took rooms for himself and his family in Winchester House, a large apartment house formerly the home of bishops, more recently used by Parliament as a prison, and now owned by a Mr Devennish. He paid his debts, took stock of his position, found it very unsatisfactory, and looked round for work.

The alternatives were to follow a trade or buy and farm some land in the country. Tithes, taxation, excise, and free quarter deciding him against the latter, it remained for him to take up some trade. But here also were difficulties. To follow a trade in a town he must be a freeman of the corporation, and was therefore limited to London. Various schemes presented themselves, to be one by one dismissèd. He thought of opening a shop, but this would bring him within the jurisdiction of the Court of Aldermen, and he knew himself well enough to conclude that he would constantly be in broils. He wondered if he might become coal-merchant in a small way, relying upon his Uncle George to supply him with coals from Newcastle. He considered the trade of soap-boiler, but found this also hedged round with oppressive regulations and restrictions.

There was the possibility of shipping cloth, which he had considered in 1646, but the Merchant Adventurers' monopoly still stood in the way of free trade. Lilburne determined, nevertheless, to try shipping in a Dutch boat, risking the opposition of the Merchant Adventurers. He swore that if they attempted to take away his goods he would board the ship " with half a dozen lusty resolved blades " and with his own hand " give the chief Monopolizer a brace of pistoll bullets in his guts," and then run the hazard of a " tryal at common Law."

" Not without the extraordinariest necessity," he determined, would he " engage in any publick contests." [14] But from Southwark the towers of Westminster were too easily seen. So experienced a navigator as Lilburne could not forbear seeing " how things stood at the helm." His observations brought him little satisfaction. The Rump, still referring to itself as " being chosen by and representing the people," although not more than ninety members were sitting in the House in January 1649, as against four hundred and ninety in November 1640, proceeded to establish the forms of a new government. Its declarations of February 6 that the House of Lords was " useless and dangerous," and of the 7th that the monarchy was " unnecessary, burdensome, and dangerous to the Liberty, Safety and public Interest of the People of this Nation," which might have heralded an appeal to the people, were followed instead on February 13 by a nominated Council of State, each member thereof binding himself to concur in " the settling of the government of this nation for the future in the way of a republic without King or House of Lords." Again, this might have been preliminary to representative government on a wide franchise, as envisaged in the *Agreement of the People*. But the new Republic made no sign, and those who had fought to set a kingdom free were saddled with a Rump and a Council of State.

Lilburne bit his lip, but said little, and went to no meeting. Some of his friends misunderstood. Not realizing how little his reparations had amounted to, they thought he had satisfied himself and then deserted the Cause. But if they needed reminding, nothing more surely showed that he was the old John Lilburne still than his scornful refusal of a post in

Government service on the grounds that to accept would be to support " so unjust and illegal a fabrick as . . . an everlasting Parliament purged twice by force of Arms." [15]

In spite of his resolution, he was attracted again to Westminster by the trials of five Royalist peers captured during the second Civil War. The High Court of Justice set up by Parliament on February 3 to try them was as illegal in his eyes as the court that tried the King—and even more damaging to liberty, for it created the precedent of bringing commoners to justice in this way. He listened to the hearing day after day with deep distress. The prisoners sought the advice of the renowned expounder of the law, who had so often confounded his judges on similar issues. Lilburne urged they should claim lack of jurisdiction of the court, and so delay the trial until a new Parliament was called. Upon which plea, he said, " I could willingly have ventured my heart bloud for them, because my interest, and the interest of all the free and honest men in England was as much concerned in that fatall president of that abominable and wicked Court, as Capell's or Hamilton's." He was disappointed that the prisoners would not do this, and would not therefore act as counsel, but willingly lent them legal books and papers, proffered advice, and even risked his own freedom by offering to appear in court as witness for them.

" Stout Capel," as Lilburne several times called him, chose to act himself before he was assigned counsel, " and so gallantly and acutely to plead the Law, and demand the benefit of it," that he won the sincere admiration of the Leveller leader. Lilburne might, indeed, have been his model as he cited statutes and the Petition of Right, " looking round about him, and saying, ' I am an Englishman, and the Law is my inheritance, and the benefit of the Petition of Right my Birth-right,' " and demanding of the President, " Where's my Jury? I see none of my Jury, that is to pass upon me, I demand the sight of my Jury legally empannelled, as my right by Law, without the verdict of whom I cannot in Law be condemned. . . . I hope you will not deny me the benefit of the Law, which you pretend you have fought this seven years to maintain."

Lilburne knew what the answer would be. His heart sank within him, he recounted, his spirit was inwardly full of fire, and he could barely contain himself from crying out in open court to hear the flagrant refusal of elementary justice to the prisoners. On March 6 all five were condemned to death, two were reprieved, but on the 9th Hamilton, Holland, and " stout Capel " were beheaded before the gate of Westminster Hall, Capel maintaining with his last words his faith in the Thirty-nine Articles and the monarchy. All Lilburne could do was to record Capel's plea in court, which he did as effectively as if he were reporting one of his own stands for liberty.[16]

He returned to Winchester House in perplexity of spirit, and resolved anew to remain solitary at home. But this was not easily done. His fame as expounder of the law had spread, and people flocked to him for advice and help, so that he was " grievously tormented " at their distress and his inability to help them. His house became " a torment " to him, and he was forced again to Westminster. There he heard the rumour that the Council of Officers was threatening civilians with martial law and about to take strong measures against him and the Whaleboneers.[17] This was the last straw. Within four days he was back at the bar of the House with several friends bearing a petition with the challenging title *Englands New Chains*.

CHAPTER TWENTY-TWO

" *England's New Chains* "

We were before ruled by King, Lords, and Commons; now by
a General, a Court Martial, and House of Commons: and we
pray you what is the difference?

The Hunting of the Foxes, March 21, 1649

*T*HE ACTION OF THE COUNCIL OF OFFICERS THAT BROUGHT
Lilburne back into the contest arose from the discontent of
the soldiers at the end of the second civil war. They had
fought without reservation a second time, but still looked in
vain for the satisfaction they had been denied previously. The
execution of " the man of blood " and the erection of the
Council of State brought relief no nearer. By February 1649
they were petitioning the Rump on the old lines, demanding
pay, arrears, the removal of free quarter, the abolition of
tithes, law reform, and provision for the poor. They also
expressed their determination, as soldiers, not to infringe
people's rights as citizens, and requested that they should not
be required to execute civil ordinances such as " seizing upon
unlicensed books or Printing Presses, or in distraining for
moneys, or the like . . . that so people may have no cause to
complain . . . of our intrenchment upon their liberties " [1]—a
significant comment upon the methods of the young Commonwealth.

While they also demanded the reinstatement of the Council
of the Army on the representative lines laid down at Triploe
Heath, rumours were spreading of the re-election of agitators
and of the presence of ' London agents ' with the troops. The
officers had for some time been considering the alarming
question of " those . . . not of the army " who " endeavour to
breed . . . discontent." [2] They now replied to the soldiers'
petition by announcing that since " some evill, scandalous, and
cashiered persons " not of the Army were " working some

discontent in the army," private meetings of officers and soldiers were forbidden, and petitioning allowed only through the officers. At the same time they would seek powers to punish by martial law civilians who dared " to indeavour to breede any discontent in the army ": " we can hang twenty before they will hang one," Colonel Hewson was reported as saying.[3] " And thus," remarked Lilburne bitterly, " after these fair blossoms of hopeful liberty, breaks forth this bitter fruit, of the vilest and basest bondage that ever English men groan'd under." [4] It was then that his resolutions were cast aside— " my spirit was all on fire," he said [5]—and on February 26 he reappeared at the bar of the House with *Englands New Chains*, in presenting which he made a short and restrained speech explaining it had been prepared in a few days, and that fear of arrest had kept him from circulating it for signature.

Its attack took two forms. It opposed the officers' *Agreement*, it wanted a guarantee against the restoration of monarchy or House of Lords, and a curb to the power of the Council of State; it asked that the Government's policy on law and religion should be made absolutely clear. At the same time it took up concrete issues. Where is that good, it asked, " or where is that liberty so much pretended, so deerly purchased? If we look upon what this House hath done since it hath voted it self the Supreme Authority, and disburthened themselves of the power of the Lords ? " A High Court of Justice instead of trial by jury; a Member of Parliament questioned concerning his religion; an Act for the impressment of seamen; ordinances against printing reinforced; new fees imposed in lawsuits; imprisonment for debt. " And lastly, for compleating this new kind of liberty, a Councel of State is hastily erected " with supreme power. Repeating all their former grievances—tithes, " that great oppression of the Countries' industry and hindrance of Tillage," excise and customs, " those secret thieves, and Robbers, Drainers of the poor and middle sort of People," monopolies, " the hinderers and decayers of Clothing," it begged for a new Parliament, the practice of the Self-denying Ordinance, a committee to examine questions concerning the Army, including its dis-bandment; the opening of the press, the reduction of law

costs, and, above all, the dissolution of the Council of State
and the management of business by committees " frequently
and exactly accountable for the discharge of their trusts."
The Moderate immediately printed both the pamphlet and
Lilburne's speech at the bar.[6]

The soldiers were hard on the heels of the civilians.   On
March 1 they sent eight troopers to deliver their protest to
the General and the Council of Officers, asserting the soldiers'
right to petition and asking the fundamental question, " Is
it not the Souldier that endureth the heat and burden of the
day, and performeth that work whereof the officers beareth the
glory and name? " [7]   The speed with which the Council of
Officers acted demonstrated the truth of Hewson's claim.
While Parliament ' considered ' *Englands New Chains*, the
Council of Officers court-martialled the eight troopers, and in
Palace Yard on the 6th cashiered five of them.   A fortnight
later appeared the memorable pamphlet *The Hunting of the
Foxes from New-Market and Triploe Heaths to Whitehall, by
five small Beagles*, being a recital of the officers' treatment of
the soldiers from the Engagement of Triploe Heath to the
cashiering of the five men.   Although the " five small beagles "
purported to be the five troopers, it is highly likely that John
Lilburne had a hand in the pamphlet.   When the five men
were examined by the Council of Officers concerning the
pamphlet and one said he would like time to write his reply
Colonel Hewson exclaimed, " Yes—and then he that wrote
the other can write that too! "

The Hunting of the Foxes complained bitterly of " the old
cheat, the transmutation of names," and asked the question
that would soon be on every one's lips : " We were before
ruled by King, Lords, and Commons; now by a General, a
Court Martial, and House of Commons; and we pray you
what is the difference? "

Lilburne was by now in the thick of the fight, his resolution
to devote himself to his private affairs having lasted for about
two months.   On Sunday, March 24, he was reading aloud a
new petition to a great crowd before Winchester House, who
found the entertainment more enjoyable than the forbidden
stage plays.   It went by the same name as the previous
pamphlet, for no title could more aptly express what he felt

about the Commonwealth—*Englands New Chains*, Part II. The crowd was hot behind when he presented it to the Commons on the same day. This time the House took courage from the Army and hastily issued a Declaration and Order that it was " false, scandalous, and reproachful . . . highly seditious, and destructive to the present Government, and tends to division and mutiny in the army, and the raising of a new war," and that the authors were guilty of high treason and should be proceeded against as traitors. The Council of State on the same day passed its instructions to Sergeant Dendy to provide himself with drum, trumpet, and a guard and make proclamation against the authors at Cheapside, the Exchange, and the Spittle in Southwark. That night the post was to be searched for copies of the pamphlet, and all letters containing it were to be stopped. Two days later the Proclamation was ordered to be made in all the market towns of England.

There is evidence here both of the wide and organized circulation of the pamphlet and the difficulty in stopping it. That the Levellers had carefully planned its dissemination is indicated by a newspaper report that Lilburne, with Henry Marten, had sent emissaries—" some pokey saints of their own propagation "—into many counties, Hertfordshire, Berkshire (Marten's own county), Hampshire, being named, to proclaim Lilburne's address and to urge the people to oppose any power which forced them to pay excise " and other unnecessary Rates and unreasonable Taxes."

On the 26th the Council of State sought for means to reply, and instructed John Milton, the newly appointed Secretary for Foreign Tongues, to do so.[8] On the 28th, between four and five o'clock in the morning, Winchester House was beset by over a hundred horse and foot soldiers, many of whom forced their way into Lilburne's rooms, took him prisoner, and marched him through the streets of the City to St Paul's. Here, also in custody, Lilburne found Thomas Prince and, to his surprise, William Walwyn, for Walwyn had not been a party to the Leveller meetings since the breakdown of the discussions on the *Agreement of the People* the previous December. After drinking " their morning draughts " at a near-by inn they were taken on by boat to Whitehall, where they were joined by Richard Overton, and the four men, whose arrests had all

been equally violent, were brought before the Council of State
at about four o'clock in the afternoon.

The prisoners were each called before the Council twice.
Lilburne marched into the room with his hat on, but, per-
ceiving Members of Parliament to be present, removed it out
of deference to the Commons.   He protested, nevertheless,
that the Council had no power to try him, for since the House
itself had no executive power it could not delegate it.   The
President assured the prisoner that the Council claimed no
jurisdiction over him, but when they asked if he was the author
of *Englands New Chains* Lilburne protested vigorously against
what he termed the revival of the Star Chamber practice of
questioning upon interrogatories, and refused to answer.   " I
know not what you intend to do with me," he told the Council,
" neither do I much care; having learned long since to dy,
and rather for my Liberties, than in my bed."

While his friends were being examined Lilburne made use
of the opportunity to repeat his remarks to the people who had
gathered outside the court door.   After their second examination, however, the prisoners were ushered into a room where
there was no audience.   Lilburne therefore occupied himself
with listening at the keyhole, and was rewarded by hearing
Cromwell " thumping his fist upon the Councel table until it
rang again and saying, ' I tel you Sir, you have no other Way
to deale with these men, but to break them in pieces . . . if you
do not break them, they will break you ! ' "   Hearing which,
recounted Lilburne, " the blood ran up and down my veines
and I heartily wisht my self in againe amongst them, being
scarse able to contain my self."

The sentence was commitment to the Tower on the suspicion
of high treason.   The four men at once defined their attitude
to the prison system by appointing Walwyn to speak for them
and inform the Lieutenant that they were resolved not to part
with an inch of their freedoms that by struggling they could
keep, and therefore would pay no fees or chamber rent above
that prescribed by law, and would neither eat nor drink at
their own charge.   " So now I have brought the Reader to
my old and contented Lodging in the Tower," remarked
Lilburne cheerfully in his account of the affair.[9]

The publication which caused such anxiety, and for which

they were committed, was a vigorous and comprehensive attack upon the Army grandees. It told of their apostacy from their original ideals, their campaign against the agitators, their trafficking with the King, their use of force against the City and of martial law against civilians, their subjection of the civil authority by force of arms, so that the House of Commons had become " but the Channell through which is conveyed all the Decrees and Determinations of a private Councell of some few officers," who muzzled the press and bribed judges for their purposes. " According to the maxime of Politicians, they judge themselves loose, where other men are bound . . . everything is good and just only, as it is conducing to their corrupt and ambitious interests." The result was that " the most hopefull opportunity that ever England had for recovery of her Freedome was spent and consumed, in . . . uncertaine, staggering motions, and arbitrary, irrationall Proceedings."

It was a heavy indictment, and merited the care which the Government took to prevent its circulation. It was impossible, however, to suppress anything in which Lilburne was concerned. Not only had he ensured an initial advertisement by reading it aloud on the day of publication, which, probably by arrangement, was a Sunday, but *The Moderate* gave full publicity to the proceedings of the House and Council, and announced that 40,000 people would support the pamphlet. The proclamations ordered by the authorities attracted large crowds, and in one case at least an entire force of fifty troopers refused their sergeant's request to read the required refutation of the Levellers.[10] Throughout April and early May petitions for the Levellers' release poured into Parliament from the citizens and women of London and from the districts and counties around. Those of April 2 and 16 were said to bear 10,000 signatures each,[11] and the presenting of each petition was also a Leveller demonstration in which the sea-green emblem was prominent. The press sang of " the bonny Besses in the sea-green dresses," of petitions for " honest John o' the Tower." [12] On one occasion the House of Commons told women petitioners " That the Matter they petitioned about, was of an higher concernment than they understood . . . and therefore desired them to go home, and look after their own business,

and meddle with their huswifry." [13]   The result was a miniature
riot as the women's tongues "pelted hail-shot against the
Members as they passed to and fro." One of the Members
they seized, not releasing him until he swore he was for the
liberties of the people.[14]   On May 5 they wrote a reply, asking
"can you imagine us to be so sottish or stupid, as not to
perceive . . . when dayly those strong defences of our Peace
and wellfare are broken down? . . . Would you have us keep at
home in our houses, when men of such faithfullnesse and
integrity as the Four Prisoners our friends in the Tower, are
fetcht out of their beds, and forced from their Houses by
Souldiers, to the affrighting and undoing of themselves, their
wives, children, and families?" [15]

The Levellers were by no means the only agitators in the
field.   The breaking down of regal government fanned the
sparks of many smouldering ideas that normally would have
been quietly smothered.   The Fifth Monarchists—people who
believed that after the overthrow of the four monarchies of
the ancient world the Fifth Monarchy of Christ would be
established—took the execution of the King as their sign, and
petitioned the Council of Officers for government by the godly.[16]
There were also a group of reformers calling themselves "the
true Levellers" who were being nurtured on the mystical
writings of Gerrard Winstanley.   At the beginning of 1649
Winstanley's visions became more practical, and on April 1
he, with William Everard and a group which grew to some
twenty people, began digging the common land of St George's
Hill in Surrey, saying they were acting upon Winstanley's
vision that the common people should sow and reap the
common land, "work together; eat bread together."

There was local opposition to the Diggers, though a reporter
for the Army declared their enterprise "not worth . . . taking
notice of."   By the following spring they had built several houses
and were supported by a similar enterprise in Northamptonshire.   But in April 1650 their local opponents destroyed their
buildings, turned cattle into their sprouting grain—the visible
mark of the success of their digging—and turned their families
on to the heath.   These simple men, planning a simple agrarian
communism that would start with the waste lands, received
more opposition from small local landowners than from the

Council of State or from the Army, who only perfunctorily
sent a few soldiers to help quell the disturbances they caused
among the local farmers.[17]

The Diggers were only one manifestation of the poverty
and discontent which still existed from one end of the country
to the other. From London, Lancashire, Cumberland, West-
morland, Somerset, Buckinghamshire, Gloucestershire, Dorset,
the petitions and complaints came pouring in. One, more
practical than most, asked that the petition be read in parish
churches and that all subscriptions be sent to the house of
William Wallis, a hosier, in Aldgate, London.[18] Small wonder
that Cromwell, at a meeting of the Council of Officers on the
23rd, harped upon his ever-present fear. " I thinke there is
more cause of danger from disunion amongst ourselves then
by any thinge from our enemies," he said.[19]

Cromwell might have gained some comfort by the fact that
there was dissension also in the Leveller ranks. Two years
previously the Independents of Goodwin's congregation had
become lukewarm and withdrawn the financial and other
support they had been giving to Leveller petitioners. Now
Independent and Baptist congregations more decisively severed
their connexion with the Levellers. They were among the few
whom the Commonwealth settlement had guided to a safe
haven. Being now free from prelate and presbyter, they were
prepared to ignore the economic and social shortcomings of
the new system, and wished to end strife.

To the Levellers' dismay, their congregations not only
refused to support the second part of *Englands New Chains*,
but their ministers drew up their own petition, which a deputation presented to Parliament on April 2. To add to Lilburne's
sorrow, one of the signatories was Edmond Rosier, his pastor
when he first came to London, and one of the deputation was
William Kiffin, with whom, years before, he had wrestled for
the Lord when they were both young apprentices seeking for
signs of grace.[20]

Although the Baptists sent Samuel Richardson to the Tower
to plead with the Levellers for unity, the four maintained their
position, offering, Lilburne-like, to debate it and continuing
the publication of Leveller pamphlets. Lilburne, Overton, and
Prince each contributed to *The Picture of the Councel of State* a

lively account of their arrest and their stand before the court,
Walwyn giving his in *The Fountain of Slaunder*. On April 14
A Manifestation anticipated the attack which was launched
a few weeks later as *Walwins Wiles ; or, The Manifestators
Manifested*, a title which indicated that Walwyn was once
again drawing much abuse to himself. On May 1 a new and
final version of the *Agreement of the People* was published from
the Tower, where John Lilburne and his " brave comrades "
were said to " sit close in Councell every day." [21]

The four prisoners, who all signed the *Agreement*, announced
it as " the ultimate end and full scope " of their desires for
reform. The troubles which led to the Civil War had been
caused by uncertain government and arbitrary power. It was
necessary for government to be certain, known, and bounded.
The Long Parliament must therefore be dissolved and new
elections take place immediately. Nothing was said about
presenting the *Agreement* to the people or making its acceptance
a condition of voting, but the general constitutional clauses
were similar to those of the preceding *Agreements*. There
should be annual Parliaments of not more than 400 Members,
of whom 200 could form a quorum. In any adjournment,
which could not exceed two months at a time, affairs should
be managed by a committee of their number, acting under
detailed, and published, instructions from the Parliament.

Members of Parliament, who would receive salaries, should
be persons of twenty-one and over who were not servants or in
receipt of alms, who were not members of the legal profession
or holders of public appointments, and they would not be
eligible for consecutive Parliaments. The electorate should
consist of persons of twenty-one and over not servants or in
receipt of alms. Royalists were disabled both from voting and
from membership of the Government for ten years.

Fear of the power of an elected representative, even if its life
were only for one year, was still strong, and the new *Agreement*
endeavoured to define the powers of the representative. It
should conduct foreign affairs and foreign trade, preserve the
" safeguards and securities " contained in the Petition of Right,
raise money and perform all things " evidently conducing " to
" the enlargement of . . . freedom, redress of grievances, and
prosperity of the Commonwealth."

The 'reserves' reappear, but this time to the number of eighteen ! The reserved subjects of religion, impressment, questioning for acts done during the war, and action contrary to, or destructive of, the *Agreement* appear much as in earlier *Agreements*. But to these are added a series of restrictions which amount to the points of the Leveller programme expressed in negatives. The Representative should not make laws restricting trade, nor continue customs or excise or tithes, nor deprive a person of the privileges of the Petition of Right— and so on to the thirtieth and final point of the *Agreement*, which stipulates that it shall not be in the power of any Representative to alter any part of the *Agreement*, " nor level mens Estates, destroy Propriety, or make all things Common." That this particular disavowal of the charge of social levelling should be expressed with such force in their programme at this time indicates not only their dislike of the charge, but their fear of the damage it was doing their cause. Their *Manifestation* had been similarly emphatic.

But it did not affect Cromwell's reaction to the new *Agreement*. He was so incensed against Lilburne that at Sir Peter Temple's he " professed passionately the Kingdome could never be setled so long as Lilburne was alive, and that either he would stop his mouth or burst his Gall, rather than run the hazard of such discontents and mutinies as are dayly contracted in the Army by meanes of his Seditious scribling." [22] Cromwell's fear of discontents and mutinies in the Army was not unfounded.

CHAPTER TWENTY-THREE

Mutiny

[The Commons] were mindful of John Lilburne . . . taking it
for granted that these Disorders and Mutinies were all occasioned by his meanes.

Mercurius Elencticus, May 7–14, 1649

*T*HE YOUNG COMMONWEALTH WAS FACED WITH NO EASY TASK.
Royalists in France, the Low Countries, and Scotland had
acknowledged the Prince as Charles II and were plotting to
restore him to his father's throne. Rupert, in charge of the
Royalist ships, was planning to use Ireland as a base for operations against England. The Army, in such circumstances,
could not be disbanded, but neither could the Commonwealth
conjure from a lean purse the money with which to pay it. A
reassessment on the counties only exasperated civilians without
settling arrears or appreciably easing free quarter, and paid
only a fraction of current wages.

Attempts to recruit soldiers for the Irish service were causing
discontent, but the trouble actually started in April 1649 over
the question of pay, when about sixty men of Captain Savage's
troop of Colonel Whalley's regiment, led by Robert Lockier,
seized the regimental colours and barricaded themselves in the
Bull Inn in Bishopsgate Street, refusing to move or surrender
the colours until they had been satisfied. When Fairfax and
Cromwell arrived some of the men had already submitted,
fifteen were easily taken into custody, and the rest dispersed.
Court martial on April 26 sentenced six of these to death, but,
following their petition for mercy, all but Lockier were pardoned.
Lockier then retracted his submission and denounced the court
which had tried him as tyrannical.

Robert Lockier was twenty-three years old, had served in
the Army since he was sixteen, and had already given active
support to the Levellers, being an agitator and one of those

who at Ware tried to push matters to a climax. He was said to be " a pious man, and of excellent parts, and much beloved." Petitions for his reprieve from citizens, and from Lilburne and Overton, were of no effect. It was clearly felt that the death of Lockier would nip in the bud a fresh mutiny and rid the Army of a dangerous Leveller. The effect, however, was the contrary. For Lockier proved to be of the stuff of heroes. After joining his fellows in their petition for mercy, not one word of supplication or appeal was heard from him.

His sisters and cousins accompanied him to St Paul's on Friday, April 27. He spoke cheerfully to them and others gathered round, finally addressing himself to the firing squad: " I did not think that you had such heathenish and barbarous principles in you, as to obey your Officers in murthering of me, when I stand up for nothing but what is for your good," he said. Asked if he would have his eyes covered, Lockier replied that his cause was so just that he feared not the face of death. Then, addressing his last words to the crowds, he said, " I pray you, let not this death of mine be a discouragement, but rather an incouragement; for never man died more comfortably then I do." And so Robert Lockier " died a very Martyr for the Liberties of England." [1]

In shooting a mutineer the Government had indeed created a martyr, to follow in the footsteps of Richard Arnold, shot at Ware. Lockier was given by the Levellers the funeral honours of a General. About a thousand soldiers paced before the hearse in files of five or six; the coffin itself, carried by six soldiers in mourning dress, was covered with a black cloth on which were sprigs of rosemary dipped in blood, and, in the middle, the dead trooper's naked sword. Behind came his horse, draped in black and led by footmen in mourning suit and cloak, while on either side marched three trumpeters. Lockier's kindred, with some two or three thousand citizens and soldiers, followed in orderly file, ranks of women bringing up the rear. All the attendants wore, besides the black ribbons of mourning, the sea-green of the Levellers. At the churchyard thousands more waited, most wearing the sea-green emblem. As the slow-pacing procession made its way through the streets, the trumpets announcing a soldier's funeral, the route became thronged with spectators, some of whom derided the mourners as Levellers, but others were heard to remark that King Charles when interred had not half so many mourners as this trooper. No disturbance was intended or occurred. It was a ceremony of consecration, and, the " sad service being performed, they returned every man to his own habitation." [2]   Nevertheless, as Whitelocke staidly remarked, many looked upon the funeral procession itself " as an affront to the Parliament and Army," [3] and *Mercurius Pragmaticus* more exultantly declared that the demonstration had sufficed " to let Cromwell and Fairfax both know . . . that this is not the way to crush the Free People of this Nation." [4]

The funeral of Lockier was the preliminary to widespread troubles in the regiments destined for Ireland. As in 1647, the question was asked: If we are neglected while undivided and in this country, how much worse will be our lot when divided and some of us in Ireland? In Somersetshire the soldiers were coupling their demands for pay with the name of John Lilburne and urging " a new Representative . . . which shall make Laws, alter such as are amisse, ease the subject," and leave religion free.[5]   Printed sheets appeared reminding the soldiers ". . . you Engaged not as a meer Mercenary Army, hyred to serve the Arbytrarie ends of a Councel of State; but took up Armes in Judgment and Conscience, in behalf of your own, and the Peoples just Rights and Liberties." [6]

Mutiny came to a head simultaneously in Salisbury and Banbury. Once again Lilburne had to watch from the Tower while the soldiers acted.

Colonel Scroop's men at Salisbury announced on May 1 that they were tired of waiting for the promised redress, that they had not left their trades and callings, spent the prime of their youth, exposed themselves to danger, and spent their estates merely in order to be deprived of their just rights by a Council of State instead of by a King.[7]   Six days later, after much preliminary propaganda, a rendezvous was called by Captain Reynolds' and other troops at Banbury, which was joined by Captain Smith and his county troop and most of the regiment of Colonel Henry Marten, the Leveller Member of Parliament. At Banbury William Thompson, a Leveller agent who already had caused trouble, was the ringleader, drawing all men after him, as the newspapers reported. At

Coventry he was less successful, for the gates of the city were closed to him, but at Towcester he seized the postmaster, and sent him to London on his parole to intercede for three Levellers taken while posting bills at Banbury.

In a spirited indictment of the Government—*Englands Standard Advanced* [8]—unanimously agreed to at the Banbury rendezvous, Thompson and the Levellers accused it of failing to keep faith with the nation on every count. The issue of this pamphlet, the declaration from Salisbury, the discovery of printed Leveller literature in the West and Midlands, the presence of Thompson with the mutineers, the issue at that time of the new *Agreement of the People* from the Tower, evidenced something more than a spontaneous resentment. When Thompson's men were seen wearing papers in their hats similar to those worn at the Ware rendezvous in 1647, with the inscription

> For a New Parliament
> By the Agreement of the People

a widespread Leveller plot was no longer doubted. It was reported that agitators were now again in every regiment.[9] Ireton's regiment joined Scroop's men at Salisbury. The day after news of this revolt reached London came reports of a rally of Levellers at Aylesbury. On the same day, May 9, Cromwell called a rendezvous of his and Fairfax's regiments in Hyde Park before marching against the mutineers. Some appeared at the rendezvous with the sea-green emblem in their hats. Many announced they would not fight their fellow-soldiers. Cromwell spoke to them as he had done many times before, roughly commanding those who wore the sea-green badges to remove them. But at the same time he declared the great care and pains which Parliament was exercising against many difficulties. And, he concluded, those who no longer liked the service were at liberty to lay down their arms and be paid their arrears even as those who remained. When he had finished most of the sea-green emblems were on the ground and the regiments docile. The following day they left for the West.[10]

Before they left London, however, Cromwell and Fairfax had secured their rear. This was all the more necessary because of rumours of an attack on the Tower to release Lilburne and his friends. Debating the mutiny on the 8th, the Commons " were mindful of John Lilburne . . . taking it for granted that these Disorders and Mutinies were all occasioned by his meanes." [11] Consequently, 400 men of Pride's and Hewson's regiments, known to be hostile to Lilburne, were on the same day sent to guard the Tower and prevent all confluences of people there. Lilburne and his friends were segregated and deprived of pen, ink, and paper, and all visitors, except their wives and servants, were denied them.[12]

When Cromwell and Fairfax left London on the 10th the whole of Colonel Scroop's and most of Ireton's regiments, both quartered near Salisbury, had declared for the Levellers, and were hoping to be joined by Colonel Harrison's regiment from Aylesbury, and from the Banbury area by most of Colonel Reynolds' regiment, some of Colonel Marten's men, Captain Smith's Oxfordshire troop, and other local men. The three bodies were to join forces north of Salisbury before marching westward. There was serious defection in both Banbury and Aylesbury, however. No more than twenty men rode in with Scroop's regiment at Salisbury, while only two troops of Harrison's regiment joined them at Sunningwell, between Abingdon and Oxford. Fairfax, by this time, was between the Levellers and Buckinghamshire, so, abandoning hope of winning more of Harrison's men, they wheeled sharply west towards Newbridge, on the Thames. They numbered about 1200 men and had twelve colours. Continuing on the south side of the river, they forded the Thames near Faringdon and made their way to Burford, where they quartered for the night, imagining they were safe from attack.

But by a splendid effort of marching the pursuing forces turned north-westward and reached Burford by midnight on May 14, only a few hours after the weary Levellers had turned in to rest. Cromwell, who was in command, immediately fell on the mutineers, aided, as the Levellers afterwards asserted, by the treachery of Quartermaster More, who was that night in charge of the guard, and of Cornet Denne, who appointed him. Taken by surprise and with their weapons laid by for the night, the Levellers had little chance of resistance. From a few windows came a little desultory shooting, but there was only one centre of active resistance—the Crowne Inn, in the centre of the town, where Sheep Street joins the High Street. Here Colonel Eyres, ex-Army officer and friend of Harry Marten, led a desperate little resistance, during which one man was killed and two wounded, before being himself taken prisoner.

Of the 1200 mutineers, many hundreds escaped, most of whom dispersed. Some 400 were captured or surrendered, and were imprisoned by Cromwell in Burford Church while a Council of War the following day condemned them to death. Some of the Levellers remained at first resolute, saying, " It is our day to-day, it may be yours tomorrow." But when, having waited in idleness and suspense, the news of the death sentence was brought they needed little persuasion to put their names to a petition of penitence. Wandering round the church, thinking of their plight, of their friends and families, perhaps of Free-born John and his teaching, many of the prisoners helped to pass the hours by scribbling or cutting their names on the woodwork and stonework of the church. In this way one at least has won immortality, for round the lead lining to the font in Burford Church, among many initials and scratchings scarce distinguishable, stands out clearly the deeply and carefully cut inscription *Anthony Sedley Prisner*, 1649.

The court martial selected four of the ringleaders to be shot as an example to the others, and on Thursday, May 17, the third day after the surprisal, Cromwell had the 400 prisoners out on to the leads of the church to witness the execution. There they could face away over the churchyard to the river and fields beyond. But against the west wall of the churchyard they could see the execution of their comrades. One was reprieved, but the other three died bravely upholding their cause, and *The Moderate* reported them honourably.[13]

William Thompson escaped and, riding north, rallied another centre of resistance, fighting with much bravery until he was killed. A Royalist newspaper, half in jest, but with some respect, called him " the great Achylles, or that Alexander of the Levellers, who wanted nothing but a Royal Cause, and a better Fortune, to have built himself a Monument as large as either of those." [14]

There remained many unco-ordinated centres of discontent

which served to indicate the extent of the design against the
Commonwealth Government. The mutineers had apparently
expected most support from the West, where they had agents
at work who, reported Whitelocke, "took much with the
people." The day after the executions in Burford churchyard
came news that 1500 Somersetshire clubmen were advancing to
join the Levellers.[15] On the same day a Leveller pamphlet
appeared in Bristol over the date "the Year of intended Parity,
1649." In June officers of the garrison at Bristol were examined
by a committee of officers; Major Cobbett was dismissed his
command, and Captain Rogers committed to prison.[16] The
presence of Cobbett at Bristol was in itself a sign of Leveller
activity, for it was probably the same Major Robert Cobbett
who had joined Lilburne in presenting the *Plea* to Cromwell
in December 1648. At Oxford, meantime, plotting was continuing not unaided by Colonel Eyres, the Leveller taken at
Burford and transferred to Oxford for trial.

In Lancaster Levellers were imprisoned at the end of May
on the charge of attempting to seize the castle.[17] From
Yorkshire came news that the Levellers were strong, and that
only with difficulty had the General prevented the seizure of
York Castle. Riots and disorders by mutinous soldiers caused
the Council of State to fear that they were "fomented by some
that lay these disorders as a foundation to greater." [18] From
Chester came news that the garrison had been much impressed
by the soldiers who had escaped from Burford. The House
of Commons issued orders for the apprehending of all concerned in the rebellion who had not been issued with a pass
by the General, and for the issue of Commissions of Oyer
and Terminer into the counties of Oxfordshire and Northamptonshire for the trial of all taken in arms against the Commonwealth.[19] They had already passed a new Treason Act, which
became law on May 14, the day the mutineers reached Burford,
and included a new clause making it treasonable for civilians
to stir up mutiny in the Army.[20] At this point a final reasoned
appeal was published by *The Moderate* at the end of June.
"Ye have subdued the outward and more visible strength of
the Levellers," it said, but "Be pleased to bethink your selves
in time, of making another conquest over them, by overthrowing their more inward strength. I mean their Reason" [21]

The Council of State tried to do this when it instructed John Milton to draft a reply to *Englands New Chains*. Since he produced nothing, John Frost again took up the pen against them, and on June 2 published the first part of *The Discoverer*. Answers came smartly from the prisoners themselves and from their friends, Lilburne's reply being *The Legall Fundamentall Liberties* of June 8, which spanned his life from youth to the beginning of 1649 in one of the longest and most impressive of his works. While these polemics continued there appeared one day in Lilburne's room in the Tower Hugh Peters. Whether his visit was part of the campaign to influence the Levellers, whether he was spying, as Lilburne believed, or whether, as he himself asserted, he just dropped in casually, the two men were soon deep in argument, in spite of the fact that his visit interrupted Lilburne's dinner with his wife. With Parliament's published *Declarations*, Coke's *Institutes*, and other law books ranged round the walls of his prison room, Lilburne was more than a match for Peters. When the chaplain remarked on the power of the sword in England Lilburne took the opportunity to read at length from Pym's speech in the Commons on the potency of law, and when Peters left it was with a message from Lilburne: " Tell your masters from me, That if it were possible for me now to chuse, I had rather chuse to live seven years under old King Charles his government (notwithstanding their beheading him as a Tyrant for it) when it was at the worst before this Parliament, then live one year under their present Government that now rule: nay, let me tell you, If they go on with that tyranny they are in, they will make Prince Charles have friends enow, not only to cry him up, but also really to fight for him, to bring him into his Father's throne." [22]

The Burford defeat had added another count to the charges laid against Cromwell and Ireton, and Lilburne was preparing a long impeachment against them when in July his wife and three children fell ill of the smallpox. The elder boy was calling for his father, and from July 18 Lilburne was allowed bail to visit his family. To his great grief his two sons died, but his wife and daughter, after being seriously ill, recovered. Lilburne, still allowed bail, took up his writing and resolved to be prodigal of his pen and his life, " being I am in manner a weary of any thing I can see abroad." He not only had to bear the death of his children, " a greater tryal of my dependence upon God, then ever I had in my life," but had to bear the reproaches of friends and family, " a company like Jobs, with many other bitter ones." If he blamed himself for his children's death he was the more determined to give renewed life to his Cause. He held up publication of the *Impeachment* in the hope of a compromise, but when it was published on August 10, addressed to his friends meeting at the Whalebone, it revealed a bitter man.[23]

An Impeachment of High Treason
by John Lilburne

O Crumwell ! O Ireton ! how hath a little time and successe changed the honest shape of so many Officers !

The Hunting of the Foxes, March 21, 1649

LILBURNE BY THIS TIME SAW THE SUCCESSIVE STAGES IN THE war as steps designed by the principal actors for their own ends. The " King's party for his Will and Prerogative . . . the Presbyterians for their . . . Covenant . . . the Independents for the peoples Liberties "—each was " meerly no more but Self in the highest." The final step was " to set up the false Saint, and most desperate Apostate murderer and traytor, Oliver Cromwell . . . to be King of England." [1]

Two pamphlets in particular focused the charges against Cromwell and Ireton—*The Hunting of the Foxes* of March 21 and *An Impeachment of High Treason against Oliver Cromwell and . . . Ireton*, completed by July 17, but not published until August 10 because of the illness of Lilburne's wife and children. The latter was certainly by Lilburne; the former was signed by the five small beagles of the Army,[a] although there was little doubt that some more experienced hand or hands had actually penned it.[2]

Both pamphlets told of the breaking of the agitators and the Council of the Army in 1647, and carried the story forward in different ways to 1649. " Clothing themselves with the glorious Garments " of the Engagement of Triploe Heath, by " fair speeches and fawning dissimulations," the grandees, led by Cromwell and Ireton, court the soldiery " even to believe their lyes, their enchantments and sorceries. Never were such Saints, such curious Angels of light. Pharaoh's Egyptian sorcerers were short of these in their art." Next they " resolve

[a] *Supra*, p. 268.

upon an Hocus Pocus trick with the King," in the course of
which Ireton reaches to high office about the King while
Cromwell aspires to the Garter [3] and seeks " to make himself
able, like Cardinal Wolsey, to say I and my King." [4] To aid
these designs they send the agitators back to their regiments,
but when their schemes fail " they cast off those robes of
Royalty " and " finding the way of an Agreement of the
People to be much affected and endeavoured after among the
Souldiery; they also invest themselves with that Robe to hide
their deformity from the Army." They then " call Fasts (a
certain forerunner of mischief with them) cry, and howl, and
bedew their cheeks with the tears of hypocrisie and deceit,
confess their iniquity and abomination in declining the cause
of the people, and tampering with the King; and humbly, as
in the presence of the all-seeing God, acknowledge the way of
an agreement of the people . . . and even then, as soon as they
had wiped their eyes and their mouths, they proceed even to
death, imprisonment, or cashierment, of all such in the Army
as promoted or owned that agreement." [5]

In this way they weakened the soldiery and opened the way
to the second civil war. After which, seeing the soldiers in a
similar temper as before, they pretended to consider an *Agreement* while Ireton was hatching the Council of State. " But no
sooner was this monster born into the world but it devoured
half the Parliament of England and set about adorning itself
with regal magnificence." [6]

Apart from anger, there was sound sense in the reasoning.
For the Army to set up Oliver, or any other, as their elected
king would bring " nothing . . . from the beginning of the
Chapter to the end thereof, but Wars, and the cutting of
throats year after year . . . and the . . . keeping of a perpetuall
and everlasting Army." As Lilburne said, " if they must have
a King, he, and the people too, would as soon have the Prince
as any other, because of his large pretence of right." [7]

It was a measure of Cromwell's desire for a settlement that
even after such an attack meetings were begun again at the end
of August between the Parliament, the Army, and the Levellers.
Walwyn, Overton, and Prince were given the freedom of the
Tower to attend the meetings with Lilburne. Little progress
was made. But Lilburne, in spite of his private grief, was

making use of his freedom for other purposes. On August 21 soldiers who came to his house to search for copies of the *Impeachment* were harangued to such good purpose by Freeborn John himself that they departed empty-handed. More important was the publication of another pamphlet, entitled *An Outcry of the Youngmen and Apprentices of London,* which few failed to attribute to Lilburne. Of all his pamphlets it was the most deliberately intended to incite to mutiny. Addressed to the private soldiers, and particularly to those who marched against the Levellers, it was signed by ten apprentices on behalf of all their fellows of the City of London.

"Do you," they asked the soldiers, "justify these actions done in the name of the army? Do you uphold the *Agreement of the People* so far as to use your swords in its defence? Do you allow [referring to the suppression of the Burford Mutiny] of the late shedding the bloud of war in time of peace?" "We earnestly beseech you to acquaint us," continued this highly seditious pamphlet, "whether from your hands . . . we may expect any help or assistance in this our miserable distressed condition. . . . You . . . the private Souldiers of the Army, alone, being the instrumentall authors of your own slavery and ours."

Shortly after the publication of the *Outcry* Lilburne met some soldiers by chance in Ivy Lane, with one of whom, Thomas Lewis, he was acquainted. The men went into the Red Cross, Newgate Street, for a drink, and Lilburne asked the soldiers how their pay was going, remarking also, "You soldiers are the men that keep us all in slavery." Then he asked Lewis if he had seen a copy of the *Outcry.* When Lewis replied no, but he intended to get one, Lilburne said he had just had a copy given him, which he forthwith took out of his pocket and passed to the soldier.[8]

These soldiers were of Colonel Ingoldsby's regiment of the garrison at Oxford, not far from the scene of the recent mutiny. The regiment had a tradition of independence, the temporary detention of Colonel Eyres at Oxford after the Ware mutiny was unwise, and when in July letters complained that he and other prisoners were poisoning most of the men with Leveller doctrines the Council of State had ordered their removal.[9] The ground, however, was prepared for Lilburne's pamphlet.

Nor was the transmission of the *Outcry* to Oxford dependent upon Lilburne's chance meeting with soldiers of the garrison. The centre of Leveller activity at Oxford was John Radman, an agitator of 1647 who was still in close touch with the civilian Levellers. A search of his quarters in the first week of September produced copies of the *Outcry* and other Leveller papers, and the soldiers subsequently chose agitators and sent a written demand to their officers for the re-election of the Council of the Army. Not trusting their officers to carry the matter further, they then presented *The Declaration of the Garrison of Oxford* to the Lord General and to Parliament, asking for the dissolution of Parliament, the circulation of the *Agreement of the People* for signature by the people, the election of a new and free representative on the basis of the *Agreement*, and the revival of the Council of the Army to manage Army affairs.[10] Agents from London and the newly elected agitators succeeded in raising resolution to such a pitch that, defying their officers, a company marched to and occupied New College, where the magazine lay, stoutly answering all expostulations by saying they would refer the matter to their agitators.

Serious as was the trouble at Oxford itself, it was feared to be part of a larger design. " The enemies of this commonwealth," reported the Council of State to the Lord General on the 8th, " have endeavoured to seduce the army, and with too much success. Their design is laid throughout the nation, and although it only appears as yet at Oxford, they are active in other places." Alarm was increased by a rumoured alliance of Levellers and Royalists which a letter intercepted by the Government seemed to confirm.[11] Officers were ordered to keep a strict eye upon their soldiers " that they may not be wrought upon by malignant insinuations to engage in any undertaking against the Parliament." [12] Instructions were sent to governors of garrisons to " prevent or suppress the first stirrings towards insurrections." [13] A force was sent towards Oxford to prevent the mutineers from receiving assistance or communicating with their confederates outside the city. Colonel Ingoldsby and three others were dispatched to Oxford to attempt conciliation. And, in order to meet propaganda by its own weapon, a subcommittee was appointed to draw up a *Declaration* to the mutineers.[14]

When Colonel Ingoldsby arrived at Oxford at 2 A.M. on September 9 he found that all the officers in the city had been rounded up and secured in New College. Later on the same day, a Sunday, amid great acclamation, the regimental colours were taken into New College and mounted cannon placed at the college gates. The men were very confident. They reckoned that within six weeks their friends in other garrisons would declare for them, and that they would have an offensive field army to command.[15]

But it never came to that. This was the situation in which Lilburne's presence would have made all the difference. Left to themselves, the soldiers, valiant in the heat of action, wavered in the cooler moments that succeeded. Observing their hesitancy, their officers at once assumed the command that came natural to them and demanded their liberty. Many of the men cried " No ! " but in the absence of unanimity the officers pushed their way through the hesitating soldiers, forced the gates open, commanded the men to give way, made their way to a cutler's shop to get swords, and continued up the street to the Inn where Ingoldsby lay. That was virtually the end of the Oxford Mutiny. The following week-end a court martial heard prisoners confess that they had expected some 6000 or 7000 men to join them from Northamptonshire, Leicestershire, and Derbyshire, 500 or 600 from the West, some thousands from Kent and other places, and that all the Army would follow. " Considerable " persons, they said, had promised supplies of money, some in Oxford as much as £4000 or £5000. Some of the prisoners declared they had been for Prince Charles. The sentences were light. Seven civilians were handed over to a civil court, and two soldiers, Biggs and Piggen, were on the morning of Tuesday, September 11, executed outside the City of Oxford near the Castle. Both men died resolutely, Piggen saying " that he died for what he acted for, the good and ease of the people, who were under great oppression and slavery." [16]

In Derbyshire, one of the centres from which the Oxford prisoners had said they expected help, there was meanwhile considerable unrest. It had begun as a dispute between the Earl of Rutland and the Derbyshire miners. The Earl had pronounced a lock-out, and in their growing poverty and distress the miners had turned to the Levellers in near-by towns, who promised assistance, while *The Moderate* published accounts of their distress and warnings of disturbances. If they were not satisfied " its much feared," said a letter of August 25 from Derby, " the Parliament may thereby gain many . . . stubborn opposites, who say . . . they must be forced to fly to the Law of Nature for reliefe."

The miners were said to number about 12,000, who, with their friends, " would make a formidable and resolved Army." In the first week of September they announced their support of *The Agreement of the People* and the Petition of September 11, but the crushing of the Oxford Mutiny ended their activity.[17]

From other parts of the country news of spasmodic disturbances and meetings of soldiers and civilians continued to cause alarm. From Pool, Plymouth, Bristol, Carlisle, Windsor, came news of Leveller activity. *The Moderate* reported each episode with lively pen. On September 21 the Levellers issued a careful statement clearly intended as a further effort to rally their forces. It directed promises to each individual who came in to the Leveller standard. He was to " be freed from all Taxes " and " have his free Vote . . . to Chuse and Elect a Representative in the County, or Burrough wherein he liveth." All soldiers who sided with them were promised debentures for past service, to be paid in full from money raised on the King's lands and goods. ". . . every free commoner " was guaranteed " Means for his Natural subsistence " and, further to encourage men to join their ranks, the Levellers promised " in the name of the free commoners " that all damage sustained through supporting them should be made good out of the estates of those who caused the damage. As the first practical step towards obtaining their demands, the Levellers suggested for the first time the application of economic sanctions: they should withold the payment of taxes, assessments, tithes, and free quarter.[18] They had never before been so specific. But the call to economic action came too late. It was never put to the test, for they were given no chance of any form of reorganization.

The Proceedings and correspondence of the Council of State in the autumn of 1649 signify its deep alarm at the state of the country. " Every day," it wrote to the Attorney-General, " we have new information that consultations are held by the party that oppose the present government." [19] Orders were given to

proceed against all disturbers of the peace and to issue warrants
for apprehending agitators in meetings of Levellers.[20]   Horse
were held in readiness in Surrey, and the guards in and about
London were doubled.   On September 20 Parliament passed a
new Act, stiffening the penalties for unlicensed printing, the
preamble conveying almost the impression of panic.[21]

It was not only that the Levellers alarmed the Government,
it was feared that they were being driven to make common
cause with the Royalists. Reports that the Levellers were getting
support for Prince Charles were certainly premature, yet there
were straws to indicate that this was a direction in which the
wind was beginning to blow. The conclusion of *The Levellers
. . . vindicated*, published a few days after the Burford defeat,
was significant. They would rather, said the signatories, choose
subjection to the King than " be vassallaged, and thus trampled
and trod under foot by such that over our backs, and by the
many lives, and losse of our blood . . . have thus stept into the
chair of this hatefull kingship." [22]   Lilburne had said as much
to Hugh Peters, and written as emphatically in the *Impeachment
of High Treason*. An intercepted letter in September left no
doubt in the mind of the Government that a united front was
being formed against it, and it circularized governors of garrisons
warning them of " designs carried on in all parts of England to
promote the interests of Charles Stuart, by the joint endeavours
of the Levellers with his own party." [23]   Shortly afterwards they
wrote to Justices and Committees of Counties warning them
that the Royalists, finding they did not always take with the
people, were insinuating themselves into the Leveller ranks, and
in this way stirring up fresh insurrections.[24]   The Prince had
hoped so much from the Oxford Mutiny, reported Whitelocke,
that he was " at a stand what to do, because the Levellers in
England were reduced." [25]   With Lilburne himself making no
secret of the fact that he would welcome a prince who would
subscribe the *Agreement of the People*, the Royalists had ground
to hope for, and the Government to fear, such a collaboration.

At the end of 1649, however, there was still one further factor
which overtopped all others—the personal influence of John
Lilburne and his " seditious scribbling." At Burford, after his
examination of the prisoners, Cromwell declared in fury that
John Lilburne was responsible for the mutiny, and vowed in

the presence of his officers " and bound it with a Solemne Thump on the Table, either Lilburne or himselfe should perish for it." [26]　Perhaps fearing that that one would finally be himself, Cromwell at last determined to settle Lilburne once for all by bringing him to trial.

CHAPTER TWENTY-FIVE

Lilburne on Trial

That which silenceth all other (the newes of this weeke) is the Tryall of Mr Lilburne.

Mercurius Pragmaticus

*I*T HAD BEEN RUMOURED SINCE THE SPRING THAT LILBURNE would be brought to trial, and he himself was prepared for this. The delay was due to the difficulty in determining the manner and the charge. " Ned Prideaux," [a] wrote *Mercurius Pragmaticus*, " is as pitifully puzzled about managing the Triall against honest John Lilburn, as they at Derby-house are to finde matter to accuse him." They could end it quickly enough in Paul's churchyard with six words and six bullets, but this they dared not do, and the Levellers taunted them:

A Fig for the Rascals, whate'er they can do
Though their plots are laid deep yet John's are so too.[1]

Contemporary opinion was nevertheless certain of the speedy dispatch of John, and *Pragmaticus* carried also the story that Lilburne's shoemaker refused to make a new pair of boots, saying that John would have but little time to wear them. Lilburne, however, commanded the immediate execution of the order, saying he would wear out his old boots and his new too as soon as Cromwell would wear out his ! [2]

The publication of the *Outcry of Apprentices* on August 29 at last induced Cromwell to act. But how? Court martial was out of the question. A charge of sedition immediately opened the way for Lilburne to point to the illegality of the Rump and the Council of State: the trials of the King and the Royalists had already shown what he could do in this way. On September 14 Lilburne was brought before Prideaux, and gave the Attorney-General a foretaste of what was coming.

[a] The Attorney-General.

His supporters lost no time in flocking to the Inner Temple
and crowding into the room where Lilburne was holding
forth with exaggerated oratory.   When Prideaux asked them to
withdraw to an outer chamber Lilburne managed to keep the
door ajar and raised his voice.   Asked if he wrote the *Impeachment of High Treason*, he denied Parliament's right to question
him, but drew from his glove a new pamphlet—the *Preparative
to an Hue and Cry after Sir Arthur Haselrig*—and provocatively
announced it was all his ! [3]

With some trepidation a warrant for the trial of Lilburne
by special commission of Oyer and Terminer was issued on
September 19, but still attempts were made to placate him.
Agents even came to the Tower to warn him he was courting
his own ruin if he refused to come to terms with the Commonwealth, but Lilburne characteristically flew into a rage and
threatened to kick them out if they ever came again to abuse
him ! [4]   There was even, so Lilburne believed, a half-hearted
attempt to implicate him with the Royalists, in which Tom
Verney, second son of the Royalist who had been killed at
Edgehill, was concerned with other agents of Scot, the Parliamentary intelligencer.   Their machinations included efforts
to get him to write letters to the King of Scots, at Jersey,
so Lilburne asserted, and when he refused letters were forged
which it was intended to produce at his trial.   Upon Lilburne's
determined resistance, however, " this cheat vanished as smoke,"
and his opponents were compelled to find other charges against
him.[5]

Four days before the trial opened Lilburne offered to submit
his case to a committee of two judges, one to be chosen by him,
one by his adversaries, and promised to abide by their ruling
provided the hearing were open, fully reported by two of
Lilburne's friends, and that the judges deliver their judgments
in writing with reasons for every point.   He even again
suggested he would go abroad on terms.[6]   But his trial could
not be stopped in this way, and at the Guildhall on October
24 Lilburne was charged with high treason under Acts of
Parliament of May 14 and July 17, 1649.   The grounds of the
charge were that by his writings he endeavoured to subvert
the Government and disturb the peace and tranquillity of the
nation by declaring the Government to be tyrannical, usurped,

and unlawful, and denying that the Commons were the supreme authority of the nation, and that he " maliciously, advisedly, and traiterously didst plot, contrive and endeavour to stir up, and to raise force " against the Government, and that " not being an Officer or Souldier . . . as a false Traytour did maliciously, advisedly and Trayterously indeavour to stir up a dangerous mutinous, and Trayterous distemper, Mutiny and Rebellion in the Army." The pamphlets named were *An Impeachment of High Treason*, *A Salva Libertate*, *The Legall Fundamentall Liberties*, the *Outcry of Apprentices*, and the *Hue and Cry*.

Lilburne's friends and supporters packed the Guildhall, outnumbering the Government's supporters by twenty to one,[7] though his wife, ill and distraught, was deliberately kept away by friends. In establishing its case the prosecution read lengthy extracts from the offending pamphlets, " which pleased the People as well," declared a spectator, " as if they had acted before them one of Ben Jonson's plays." [8] The noise throughout the trial was considerable, the prisoner having to ask for the repetition of certain statements, and, when the indictment was being read, to appeal direct to the people for quiet.

The trial was noteworthy for the patience of the judges, their anxiety not only to be fair, but to be quite sure their audience knew they were fair. They gave Lilburne more than enough scope: they openly appealed to the populace, they excused themselves on various points when challenged by Lilburne, and made the court look foolish as they allowed him to make mountains of trivialities. Time and again he won his point, he continued talking when he had been commanded to stop, at times both judge and prisoner were shouting at each other. The expected denial of their jurisdiction, the flourishing appeal to principle, never came; but the nerves of his judges were worn to shreds as, surrounded by tight-packed Leveller supporters, they waited for the grand denunciation.

For Lilburne realized well enough that, difficult as the trial was for his judges, for him it was a matter of life. He had long ago decided that he must take them unaware and meet them, not with the expected denial of their authority, but with a tenacious opposition to each point of procedure as it arose. It needed an iron nerve to do this, and the success of the scheme

depended on taking his judges by surprise. " I neither did nor
durst tell any man or woman in the world what was my intentions," he afterwards wrote, " till I came to the Barr;
least my adversaries should get a hint of it, who I beleeve never
expected but I would have dealt with them upon a ranting
high-flown score, in totally denying their jurisdiction, and the
authoritie of those that constituted them but through the
strength of the Almightie, I went beyond their expectations,
and gave them such a cuff under their other eare, as I belieeve
they wil never throughlie shake of the smart and paine of it." [9]
His " high-flown " statements before Prideaux, with the crowd
on the other side of the half-opened door, his offers to accept
mediation or to go abroad, were probably designed to further
his scheme.

Not that he kept to simple questions or objections. He
managed to relate a great deal about his trial by the Royalist
Judge Heath at Oxford, and claimed liberty of speech as his
right by the law of God and man and the law and light of
nature. He kept this subservient to his main points, however,
and made no attempt to deny the jurisdiction of the court,
as he had advised Capel to do in similar circumstances.

When the crier commanded him in the traditional way to
answer to his name by holding up his hand Lilburne turned to
Judge Keble, who presided over the court with the assistance
of seven of the common-law judges, and in a speech of considerable length claimed a free and open hearing. When Judge
Keble bade him look behind him he found that the door of
the court was, in fact, open. He then demanded a copy of the
indictment, for he could not read the illegible Latin in an
" unusual strange " hand on the piece of parchment which
brought him there, and neither, he said, could the Lieutenant
of the Tower who gave it him ! Prideaux remarked that
Lilburne could not complain of Keble's patience in hearing
him. Since the printed report of proceedings up to this point
occupies fourteen and a half pages, and Lilburne had not yet
consented to hold up his hand, this was manifestly true. But
at last he came to the point: " I know not what it meanes,
neither what in law it signifies." If they will explain he will
consider it. He does not wish to throw away his life upon a
punctilio. Finally, he decided he would not hold up his hand,

but acknowledged himself to be John Lilburne, and the indictment was at last read. Lilburne then refused to answer Guilty or Not Guilty, lest thereby he incriminate himself, asking first to have a copy of the charge and be assigned counsel.

There was a struggle to speak at several points. " Let me speak, it is upon life ! " cried Lilburne as he struggled to say that by the laws of England a man could not answer questions concerning himself. He was just starting again upon an account of his trial before Judge Heath when Judge Keble broke in: " Mr Lilburne, we do remember it." This made Lilburne so angry that a shouting match developed between the two, Keble crying out, " I will not be outvoiced by you ! "

At one point Lilburne accused Prideaux of whispering with the judges on the bench. Prideaux assured him his conversation had nothing to do with the case. Never mind, said Lilburne. Judge Thorpe mildly assured the prisoner that the Attorney-General could talk with any in the court of law. " Not in hugger-mugger," announced Lilburne calmly. He accused Prideaux of consulting with the judges before the trial. They attempted to explain.

Lilburne was doing well. He kept craving " one word more " on the grounds it was " upon life," while his judges reasoned with him, imploring him to be quiet. " I would not have you believe," said Justice Thorpe, justifying himself upon some point, " nor the rest that hear it "—the crowded Guildhall was never out of their minds. On one point only were they firm. Lilburne claimed that the indictment was a matter of *law*, and that, as such, he should be allowed counsel. The court insisted that it was a matter of *fact*, and that Lilburne could have counsel only when matter of law arose.

" It is but words and flourishes, Sir, that you are so willing to die as you say you are ! " expostulated Judge Keble. Lilburne again furiously demanded a copy of his indictment— if the judges wished to murder him they might ! " We are willing to die too ! " wryly remarked Judge Keble, with a glance round the crowded court. But the day's proceedings were drawing to a close. The prisoner was given until seven o'clock the following morning to prepare his own defence and find witnesses. Standing up and speaking to the people, Judge Keble commanded " all that are here are to take notice . . .

that the prisoner . . . hath had more favour already, then ever any prisoner in England in the like case."

On the second day of the trial Robert Lilburne, who had been staunchly supporting his brother, and Sprat, a solicitor, appeared with Lilburne. Proceedings began sharply when they were both ordered out of the bar where they were standing with the prisoner, and in this preliminary skirmish Lilburne lost. He again asked for counsel, this also vainly. The jury were then sworn, Robert and Sprat advising John in his exceptions.

The witnesses for the Crown were then called—Thomas Newcombe to testify that Lilburne and a Captain Jones brought him the manuscript of the *Outcry* for printing, and that Lilburne later held a proof in his hand; the three soldiers to witness that Lilburne gave them a copy of the *Outcry*; servants of Prideaux to certify that he gave a copy of the *Salva Libertate* to their master, claiming it as his work; the Lieutenant of the Tower to witness that he also received a copy of this tract, which denied the Government's authority, from Lilburne's hands; Prideaux's servants and Colonel West to testify that Lilburne in his interview with Prideaux had acknowledged the *Preparative to an Hue and Cry*, which would prove him also the author of the *Impeachment of High Treason* and the *Legall Fundamentall Liberties*, since both were acknowledged therein.

After four or five hours of this evidence and the reading of inciting and stirring passages from the offending pamphlets Lilburne, who was following proceedings closely, cross-examining the witnesses on point after point, again demanded counsel on the ground that matters of law had arisen. "I cannot conceive," he said, "upon what ground it can be apprehended I can go on, for my time and strength now it is far spent, that I conceive you cannot thinke my body is made of steel, to stand here four or five hours together spending my spirits to answer so many as I have to deal with, and be able after all this, to stand to return an answer to above five hours charge, and that upon life." In vain he pressed for a little respite—a day, an hour—he was refused and told he must proceed immediately to clear himself from the charge of writing the pamphlets named.

"Then," said Lilburne, with a mighty voice, "I appeale

to the righteous God of heaven and earth against you!"
As he uttered these words there was a splintering crash as
scaffolding in the court came hurtling down, hurling people
to the ground and causing great noise and confusion. The
Lord had not always answered Lilburne so directly, but he
seized the opportunity given, and when at last silence and order
were restored the prisoner was perceived busy with his books
and papers.

The court pressing him to begin, Lilburne made one more
effort at delay. "Sir," he said to the judge, " if you will be
so cruel as not to give me leave to withdraw to ease and refresh
my body, I pray you let me do it in the Court. Officer, I
entreat you to helpe me to a chamber-pot." While it was
fetching, said the reporter, the prisoner followed his papers
and books very closely. He then made water, returned the
chamber-pot, and asked for a chair to sit on. The judge
complaining that he could not see the prisoner if he used a
chair, Lilburne at last stepped to the bar, set the chair before
him, and laid his law books upon it, in the order in which he
intended to use them.

His plea to the jury was based on his contention that they
were judges of law as well as of fact. " You," he said, turning
to the judges, are " only the Pronouncers of their Sentence, Will
and Mind. You that call your selves Judges of the Law, are
no more but Norman Intruders, and indeed and in Truth, if
the Jury please, are no more but Cyphers, to pronounce their
Verdict."

" Was there ever such a damnable blasphemous Heresie as
this is," exclaimed Judge Jermyn, " to call the Judges of the
Law Cyphers? You cannot be suffered to read the Law," he
commanded, as Lilburne turned to Coke's *Commentary upon
Littleton* for confirmation. " You have broached an erroneous
opinion that the Jury are Judges of the Law, which is enough
to destroy all the Law in the Land; there was never such a
damnable Heresie broached in this Nation before."

But Lilburne had his way, read from Coke, and proceeded
to deal with the facts of his indictment. There was no evidence
to show him to be the author of the books specified: holding
in his hand a proof, giving away copies of a book, in no way
incriminated him. Moreover, and with profound satisfaction

he produced a piece of antiquarian lore, the section of the Tower where he was alleged to have given a pamphlet to the Lieutenant was not in the City of London, but in Middlesex, and a London jury was not therefore empowered to try him on that charge ! Furthermore, he had been in prison for seven months on the original charge of treason, yet the Acts upon which he was now indicted were made after his arrest—on May 14 and July 17.

At last, after many passages of arms with the judges, Lilburne concluded by speaking direct to the jury as his fellow citizens and judges of law as well as of fact. ". . . and therefore, you Gentlemen of the Jury, my sole Judges, the keepers of my life; . . . I desire you to know your power, and consider your duty, both to God, to Me, to your own Selves, and to your Country; and the gracious assisting Spirit, and presence of the Lord God omnipotent, the Governor of Heaven and Earth, and all things therein contained, go along with you, give counsell, and direct you, to do that which is just and for his glory."

The people then " with a loud voice cryed Amen, Amen, and gave such an extraordinary great hum " that the judges looked apprehensively around, and Major-General Skippon sent for three more companies of foot soldiers.

The jury retired at five o'clock. At six the court reassembled.

" Are you agreed of your verdict ? " asked the Clerk.

" Yes."

" Who shall speak for you ? "

" Our Fore-man."

" John Lilburn, hold up thy hand, what say you, look upon the Prisoner, is he guilty of the Treasons, charged upon him : or any of them, or not guilty ? "

" Not guilty to all of them."

" Nor of all the Treason, or any of them that are layed to his charge ? "

" No, of all, nor of any of them."

" The juryman's ' No ! ' being pronounced in a very loud voice, immediately the whole multitude of People in the Hall, for joy of the Prisoner's acquittal gave such a loud and unanimous shout, as is beleeved, was never heard in Yeeld-Hall, which lasted for about halfe an hour without intermission : which made the Judges for fear, turne pale, and hange down their heads; but the Prisoner stood silent at the Barre, rather more sad in his countenance than he was before." [10]

The man who stood thus silent at the bar was now thirty-one years old. He showed nothing of the emaciation that had been noted earlier. On the contrary, he appeared to be rather over middle height and thick-set. Dressed carefully in doublet buttoning down to the hips, with lace at the neck and cuffs, trousers slashed and decorated, good boots and spurs, there was nothing at first glance to indicate the struggle he had been through. It was apparent, however, that strife over the years had coarsened his features, that the delicacy of the young man's face had gone. The disfigurement caused by his eye injury many years before gave his face in repose a slightly saturnine look. He no longer curled his hair back from his ears, as he had done as a young man, but let it hang to his shoulders, slightly grizzled and somewhat unkempt. The expanse of forehead was moie apparent than ever, and the profile still showed the high ascetic nose. It was perhaps in the eyes and the mouth that the greatest difference showed. At twenty-three Lilburne held the simple belief that the demonstration of an injustice led to its abrogation. Seven years later disillusionment and bitter struggle had left their mark in the set of his mouth and the challenge in his eyes.

Lilburne, though acquitted, was conveyed back to the Tower, the people accompanying him with cheering and acclamation, the very soldiers who guarded him " hollowing and shouting as they Rid in the streets for joy at his deliverance." [11] If he had not been acquitted he would have been rescued, it was said, by his supporters. That night bonfires were lit up and down the streets to signify the people's joy at their hero's acquittal. They appointed a day of thanksgiving, and when, with the other three Levellers, he was released from prison on November 8, they all, Lilburne included, marched in troops and companies to a great feast in the King's Head Tavern in Fish Street.[12]

Nothing demonstrated more than Lilburne's trial the esteem in which he was held by the people. To commemorate his acquittal a medal was struck by the Levellers showing on one side the head of Lilburne and on the other the names of the jurymen. Round the head of Lilburne were inscribed the words: " John Lilburne saved by the power of the Lord and the integrity of his jury who are juge of law as wel as fact. Oct. 26. 1649." The medal, which was struck in silver, copper gilt, and copper, was perhaps the work of Thomas Simon, the medallist. There was also a much smaller medal, with Lilburne's head on the obverse and his arms and the date on the reverse. This smaller medal had a ring by which it could be suspended from a cord (or from a sea-green ribbon ?) round the neck.[13]

What his enemies had hoped would be the end of John Lilburne proved to be one of his major triumphs. As a personal feat of skill and endurance in arguing single-handed with his judges, and as a testimony by the jurymen, soldiers, and populace of the popularity of Free-born John, the trial was emphatic. It did not necessarily imply an equal enthusiasm for the Leveller movement. After 1649, although Lilburne himself could still arouse enthusiasm, the Leveller movement declined. Perhaps he realized something of this as he stood silent at the bar and heard the verdict. Perhaps it was merely the strain of the months of preparation and the two days of single-handed wrestling with the law for his life that kept him silent in the moment of victory. Was he perhaps thinking of his old friend Jehovah, who once more had entered into him with his own self? Or was he merely humble in the presence of such support and affection as the people gave him?

CHAPTER TWENTY-SIX

Jack of All Trades

...had he been ... a Selfe-Seeker, crafty and deceitful, he might have feathered his nest ten times better than he hath done.

SAMUEL CHIDLEY, *The Dissembling Scot*, February 1, 1652

LILBURNE RETURNED TO WINCHESTER HOUSE AND HIS FAMILY, resolved, it would seem, to implement the resolution he had felt compelled to break at the beginning of 1649. For more than eighteen months he published nothing contentious, and shortly after his release moved from Southwark to the City of London, where he was a freeman and could more easily follow a trade.

It was a matter of pride to him that by a clear majority he was elected Common Councillor in the City elections on December 21, 1649. But there was a hurdle to surmount before he took his seat. The Engagement, taken by most of the Council of State, was now being extended to all office-holders, those who took it undertaking to be true and faithful to the Commonwealth without King or House of Lords. There was some surprise when Lilburne consented to take the Engagement, those who elected him probably hoping for some display on the old lines. He did not disappoint them, immediately craving permission to say a few words of explanation. No official ever voluntarily permitted Lilburne to speak to the people, and naturally enough the Aldermen refused his request. But amid cries of "Heare him! Heare him!" Lilburne, as usual, had his way, and explained that by 'Commonwealth' he understood "all the good and legal people of England," and not "the present Parliament, Council of State, or Council of the Army." He was not allowed to say more, nor was his election allowed to stand, and his chief sponsor was disabled from being a foreman and committed to Warwick Castle. But Lilburne contented himself with elaborating his point in a pamphlet which stated that the Commonwealth as he understood it comprised annual and successive Parliaments, trial by jury, and the rule of law.[1]

Perhaps with some relief his wife saw the election quashed [2] and her husband turn to the trade of soap-boiling, believing with the newspaper reporter that " the wild levelling representative is at an end since John Lilburne turned off the trade of State-mending to take up that of soap-boiling." [3] Twenty people, including Lilburne, signed a petition to Parliament in November 1650 begging that the excise of 4s. 8d. a barrel should be taken from soap on the grounds that excise had already been paid on the potash, oil, and tallow used in manufacture, and could thus only be a tax on the labour of their hands, and pointing out that since the excise had been increased the revenue therefrom had decreased. The soap-boilers offered to support a tax on all the imported materials used in soap-manufacture if they could collect it themselves.[4] The chairman of the committee for regulating the excise on soap making counter-proposals, the old John Lilburne leaped out in a challenge to debate—with shorthand writers present, naturally, to record the session ! [5]

Apart from soap, Lilburne's private affairs were going badly. His family had been increased by the birth of another son, John, on October 12, 1650,[6] and he needed money. Haselrig, while Lilburne had been in prison, had withheld rents from the lands granted to him as reparations. Meeting Haselrig's clerk in London, Lilburne bade him tell his master that he would have his rent although it cost him his heart's blood! He knew it vain to sue so powerful a man at law, or to complain of him to the House of Commons, but he sent the message that Lilburne wore a good dagger by his right side and a good rapier by his left, and unless he received some satisfaction within eight days Haselrig must look to himself! Shortly afterwards Lilburne received £800 from Haselrig as arrears of rent, and Cromwell, returning in May from the subjection of Ireland, was influential in getting a grant of sequestered Dean and Chapter's lands for Lilburne, which was confirmed on July 30, 1650.[7] Lilburne was grateful to Cromwell. He accompanied him twenty-five miles northward in the same month, when, having been named Commander-in-Chief of all the forces of the Commonwealth, Cromwell set out to destroy the Royalist forces which were again rising in Scotland.[8]   Lilburne wrote to him in the following January to express, with atrocious spelling, his " reall graitfull acknowledgment of your Excilencys most obliging and nobell favours manifested unto myselfe." [9]   Cromwell had by then won a victory at Dunbar on September 3, 1650, Lilburne's brother, Colonel Robert, utterly defeated the Earl of Derby in August 1651 at Wigan, and on the first anniversary of Dunbar Cromwell defeated Charles himself at the battle of Worcester. He returned to London in triumph on September 12, and it may be imagined that John and Elizabeth Lilburne, with their children, joined in the citizens' joyous welcome, for a brief while united as a family, in harmony with Cromwell, and claiming, through Robert, some share in the victory. Lilburne visited Cromwell at his house in the Cockpit shortly afterwards, where they spoke alone together, cordially and in friendship. It was then that Lilburne told Cromwell of Scot's attempts to implicate him in Royalist intrigue, and Cromwell promised never to believe what Scot said about Lilburne until the two men had been brought face to face.[10]

It was Haselrig who incurred the tempest which, after eighteen months' unnatural docility, was rising in Lilburne's breast. He had built a long and severe count against Sir Arthur, which included all he had heard from his family in the North in 1649. His brother Henry's disaffection he laid at Haselrig's door. Robert, who had secured Newcastle for the Parliament, and afterwards governed it " effectually and honorably like a Soldier . . . in Justice, honesty and peace "—witness the two silver flagons presented to him by the Corporation—was " privately undermined and worm-eaten " out of his governorship by Sir Arthur Haselrig, and — apparently of softer mettle than John—gave way " like a soft and quiet spirited man . . . without so much as one rustle." [11] George Lilburne had incurred Haselrig's enmity when he refused, as surveyor of bishops' lands, to make some reprisals which Haselrig wanted. He refused also, without Parliament's authority, to lay 4s. a chauldron excise upon coals in Sunderland, as Haselrig had done in Newcastle. Further trouble arose between the two

men when early in 1649 George Lilburne had accused John
Blackston of protecting his malignant relations from sequestration. When the charge was heard before the committee of
which Haselrig was chairman John rushed in to accuse Haselrig
to his face of partiality for Blackston, but was imprisoned for
Englands New Chains before the matter could go further.
George Lilburne was voted a clear and honest man by the
committee, but John stored up the count against Haselrig.
His will, he declared, was a law to all the committees in the
North, so absolute that he would not allow the Members to
vote or even state a question, but resolved everything himself.
Haselrig seems to have turned his traditional feud with the
Lilburne family full upon John from that point.[12]

The Dean and Chapter's lands which Lilburne acquired in
place of those disposed of while he was in prison led to more
trouble. He had promised to keep them as inheritance for
himself and his heirs, and set about collecting rents from the
five farms in question in County Durham. Fourteen families
were involved, some of whom—largely because the rent was
raised from £13 to £18 a year on the official evaluation—
proved recalcitrant. In particular, two tenants who were out
of lease were troublesome because Lilburne wished to acquire
their farms for his own family. William Huntington, especially,
caused a great deal of trouble. A large part of the Lilburne
family and many neighbours endeavoured to see that justice
was done. Lilburne offered the Huntingtons the agreed value
of the corn they had sown plus £5 if they would quietly render
possession, and offered also to take one of the Huntingtons'
children, " new clothe him from the crown of the head to the
sole of the foot," and bring him up as his own son until he
was twenty. He even offered to let them stay as tenants and
waive his right to an increased rent if they would consent to
pay it. But in April 1651 the family had still not moved, and
the Committee of Sequestrations ordered payment of rent to
date and immediate surrender of possession. When Lilburne's
agent served the order he was set upon by Huntington's friends
and beaten with cudgels. In a final effort Lilburne sent his
brother-in-law, Cornet Thomas Dewell, to arrange a settlement,
but still to no avail. The Huntingtons remained, and they paid
no rent. On June 25 Lilburne took the final step. Acting

upon an order from the Committee, the sheriff and his men arrived to eject the family by force, and Huntington and his wife drove them to the " utmost extremity " before Lilburne gained possession.

It was a regrettable episode, the causes of which are not entirely clear. Huntington, who appears to have been a persevering and honest man, not afraid of hard work, had married a widow, a tenant to the Dean and Chapter, who had a house, a farm, goods and household stuff, two cows, and four children. He borrowed money to plant and sow, they had a child, and all seemed to be going well until Lilburne, as Huntington claimed, took all and turned them out of doors. It seems they both believed her tenancy to be a " birthright," unaffected by sequestration, but whether by this they meant a freehold or a fixed, low-rent lease is not clear. They had rather counted, it seemed, on the farm going to an officer who had agreed to return part of it to them on very favourable terms, and Lilburne by stepping in had ruined this plan.

In pursuit of the justice he claimed, Huntington not only applied several times to Haselrig in Durham, but three times he went on foot to London and back. There was a determination about this not unlike Lilburne's own, especially when on his first visit to London he was found delivering copies of a printed petition to assembling Members of Parliament. This, he declared, moved Lilburne a little, who suggested a committee of three to report on the case. But they were too long in coming to a decision, and Huntington trudged back home.

For Lilburne the Huntington case meant his first taste of popular disapproval, for the family was large and obviously very poor, and Huntington himself a worthy man. It was a new experience to find the local people incensed against him and the Huntingtons keeping up a continuous sniping of the kind he was used to deliver himself. He was given a unique opportunity of replying to them. Finding one Sunday when he was in the district that the church was shut and the parson out of his living, he had the door opened, took the parson's place, and, besides preaching a sermon, took occasion to give his version of the dispute. Perhaps it is unnecessary to add that he also offered to submit the case to an inquiry of two persons chosen by the tenants and himself ! It was unfortunate

that when Lilburne acted for the first time in many years with
the weight of authority behind him, and for his own interest,
it should have been in a cause which had so little to commend
it, and should have involved the disinheriting of people of the
very kind the Leveller movement spoke for. Perhaps justice
was on Lilburne's side. But years afterwards Huntington was
still plodding backward and forward from Durham to London,
maintaining his right to his farm, and the pamphlet explaining
his case was simple and dignified.[13]

It was about this time, probably with money acquired from
his reparations, that Lilburne bought property in the City of
London. When he wrote to Cromwell in January 1651 it was
from his house at the end of Old Bailey without Ludgate, and
some years later his wife was selling his " interest in one
house in London." [14] It was not soap-boiling which had
enabled him to do this, for already he had abandoned that
uncongenial occupation. He could not in conscience pay the
excise, neither could he stomach the evasions which were
widely practised. Instead, with people constantly coming to
him for legal advice, he " resolved to undertake men's honest
causes, and to manage them either as Sollicitor or Pleader." [15]
Wishing to equip himself more adequately for the profession,
he tried to enter the Inner Temple, but the lawyers were not
likely to admit " poor upstart John," and, headed by Edmund
Prideaux, they denied him entry.[16] He modestly recorded that
he nevertheless " gave satisfaction " to his clients,[17] and in the
welter of litigation which succeeded the Civil Wars he might
have settled down to a not unprosperous and not unexciting
existence, acting for clients and pleading at committees.

There was the case of Morris, alias Poyntz, who complained
of being swindled out of some property by enemies who
included John Browne, Clerk to the House of Commons.
Lilburne had championed Morris in 1648, and took up his
case again in 1651. Another case in which he was asked to
act concerned the manor of Epworth, in the Isle of Axholme,
and here John Wildman joined him. Axholme was one of the
few islands of comparatively solid land amid 400,000 acres of
boggy waste which comprised the Great Fen of Lincolnshire
and adjacent counties. Charles I in 1626 had employed the
Dutchman Vermuyden to drain part of the Fens, and in the

course of the work it had been found necessary to drain through Epworth. For this reason about 8000 acres of land in the Isle of Axholme were enclosed, the commoners' plea that they kept cattle on this land for many centuries being overruled by the Exchequer, which gave possession to the drainage company. The commoners took advantage of the Civil War to get back 3000 acres, and after the war many of the poorer sort were " impatient and took their possession of the whole by force of multitudes," pulling down houses set up by the Commissioners and tearing down enclosures. Though every one did not approve of this violent action, the chief tenants were willing enough to enter on possession again, and asked nothing more than a fair trial.

Acting for the tenants was Daniel Noddel, called a ' solicitor,' but laying as much stress on direct action as on law. He naturally turned to Lilburne and Wildman as offering the combination of both, and after giving some legal advice these two appeared in person in Lincolnshire in the autumn of 1650. Those who spoke for the drainage company asserted that they had made the land better for corn and needed reimbursement for the expense of drainage. The tenants replied that the land had always been very good pasture, and that this was the more profitable, and that in any case drainage through Axholme was unnecessary to the general scheme. This was the position which Lilburne undertook to defend in return for a grant of 1000 acres of land at Epworth. On November 18, 1651, he published, with some of the others concerned, a fairly concise and clear account of the complicated issue,[18] but the affair yielded also more excitement. There was a great riot on October 19, 1651, when Lilburne, Nodell, and others took possession of Sandtoft church and ejected the preacher, Lilburne actually using the church, so it was reported, as a barn and cattle-shed, installing his own servant in the minister's house.[19]

Five years later the affair was still dragging on, but by that time an even more unfortunate case had ended Lilburne's interest in the Axholme affair. Again the issue was complicated, the ramifications immense, the arguments in speeches and pamphlets tortuous. Again it resolved itself into a duel between Lilburne and Haselrig. The case concerned the

Harraton colliery in County Durham, part of which had been owned by John Wray, a Royalist, and part by Josiah Primate. George Lilburne and George Grey had taken a lease of his part of the colliery from Primate, but in 1649 Sir Arthur sequestered the whole of the colliery as Royalist property and leased it back to himself at, it was alleged, a low rent. So Primate opposed Haselrig, George Lilburne and Grey supported Primate in the interests of their own lease, and John Lilburne was brought into the affair as counsel by his uncle. It continued with as much acerbity as any other branch of the Lilburne-Haselrig quarrel. But Haselrig was a difficult man to flout. When the Committee of Haberdasher's Hall—the central body responsible for sequestrations, which, like many other committees, took its name from its place of meeting—decided in favour of Haselrig's claim, Lilburne at once published *A Just Reproof to Haberdashers Hall,* couched in his old style, accusing Haselrig of unjustly influencing the Committee. He also prepared a petition to Parliament repeating the same charges, which with Primate and others he signed and presented on December 23, 1651. Parliament treated both petition and pamphlet as libellous, and, assuming the judicial powers which had been so often condemned in Star Chamber, imposed the monstrous sentence of fine and damages amounting to £7000 each on Primate and Lilburne. Seizing their opportunity, they also banished Lilburne from the country on pain of death if he returned.[20]

Waiting outside the House after candles were lighted, Lilburne could hardly believe the sentence. Its suddenness, its flagrant injustice by any standard, its justification by no known concept of law, its complete lack of proportion to the crime it was allegedly punishing, took every one by surprise, and Lilburne, for once, appeared stunned. The explanation can only lie in pent-up exasperation and in renewed rumours of Royalist intrigue. A Royalist agent named Coke had deposed in April 1651 that since the trial of Lilburne Levellers had been in communication with the King and that Lilburne, with Wildman and Marten, had actually promised him aid in return for an assurance of a full and general liberty.[21] The stories had been revived towards the end of the year, and Cromwell, in spite of the promise made to Lilburne only three months earlier, acted without giving the Leveller a chance to defend himself. Lilburne heard later through his wife that Cromwell had said that Lilburne might think his sentence greater than his offence, if they did not fear other things by him.[22] The House passed sentence without formal charge, Lilburne was not heard in his defence, and refused to kneel at the sentence.[23] Everything possible was done to make his departure more difficult. The original thirty days' grace was reduced to twenty; a pass to leave the country was withheld in order, it was believed, to trap Lilburne in the country after the time-limit had expired.[24]

On Monday, January 20, his friends petitioned the House for him, for Primate, and for their " fundamental Native rights " at law, but the House read the petition and set it aside. A petition presented the following day was not even read. That night Lilburne supped with some two hundred of his closest supporters in a house behind the Exchange, and on Wednesday morning went to the Speaker for his pass, but, being unable to get it, took horse for Dover on Thursday the 29th at Finsbury stables by Moorfields. Many of his friends rode out through Southwark with him. At Dover on the 31st he wrote to William Kiffin, in whom the ties of old friendship had survived the feud with the Leveller leader, and to the ministers Christopher Feake and John Simson, begging them to pray for him at their meetings and to look after his wife and children.[25] He was still without a passport, but the Mayor's wife, bursting into tears, interceded to let him board ship for Ostend.[26] He was violently sick on the journey, it was reported—" this was he that set himself against Bishops, against Kings, against the House of Lords, against Generals, yea and Parliament itself "[27]—but by February 8 he had reached Amsterdam by way of Bruges, where he found a room in the house of Mrs Beza in Sheepes Alley, Holyway Street,[28] the ease with which he did this perhaps indicating a renewal of a friendship made in 1637 or the taking up of a contact made through Leveller printing.

CHAPTER TWENTY-SEVEN

The Exile

I long to see London.
> JOHN LILBURNE, Letter to Elizabeth Lilburne, May 1653

*A*T DOVER THERE BOARDED THE SAME BOAT AS LILBURNE CAPTAIN Wendy Oxford, who, with his wife and an Irishman, Hugh Riley, dogged Lilburne's footsteps all the time he was in exile. As Lilburne readily guessed, the men were spies, the woman a 'go-between' who travelled monthly between the Low Countries and Thomas Scot, the Commonwealth intelligencer.[1] With the Royalists, who were spending their exile in Holland and Flanders, the spies added considerably to the excitements of Lilburne's banishment. The Cavaliers still regarded him as largely responsible for the King's death—a belief fostered by Wendy Oxford. Since the Commonwealth's accredited agent at The Hague, Dr Isaac Dorislaus, had been murdered by Royalists in 1649, it was not a far-fetched fear that Lilburne also would be " Dorislaused," as he put it. At Bruges, where he stopped on his way to Amsterdam, he narrowly missed an attack from armed and drunken Cavaliers, who came to his lodging when he was out, and he believed there were others.[2]

Cromwell could more easily banish Lilburne than deprive him of his pen, and Lilburne, in exile, found comfort in writing. By April 3 he had finished a biographical pamphlet directed to the people of the United Netherlands, which was published immediately in English and Flemish.[3] He wrote to William Kiffin on April 2, thanking him for his kindness to Elizabeth[4]; he wrote to Cromwell in May.[5] He was certainly not compounding for his return, and would have made an appeal in print direct to the people of England, but according to his principle of not hitting a man when he was down, and not wishing to hurt England when she was at war, desisted when hostilities between England and Holland broke out in June

1652. His wife and friends at the same time were begging him
to live quietly and abstain from writing. So after a little travel
—he was at Vianon, on the Rhine, in May 1652—he left
Amsterdam,[6] probably on the outbreak of war, and moved to
Bruges, where he lived in rural style in what he termed a
" little garden-house " in Mary Brugh, obtained through a
friend, Thomas Lambert.[7]

What else could occupy so restless a spirit in banishment
from his home and his friends and the struggle which had been
his life's blood since he reached manhood? He considered
himself too old to learn the Dutch or Flemish language,[8] but
he read avidly in English. Like most of his contemporaries,
he had freely used the term ' Macchiavellian ' to describe people
and practices he disliked. Now he read *The Prince* for himself,
and was struck by its " real usefulnesse in my streits to help me
clearly to see through all the disguised deceipts of my potent,
politick . . . adversaries." Raleigh's *History of the World* and
the *Life of Amurath the Second King of the Turks* he had
already read in prison. Now Plutarch's *Lives* occupied much
of his time as he read and took notes on fifty pages a day. His
letters were full of allusions to Greek history. He read Milton's
Defence of the People of England, and praised the poet for his
" faithfullnes and Freedome " in urging the Commonwealth
to examine its own shortcomings. He concerned himself with
economic questions, suggesting in a letter to Henry Marten
that a convoy should be provided for the British ships blockaded
in Ostend by the Dutch.[9] His wife made the journey to see
him. She had again been pregnant, but anxiety and ceaseless
activity for her husband's freedom had caused a miscarriage,
and she was reduced to an extremity of anguish.[10] She had
nevertheless gone to committee after committee with Haselrig
and Huntington, trying to sort out the interest in the land
assigned her husband. Haselrig, for all Lilburne's bitterness
against him, showed himself a fair and helpful arbiter. The
Huntingtons should have possession of the farm, and Mrs
Lilburne should have her £18 yearly rent, for her case was as
hard as Huntington's.

But nothing the Lilburnes touched went smoothly. Richard
Lilburne had been in possession of the farm since the ejection
of the Huntingtons, and in spite of the new agreement he still

refused them entry. Neighbours then threw him out, and he
called in the sheriff to help him re-establish possession. By
this time Elizabeth had heard from her husband, and he instructed her to do nothing in the case and to refuse any compromise short of a full recognition of his rights. So to all
subsequent offers Elizabeth replied " she was John Lilburne's
wife " and would do nothing further. She still refused when
Haselrig asked her to compute at £1000 with £100 a year in
perpetuity, so that she was certain of maintenance for herself
and her children when her husband died. Haselrig could do
no more. Whatever arrangement was made with the tenants,
they were satisfied, for they offered a breeding mare to Sir
Arthur, which he decently refused to accept.[11]

Elizabeth meanwhile was forced to borrow money, to sell
or pawn her household goods, to part with the interest of one
of their London houses on bad terms. Her husband was
earning no money; he was saddled with a fine and damages of
£7000. He himself was forced to borrow money in order to
live,[12] in spite of his publications in Dutch and Flemish which
might have been intended to earn money. She was ill and
wretched when she undertook to travel oversea, and distraught
when she arrived. Lilburne had much ado to comfort her. He
treated her like a child, remembering all her long years of
devotion to him and the great love they bore one another.
When she begged him again and again to get back to England
he promised not to be provocative, but asked her to send him
books on her return, that he might the better prepare a new
plea for his deliverance. She promised, but once back in
England her resolution failed, and she could not bring herself
to put into her husband's hands the means to fresh temptation
and renewed trouble. In vain he wrote expostulating and
beseeching her. She was angry, rebellious, resentful, entering
into " new paper skirmishes " with her husband, the pages
" filled with womanish passion and anger." The children
were again ill, so he bore with her, trying to reason in long
letters written day after day. For once womanish unreason
prevailed. Lilburne did not get his papers and was bitterly
angry with his wife.[13]

Lilburne could not keep wholly within doors, writing and
reading, and when he walked the streets he inevitably met with

the Royalist exiles and the Commonwealth spies. It was
almost impossible to have no intercourse with either. While
the Royalists were writing that his banishment was a counterfeit
and that he was one of Cromwell's chief spies—" It is now
evident to all men that the rogue Lilburne was banish'd England
merely to gain him credit and trust on this side," as Sir Edward
Nicholas wrote [14]—the spies were soon reporting that he was
plotting with the Royalists. In " sheer rationality," as Lilburne
put it, he was compelled into a " friendly familiarity " with the
more moderate of the Cavaliers, and he named the Lords
Percy, Hopton, Culpepper, and the Bishop of Londonderry—
whom he found " a wise and shrewd blunt man "—as his
associates. In particular he conceived great liking and respect
for the Duke of Buckingham, whose protection, he believed,
saved him from further attempts on his life.[15]

This friendship helped the spies to build up a consistent
story, repeated from several sources, including Nicholas, who
heard it while he was in Amsterdam, that Lilburne had offered
for £10,000 to undertake the destruction of Cromwell, Parliament, and the Council of State and the restoration of Charles
II. Nicholas added that he had boasted of 40,000 men in
England who would rise for the King if he would guarantee
that the militia should remain under popular control and that
there should be constant Parliaments. It was frequently added
that Lilburne had said that he would have a piece of him nailed
to every gatepost in Bruges if he failed in such an enterprise!
He spoke, it was said, of his agents who would give him a
continual account of events in England, and through whom he
would spread his papers abroad and so work on the people
against the Government that the Parliament, the Council of
State, and the Lord General would be destroyed in half an
hour. His reported boasting to the Duke of Buckingham had
an authentic ring: he had bought a press at Amsterdam and
would set it to work to send papers over to England, which
would there be distributed by his agents " all over the nation "
and in the Army; I have agents enough for this, he said. The
soldiers would then " fly in the faces " of their officers, and with
the help of Lilburne's " particular interest " would carry the
enterprise through while Lilburne did nothing but sit in his
chair and use his pen. When Buckingham spoke of Cromwell's

power Lilburne replied that " heretofore . . . all his Business was mannaged by Ireton, and is since by others " ; he inferred that Cromwell was less formidable without his son-in-law's stiffening, and added somewhat inconsequentially, " I had once as great a power as he had, and greater too, and am as good a Gentleman, and of as good a family." Sometimes Lilburne's reported proposal was pin-pointed to " an Arbor in Placingdoll," where he was said not only to have promised to restore the King for £10,000, but to have averred that the King would never return without Lilburne's aid.[16]

It is clear there was scope for intrigue within intrigue, for plot, counter-plot, suspicion, and betrayal. Most of these men were either spies or exiles, bitter and quarrelsome, suffering all the evils of a small shut-in society turned in on itself. The advent of the Leveller leader was an event of great importance to such a group, and his words were subject to report and endless repetition in varying forms, while even his simplest movements were watched and reported—whether it was bringing the latest news bulletin from England to Culpepper's lodging,[17] where he had a " brief silent encounter " with Richard Watson, a chaplain to Lord Hopton who kept up a voluminous correspondence with Hyde's secretary, William Edgeman, or whether it was merely delivering his own private letters to the post.[18] More than one cypher was used by the Royalists to conceal his name. Lilburne was not at his best in such a society. He could understand an attack on his life by the Cavaliers, he understood that the Commonwealth spies were out to ' frame ' him, and he retaliated by attempting to ambush them and repay them in their own coin.[19] But the finer nuances of the situation were beyond him. Buckingham he took at his own expressed face-value—a man who sided with the Royalists and went into exile with them merely because his family had been raised and honoured by the Stuarts. Now that he had repaid that debt he wished to return to his native land and take possession of his estates and live in peace under the Commonwealth.[20]

One of the threads of intrigue involved a deal between Buckingham and Captain Wendy Oxford for a pass into England for the Duke. Although Buckingham had paid money for it, Oxford refused to hand it over unless Buckingham revealed the substance of conversations between himself and Lilburne. Buckingham refused, and won Lilburne's enthusiastic praise. " I do as immediately and instrumentally owe my life and being to him, as ever David owed his to Jonathan," he wrote. His " powerful influence among the desperate cavaliers being such, as that instrumentally under God he principally preserved my life, from those many complotted designs that the said Oxford had cunningly laid by their hands to get me murdered. . . ! " He was more beholden to Buckingham than to friends and kindred, and found in him " so much reason, sobriety, civility, honour, and conscience " that he would do him any service that did not involve disservice to his native country. He was so sure of his integrity that he offered to be bound body for body for Buckingham's good behaviour if the Duke returned to England, and according to a Royalist correspondent he wrote to the Council of State to this effect, giving Buckingham " a most high character " " as a person both conscientious and honorable." [21]

The Cavaliers themselves were divided in their attitude to Lilburne. There were those who merely saw in him a murderer of the King. Another group, led by the Duke of Buckingham, were said to resort for counsel sometimes to Lord Culpepper, but more frequently " to infamous John Lilburne." [22] " There is no question but the Duke of Buckingham believes he hath notable interest in that Saint," as Hyde wrote to Nicholas,[23] though no one was ever quite sure if that interest concerned more than the return to England of Buckingham on favourable terms. Lord Percy and some others were even of opinion that Lilburne was " more able to set the crown on the King's head than ever Scotland was." [24]

Buckingham, Colonel Leighton, young Titus, and Lilburne were in " great privity," reported Watson to Edgeman in carefully concealing cypher, but Lord Hopton refused to be drawn,[25] and Hyde and Nicholas both remained sceptical of Lilburne's genuine interest in the Royalist cause and in his ability to aid it. His banishment was " but a counterfeit to give him an opportunity of doing mischiefe in Holland and serve the Independents in their treaty with the States," wrote another Royalist correspondent, putting a new angle on the affair.[26] When Nicholas wavered in his condemnation of Lilburne Hyde stiffened him:

" Lilburne is not without reputation with some great persons here," he wrote from Paris, " as well as with you, and I am thought an obstinate fool for not understanding that he will ever be able or willing to do good." [27]

The agents made great play with the fact that both Lilburne and his wife supped with the Royalists, and that Lilburne rode every Saturday from Bruges to Ostend, where he wrote letters for the packet, which were taken by Prynne's man, and returned on Monday.[28] Lilburne was writing letters, but it is unlikely that they were concerned with the cause of Charles Stuart. He never, however, unreservedly denied the suggestion that given the means he would restore the King to his throne: all he had said over the last four or five years emphasized that he would prefer a King who reigned according to the *Agreement of the People* to a Parliament or Protector who did not. He maintained that in his intercourse with the Cavaliers he never abandoned his original opposition to " unlimited Regall Prerogative " or " Parliament's unknown unfathomable priviledges," and " never . . . entered into the least contract, agreement, oath, or confederacy " to act as agent to the King or advance his ends or interests." [29] None of this precludes an offer to the Royalists by Lilburne or much discussion on the subject; it merely indicates that no agreement was reached. Later he made his denial more explicit. Answering the charge that upon the procurement of £10,000 he would destroy the Lord General, the Parliament, and the Council of State " in half an hour," he asserted " that never any words of this nature passed from my mouth or any such thoughts entered into my heart, the Lord the Almighty God is my witness." [30] Lilburne did not lie, but he would prevaricate. " Half an hour," or even the precise sum of £10,000, may be the governing clause of this denial. Again he declared to one of Cromwell's associates, and swore upon the Bible, that he " never was guilty of any the least ingagement " with Charles Stuart, " or any of his party, to promote his Regall interest, against the welfare of the present declared Commonwealth of England," and would make this assertion good with the last drop of his heart-blood.[31] Again there is the loophole. Of course he would never act against what he considered " the welfare of the present declared Commonwealth of England." Even if he had entered into negotiations with the Cavaliers upon conditions his principles would still have remained unimpaired. What is more likely, however, is that Lilburne, as usual, talked too much, and that the matter never reached the point of a definite proposal. Buckingham's interest may, indeed, have been as Lilburne explained it, that he was seeking means of making his peace with the Commonwealth and sounding Lilburne as to the best approach.

In the month Lilburne left England attempts at reform had begun with a committee to consider law, led by Matthew Hale, and the following month John Owen, once Cromwell's chaplain in Ireland, and a group of fourteen ministers presented a scheme of church reform, which a committee was appointed to consider. But the promises held out were never fulfilled. The Rump of some sixty or seventy Members still refused a dissolution, and although by the spring of 1652 the Navy under Blake had won supremacy for the Commonwealth at sea and in all the lands oversea where the Stuarts had been recognized, in November the Dutch Admiral Tromp defeated Blake off Dungeness, and the year ended gloomily with an Army costing £1½ million annually and the Navy £1 million, with taxation and fresh confiscations of property stretched to the uttermost to pay them, and social distress still unrelieved. The recognition of the Republic by France in December and the victory of Blake and Monk over Tromp off Portland in February 1653 brightened the prospect, but Cromwell and the Council of Officers were still left with the anomaly of a self-perpetuating Parliament over twelve years old which was the only instrument that could be used with any show of legality to re-establish the kingdom. It was basically opposed to the Army, and basically opposed to reform, and rumours reached Lilburne that its expulsion was again being discussed by the Army. This was sufficient to make him break silence, and in March 1653 *L Colonel John Lilburne Revived* indicated that he was back in the struggle. The people of England, he urged, must now contest even to the death for the election from among themselves of tribunes, or keepers, or defenders of the peoples' liberties such as would defend them against the " annihilating incroachments that their present Tyrannicall Riders have already made upon them." He had seen the names of the

officers of the Army who were again talking of expelling the
Rump, and he hastened to advise that they were mostly
knaves or neuters, and their general intention " a perfect
cheat." But it was Cromwell who incurred his hottest anger.
He judged him " to be as false as the Devill himself," and he
resolved " never to see England, so long as Cromwell's most
hatefull and detestable beastely Tyrannie lasteth, unlesse it be
in a way to pursue him, as the grandest Tyrant and Traytor,
that ever England bredd."

But in the letter to a friend in Scotland in which he spoke
thus of Cromwell he also wrote tenderly and delicately of
his wife. If the journey from Scotland had not been so long
he would have pressed him " to have lent my honest Besse
your wonted assistance." His anger had spent itself against
Cromwell, and once more she was the helpmeet " who for
twelve years hath many times with a good proportion of
strength and resolution, gone through so many miseries with
me, with so much affection." He also allowed himself the
only touch of playfulness in all his writings. Is it viewing the
new forts and fine monuments of Scotland—" that rare
Nation "—which has kept him from writing? Or is it that
" the imbraces of your lately married delight, hath so taken
up your time, that you have had no leasure to think of an
exiled and banished man in Flanders? " [32]

The growing unrest in the Army in the spring of 1653
produced from Parliament a scheme which proposed new
elections for vacant seats, but the continuation in their places
of sitting Members. When a compromise scheme proposed
by the Army was under consideration no less a person than
Sir Arthur Haselrig came hastening down from the North to
counteract it. He was powerful enough to deal with Lilburne
and to influence Parliament, but not to stand against Cromwell.
On April 20, 1653, Cromwell, sitting in his place in the House
clad as an ordinary citizen, and with Colonel Harrison outside
with a troop of soldiers, dissolved the Rump of that Parliament
whose assembling had cheered Lilburne in the Fleet thirteen
years earlier. Now its dissolution gave him hope of the end
of his banishment.

Elizabeth herself arrived unexpectedly at Bruges on May 3
to confirm the total dissolution of the Parliament and to discuss

the possibilities opened by the fact that the Parliament which had exiled her husband was now dissolved.[33] On the following day Lilburne's letter desiring a pass was on its way.[34] But in due course he was informed that such an address could be made only to the authority that would succeed the Long Parliament. At the same time " some of great power " were inquiring if Lilburne would be quiet if he came home. The answer was what might have been expected: " I am as free born as any man breathing in England (and therefore should have no more fetters than all other men put upon me)." [35]

Elizabeth returned to England in the care of a friend primed with " full instructions " from her husband to procure the pass and send a copy to him at Dunkirk. He was confident and buoyant: " I long to see London," he wrote after her, instructing her to send horses for him at Canterbury; and he wrote obscurely of " something of very great consequence " he had to say to " a great faithful man as I shall trust " if " I find things in a handsome way to my liking." [36] He wrote " many humble addresses " to Cromwell. That of May 14 he had printed in Dutch and English, and sent a copy to Paris to be printed in French and English, and one to Amsterdam to be printed in Latin and English. One he sent to his wife to get printed in England.

But Elizabeth knew too well her husband's " provoking pen," and to his mounting anger " most irrationally hindered it." He blamed Cromwell for reducing her to such lowness of spirit. " Your late barbarous tyrannical dealing with me," he wrote, " hath exposed her to so much folly and lowness of spirit in my eyes, in some of her late childish actions, as hath in some measure, produced an alienation of affection in me to her." Never had Lilburne been so unjust or so cruel as when he wrote of " that tenderness of affection that I owe her, whom I *formerly* entirely loved as my own life." [37]

Even so flamboyant a use of the petition—was he hoping to make money by their sale?—brought no reply. By May 29 he was waiting at Calais for the next boat in a state of growing tension. Asked what he would do if his pass failed to come, he replied it was in Cromwell's power to send or hinder it, so he would either kill Cromwell himself or send some one to do it for him ! He made one final bid to attract the required permission by writing to his friends from the Silver Lion in Calais offering to show on his return how England could become more flourishing in trade than ever before, with taxes lightened, land settled on soldiers and decayed householders, the old and lame provided for, and not a beggar in England.[38]

So, after final letters to Cromwell and the Council of State from Dunkirk and from Calais, Lilburne prepared to risk all on a personal stand. After, so it was alleged by the spies who still dogged his footsteps, a farewell supper with Buckingham and the Cavaliers at the Silver Lion, he crossed on the morning of June 14 and made his way with speed to London via Canterbury, where his wife had fresh horses awaiting him. Challenged here in the Lord General's name for his pass, he replied he was as good a man as Cromwell and needed no pass, and galloped off, making the journey from Calais to his home in a day.[39]

William Kiffin was there to help, and went immediately with Elizabeth to Cromwell, but, failing to obtain an audience, left the letter which Lilburne had written from their lodging in Little Moorfields immediately he arrived. His position was desperate, he pleaded; he must either go to a foreign country where he was not known and try there to earn a living or else return home. He was conscious of the hard things he had said of Cromwell, yet hoped and believed these would be " construed to be the fruits of my highest passions when my reason was clouded, not only by my sad and most heavy sufferings, but also by the misapprehensions of your Excellencies actions and intentions." He was now resolved to live " quietly and submissively," " godly and peaceably," with his " poor distressed Family." I will, he said, " studie to serve the Commonwealth, if those trusted with the Government thereof, should at any time conceive me fit for their Service; or otherwise to confine myself to the most private life." [40] If Lilburne had decided that Cromwell's efforts at reform were genuine and were worthy of Leveller support he said so too late. Unwonted humility was now of no avail. Cromwell's burdens were too great for him to risk augmenting them. On the 15th Lilburne was taken into custody by the sheriffs, and on the following day the Council of State ordered him to Newgate.

The three and a half years that had passed since Lilburne's

acquittal at the Guildhall were the least heroic part of his life. His energies were dissipated—he was too restless to settle down as a family man, ill-equipped by temperament to make money, not strong enough to alter the trend of events, yet fighting a series of private rearguard actions, still toying with the possibility of a Royalist acceptance of the *Agreement of the People*—and he was in addition for seventeen months removed from the English scene. That the onlooker is left with a sense of disappointment or anticlimax is due perhaps to the contrast with the heroic issues that occupied the rest of his life. It is partly due also to the sense of the dramatic that looks to the hero to play a part larger than life in every scene, and cannot bear the entr'acte where all is subdued. But when the curtain went up on the penultimate act Lilburne was back, full centre, playing not the subordinate rôle of father or husband or public attorney or exile, but that of Free-born John making his last appearance. As Hyde expressed it: " Lilburne appeared undaunted, and with the confidence of a Man that was to play a Prize before the People for their own Liberty." [41]

CHAPTER TWENTY-EIGHT

" *Long Live Lilburne !* "

And what, shall then honest John Lilburne die ! Three-score thousand will know the reason why !

ANON, July 1653

Whatsoever is the issue of my trial, will hereafter be drawn into a precedent, either for the good or evil of all the people of England.

JOHN LILBURNE, Trial, Old Bailey, August 1653

LILBURNE COULD NOT HAVE RETURNED AT A WORSE TIME. With the Rump dissolved, the Government of the country was wide open to the winds of dissension, any one of which might blow into a hurricane before a new Government was settled. Ireton, whose statesman's mind would have risen at once to the challenge of a new constitution, had died of plague-fever in Ireland nineteen months earlier, while Lilburne was rioting in the Fens. Cromwell hesitated between the proposals of Major-General Harrison for a nominated Assembly of the righteous, and of Major-General Lambert for an elected Parliament governing within the framework of a written constitution not unlike the officers' *Agreement of the People*. His temperament inclining him to a Parliament of Saints, on May 6 the congregational churches were asked to nominate " persons of approved fidelity and honesty " from whom the Council of Officers might select representatives. While the churches were considering their nominees the firebrand Leveller began to petition for return. On June 14, with the Council of Officers still selecting the Members of the new Parliament, amid petitions for Cromwell to assume the supreme authority, verses in praise of Charles I, sermons on " The Crying Sin of England of not caring for the Poor," Lilburne himself reappeared in London, bastioned by a core of old supporters and new, all ready to fling into his defence every one of the old devices and many more.

The Royalist and other correspondents were agog. Rumours flew from mouth to mouth and from pen to pen, letters and news-sheets mingling pleasure that Lilburne and Cromwell were again at grips, with expectation of Lilburne's end, Cromwell's discomfiture, and even of widespread disturbance. It was variously reported that Lilburne was acting for the Dutch, that he intended to prosecute Haselrig, that he came as leader of the Levellers to embroil the nation,[1] that there was " some great design in hand " in favour of the King.[2] Twenty eminent citizens offered to stand bail for him for £20,000 apiece, it was reported.[3] In the conventicle at Black-friars Samuel Highland led prayers for him. A woman preached at Somerset House in his behalf.[4] The Government was at a loss. Some thought he should be brought to trial by special warrant; others would have him tried by a Council of War as having endeavoured since his banishment to disaffect the Army and the fleet. The Council of State was divided. Some favoured leniency to placate the country and Army, but Cromwell was violent against Lilburne " to the prejudice of his wisdom." [5] " Legislative John Lilburne has almost brought his neck into a noose," gloated Theodorus to Lord Conway.[6] Hyde expressed the calculated interest of the more sober Royalists when he wrote to Nicholas: " I shall judge much of Cromwell's power and interest both in their Council and Army, as John proves to be hanged or not hanged; and I see letters from no ill hands in England, that it is a measuring cast between them, and infallibly that one will hang the other." [7]

It was an inappropriate time for Isaac Walton to publish on May 20 *The Compleat Angler; or, the Contemplative Man's Recreation*. If Lilburne were inclined to humour it might have made him smile as he prepared the pleas that could bring him life or death. If the authority of the late Parliament was taken from them for misgovernment, he was saying, then surely he could crave the suspension of their Act against him; he had no design, end, or intention, he averred, to interfere with the new Government. Cromwell promised a fair trial, which was fixed for June 21. Lilburne then petitioned for postponement until the new authority had assembled on July 4, and this was granted.[8]

Lilburne made good use of his time. If he was not to be released, but was to stand trial, it should be after the old fashion in the full light of publicity. Back in action, he was the same John Lilburne still, his vitality and his endurance unimpaired. " John Lilburne keeps a filthy stir stil with Petitions and Addresses one in the neck of another," wrote *Pragmaticus* on June 19. " He invites daily all his friends and those of his Levelling faction to petition for him." [9] " It cannot be expressed what posting here is up and downe about John Lilburne in Citty, Country, and Army," said a newswriter.[10] Not only from London, but from his friends in Hertfordshire and Bedfordshire, from soldiers, from Mrs Lilburne and other women, the petitions and deputations came. Praise-God Barebone, acting for the House of Commons, found himself quite unable to deal with a deputation of twelve women, headed by the militant Mrs Chidley, mother of the gentle Samuel, who brought a petition signed by 6000 women.[11]

Lilburne himself printed pamphlet after pamphlet. He borrowed money to pay for the printing of thousands of copies of *A Jury-man's Judgement*, a supporting pamphlet which he liked well, and for his own *Plea in Law*. Many hundreds were given away, but when the cost became too great they were sold.[12] Though many pamphlets and petitions were confiscated and some probably never found their way into his collection, Thomason lists thirty-two tracts supporting Lilburne in the two months between the Leveller leader's return and the end of his trial, not including the newspapers.

The Nominated Parliament when it met on July 4 did not repeal the Act under which Lilburne was banished, and he was therefore brought to trial before the regular sessions at the Old Bailey on July 13, 1653. It was necessary only for the court to prove that he, John Lilburne, had returned, in order to secure conviction and death under the Act. But on the morning of the trial Lilburne sent yet another petition to Parliament asking for an examination of the whole issue on which that Act had been based,[13] and his first object was delay until that petition had been considered. Delay was a tactic of which Lilburne was past-master.

When proceedings opened the court was thronged with an
excited crowd, many of whom were said to be armed, while
outside the streets were dense with Lilburne's supporters.
Flung among the crowds was the text:

> And what, shall then honest John Lilburne die !
> Three-score thousand will know the reason why ! [14]

Closely supporting him in court were his father, father-in-law,
cousins, and his brother-in-law, Thomas Gore; Richard
Overton, John Prince, Samuel Chidley, Mrs Mary Dorman,
who had seen his cruel whipping and had visited him in the
Fleet, Thomas Hawes, who had stood by him at the pillory,
and Henry Clarke, a Quaker friend. According to a newsletter
written from London while the trial was taking place, there
were " daily " petitions to Parliament on his behalf, and
" infinite numbers of Pamphlets . . . hourly printed and
dispersed by his friends about the Towne." [15] The Government would not dare to condemn him to death, reported the
Venetian Secretary in England. He himself, " with a courage
exalted both by warfare and by literature," " did not scruple
to declare . . . that his death would find 20,000 avengers." [16]
On a peaceful bowling-green in Highgate a judge predicted his
execution, but a merchant standing by replied that that would
prove the bloodiest day London had ever seen ! [17]

The Government was taking no chances. Three regiments
of horse were held about St James's to deal with trouble.[18]
The Army's march to Scotland was delayed, wrote the Venetian
Ambassador, because of the Government's apprehension.[19]

It seemed almost as if the trial of 1649 were to be repeated
when the clerk commanded Lilburne to hold up his hand
and Lilburne, with assumed naïveté, turned to Lord Chief
Baron Wylde asking him to explain what was meant by holding
up the hand at the bar. After what reporters termed a " large
dispute between the Court and him," which consumed much
time, Lilburne acknowledged his name and heard the indictment read. Was he guilty or not guilty of returning to
England? he was asked. After a further struggle Lilburne
obtained leave to speak against " the insufficiency and
illegality " of the indictment before pleading to it. " Now is
the time," he maintained, " to assign my errors against the

Indictment before I plead to it," and in order to do this he
demanded a copy of the indictment and counsel to advise.
This was the point at which the *Institutes* were produced and
" pregnant and pertinent passages . . . were distinctly read by
the prisoner at the Bar." On the 13th he was allowed counsel
on one point, on the 14th he was still struggling for a copy
of his indictment, by the 16th he had wrung a copy from the
court, doing what no prisoner had ever done before, and had
won counsel at large. He then demanded also an Oyer, or
hearing, of the Act under which he was banished, and started
to make his objections to his indictment.

All this was effected with the help of even more argument,
noise, and what a reporter called " hurley-burleys " than had
accompanied his trial in 1649. When a new figure appeared
in court and mumbled something that the prisoner could not
hear he immediately demanded to know what that newly come
gentleman was that was so far afraid to speak his mind?
When it was attempted to stop his spate of words, " Good
Mr Recorder, interrupt me not," he requested. When on the
16th Prideaux attempted to hold him to the question of whether
he was the John Lilburne named in the Act of Banishment
Lilburne " fell upon Mr Prideaux " : In what capacity was he
there? He was no judge, no citizen, and could not therefore
sit on the bench as one of John Lilburne's judges. As
Attorney-General he was prosecutor, and could be no more.
Therefore, cried Lilburne to the judges, " do that which
becomes you, and thrust him down to the bar, and there let
him (as I do) stand with his hat in his hand, and know his
office and duty! " Lilburne had paid back an old debt!

Lilburne was obviously playing to the people in a way he
had not done before. It was as though he realized that this
was to be his last public stand, and he would portray Free-
born John, the leader of the populace, with an abandon he had
never before displayed. The people responded, applauding
everything he said.[20] As he demanded his Oyer he " cried
out again and again, My lord, rob me not of my birthright, the
benefit of the law . . . if you will be so audacious and unjust
in the face of this great auditory of people, to deny me, and
rob me of all the rules of justice and right, and will forcibly
stop my mouth, and not suffer me freely to speak for my

life according to law, I will cry out, and appeal to the people, and do cry out, and appeal to all the people, that hear me this day, how that my lord-mayor, and this court, by violence rob me of my birthright."

The court continued in great heat and rage, said the reporter. The Recorder told him he was trifling away the time of the court, some one cavilled at Lilburne's pronunciation of *certiorari*, Sir John Maynard, Lilburne's counsel (who had been chairman of Lilburne's committee in 1647), gave some verbal instructions which Thomas Gore, Lilburne's brother-in-law, wrote down. Gore and Lilburne's father then tried to speak, Mrs Dorman, accused of admitting to receiving printed petitions from John Lilburne, cried out, " That's false, my lord, I never said any such thing! " and the most " furious hurley-burleys " continued between the Lord Mayor, the Recorder, the Attorney-General, " mumbling Mr Hall the Attorney of the Dutchy," and Mr Lilburne, his father, brother-in-law, Mr Thomas Hawes, and Thomas Prince. Prince made the most noise, and " pressed hard on " urging the right of the bystander to speak for the prisoner at the bar, while the clerk to the court called to have Lilburne gagged. Lilburne then, exerting himself, with a mighty voice made himself heard over all:

" My lord, will you murder me without right of law . . . are you afraid, and ashamed to produce that Act of Parliament upon which you pretend to ground your indictment . . . you will give me and the people cause to believe, that there never was such an Act . . . but that rather all your proceedings against me, from first to last, is a malicious packed conspiracy . . . to take away my life! "

" The officers crying out ' Hear the Court !' and the said mumbling Mr Hall still singing his pitiful ill-tuned song of pressing for Judgment against the prisoner," Colonel Okey was sent to get more troops, and a guard of horse forced its way into the court and restored order. Lilburne refused to continue until all the soldiers had departed from the place of justice.[21]

In the end a compromise was reached, Lilburne agreeing to hand in his exceptions to the indictment and the court agreeing to grant him an Oyer of the Act of Banishment if

the request were signed by his counsel, who by that time had
left the court. With Lilburne calling on the people to witness
this promise, and maintaining that he had still more exceptions
to make, the court rose on July 16, and the rest of the hearing
was postponed until the next session on August 10.[22]

Against the time gained, Lilburne had to set an adverse
factor. On the day his trial opened a printed deposition of the
spies who had been tracking Lilburne in the Netherlands was
published, read to the Commons, issued to the judges, and
distributed among the soldiers.[23] Five different people produced
similar testimony of Lilburne's Royalist activities. Lilburne
hastened to reply in *Malice detected, in printing certain Informations and Examinations concerning Lieut. Col. John Lilburn
the morning of the Tryal . . . which were not brought into his
Indictment*, and the pamphlet was in print two days later.
Lilburne swore by Almighty God that the stories as recounted
were not true, but their publication did him harm. The
Government laid aside his petition, and when the Court
reassembled on August 10 it refused him Oyer of the Act of
Banishment. In vain he pointed out that such charges were
" a poysonous ingredient that his Adversaries have always in
readiness to cast into his Dish, although they know it is false
as Hell," and that similar charges had circulated before his
1649 trial.[24]

Petitions continued to stream in, including one of July 29
from women supporters and one of August 2 from apprentices.
The first session of the trial was well reported, Lilburne's
Exceptions were published as well as other pamphlets by him,
including an expostulation to the troop of horse who were
called in to restore order in the court: " What are you? Are
you Englishmen and true English souldiers raised for maintenance and defence of the ancient Rights and Liberties of
England . . . how is it you enter the place and legal Courts of
Justice, with horse and swords drawn? " [25]

When the court reassembled six or seven hundred men were
reported to be present, armed with " pistolls, bills, daggers,
and other instruments," to rescue him if the verdict went
against him.[26] The Government responded by posting two
companies of foot near the Old Bailey, while horse and foot
paraded the streets.[27] Although Oyer of the Act of Banishment

was refused, a copy of his present indictment was read and a
jury impanelled. Lilburne tried every trick to prevaricate
and delay before coming to his exceptions and making his
final plea. "His arguments and subtle wit," reported the
Venetian Secretary, drew "immense crowds and plentiful
sympathy." [28] Colonel Baxter, in charge of the guard, was
drawn to exclaim that there was a necessity of taking away
his life, for that he was a pestilent fellow and seducer of the
people! Lilburne replied tartly that it would be better for
Baxter to be selling his bodkins and thimbles than presuming
to pass judgment on his superiors! [29] It "was apparent to all
honest Christians," he continued, "that he himself had (ever
since his coming to maturity of knowledge and understanding),
been a constant Sufferer for, and Assertor of the Fundamental
Rights and Liberties of the free-born people of England, and
that he would seal the same with the price of his precious and
innocent bloud; desiring that what he died for, might be
recorded to future Ages and posterities." He was continuing
in similar strain—that he would be pleased to shed his innocent
blood if the free-born people of England could but know that
John Lilburne died for the fundamental laws and liberty of all
free-born Englishmen—when he was made to stop.

On the 13th he was allowed to start again, telling the court
that he had consulted with God and his own soul and his chief
friends and the laws of England, and could see that they were
determined he should die. Therefore, he said, do your
pleasure! But his counsel were fearful that the court would
seize its chance and pass sentence out of hand, so they whispered
to the prisoner to go on, which he did! On the 19th he was
still holding off his accusers. A month previously he had
written that he was weary and spent in spirit, with little leisure
to sleep or eat. Perhaps he was not sorry when on the 20th
he was told that he could prevaricate no longer, but that he
must plead to the indictment or be judged worthy of death.

Lilburne then put in a plea of Not Guilty. He made several
technical exceptions to the charge against him—that the Act
under which he was banished was insufficient in matter and
form, that it was not clear that it was an Act of the English
Parliament, that it recited an illegal judgment since Lilburne
had never been indicted, summoned, or set to plead to an

indictment, that the Act did not agree with the judgment, the one giving him twenty days to leave the country, the other thirty, and that his present indictment did not prove that he, John Lilburne, was the Lieutenant-Colonel John Lilburne named in that Act.

But his main defence was that as he was condemned by the Rump his release was the necessary consequence of its dissolution for injustice, irregularity, and maladministration. If, on the other hand, that Parliament was adjudged lawful and its administration upright, then punishment ought first of all to be inflicted upon Cromwell as the principal agent of its unjust dissolution. " Close reasoning," commented the Venetian Secretary, " whereby the prisoner aims at his chief enemy." [30]   Lilburne also appealed to the jury to consider what would happen if such an Act as that which banished him could do him to death. Neither they nor their wives nor children would be safe. He appealed to them not to look only to the fact of John Lilburne's return, but to regard themselves as judges of law as well as of fact and ask themselves if that was good law. " Whatsoever is the issue of my trial, will hereafter be drawn into a precedent, either for the good or evil of all the people of England," he concluded.

Lilburne spoke direct to them for about two hours. They were a long while considering their verdict. When they returned it was on no technical flaw that they delivered judgment. " John Lilburne," they announced, " is not guilty of any crime worthy of death." [31] The shout of joy within the court-room spread to the soldiers who were guarding it and the crowds outside, and was heard a full mile off. The soldiers beat their drums and sounded their trumpets.[32] " Long live Lilburne ! " was heard on every hand.[33] In Hertfordshire they gave solemn thanks to the Lord.[34] Again Lilburne had made his stand, rallied his supporters, and worsted his enemies. The verdict was the more unwelcome to Cromwell because he had expected otherwise.[35] But Lilburne's very triumph spelt not liberty, but renewed imprisonment. His acquittal was interpreted in terms of criticism of the Government. In itself it caused apprehension, but, as the Venetian Secretary noted, " what matters more is the discovery thus made of the unpopularity of the present government." [36] In short, as another observer noted, the "Lord General's intended government . . . and Lilburne's turbulent restless spirit" were "altogether incompatable."[37] It was because he at last realized this that Cromwell kept Lilburne in prison while the Council of State was required to examine the judges and jury and report with all speed upon "scandalous, seditious and tumultuous Papers" which had been dispersed during the trial, and to examine the shorthand reports of Lilburne's speeches.[38] After this had been done, and the jury had shown no sign of regretting its verdict,[39] it was ordered on August 27 that John Lilburne should be held prisoner "for the peace of this Nation." Quietly, that night, he was removed to the Tower, guarded by a party of horse, the Lieutenant having orders to keep him close.[40] This time there came no jaunty remark to signify his return to the prison he knew so well, but on September 3 his wife was allowed to go to her husband, provided she remained there with him and no access was occasioned to him or to herself by her being there.[41] Cromwell, it seemed, had learned to do what the Long Parliament failed to accomplish, for Lilburne remained quiet. The Lieutenant of the Tower was instructed to refuse the application for *habeas corpus* that was made in October,[42] but Lilburne must have been brought once to the Upper Bench, for the Lieutenant's application for the quarter's expenses in December included an item for taking Lilburne by barge there and back.[43]

The Royalists had hoped for much from Lilburne's trial. A newsletter from London in July told of a "great and formidable conspiracy by the Levellers in City, country, gathered churches and army," the knowledge of which came from several reliable sources. Cromwell, it was said, knew of it, and was so apprehensive that he would be willing to treat with the King: he was "so perplext" with the threats of the Leveller party on the one hand and "the Presbyterian stifnesse" on the other, said the writer, that he "knoweth not how to steere."[44] In the event there was merely one final moment of Leveller agitation when a pamphlet attacking Cromwell was scattered in the streets on the night of September 14. It accused him of high treason to "his lords the people of England" in not entrusting them with the choice of a new representative when he expelled the Rump, and called upon the people to elect a new Parliament on October 16 by voting in their counties by manhood suffrage.[45]   Once again there was an appeal to the soldiers, and Cornet Joyce was prominent in the agitation, saying that he wished that the pistol aimed at Cromwell on Triploe Heath had been actually discharged ! He was cashiered, the agitation was easily suppressed,[46] and Lilburne made no sign.   In the attempted reforms of the Nominated Parliament, in its abdication, in the Instrument of Government and the installation of Cromwell as Protector in December, he showed no interest.   By January 1654 he was being allowed visitors at the Lieutenant's discretion, and an allowance of £2 a week.[47]

There occurred at this time, however, a case which it was feared might serve as a model for Lilburne.   A Captain Streeter, imprisoned by the Council of State for publishing seditious pamphlets, obtained a *habeas corpus* in January 1654 on the grounds that an Order of Parliament ceased to be of force after a dissolution, and on February 11 he left prison a free man. Cromwell knew there was only one way to prevent Lilburne following this precedent—to remove him where the writ of *habeas corpus* did not run.[48]   He was sufficiently worried by Royalist plotting early in the year, and mindful enough of the power that still lay in his adversary, to take this step.

On March 16, 1654, the Council of State made an order to remove John Lilburne to Jersey.   On March 23 Captain Lucas was ordered to find a vessel at Portsmouth to receive John Lilburne and a guard and proceed thither.   The Governor of the island was commanded to keep Lilburne close prisoner within the compass of the castle, and to command some trusty person to keep a strict eye over him: the Protector and Council had thought fit " for the public peace " to make this transfer from the Tower to Castle Orgueil.   Little more than a week after he landed his wife, in London, gave birth to her ninth child, Benomy.   Three months later the Governor was commanded to disregard any writ for *habeas corpus*.[49]

Lilburne had written only one pamphlet after his trial.   He was weary, spent, something of the old assurance was gone, in spite of the verdict in his favour.   He knew that Cromwell would not release him.   He knew at last that reason and conviction were not enough to change a political system and reform a social code.   Yet he felt the need, once more, to justify the career of John Lilburne. He was troubled at criticisms of turbulence and quarrelsomeness when he knew he had acted throughout from a burning conviction of justice. "Frailties and infirmities I have," he wrote, "and thick and threefold have been my provocations; he that hath not failed in his tongue, is perfect, so am not I. I dare not say, Lord I am not as other men; but, Lord be merciful to me a sinner; But I have been hunted like a Partridge upon the mountains; My words and actions in the times of my trials and deepest distress and danger have been scanned with the spirit of Jobs comforters; but yet I know I have to do with a gracious God, I know that my redeemer liveth, and that he will bring light out of this darkness, and cleer my innocency to all the world." [50]

CHAPTER TWENTY-NINE

Requiescat

His impatient spirit, wearied out with long and sore afflictions.
ELIZABETH LILBURNE, to the Protector, July 31, 1655

MOUNT ORGUEIL WAS A GLOOMY NORMAN FORTRESS HIGH ON
the rocky coast of the eastern end of the island of Jersey. With
fierce seas below and high hills behind, it was dark and cold,
and the scattered habitations below gave little promise of
friendliness or cheer. As a young man Lilburne had found
satisfaction in following his spiritual leader, Dr Bastwick, into
the Gatehouse prison. Now, a weary veteran of thirty-nine, he
experienced no such cheer when he entered the castle from
which William Prynne had been released when he himself left
the Fleet. Nor could Prynne's laboured description in verse
of the castle render either solace or amusement.[1] Cut off from
communication with home except through irregular shipping,
this prison, unlike the Tower, could crush his spirit. There was
no audience outside to hear his words, no printers hurriedly
and secretly to print them, no " straggling soldiers'" to come
to him, no Judge Jenkins to learn from or Lewis Dyve to plot
with—only the waves beating on the rocks like the thoughts
beating in his brain. Imprisonment then had been a life on
its own, an excitement full of hope. This was a hard and lonely
exile, made the more bitter since it spelt the failure of his cause
and the end of his personal following. Thousands had sworn
to die if he were convicted at his trial; no one stirred when he
was removed equally effectively from the political scene. The
splendid democracy in the Army in 1647, the stirring pamphlets
and petitions, men and women with high hopes and eloquent
pens, asking only for justice and a political framework in which
to realize it, had faded into acquiescence before an Instrument
of Government and a Protector. With fire in his belly and

Jehovah his spirit, Lilburne had thought it only necessary to denounce the wrong and proclaim the right. The bitterness of Castle Orgueil was that he now knew this was not enough.

He tried at first to enlist the support of the garrison and to make contact with home. He had not been in Jersey a couple of months before there were rumours in England of his being put to death following the discovery of papers prejudicial to the Protectorate.[2] The following April a newsletter told how he had endeavoured to send a packet to England, but the person who had it threw it overboard when the ship's officer approached to search him.[3] Captain George Gibbon, the Governor, was clearly worried over Lilburne's presence: he fell into no such friendliness with him as Sir Philip Carteret had with Prynne. Lilburne's railing and what the Governor described as his " ill language and threatnings " caused " many disorders " among the garrison, and brought him close imprisonment without the benefit of air or exercise.[4] In similar circumstances in 1639 Lilburne was rumoured to have set the Fleet on fire. No such opportunity offered here. In the " unparalelled extremity " of his " outward desires " an old woman named Elizabeth Crome looked after him, her " faithfulness and tender compassion " his only comfort.[5] No other approach proved possible, and his health and reason suffered. Gibbon thought it better to end Lilburne's close imprisonment and let him walk abroad again within the castle precincts accompanied by a keeper, " that so his spirit may be a little qualified, and the fitter to be dealt with." But Lilburne refused to take the air unless he could go along without " a dogg at his heeles." [6] " He is more trouble than tenn such as Ashburnham ! " exclaimed Gibbon, and suggested that the only way to bring Lilburne's spirit to be meek and quiet was to bring him nearer home, where some of his soberer friends might reason with him.[7]

If Lilburne received news from home it would not have cheered him. The Leveller party had lost all coherence, its failure to take action after his trial being symptomatic of its general decay. When Cromwell's first Protectorate Parliament met on September 3, 1654—the first elected Parliament for fourteen years—it was returned on the old franchise, but with a new property qualification of £200 *per annum* for Members. Wildman was elected for Scarborough, but on a technical flaw was refused his seat; in Southwark a little of the old spirit revived, and Samuel Highland, who had acted as messenger for Lilburne in 1648, and led prayers for him in 1653, was returned; Lenthall, Haselrig, the elder Vane, were there, with Skippon, Fleetwood, Lambert, Fairfax. Cromwell spoke on the 4th of liberty of conscience and liberty of the subject— " two as glorious things to be contended for, as any God hath given us "—yet both could be abused to the peril of the Commonwealth, the one to prevent the magistrate from acting in cases of disorders, the other to overturn the ancient ranks and orders of England—" A nobleman, a gentleman, a yeoman "; he signalled out the Levellers and the Fifth Monarchists for castigation.[8]

The Republican movement had hardened with Cromwell's assumption of the office of Lord Protector, and when Cromwell required Members to sign a pledge not to amend the Instrument of Government about 160 were excluded, including Haselrig, Vane, and Bradshaw. The Fifth Monarchists prepared a petition, some Army officers, together with John Wildman, prepared another in the old style for popular support and signature, but were betrayed by a spy and arrested, leaving Wildman to publish the petition in October 1654. The Navy talked of sending up its grievances by way of petition.[9] But these were merely echoes of the earlier enthusiasm.

On June 29, 1655, fifteen months after Lilburne's arrival, old Henry Dewell, his father-in-law, made the long journey to visit him. In the presence of the Governor he had two long interviews with Lilburne, trying to get some assurance of compliance. But Lilburne continued to protest against any way of gaining his liberty but by the law. When his father-in-law pressed him " to forbeare determyneing to have all things his owne way, and to refrayne his reproachful words " he replied, " The lawe is my way," and—the same John Lilburne still—said he would be willing to refer the " difference " between himself and Cromwell to four understanding Christians, and would undertake to accept their decision. That, reported Gibbon, " was the summe of all that his father or myselfe could have of him." " I cannot but report," he said, " that he is the very same man as formerly." In only one suggestion did he show any interest. When Mr Dewell mentioned that Cromwell might remove him to the Isle of Wight " that," said Lilburne, " I will assent unto." [10]   He also unbent sufficiently to ask his father-in-law if he could get permission for his own father to come over to see him. This caused the Governor great anxiety. Should he allow them to speak together alone? he asked the Council of State. He was afraid Lilburne had something secret to say and that he would try to send over some papers to England.[11]

Richard Lilburne did not come to Jersey. On July 31 he and Elizabeth again petitioned for John's release. Knowing his disposition better than any other, wrote his father, I am confident that his rash words proceed only from restraint, hard usage, and affliction [12]; my husband's restraint is still most severe, wrote his wife, " and his senses, health, and life endangered, and all because he is represented as violent and rash, and not to be trusted with liberty. I appeal whether his extreme sufferings after trial for life, and all converse of friendship withheld, are not such matter of provocation as to have caused the expressions reported. I am confident that if you would enlarge him, he would be quiet and thankful, for no one has ever received an act of violence at his hands. . . . I beg you to take away all provocation from his impatient spirit, wearied out with long and sore afflictions, and enlarge him, in pity to me and my children. I durst engage my life that he will not disturb the state. I should not else desire his liberty." [13]

In September Cromwell promised Elizabeth that her husband should be brought home.[14]   In October the *Cornelian* put into Weymouth with Lilburne and his old nurse on board, and as fellow-passenger William Harding, the Mayor of Weymouth, who had been visiting Jersey. Lilburne had been allowed some converse with Harding, probably when he had quietened down with the knowledge of his return to England. They talked of spiritual matters, and in particular of the Quakers, with whom, it seemed, Harding was in sympathy. Now he took Lilburne to stay for a few days at his house before the *Cornelian* proceeded to Dover.[15]

It was on October 10, 1655, that Captain Cornelius brought his vessel into Dover harbour and reported arrival with John Lilburne and several hogshead of cider from the Governor of Jersey.[16]   Lilburne's wife was prepared to move heaven and earth to obtain his release now that he was so near, but Lilburne, occupied with the spiritual crisis that he knew was rising within him, and still loftily determined to accept no favour that was not his by law, was a difficult man to deal with. Not only did he remain aloof from efforts of his friends and family to obtain his release, but he was incensed when he learned that Elizabeth was about to accept what he regarded as a favour at the hands of Sir Arthur Haselrig.

After her refusal as " John Lilburne's wife " to accept any interest in the Durham lands that was not given as a right Elizabeth had been living in poverty at the house of a friend, George Wade, in the City near the Guildhall, only rousing herself sufficiently to get little Benomy christened on his first birthday at Stoke Newington. Shortly before her husband's return Haselrig had made a further effort to help her, and she had agreed to take the land which he now proceeded to convey through his agent, Antony Pearson. While Elizabeth and her father-in-law were thankful that at last she could enter into some reliable means of subsistence, to John Lilburne the transaction spelt nothing but patronage. Haselrig could not rob him of his lands and then return some of them as a favour. Only if Lilburne's right in law were established should his wife enjoy them. Bitter were the quarrels between Lilburne and his wife and father, marring the homecoming that might have been the beginning of a happier life. For Dover Castle on its chalk cliffs and grassy downs, looking over the English Channel and with the little town clustering at its feet, promised a kinder home than Mount Orgueil. Not until Elizabeth visited her husband in Dover in November was an emotional reconciliation effected, when Lilburne spoke at length of his spiritual unrest.[17]

Elizabeth had an adventurous journey back to London, being wrecked and nearly losing her life in an accident on the Thames, as she told him when she wrote on November 29. But her letter then reflected his mood, as she herself had done throughout his career. " My Dear," she wrote, " Retain a sober patient Spirit within thee, which I am confident thou shalt see shall be of more force to recover thee, then all thy keen mettal hath been; I hope God is doing a work upon thee and me too, as shall make us study ourselves more then we have done." [18]

God was indeed " doing a work " upon Lilburne, who was

reading the works of " those preciousest . . . people called Quakers," and fighting, as he described, " for divers hours in several nights, one after another, when my God denyed sleep unto my outward eyes, and caused my soul to be awake with himselfe, and to be really exercised in an interchange of divine conference, contemplation and parley with him." [19] At his second trial he had been supported by Henry Clarke, one of his Southwark friends who became a Quaker,[20] and it may have been then that the seed was planted. In Jersey it was of the Quakers that he talked to Harding, and it may well be that the violence of his passion at that time found its antidote in the quietism of their creed. On his arrival at Dover he immediately sent to Giles Calvert for Quaker literature both for himself and his wife, and found particular comfort from the works of Dewsbury and James Nayler. Twenty years earlier Sibbes had called upon the militant Christian, exhorting his hearers to carry themselves above all threatenings, for all the devils in hell could not hurt one hair of their heads. Now Lilburne learned from Nayler of a meek Christianity, of a cross " to be daily taken up, whereby all the unruly nature must be crucified, for all must be brought subject to the yoke, even the most rebellious and stifnecked." [21] In the Fleet, when he had suffered such spiritual upheaval as he knew now, he had been helped to sanity and peace by a woman he described as " a poor dispised (yet understanding) Priscilla, to instruct me in, or expound unto me the way of God more fully." He does not name her—perhaps it was his old nurse, Katherine Hadley. Now to Dover Castle there came Luke Howard, an " Aquila, being a contemptible, yet understanding, spiritually, knowing, and single-hearted Shoomaker." [22]

Luke Howard, born in Dover in 1621, was a little younger than Lilburne, coming to London after his apprenticeship when the fortifications were being dug at the outbreak of the Civil War. Like Lilburne, he wrestled for truth and visited many of the congregations where Lilburne himself must have been. William Kiffin baptized him on a February day " when the Ice was in the water." He had not been included in the first levies of the Civil War, a fact for which he was later thankful, for he was thus " clear of the blood of all men." Not until 1655 did his soul-searching end in his embracing of

Quakerism, and he was one of the first to attend the meetings of Friends in Dover.[23]

The Quakers, or Friends, as they called themselves, were the followers of George Fox, son of a Leicestershire weaver, and apprenticed, like Luke Howard, to a shoemaker. Finding no satisfaction in any of the congregations or in any of the "mechanik preachers," he wandered for four years up and down England while armies were marching, Levellers were organizing, and Lilburne was pouring his pamphlets from the press. In 1647 he came to the simple realization that the spirit of God was within each man, and that the knowledge of Christ was an inner light that could reveal itself at any time without the help of dogma, form, or ceremony. A man need be equipped with nothing but a humble spirit and a belief in God and Jesus Christ. No prayer-book, no preacher, no sacrament, no church, was needed to guide him—only the witness in his conscience. It was a direct antithesis to Laud's belief that "the external worship of God and His Church is the great witness to the world, that our heart stands right in that Service of God." It was a natural development from Congregationalism, and many of the people called "Seekers," who, like Fox, had been searching for spiritual satisfaction, joined him as he travelled round the country. The "witness" would attend them in earthly matters: it guided Luke Howard in his relations with the master shoemaker to whom he was apprenticed; it would attend them in spiritual matters; it brought Howard to the conviction "that singing of Psalms in Rhyme and Meter" was to him a lie and a "Mock Service to the Lord," and guided him until he fully received the Truth.[24]

The simplicity of their belief caused the Quakers to denounce not only church forms and ceremonies, but all earthly vanities, such as ostentation in dress, bowing, or uncovering the head in homage; they would not swear an oath, but according to the Scripture their Yea was Yea and their Nay, Nay; they recognized the authority of no magistrate in any matter touching their spiritual beliefs; many of them were already pacifist, believing it wrong to take life. But the picture of their meetings in bare rooms where they would sit in silence until the spirit moved one of them to speak can be misleading. This they did, but they also held meetings in churchyards to witness against the service that was proceeding inside the Steeple House, and Friends tramped the country bearing witness in vigorous speech to the Truth that was within them. Although they were not politically active and did nothing concerted to oppose authority, magistrates found the visits of such Friends highly troublesome, and sectaries and others who had developed their own dogma, as well as Presbyterians and Baptists, found them strangely disturbing. They would even attend worship in church and act and speak as the spirit moved them against the forms of worship there practised. Many suffered imprisonment for their attempts to witness to the light, and for their refusal to take an oath when charged.

But it was their emphasis on the witness within which made such a strong appeal to Lilburne, when he abandoned his efforts to change the outward face of society. The witness of many Friends to their own conversion had echoes in his own experience. " But for a season and time my State and Condition was Death, Blackness and Darkness, yea, such as might and was indeed felt. . . . In which dark Condition, I sat waiting to see something Outwardly, and then was the word of the Lord within me, *Waite*." [25] It was Luke Howard speaking, but it might have been Lilburne in the Fleet, or in Mount Orgueil. In Dover Castle he was waiting when Luke Howard came to him.

Lilburne was prepared to find humility and directness of speech in the Quakers, yet hardly for such an answer as he got to his opening question to Luke Howard, " I pray, sir, of what Opinion are you? " " None," answered Luke Howard. The reply was so unexpected to one used to contention that it struck Lilburne into silence. This was the first of many visits, and when Lilburne was granted liberty on parole he went to Quaker meetings in the town, where, again, he met with a perspicacity and directness of speech that bore into his spirit as no words had done since the thunderings of Gouge and Sibbes twenty years earlier. On one occasion as he left a meeting, still without the full realization of conversion, the speaker, George Harrison, ran after him, exclaiming, " Friend, thou are too high for Truth! " Lilburne had been told many times he was wrong, quarrelsome, contentious, unruly—but never, since he thrust old Warder White down the stairs at Newgate, had he been accused of spiritual pride. The thought that pride was keeping him from salvation gave him, as he said, such a box on the ear that he was stunned.[26]

But Harrison had seen into one side of Lilburne's character, and his words achieved the full conversion of the Leveller leader. In December 1655 Lilburne was writing to his wife of his " indeared, spiritual, and faithful friend, Luke Howard," and telling her that he had " become dead " to his " former bustling actings in the world." He had Quaker books sent her. He begged her to give up her " many toilings and journeyings " for his outward liberty and to " sit down a little, and behold the great salvation of the Lord."

" O my dear love," he wrote, " I am already entered into my part of it, the mighty power of God inable thee to get in too, and also to go through thine, and effectually to go cheerfully and willingly along hand in hand with me."

It was in many ways a poor return for all she had suffered for him, but she saw in the letter renewed hope of his liberty, and took it to Cromwell and Fleetwood. But the Protector was not convinced. His wife then begged Lilburne to sign an engagement to do no harm to the State. But Lilburne had not yet entered into the final phase of complete renunciation of the world, and refused to do so. Yet he simplified his life further by sending his old nurse back to her husband, and wrote to Elizabeth that he could cheerfully live on bread and small beer. By May 1656 he was fully convinced, and marked his full conversion by *The Resurrection of John Lilburne now a Prisoner in Dover Castle*, which Giles Calvert published and which went into a second edition in less than a week. I wish, he said, " to make a publike Declaration in print, of my real owning, and now living in . . . the life and power of those divine and heavenly principles, professed by those spirituallised people called Quakers."

" I am," he said, " led up into power in Christ, by which I particularly can, and do hereby witness, that I am already dead, or crucified, to the very occasions, and real grounds of all outward wars, and carnal sword fightings and fleshy buslings and contests; and that therefore I confidently now believe, I shall never hereafter be an user of a temporall sword more, nor a joyner with those that so do." [27]

Of the earthly affairs with which he had struggled for so
many years only one troubled him, and that concerned the
lands which he felt rightfully belonged to him, but which had
wrongfully been offered to Elizabeth as charity. Haselrig's
agent in the matter, Anthony Pearson, was a Quaker and a
friend of Margaret Fell and her daughters. So, after consulting
his Quaker friends, Lilburne on May 28, 1656, wrote to
Margaret Fell at her home in Lancashire.[28] This woman,
who four years previously had been converted by George Fox
himself, and who would marry him years later, was devoting
her life to helping Friends in prison, and her legal experience
combined with her religious beliefs and her friendship with
Pearson seemed to offer just the help and advice that Lilburne
needed. But the land question apparently still proved in-
tractable, and no further sign came from Lilburne concerning
this or any other public matter.

There were attempts on the life of the Protector: Miles
Sindercombe, an old soldier, failing to find an opportunity for
direct assassination, set fire to Whitehall Chapel, but was
caught, imprisoned in the Tower, and took poison secretly
conveyed to him by his sister. Wildman, imprisoned in the
Tower from February 1655 to July 1656, became involved with
Sexby in a series of intrigues involving cross and double-
crossing between the remnants of the Levellers, the Spaniards,
the Royalists, and Thurloe, the intelligencer of the Protectorate.[29] Sexby, possibly with the collaboration of Captain Titus,
one of the spies who operated against Lilburne in the Netherlands, wrote *Killing No Murder* in the spring of 1657 to justify
attempts on Cromwell's life, was captured and imprisoned in
the Tower, where he died on January 13, 1658. But Lilburne
was already dead to the outward struggle.

He was not released, but in the spring of 1656 his wife and
children lived for a while in Dover, and he was frequently
allowed out on parole, even spending nights away from the
Castle, and would preach for the Quakers at Woolwich and
Eltham and other places in Kent.[30] The Quaker Richard
Hubberthorn found Lilburne in 1657 " zealous and forward
for the truth, with a sight and comprehension which is deep." [31]
He was back in Hixon country, treading probably the lanes
and fields his grandfather and his parents knew, and he and

his wife both had friends in the pleasant villages near the
Thames. When the birth of another child drew near it was at
Eltham that he took lodgings for his wife and family, and he
was allowed to join her there for her lying-in. He was due to
return to Dover Castle on August 29, but his health was failing,
and as the term of freedom drew to a close he grew sick and
weaker. He died on August 29, 1657, on the very day he was
due back in captivity.[32] " His impatient spirit, wearied out
with long and sore afflictions," turned away from the prison
cell, and he breathed his last in the arms of the woman who
had loved him with faith and devotion, who had served him
with courage and a conviction that yielded only to his own, and
who knew no greater pride than that of being " John Lilburne's
wife."

Two miles away to the north-west the old Palace of Greenwich lay deserted of all the pomp and bustle his grandfather
and his mother had known. Thomas Hixon, household servant
to Elizabeth and James, would not have understood the issues
for which his grandsons had fought, nor the religion in which
this one had died. He would hardly have thought that the
England which resulted was worth their struggles. A Protectorate substituted for a Crown, the gaiety of Court life
shrunk to a little music and a few insubstantial masques, the
intrigue of rising favourites and falling fortunes replaced by
wary intelligencers watching the French coast. Marvell and
Milton were a poor substitute for Marlowe and Shakespeare,
political pamphlets and religious discussions a bad second to
Ben Jonson and the love lyrics. The only constant was the
familiar cycle of poor harvests and rising prices. Perhaps the
wars with Spain and Holland would have been to Thomas
Hixon the most easily intelligible of the events of the fifties,
but could Blake hold a candle to the Sea Dogs on the Spanish
Main? The Navigation Act of the Commonwealth and other
measures to protect English trade and commerce, foreshadowed
when the East India Company was formed in the year his
daughter married Richard Lilburne, complicated a simple
issue of fighting for trade and treasure. Yet the trade grew,
and down in the Thames off Greenwich the shipping clustered
thicker than before, and merchantmen and colliers still came

and went with noisy bustle. The view from Duke Humphrey's hill over fields and river to the City was unchanged. The church of St Alphege remained, with its memorials of Hixons and household servants. But Thomas Hixon's grandson, though dying but two miles away, could not lie here with his mother and his grandfather. Neither as Leveller nor as Quaker could John Lilburne be recorded in the little church.

Two days after his death his body was taken instead to the Mouth, at Aldersgate, the scene of many Leveller discussions and the usual meeting-place of Quakers in London. Some of the mourners wished to cover the coffin with a hearse-cloth, but the Quakers prevented this, and at five o'clock in the evening carried it out into the street. At the door stood a man who tried again to throw a velvet pall over the coffin, but after a short struggle the Quakers raised it upon their shoulders and bore it unadorned to the burial. About 400 people followed it to the new churchyard in Bethlehem by Bishopsgate. There was no more disturbance. Lilburne's funeral was as quiet as the last two years of his life and left as little record; the friend of earlier days who stood by the door to honour him with a velvet pall passed unrecognized by the reporter.[33] His wife and three children carried on the struggle to live, and two months later the Protector received a petition from Elizabeth begging for payment of the £2 weekly pension which her husband had received while in prison, for the arrears due and for the repeal of the Act which still burdened his estate with a £7000 fine. Cromwell acted immediately, and on the same day ordered the continuance of the pension and a payment of arrears of £15.[34] He did more. Professing, as he always had, very great tenderness for Elizabeth, he arranged with Haselrig that she should at last take possession of the Durham lands.[35]

Cromwell outlived Lilburne for only a year. With his death the Commonwealth crumbled as Lilburne's democracy had done. But the woman who more than any other person had suffered from their long antagonism was still struggling to support her family. " Having long suffered heavy afflictions," she wrote to Richard Cromwell in January 1659, " I hoped that my husband's death would have been the last of my piercing sorrows." Richard Cromwell continued her pension,

but the tenants on the Durham lands still proved " perverse,"
and she was still saddled with much of the £7000 fine. She
begged Parliament to repeal the Act, that after seventeen years'
sorrows she might have a little rest and comfort among her
fatherless children.[36]   Primate, she added, was fined £7000
and sent to the Fleet, " but he soon got out, and gained his
colliery, and this adds to my vexations."   Some beneficiaries,
including Haselrig, had remitted their portions of the fine,
the State now agreed, " in respect of Mrs Lilburne's poverty,"
to discharge its share of £3000, and on August 15, 1659, the
Act of January 15, 1651, was made void.[37]   On March 15,
1660, her pension of £2 weekly was still being continued.[38]
Haselrig had shown himself fair and helpful to Elizabeth—it
was he who moved that her last petition be read—yet her
husband would have turned in his grave if he had known that
she agreed to surrender all the papers concerning the case, to
be burnt, without keeping any copy.[39]

CHAPTER THIRTY

England's Touchstone

He is thy true touchstone, O England, thou needest no other
to try either thy Gold or drosse.

Englands weeping Spectacle, June 1648

*E*VEN IN THE CONFUSED ENDINGS OF THE PROTECTORATE IN
1659–60 the Levellers never regained their cohesion. They had
splayed out into Fifth Monarchists, Royalists, Republicans;
some, probably, like Lilburne, had become Quakers. Wildman
and Maximilian Petty joined the Rota, a political club founded
by James Harrington in 1659, and perhaps brought some of
the Leveller principles to its discussions. In the Restoration
itself they played no part, and the very name of their party
died away. Neither in Restoration settlement nor in the
Revolution Settlement of 1688 was there any hint of a written
constitution or a wide suffrage. But the classic enunciation of
the principles of representative government came less than half
a century after the publication of the first *Agreement of the
People* in the work of Locke. Yet Locke, though extolling
representative government and speaking in terms of the
sovereignty of the people and the responsibility of Parliaments,
though using some of the premises and at times even the
language of the Levellers, was in the tradition not of Lilburne
or Wildman, but of Cromwell and Ireton. The principles
which triumphed in 1688 and which he enunciated in the
Essays on Civil Government two years later, were largely those
expressed by Ireton in the Putney debates and the *Heads of the
Proposals*.

For echoes of the Levellers themselves the historian must pass
over nearly two centuries of British history to the Chartist
movement. Here again he will find a social and economic
movement expressing itself in the demand for political reform;
again he will find the tactic of the signed petition presented

to Parliament by crowds of supporters, the sending out of emissaries to preach the word; and in the six points of the people's charter, including manhood suffrage and annual parliaments, he will find again Leveller ideas. But their name did not reappear; nor was any debt to the Levellers recorded except a note on the fly-leaf of a page of Lilburne's tracts belonging to William Hone [1]; nor was there any manifesto or pamphlet which in language or sentiment or principle echoed the magnificent voice of the seventeenth-century pamphleteer.

Of the separate ideas embodied in the Levellers' proposed constitution and considered so revolutionary in their own time, manhood suffrage was, in effect, achieved in 1884, without the exemption of servants or wage-earners or receivers of poor relief; while annual Parliaments, with the practice of quin-quennial, have ceased to be an issue. A virtually complete toleration has been achieved piecemeal, partly through a grow-ing indifference, partly through the abdication of religion from the realms of economics and politics, but not through the reservation of religion from the sphere of parliamentary activity. The idea of the written constitution, though never again a practical issue in this country, was actually implemented by the United States of America in 1787. Of the Levellers' proposed social legislation there is little that would not stand to-day. In their demands for freedom of speech and of the press there is nothing that the modern liberal would not endorse.

The general impression left by the Levellers is, indeed, one of an almost fierce individualism. It is their " rights " and " privileges " as " free-born Englishmen "—not " halfe-penny Charities "—which they demand. Freedom for the individual at his work, in his worship, in his choice of government, is essential to their idea of a good society. Their frequent use of the word ' liberties ' or ' freedoms,' in the plural, indicates the specific and positive content which they gave to the term. Freedom was understood by them to imply powers and rights, as well as an absence of coercion. Consequently, the cry for liberty was accompanied by the constantly expressed desire to check the strong and to protect the weak. Though this involved the infringement of liberty in the sense in which that idea was interpreted by some of the individualist thinkers of a later age, it was in complete accord with the positive content which the Levellers gave to the term. Their passionate belief in freedom, their defence of civil liberties, their protection of the weak and safeguarding of minorities, characterize them as true Radicals. They breathed the spirit of radical humanitarianism into an age which already was so much occupied with worldly success as to be in danger of forgetting the human values which underlay the mounting assets of its balance-sheets.

Yet the links with the Levellers are tenuous. In the forcing-house of the Civil Wars their party grew with startling precocity. Their decline after 1649 was equally emphatic. The reasons for their growth are apparent in the story of Lilburne. The reasons for their failure are harder to find. There was, perhaps, too much that was ephemeral in the very nature of their support; the splendour of the pamphlets and the spectacles provided by Lilburne created immense enthusiasm without providing corresponding action: there was too much unco-ordinated petition-ing and rioting. Not until 1649 was any economic action proposed, and then it was too late. The propaganda effort of 1647–48—so like the Chartists' later organization—might have developed into something really big if betrayal had not nipped it in the bud and swept away the two leaders. Moreover, what was true of the wider struggle against the King—that it was composed of groups united in opposition but diverse in aim—was true to a less extent of the Levellers. Goodwin's con-gregation early became lukewarm. The Baptists and some of the Independents who joined the Levellers in demanding re-ligious toleration withdrew their support when the establishment of the Commonwealth promised them freedom from persecu-tion. The very breadth of the Leveller programme indicates wide, if not conflicting, aims. It cannot be expected, said the astute *Pragmaticus* in November 1647, that " the soveraigne Hob-nails will drive all one way, and so come to a miraculous agreement." The support of the Army—in spite of the detailed organization of the agitators—was never really possible while Cromwell was in the saddle, as was proved at Corkbush Field. And once he held the powers both of legislature and executive in his own hands the Levellers never had a chance, as was proved by his suppression of the disturbances of 1649, his tightening of press restrictions, and his refusal to allow freedom to Lilburne.

At the same time, Leveller philosophy was too confused, too eclectic, to give a firm foundation to their party. They were both anarchist and authoritarian, believers at the same time in *vox populi* and *salus populi*; as democrats they believed in *vox populi*, but their stress was upon *salus populi*, and this brought them either to an individual interpretation of the public good, and so to the anarchy they repudiated, or else to Ireton's authoritarianism, which they denied with equal emphasis. The Levellers were splendid, and sometimes devastating, in attack, but placed on the defensive, as they were by Ireton and Cromwell, their case was not so strong. If they appealed to authority—and their appeals to the past made them frequently authoritarian—Ireton could with equal confidence pose a conflicting authority. Why natural law and the will of the majority any more than civil law and the will of the propertied interests? The Levellers preferred the former because it protected the mass of the people; Ireton preferred the latter because it protected property. If the Levellers deduced an inherent power in the people Ireton could deduce an inherent power in magistracy.

In posing their respective authorities the grandees and the Levellers were, at bottom, appealing to their own sets of values; and as polemical weapons the Levellers' criteria were of no more use than anyone else's. Their appeal to nature broke on the accusation of anarchism, which the Levellers were neither able to refute nor willing to accept. The appeal to reason broke because the Levellers were denied a monopoly of reason. They were on weak ground if they appealed to Saxon law—for why should the Parliament of 1000 be any more competent than the Parliament of 1640 to deal with the affairs of 1640? Magna Carta was of infrequent and doubtful assistance (" but a beggarly thing "). If they appealed to the body of post-Conquest law they were on Ireton's own ground. If they claimed the law of God, as ' Buffcoat ' did at the Putney debates when he asserted that he would be guided by the revelation of God, a counter-revelation could be claimed. There remained only *salus populi*. But this brought the disputants back to a personal evaluation. When Wildman

claimed at Putney that laws should be judged by their consequences—" I conceive wee looke to prophecies and looke to
what may bee the event, and judge of the justnesse of a thinge
by the consequences "—he was prepared to judge by what he
considered the good of the people. But Ireton would have
judged in accordance with the good of property-owners. The
issue remained, therefore, one of values. The *Agreement of
the People* itself, with its proviso " that as the laws ought to be
equal, so they must be good, and not evidently destructive to
the safety and well-being of the people," could appeal to no
more ultimate authority. The issue was between two sets of
values—dependent, as Ireton emphasized, largely upon the
social interests of the participants, and determined, as
events proved, in accordance with the strength of those rival
interests.

And here lies the most fundamental reason for the failure of
the Leveller party. In their programme there was much that
appealed to the lower-middle classes and the small industrial workers of the towns, and to the small landholders of
the country. What was there, however, to appeal either to the
landless labourer or to the industrial wage-earner? Not the
offer of land, for property was to be maintained. Not a share
in the direction of industry, for private ownership was to be
preserved. Not the certainty of the suffrage, for servants and
wage-earners and those in receipt of alms were to be excluded
on the ground that their interest was expressed through others.
They were promised, however, the relief of poverty by social
legislation, the reduction of taxation, the abolition of tithes,
the ending of " base tenures." Moreover, the *spirit* of Leveller
teaching was more revolutionary than its *content*, and there
was a spirit of equalitarianism in their doctrines which existed
not merely in the apprehensive imagination of the Army
grandees.

This spirit of equality was not strong enough, however, to
induce the Levellers to ally themselves wholeheartedly with the
class below them. Yet, ironically enough, it was at the expense
of members of the Levellers' own class—the small and medium
freeholders and leaseholders and the independent craftsmen—
that the ranks of the agricultural labourers and the factory
proletariat were to grow. The Levellers, representing a

decaying lower-middle class, shouldered aside by the vigorously developing middle class, to whom fell all the advantages of economic progress, remained the anti-equalitarian defenders of property, refusing to associate themselves with the coming proletariat, and thereby depriving themselves of a valuable ally. If the Levellers, instead of repudiating, had entered into alliance with the dispossessed, represented by the Diggers, would the issue have been any different?

But whatever is said of the Leveller movement in praise or criticism or explanation, nothing dims the lustre of the remarkable man who was its leader—a man whose life and experience reflected sharply the developments which made men successively rebels against the bishops, the King, the Parliament, and the Commonwealth. His clear-cut antagonisms, uncompromising battles, and sharp distinctions between right and wrong epitomize the less precise reactions of a large section of his fellow-countrymen. He had most of the qualities of leadership —courage, audacity, a quick and lively mind, a good memory, a strong personal charm, the ability to popularize and make an easily understood slogan of the question at issue, to give to his cause the full light of a profitable publicity, and himself to stir to action through telling words and personal example. His ready apprehension of the point at issue, his flair for popularization, his fluency of speech and pen, mark him as the natural leader of Leveller campaigns.

Each of his struggles was carried on in the full light of publicity. He was a born showman; a champion who made of each issue a spectacle. His energetic adoption of a dozen causes (not only his own), his unremitting campaign against any injustice (not only to himself), won him the enthusiastic support of all who had a grievance to right or a trouble to air. The poor, the oppressed, the unhappy, anyone who was ' down,' could claim the assistance of this great-hearted champion of the underdog. Conversely, he never hit a man when he was down, as he told Cromwell on several occasions. It was only when Cromwell was ' high,' remarked Clarendon, that Lilburne " thought him . . . an enemy worthy of his displeasure." [2] Once having adopted a cause or a principle, he would not swerve in his support of it. " I will not depart," he once said, " the breadth of one-hair of what I know to be my birthright," and his birthright undoubtedly included the right of a general partisanship of the oppressed.

Because of his frequent clashes with authority some likened Lilburne to a rainbow—never on the same side as the sun.[3] Others regarded him as naturally quarrelsome, fractious, quick to take offence:

> Is John departed? and is Lilburn gone?
> Farewel to both, to Lilburn and to John.
> Yet being dead, take this advice from me
> Let them not both in one grave buried be.
> But lay John here, lay Lilburn hereabout.
> For if they ever meet they wil fal out.[4]

The designation of *Mercurius Pragmaticus*—the " lunaticke Lieutenant Colonell " [5]—must often have appeared remarkably apt.

There is an element of truth in these judgments. Quick to take offence he probably was; quick to realize when his liberties were being infringed; possessed of an inherent suspicion of authority which made him fundamentally anarchist. He was, perhaps, too quick to jump to conclusions, too prone to pour out words of condemnation in conversation or in print. Neither his tongue nor his pen could be still for long.

> Here lies a man; no Woman can deny it
> Which dy'd in peace, but never liv'd in quiet.
> Here's a man so skil'd in Law and Reason,
> He could convert the sense o'th Law to Treason;
> The People pray, if o're his Grave ye walk
> For to tread softly, if he wake heel talk

read a fictitious epitaph.[6]

Similarly, Lilburne's intervention in a variety of issues caused some to regard him as " never well but when fishing in troubled waters . . . a busie body medling with other men's matters." [7] Another hostile critic remarked that Lilburne brought his sufferings on himself, and wanted to know: " Is it any reason that when a man shall wilfully set fire on his house and goods, his neighbours should be constrained to make him reparation? " [8] But the gentle Samuel Chidley, who had known Lilburne from the time of his Star Chamber imprisonment, saw him with other eyes—". . . he was like a

candle lighted, accommodating others and consuming himself." [9]

Lilburne was possessed of a very real sense of political
expediency. He foresaw the dangers of rule by the sword and
of the execution of the King by an illegally constituted court.
He cut through a great deal of woolly thinking and airy talk
when he announced that the substance of government mattered
more than its form, and that a monarchy, on terms, could
bring more benefit to the people than an unbridled Commonwealth. Lilburne was essentially practical, in spite of the
periods of spiritual emotion, in much the same way as most
Puritans were excellent men of business. He even showed,
in the negotiations of 1648, that he could compromise. Yet
compromise, in general, was alien to his disposition. His
certainty of being right sprang not from mere personal conceit,
but had in it much of the arrogance of the elect. He was in
touch with Jehovah, who entered into him with His Own Self.
Lilburne never lost this sense of election, even when he had
moved from the Congregation of Saints to the political battle-
field; he was as certain of the Lord's assistance in fighting for
law reform and an extension of the suffrage as in fighting
for freedom of conscience.

Of all his assets, none was more valuable than his pen. He
early realized that he had been given " a talent of the Lord,"
and did not hesitate to use it. Never at a loss for words, at
worst his sentences were long and involved as words and
phrases tumbled one upon another, abstract ideas jostling with
personal invective, historical allusion, and Biblical imagery to
clothe his blistering anger. Yet he always found his way out,
and left little doubt as to his meaning. At best, his style was
vital and hard-hitting, full of telling phrases that could scorch
or infuriate his adversaries. No one pricked the bubble of
Prynne's windy rhetoric more effectively than Lilburne, referring casually to " William Prynne, who takes so much elbow
roome to tell untruths." [10] No one exposed more devastatingly
than Lilburne the streak of ambition in Cromwell—" seeking
to say like Cardinal Wolsey, 'I and my King.'" [11] His
spelling was so atrocious—as his two extant letters reveal [12]—
that he must have been dependent on a good printer or reader
to edit his work, a fact which makes even more amusing

Samuel Chidley's story of one of Lilburne's printers who
would add long, irrelevant passages of his own to Lilburne's
manuscripts, with even worse spelling, giving Lilburne much
trouble in altering it all back to his original version! [13]

Early in his career, Lilburne had to reconcile his duty to
his family with his convictions. If law and justice were
destroyed his family, with the whole nation, would perish.
His stand was for them, too. If he should die God would take
care of them. And would they, he asks, wish him to sin
against his own soul for love of them? [14] It was a stern doctrine
to which he asked them to subscribe; it condemned them to a
life of little comfort and less repose. It did not prevent him
fathering ten children. For Elizabeth it meant " seventeen
years' sorrows." Yet she never hindered her husband's resolve,
nor ever tried to alter his decision, except to bring him back to
her from exile.

In all his public combats Lilburne laid himself open without
reserve, yet he told little concerning his private life. He never
mentions the birth of any of his children or refers to any of
them by name. Elizabeth as a person—apart from the work
she did for her husband—appears only fleetingly. He never
mentions Shakespeare, refers only once to Milton, gives no
indication of any general reading: Plutarch's *Lives* and Raleigh's
History of the World are his nearest approach. Poetry and
music he never mentions. His humour was not robust.
Did he join the apprentices in the " football war " up and
down the Strand, or take Elizabeth to Spring Gardens? The
portrait of 1641 and Bastwick's description of him when he
came to the Gatehouse in 1636 give a clear picture of the
handsome, impetuous youth from the country; the portrait of
1649 and his writings give a general picture of the man in
middle life. Occasional references show the conventional side
of his life—his call for " morning draughts " to the captors
who carried him from bed to prison in 1649; his drinking wine
with friends in 1648 after a meeting with Independents;
Edwards's picture of him in *Gangræna* as " profaning the
Lord's day in sports, one who is a player at cards, and who
will sit long with company at wine and tippling." [15] He is
reported as sitting with the agitators over " capon and cock
broth," [16] there was a feast after his trial in 1649, and he

supped with his supporters before he went into exile in 1652.
Here is a Lilburne who could enjoy his friends and family,
who mixed with the people and could relax in the comradeship
of the tavern.   But, for all this, there is something that escapes
—a picture of the Lilburne family at home; badinage between
husband and wife; the entertainment of friends; play with the
children.   The references to his children—" my tender babes "
—are always conventional.   It is only when he speaks of his
wife that a man with strong private affections shows through
the party leader dedicated to public ends.

Yet he was a man who could arouse deep and lasting affection.   At least two people who followed him to the pillory in
1638 and whose names are known came forward in 1653 at
his second trial.   The faithfulness of the two old women,
Katherine Hadley and Elizabeth Crome, the latter coming all
the way with him from Jersey to Dover, is remarkable.   William
Kiffin, in spite of differences in religion, remained his friend;
William Harding, whom he met in Jersey, welcomed him to his
home in Weymouth;   Overton and Prince and Chidley were
still his friends in 1653;   his family rallied to him;   there was
always a gaoler or prison-keeper to show him kindness;
" D. D." in the United Provinces was a faithful friend during
Lilburne's exile;   Thomas Lambert found him lodgings and
looked after his belongings when he returned hastily to
England;   the friendship of Sir John Maynard was enduring;
Maynard's daughter Elizabeth, with her husband, Sir Edward
Honeywood, of Elmstead, Kent, befriended him when he was
in Dover Castle.   Cromwell showed time and time again that
he held him in high regard.   And beyond his personal friends
the people as a whole loved and believed in John Lilburne more
wholeheartedly than they supported the Leveller movement
itself.   He had the qualities—including even those which his
enemies deemed his faults—of popular appeal.   Impulsive,
warm-hearted, entirely reckless of his personal comfort, from
the time when the news flew round London that Hewson's
apprentice, young Lilburne, had claimed the right of a free-
born Englishman to refuse to answer to interrogatories, to his
trial fourteen years later, when his triumphal acquittal was
greeted with such cheering as was heard an English mile, John
Lilburne's name stood for freedom against oppression.   In all

those years he never forfeited the proud title he won as an apprentice, and he himself would have asked for no finer epitaph than that of Free-born John.

Such a life as Lilburne's cannot be lived in vain. In word and action he witnessed to the truth as he believed it. He could be called the first English Radical—a great-hearted Liberal—a militant Christian—even, if the *spirit* of his teaching were taken fully into account, the first English democrat. But it is better to leave him without a label, enshrined in the words he spoke for his party: " And posterity we doubt not shall reap the benefit of our endeavours, what ever shall become of us." [17]

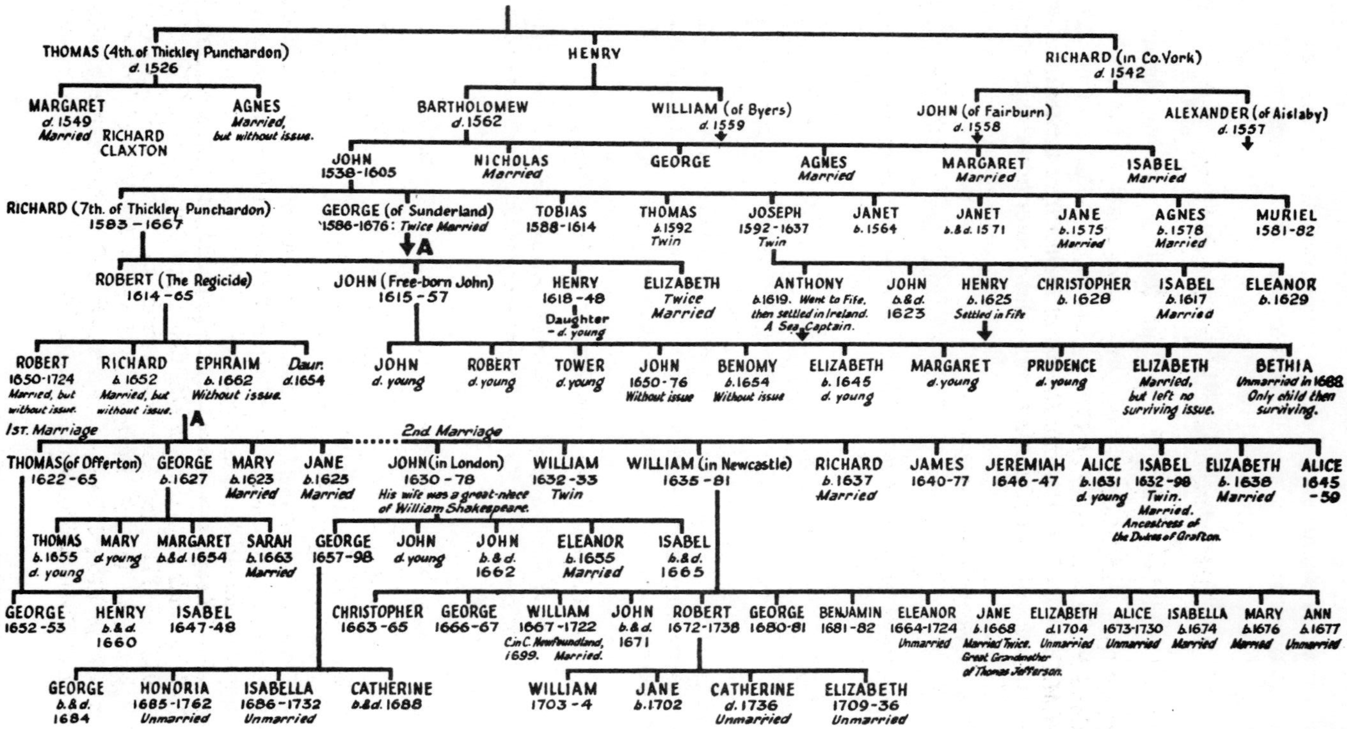
THOMAS (4th. of Thickley Punchardon) d. 1526
HENRY
RICHARD (in Co. York) d. 1542
MARGARET d. 1549 Married RICHARD CLAXTON
AGNES Married, but without issue.
BARTHOLOMEW d. 1562
WILLIAM (of Byers) d. 1559
JOHN (of Fairburn) d. 1558
ALEXANDER (of Aislaby) d. 1557
JOHN 1538-1605
NICHOLAS Married
GEORGE
AGNES Married
MARGARET Married
ISABEL Married
RICHARD (7th. of Thickley Punchardon) 1583 – 1667
GEORGE (of Sunderland) 1586-1676: Twice Married
A
TOBIAS 1588-1614
THOMAS b. 1592 Twin
JOSEPH 1592-1637 Twin
JANET b. 1564
JANET b. & d. 1571
JANE b. 1575 Married
AGNES b. 1578 Married
MURIEL 1581-82
ROBERT (The Regicide) 1614 – 65
JOHN (Free-born John) 1615 – 57
HENRY 1618 – 48
Daughter – d. young
ELIZABETH Twice Married
ANTHONY b. 1619. Went to Fife, then settled in Ireland. A Sea Captain.
JOHN b. & d. 1623
HENRY b. 1625 Settled in Fife
CHRISTOPHER b. 1628
ISABEL b. 1617 Married
ELEANOR b. 1629
ROBERT 1650-1724 Married, but without issue.
RICHARD b. 1652 Married, but without issue.
EPHRAIM b. 1662 Without issue
Daur. d. 1654
JOHN d. young
ROBERT d. young
TOWER d. young
JOHN 1650-76 Without issue
BENOMY b. 1654 Without issue
ELIZABETH b. 1645 d. young
MARGARET d. young
PRUDENCE d. young
ELIZABETH Married, but left no surviving issue.
BETHIA Unmarried in 1688. Only child then surviving.
A
1st. Marriage
2nd Marriage
THOMAS (of Offerton) 1622 – 65
GEORGE b. 1627
MARY b. 1623 Married
JANE b. 1625 Married
JOHN (in London) 1630 – 78 His wife was a great-niece of William Shakespeare.
WILLIAM 1632 – 33 Twin
WILLIAM (in Newcastle) 1635 – 81
RICHARD b. 1637 Married
JAMES 1640-77
JEREMIAH 1646 – 47
ALICE b. 1631 d. young
ISABEL 1632 – 98 Twin. Married. Ancestress of the Dukes of Grafton.
ELIZABETH b. 1638 Married
ALICE 1645 – 59
THOMAS b. 1655 d. young
MARY d. young
MARGARET b. & d. 1654
SARAH b. 1663 Married
GEORGE 1657 – 98
JOHN d. young
JOHN b. & d. 1662
ELEANOR b. 1655 Married
ISABEL b. & d. 1665
GEORGE 1652 – 53
HENRY b. & d. 1660
ISABEL 1647 – 48
CHRISTOPHER 1663 – 65
GEORGE 1666 – 67
WILLIAM 1667 – 1722 C. in C. Newfoundland, 1699. Married.
JOHN b. & d. 1671
ROBERT 1672 – 1738
GEORGE 1680-81
BENJAMIN 1681-82
ELEANOR 1664-1724 Unmarried
JANE b. 1668 Married Twice. Great Grandmother of Thomas Jefferson.
ELIZABETH d. 1704 Unmarried
ALICE 1673-1730 Unmarried
ISABELLA b. 1674 Married
MARY b. 1676 Married
ANN b. 1677 Unmarried
GEORGE b. & d. 1684
HONORIA 1685 – 1762 Unmarried
ISABELLA 1686 – 1732 Unmarried
CATHERINE b. & d. 1688
WILLIAM 1703 – 4
JANE b. 1702
CATHERINE d. 1736 Unmarried
ELIZABETH 1709 – 36 Unmarried

Notes

Main Abbreviations used in the Notes and Bibliography

C.J.=Journals of the House of Commons.
L.J.=Journals of the House of Lords.
Cal.S.P.Dom.=Calendar of State Papers Domestic.
Cal.S.P.Ven.=Calendar of State Papers Venetian.
H.M.Comm.=Reports of the Historical Manuscripts Commission.
Rushworth=Historical Collections of John Rushworth (eight vols.; 1721).
Whitelocke=Memorials of the English Affairs (1682).
Acts and Ordinances of the Interregnum=the three vols. edited by Firth and Rait.
Clarendon's *History of the Rebellion* is cited in the six vols. edited by W. D. Macray, 1888.

To save confusion through the use of too many brackets I have throughout used a / instead of ( ) in the familiar Thomason reference numbers. Thus Thomason references E.000(0) and 669.f.00(0) become E.000/0 and 669.f.00/0. In the Bibliography all Thomason tracts are given their references. In the Notes only important tracts not appearing in the Bibliography are assigned their Thomason numbers.

Chapter One : THE HIXONS OF GREENWICH

1. Pat. 11 Hy. VI, quoted in Hasted's *History of Kent* (ed. Henry H. Drake), Part I, *The Hundred of Blackheath* (1886), p. 54 (cited as Drake's *Hasted*).
2. Drake's *Hasted*, pp. 54 and 55, note 1.
3. Sketches by Antonie van den Wyngaerde (1558) in the Ashmolean Museum; Drake's *Hasted*, p. 67, based on works accounts and plans of survey made in 1694–95; *Lansdowne MSS.*, Vol. 18, ff. 73, 74, in the British Museum, gives lists of persons lodged in the Court in 1574.
4. Drake's *Hasted*, p. 57, based on Hall's *Chronicles* and Holinshed.
5. Francis Peck, *Desiderata Curiosa*, Book II (1779), *Queen Elizabeth's Annual Expence, Civil and Military*, p. 69.
6. List of Keepers in Drake's *Hasted*, pp. 279–280 and p. 62, note 8.
7. *Memorials in Greenwich Old Church*, in *Lansdowne MSS.*, Vol. 938, ff. 111–126, contains records of Greenwich household servants. Drake's *Hasted*, p. 280 and p. 60, note 5.
8. Pat. 35 Eliz., 4 Jas. I, p. 19, quoted in Drake's *Hasted*, p. 280.
9. *Lansdowne MSS.*, Vol. 18, ff. 73, 74.

10. *Queen Elizabeth's Annual Expence* (supra), pp. 62, 63, 69; *An Abstract or Brief Declaration of the present state of His Majestie's Revenew*, bound in volume *Truth Brought to Light and Discovered by Time, a Narrative History of King James for the first fourteen years* (printed for Michael Sparke, 1651), pp. 52–55. This would indicate that James had reduced salaries.

11. A Thomas Hixon, student of Christ Church, was involved in brawls in the City of Oxford in 1575 (*Cal.S.P.Dom.*, *Addenda*, *1566–1579*, p. 483; *1547–1580*, p. 498), and took his degree of B.A. on February 17, 1569, and his M.A. on March 29, 1572 (Foster, *Alumni Oxonienses*).

12. *Memorials in Greenwich Old Church*, in *Lansdowne MSS.*, Vol. 938, f. 112: " On a stone in the wall of the North Side of the North Isle of the Church

" In the never dying Memory of Thomas Hixon of Greenwich Esq Ward-rop Keeper to Qu. Elizabeth and K. James; married Margaret daughter to Thomas Manley and had issue 5 Sons and 3 daughters viz. Robert dyed young Humphry Hixon of Greenwich Esq Keeper of the standing ward-rop there now, who married Mary daughter to John Bradshaw of Bradshaw in com. Lanc and hath issue Robert, John, Tho. Franc. Elizabeth, Beatrix, Jane, Susanna, Care and Mary Hixon.

" Thomas Hixon married Anne Daughter to John Marselyne of Roydon in com. Suffolc Batchelour of Divinity and had Tho. Mary and Rebekka.

" John Hixon married Elizabeth daughter to Sir Thomas Cave of Stanton in com. Leicester Kt. and hath no issue. William Hixen was unmarried. Elizabeth died young.

" Margaret married to Richard Lilbourne of Durham Esq. who died An. Dom. 1619 and was here also buried and Catherine dyed unmarried. A.D. 1624."

I do not know when Thomas Hixon married Margaret Manley.

In Strype's *Circuit Walk*, appended to Stow's *Survey of London*, there is recorded an inscription over the east door not mentioned in *Lansdowne MSS.*, Vol. 938; " Thomas Hixon of Greenwich, Esq., Soldier under Henry IV, K. of France, Gentleman of the Bedchamber to Q. Elizab. and Keeper of the Wardrobe."

13. *Lansdowne MSS.*, Vol. 18, ff. 73, 74: " List of Persons lodged within the Court."

14. This was still so in Evelyn's day. His wife went there on April 23, 1701, " thinking to have the benefit of the aire on the heath, for the recreation of her breath and lungs exceedingly still afflicted of the Cough " (*Diary* (ed. E. S. de Beer), Vol. V, p. 456).

15. *Supra*, note 12.
16. See a description of Greenwich in Chapter II of John Barclay's *Icon Animorum*, published in Latin in 1614, translated in 1631 by Thomas May as *The Mirrour of Mindes*.
17. *Supra*, note 12.
18. Drake's *Hasted* gives many details based on original accounts of life in and around Greenwich Palace (pp. 57–62 and notes).
19. Thomas Mayneman, Keeper of the Wardrobe before Thomas Hixon, describes the furniture in the time of Queen Mary (*Harleian MS.*, Vol. 1419*A*, f. 37).
20. Paul Hentzner, *A Journey into England in the Year MDXCVIII.*
21. *Supra*, note 12. Was Anne the daughter of John Marcellan, incumbent of Layham in 1595? (See " Catalogue of the Beneficed Clergy of Suffolk, 1555–1631," in *Proc. of the Suffolk Institute of Archaeology*, Vol. 22 (1934–36).) Was Elizabeth one of the Caves of Stanford? The manuscript gives 'Stanton,' but the Caves of Stanford were a well-known family, Thomas Cave being knighted by Charles I on June 30, 1641.
22. The evidence for this rests on his son's statement that his father had worn the gold chain of a very illustrious and noble earl. The Percys and the Lilburnes were traditionally connected, and Henry Percy, the ninth Earl, who succeeded to the earldom in 1585, had a London residence as well as his house in Alnwick.
23. Richard Lilburne, baptized July 14, 1583 (parish registers of Auckland St Andrew).
24. *Wills and Inventories*, Surtees Society Publications, Vol. 2 (1835), p. 192 and note. This grandfather was Bartholomew Lilburne, who left, besides his freehold lands, his horses and harness and a considerable quantity of valuable body-armour. See Chapter Two, p. 23, and note 27 to Chapter Two.
25. Parish registers of Eltham, Kent, at the church of St John the Baptist, Eltham.
26. Grant to Humphrey Hixon of office of Wardrobe Keeper at Greenwich for life, July 23, 1606, *Cal.S.P.Dom., 1603–1610*, p. 327.
27. Parish registers of Auckland St Andrew.
28. J. Foster, *Durham Visitation Pedigrees, 1615*, p. 215; Ian Lilburn.
29. *Note on the movements of the Lilburne family and the birth of John Lilburne.* The statement in the *Durham Visitation Pedigrees* as recorded by Norroy King of Arms in 1615 says that Richard Lilburne reported Robert, aged two, John, and Elizabeth. In the records of the church of St Andrew's, Auckland, Robert is recorded as being baptized in February 1614. John and Elizabeth are unrecorded in the registers, although there is an Anne *Liber* baptized on December 28, 1611. Other local

references indicate an Elizabeth Lilburne, who must clearly have been older than Robert, since two children could not have been born to the Lilburnes between February 1614 and 1615.

As it was traditional for Lilburne births to be registered in St Andrew's, Auckland, some reason must be found for the absence of the names of Elizabeth and John. John himself said he was born at Greenwich, and round one of his portraits allowed the inscription " aetat suae 23 Ano 1641," which would make the date of his birth 1618. But this is impossible in face of the report to Norroy King of Arms. It is just possible that the John reported in 1615 was an elder brother who died, but 1618 is ruled out for John Lilburne's birth by the fact that his acknowledged younger brother was baptized in the church of St Alphege, Greenwich, on October 21 of that year. But John may have got the year wrong but the place right. The family may have returned to Greenwich by 1617, and John may have been born then and not recorded—though this is unlikely, since the parish registers had begun by that date, and it would still have to be assumed that the John who was alive in 1615 had died and another son had been given the same name. There is indeed the possibility that the family had come south after Robert's birth and baptism on February 2, 1614, and had not returned to Thickley Punchardon by the time Norroy King of Arms arrived, and that this was the reason for the signature of George Lilburne, and not of Richard, on the herald's return. John, it would then be assumed, would have been born just too soon for the St Alphege register, which began in 1615. Or, finally, to substantiate John Lilburne's assertion that he was born at Greenwich, it could be assumed that the Lilburnes never went north in 1605, that they remained at Greenwich until after the death of Thomas Hixon and of Margaret Lilburne, that the family were born at Greenwich, but not recorded because of the absence of any parish register at St Alphege, and that the baptism of Robert in 1614 occurred during a visit to the North. This, however, is a highly improbable assumption. The Lilburnes may not have lived permanently in the North. But a brief baptismal visit is unlikely. That Richard did not live at Thickley is indicated by the absence of his name from baptismal sponsorings between 1603 and 1626, and perhaps by a repetition early in 1621 of the inquisition post-mortem of 1606. This absence is easily explained by the burning of his manor-house by the Claxtons in 1604. Moreover, it is most unlikely that Richard, the son and heir, never took up his patrimony. The inquisition post-mortem of his father names him as the son and heir, and there is no indication or reference anywhere to Richard's not assuming his responsibilities. If he had not done so this would, I think, have come out in the Lilburne-Claxton lawsuit (see pp. 72–73). But if John Lilburne were not born at Greenwich, why was he not recorded in the family church of St Andrew's, Auckland, where generation after generation of Lilburne births, baptisms, marriages, and burials were recorded ? The answer, I think, is the simple one that John was born elsewhere in the North. On one of Lilburne's tracts in the Bodleian Library, *A Copie of a Letter . . . to William Prinne* (ref. no. C.14.7 Linc/10), there is a statement written in ink, probably by Bishop Barlow (1607–91), to whose collection the tract found its way and whose handwriting it appears to be, that John Lilburne was born at Sunderland when his father was residing there for a time. The statement was repeated by Mackenzie and Ross in 1834 in their *History of the County Palatine of Durham*, Vol. I, p. 264 (note); they add the date 1618 as the time of Richard Lilburne's residence in Sunderland. John Brand, in his *History of Newcastle*, Vol. II, p. 486, names " Bishop-Wearmouth " as the place of John Lilburne's birth. Bishopwearmouth was one of two parishes into which Sunderland was divided before the eighteenth century, the other being Monkswearmouth. Bishopwearmouth parish registers reveal no Lilburne birth, although John's sister, Elizabeth, is recorded as marrying Robert Chambers of Cleadon on February 4, 1638. Monkswearmouth parish registers were burnt in 1791, the existing records going back only to 1730. So there is no more proof of John Lilburne's birth in the North than of his birth in Greenwich.

There is, finally, a legend in the North, whose source is unknown, that John Lilburne was born in Westminster Hall. For drawing my attention to this charming fantasy I am indebted to Theodore Gang, who had it of Angus Macdonald. But such a triumph at such an early age could hardly have passed unrecorded—least of all by John Lilburne—and I feel reluctantly compelled to set aside this location and assume that Lilburne was born at Sunderland in 1615, and that the family came south very shortly afterwards, so that his first associations would have been with Greenwich, and it might have been said he was " practically born " there.

30. Parish registers of St Alphege, Greenwich.
31. *Ibid.*
32. *Ibid.*
33. *C.J.*, Vol. VII, p. 222; Drake's *Hasted*, p. 63, note 8. There is no proof that this was the Leveller, who was, in fact, out of the country from the autumn of 1651 to August 1653, but the name is not common, and Samuel Clerke, who purchased jointly with Sexby, could have managed the transaction.

Chapter Two : THE LILBURNES OF DURHAM

1. J.C., *The Compleat Collier.*

2. Henry Bourne, *History of Newcastle-upon-Tyne* (1736), p. 157. The descriptions of Newcastle and the Tyne in this chapter are based largely upon Bourne.

3. *History of Northumberland* (Northumberland County History Committee, 1893–1935), Vol. XIV, p. 434.

4. *Archaeologia Aeliana,* fourth series, Vol. XI (1934), p. 24.

5. *Ibid.,* p. 73.

6. *Bishop Hatfield's Survey,* Surtees Society, Vol. 32 (1856), pp. 26–28; *Northumberland and Durham Deeds,* Newcastle-upon-Tyne Records Series, Vol. VII (1927), p. 260.

7. *Wills and Inventories,* Surtees Society, Vol. 2 (1835), p. 192 and note. See Chapter One, note 24.

8. J. Foster, *Durham Visitation Pedigrees, 1615,* p. 215.

9. Richard Welford, *History of Newcastle and Gateshead* (1884), Vol. I, p. 357.

10. *Ibid.,* Vol. II, p. 21.

11. *Ibid.,* Vol. II, p. 189.

12. Pat. R 4 Chas. I, p. 9, quoted in *History of Northumberland,* Vol. XIII, p. 33.

13. Welford, *op. cit.,* Vol. III, p. 138. When he moved to Sunderland is not certain, but in 1625 he was described as " of Sunderland " when, with George Grey of Southwick, he disposed of a twenty-one-year lease of Lumley colliery, dating from the previous year, for the whole of the unexpired term at an annual profit of £90 (*S.P.D., Charles I,* Vol. Dii, No. 78, quoted by J. U. Nef, *The Rise of the British Coal Industry* (1932), Vol. I, p. 323, note 4).

14. Welford, *St Nicholas' Church, Newcastle-on-Tyne, its Monuments and Tombstones,* (1880), p. 69; pedigree of the Ellison family in Surtees, *History and Antiquities of the County Palatine of Durham* (1816), Vol. II, pp. 78–79.

15. *Proc. Soc. of Antiquaries of Newcastle-on-Tyne,* third series, Vol. 7, p. 203 n.

16. Edward Peacock, *A List of the Roman Catholics in the County of York in 1604,* p. 26, transcribed from the original manuscript in the Bodleian Library, 1872.

17. Bourne, *op. cit.,* pp. 10, 132.

18. Nef, *op. cit.,* Vol. I, p. 25.

19. *Ibid.,* Vol. I, p. 26.

20. John Brand, *The History and Antiquities of the Town and County of Newcastle-upon-Tyne* (1789), Vol. I, pp. 86–90. Francis Grey was master from 1629 to about 1637.

21. *Archaeologia Aeliana,* second series, Vol. XX (1898), p. 134.

22. *Proc. Soc. of Antiquaries of Newcastle-upon-Tyne,* third series,

Vol. I, p. 26: "Cuthbert Carr buried on the XXth day of December, 1697." He was one of the governors of Bishop Auckland Grammar School, having been elected by the governors in place of Richard Lilburne, on June 7, 1661. Richard Lilburne died in 1657. It is reasonable to assume that the office was not filled until after the Restoration.

23. Nef, *op. cit.*, Vol. I, p. 31 and map opposite p. 25.

24. Surtees, *op. cit.*, Vol. I, p. xxxiv.

25. Mackenzie and Ross, *History of the County Palatine of Durham*, Vol. II, p. 299, note, give Shildon as leased to the Bellasis family, though without saying when (they wrote in 1834). The family was important locally in the seventeenth century, and the Lilburnes never mention Shildon as part of their property.

26. "Inquisition Post Mortem John Lilburne," in H. Conyers Surtees, *History of New Shildon and East Thickley* (Newcastle, 1923).

27. Bartholomew Lilburne's will in Surtees Society Publications, Vol. 2 (1835), pp. 192–194 (see Chapter One, note 24). In making this rough guess at the nature of the Lilburne property in Thickley Punchardon I am much indebted to Dr Constance Fraser and to Mr Mervyn James, both of the University of Durham. Among other things, Dr Fraser pointed out the value of the tithes in the Middle Ages, and Mr James made the suggestion that the Lilburnes were cattle or hay merchants.

28. Nef, *op. cit.*, Vol. I, map opposite p. 25.

29. Reports by Dr William James to Secretary Cecil, January 1597, in *Cal.S.P.Dom.*, *1595–1597*, pp. 347–348.

30. *A Catalogue of the Knights, Citizens and Burgesses that have served in the last four Parliaments*, November 21, 1656 (E.1602/6).

31. November 29, 1595, *Cal. Border Papers*, Vol. II (1595–1603).

32. Report of an Agent, *Cal.S.P.Dom.*, *1611–1618*, p. 395.

33. See *Dictionary of National Biography*.

34. *Innocency and Truth Justified*, p. 8.

35. On Bishop Barlow's copy of the *Copie of a Letter . . . to William Prynne* some one, and the writing seems to be that of the Bishop himself, has written a note to this effect. The pamphlet concerned is in the Bodleian Library (ref. no. C.14.7 Linc/10). (See also note 29 to Chapter One.)

Chapter Three : THE LONDON APPRENTICE

1. John Stow, *A Survey of London* (1598) (ed. C. L. Kingsford, Oxford, 1908), Vol. I, pp. 59–60.

2. William Camden, *Britannia* (trans. Philémon Holland, 1610), p. 422.

3. Lilburne, *The Legall Fundamentall Liberties*, p. 20; *Innocency and Truth Justified*, p. 8.

4. John Bastwick, *A Just Defence of John Bastwick*, p. 15.

5. *The Legall Fundamentall Liberties*, p. 21.

6. " A Sermon Preached before the Queene's Majestie " (1570), quoted by W. Haller, *The Rise of Puritanism*, p. 13.

7. William Kiffin, *Remarkable Passages in the Life of William Kiffin* (written by himself; not published until 1823), p. 10.

8. *The Sufficiencie of the Spirits Teaching without Humane Learning or A Treatise, tending to prove humane learning to be no help to the Spirituall understanding of the Word of God.* Originally spoken January 25, 1639, printed many times. William Kiffin was " well acquainted " with How, and tasted that " Spirit of Light and Truth which God in his day did more than ordinary pour out upon him " (Postscript to the 1683 edition of *The Sufficiencie of the Spirits Teaching*). It is probable that Lilburne also knew him personally. He spoke of " the coblers Sermon " in his *Letter to the Wardens* (p. 8) : ". . . if there be but a Printing house in any of the Cities in the Provinces of Holland, I will cause this Letter to be Printed . . . and made as publique as the Coblers Sermon." He is also ready for death, he tells the Wardens, and if the priests will not suffer his body to be buried in the churchyard, " then would I have it laid beside the Coblers in Finsbury Fields " (p. 4).

9. August 5, 1637, " upon a special solemne occasion." Published as *The Saints Safety in Evill Times* in a collection of Sibbes' sermons entitled *The Saints Cordialls* (1637), pp. 171–172.

10. Douglas Bush, *English Literature in the Earlier Seventeenth Century* (1945), p. 294.

11. Helen C. White, " English Devotional Literature, 1600–1640," in *University of Wisconsin Studies in Language and Literature*, No. 29 (Madison, 1931), p. 13.

12. *Institutes*, passim.

13. *A Case of Conscience, the Greatest that ever was* (1597); *A Graine of Mustard-seed* (1597).

14. *A Treatise on Christian Religion* (1611).

15. *A Discourse of the true and visible markes of the Catholique Churche.*

16. *The Acts and Monuments of John Foxe* (fourth edition, ed. Rev. Josiah Pratt), Vol. VIII, pp. 334–335.

17. *A Relation of the Conference between William Laud and Mr Fisker, the Jesuit* (1901 edition, ed. C. H. Simpkinson), " The Epistle Dedicatory," p. xxix.

18. *The Legall Fundamentall Liberties*, p. 21.

19. William Kiffin, *op. cit.*, pp. 4–12. Kiffin does not mention

Lilburne here, but it is more than likely that Lilburne was one of them. See also W. Haller, *The Rise of Puritanism*, p. 275.

20. Bastwick, *A Just Defence*, passim. Eleven years later Lilburne, or a close friend, explained his motives: " When first he began to understand himself, had he been like unto most young men of his age and time . . . no doubt he might soone have come . . . to have been some body in the City and place where he was bred; and have enjoyed those contents, which most men seeke either in honour or profit.

" But it seems his conscience was soon awakened upon his Master's call. God to whose service he had dedicated himself, made him to know betimes, that he had other work for him to doe, and being called . . . he chused rather to suffer affliction in pursuance of a just cause, then to injoy the pleasure of sin for a season " (*Englands weeping Spectacle* (1648), pp. 1–2).

21. Henry Burton, *For God and the King*, passim.

22. *A New Discovery of the Prelates Tyranny*—the account, printed at the time of the sentence, brought up to date upon the release of the prisoners by the Long Parliament, 1641. " The manner of the execution " is at pp. 33–60.

Chapter Four : STAR CHAMBER VICTIM

1. The Polehead tavern was near the Doctors' Commons, according to Lilburne (*The Christian Mans Triall*). The Doctors' Commons, St Bennet's Hill, St Paul's Churchyard, was a college or " common house " for doctors of law, where they studied and practised the civil law. (See Wheatley and Cunningham, *London Past and Present*, Vol. I, p. 507.)

2. Lilburne, *The Christian Mans Triall*, pp. 1–6, gives the story of his capture and examination.

3. R. G. Usher, *The Rise and Fall of the High Commission*, pp. 23–24, p. 76, note 1; *Rushworth*, II, p. 463. Lilburne's speech in the pillory against the *ex officio* oath is in *A Worke of the Beast*, pp. 14–15.

4. Usher, *op. cit.*, pp. 127–128.

5. *Ibid.*, p. 132, note 3, pp. 132–136.

6. " Cases in the Courts of Star Chamber and High Commission," in *Camden Society Publications*, New Series 39 (1886), pp. 294, 295, 309, 315.

7. *The Christian Mans Triall*, pp. 7–16; *Rushworth*, II, pp. 463–466.

8. *Letter to the Apprentices*, May 10, 1639.

9. *Rushworth*, II, p. 463.

Chapter Five : THE PURITAN MARTYR

1. *Rushworth*, II, p. 466; report and evidence of the Committee appointed to examine the case of John Lilburne, published February 13, 1646, as *A true Relation of the materiall passages of Lieut. Col. John Lilburnes sufferings as they were represented before the House of Peeres.*

2. *A true Relation*, evidence of Mrs Mary Dorman, who saw the whipping from the Fleet to New Palace Yard. The evidence from *A true Relation* and *A Worke of the Beast* does not make it clear whether Lilburne's wounds were dressed before he went to the pillory or not until he returned to the Fleet.

3. *A true Relation*, evidence of Mr Thomas Hawes, who was in New Palace Yard, and of Mrs Mary Dorman.

4. Lilburne, *Come out of her my people*, p. 4.

5. Lilburne described his punishment and his sufferings in prison in *A Worke of the Beast*; *Rushworth*, II, pp. 466–467.

6. *A true Relation*, evidence of Mr Higgs, surgeon. He was perhaps the surgeon sent by Mrs Bastwick, for his persistence and his testimony before the Committee point to an interest more than professional. See Bastwick, *A Just Defence*, p. 14, and *infra*, note 15.

7. *A Worke of the Beast*, pp. 27–29; *Rushworth*, II, p. 467. The sympathetic porter who came to Lilburne at the gate of the Fleet prison to tell him he must strip to prepare for his whipping was named John Hawes (p. 64). Thomas Hawes was in New Palace Yard, visited Lilburne in the Fleet, and later testified on Lilburne's behalf to the Committee which reported on his case in 1646 (note 3, *supra*). Thomas Hawes was still a supporter of Lilburne in 1653 (pp. 327, 329). He was himself a troublesome sectarian, imprisoned in 1646 on the charge of speaking " foul blasphemous words " against the second and third persons of the Trinity, and was the author of two pamphlets vindicating himself—*A Christian Relation of a Christians Affliction*, May 31, 1646 (E.506/24), and *The Afflicted Christian justifyed*, May 18, 1646 (E.337/26). Hawes was not an uncommon name, but may there perhaps be the possibility that John and Thomas Hawes were related, and that Lilburne received the pamphlets from the porter John Hawes at the gate of the Fleet? He may, of course, have received them at any time when the crowd was thick about him. Or they may have been brought to him in prison, as the Warden suspected.

8. *A Worke of the Beast*, pp. 33–34.

9. *Rushworth*, II, pp. 466–467.

10. *Ibid.*, p. 467.

11. *A true Relation*, evidence of Mr Higgs.

12. Petition of Katherine Hadley, December 21, 1640, *MSS. House of Lords, H.M.Comm.*, Vol. 3, p. 33.
13. *A true Relation*, evidence of Mr Hawes.
14. *Ibid.*, evidence of Mr Ellis.
15. *Ibid.*, evidence of Dr Hubbard. He may have been sent by Mrs Bastwick, but see note 6, *supra*.
16. *The Poore Mans Cry.*
17. *Bankes Papers*, 18/2 (Bodleian Library). The works he named were the *Letany*, the *Answer to Sir John Bankes' Information*, and *Certain Answers to some Objections made against the Letany*. (See plate between pp. 328 and 329.)
18. *Come out of her my people*, p. 27. I take this to be an extension of the order of the previous month reported by Rushworth (note 9, *supra*). Haller, *The Rise of Puritanism*, p. 435, assumes he was not shackled until after his examination by the Attorney-General on May 17. But Rushworth is quite explicit.
19. *Come out of her my people*, pp. 6–7.
20. *Ibid.*; *Letter to the Wardens*, p. 6.
21. *Coppy of a Letter to one of his special friends*, pp. 14, 8, 12.
22. Lilburne dates it 1638, but it may not have been written until the spring of 1639—see Haller's bibliographical notes to *The Rise of Puritanism*, p. 437. Two women who are known by name to have visited him are Mrs Bastwick (Bastwick, *A Just Defence*, p. 14) and Mrs Mary Dorman, who declared that after he had suffered she went often to visit him " who was laid in irons " (*A true Relation*). But this does not make clear if she went while he was kept close prisoner.
23. Bastwick, *A Just Defence*, p. 14; *A true Relation*; *Coppy of a Letter*, passim, note 22, *supra*.
24. *Letter to the Wardens*, p. 8.
25. *The Poore Mans Cry.*
26. " Lord Harley's Journeys in England," *H.M. Comm. Portland MSS.*, Vol. VI, p. 100; Petitions of Ralph Claxton, September 22, 1636, and of Richard Lilburne, November 5, 1636, *Cal.S.P. Dom., 1636–1637*, pp. 136, 181; Petition of Richard Lilburne, August 11, 1641, *MSS. House of Lords, H.M.Comm.*, Vol. 3, p. 95. The last recorded case of trial by combat (Ashford v. Thornton, 1818) was for a charge of murder. A Bill to abolish trial by combat was proposed but not carried by the Long Parliament. Not until 1819 was it abolished for all purposes. See W. S. Holdsworth, *History of English Law*, Vol. I, p. 310; Lilburne, *The Poore Mans Cry*, p. 7; *Innocency and Truth Justified*, p. 39. (See p. 398.) For Elizabeth's marriage see Bishopwearmouth parish registers. She later married Thomas Gower, Baptist minister of Newcastle.
27. *Rushworth*, II, pp. 467–468.

28. Until 1730 the office of gaol-keeper was the subject of purchase and sale. In 1729 a House of Commons Committee found that the office of Warden of the Fleet had been sold by the previous occupant to the then holder for £5000 (S. and B. Webb, " English Prisons," in *English Local Government*, Vol. VI, p. 5, note 2).
29. *Letter to the Wardens*.

Chapter Six : THE PARLIAMENTARIAN

1. For George Lilburne and ship-money see *Cal. Cttee for Compounding with Delinquents* (Domestic), 1643–1660, Part III, p. 1920.
2. Sir William Bellasis, Sheriff of County Durham, to Secretary Nicholas, September 6, 1638, *C.S.P.Dom.*, *1638–1639*, p. 4.
3. Gardiner, *History of England*, Vol. VIII, p. 391.
4. Lilburne, *Letter to the Apprentices*, passim.
5. Lilburne, *Letter to the Wardens*. In this he refers to other publications. See Haller, *The Rise of Puritanism*, pp. 438–440.
6. *The Prisoners Plea for a Habeas Corpus*; *Innocency and Truth Justified*, p. 74.
7. " Diary of Archbishop Laud," in *Rushworth*, III, p. 885.
8. *MSS. House of Lords*, *H.M.Comm.*, Vol. 3, p. 33.
9. *E.161/1.*
10. *Rushworth*, III, p. 1128.
11. Thomas May, *History of the Parliament of England which began November the third*, MDCXL (1647), Book I, p. 60.
12. *Ibid.*
13. E.105/3; this is a later edition, printed in 1643.
14. Godfrey Davies, *The Early Stuarts* (1937), p. 92.
15. Secretary Vane to Secretary Windebank, September 7, 1640, *C.S.P.Dom.*, *1640–1641*, p. 23.
16. Gardiner, *History of England*, Vol. IX, p. 130.
17. *Ibid.*
18. *Ibid.*
19. " Diary of Archbishop Laud," in *Rushworth*, III, p. 1085.
20. May, *op. cit.*, p. 64.
21. *Ibid.*, p. 63.
22. Gardiner, *History of England*, Vol. IX, p. 202.
23. *C.S.P.Dom.*, *1640–1641*, pp. 18, 68. See also pp. 23, 28–29, 50, 141.
24. *Ibid.*, p. 23.
25. Gardiner, *History of England*, Vol. IX, p. 215.
26. *Rushworth*, III, pp. 1336–1337 *passim*.
27. *Memoirs of Sir Philip Warwick* (1813 edition), pp. 273–274. Warwick does not refer to Lilburne by name, but as the servant of Mr Prynne—an erroneous assumption frequently made at

the time. This was probably the petition printed in *Innocency and Truth Justified*, p. 66.

28. November 9, 1640, *C.J.*, Vol. II, p. 24.
29. *Englands weeping Spectacle*, p. 3.
30. May, *op. cit.*, p. 80; " The Manner of Mr Burton's, Mr Prynne's and Dr Bastwick's Returne from exile," in *A New Discovery of the Prelates Tyranny*, pp. 113–115.
31. *Innocency and Truth Justified*, p. 74; *L.J.*, Vol. IV, p. 113.

Chapter Seven : CAPTAIN JOHN LILBURNE

1. *Lord Braye's MSS. H.M.Comm.*, Vol. 15, pp. 140–141.
2. May 4, 1641, *C.J.*, Vol. II, p. 134.
3. *L.J.*, Vol. IV, p. 233.
4. Lilburne, *Picture of the Councel of State*, p. 10.
5. *John White's Defence*, p. 6.
6. Triplet to Hyde, *Clarendon MSS.*, Vol. 19, f. 274.
7. Lilburne, *Innocency and Truth Justified*, p. 39.
8. Gardiner, *History of England*, Vol. X, pp. 107–108.
9. *A Bloody Massacre by the Papists* (E.181/9).
10. *Rushworth*, V, pp. 463–464; Lilburne, *The Legall Fundamentall Liberties*, p. 22; *Englands weeping Spectacle*, p. 3. Giustinian to the Doge and Senate, January 10, 1642, *Cal.S.P.Ven., 1640–1642*, pp. 271–272.
11. *L. Colonel John Lilburne Revived*, p. 1.
12. *Englands weeping Spectacle*, p. 4.
13. *Ibid.* Her father was Henry Dewell, a London merchant.
14. D. Brunton and D. H. Pennington, *Members of the Long Parliament*, p. 1.
15. *A Remonstrance against Presbitery*, May 28, 1641 (E.163/1 and 2).
16. *The Discovery of a Swarme of Separatists*, December 19, 1641 (E.180/25), and *Catalogue of the Thomason Tracts*.
17. *The Journal of Sir Simonds D'Ewes* (ed. W. Notestein), p. 339.
18. *Ibid.*, p. 382.
19. There are many petitions in the Thomason collection, two of the most remarkable being those of August 9, 1641, and January 31, 1642 (669.f.4.27; 669.f.4.54).
20. *H.M.Comm., Portland MSS.* I, p. 87.
21. May 5, 1640 (E.203/1).
22. December 15, 1640, Ayes 135, Noes 83, *C.J.*, Vol. II, p. 344.
23. E.159.
24. *Catalogue of the Thomason Tracts.*
25. August 1641 (E.167/10).
26. *Catalogue of the Thomason Tracts*, Preface by G. K. Fortescue, Vol. I, p. xxi.

27. Brunton and Pennington, *op. cit.*, p. 177, Appendix I, Table I *B*.
28. *History of the Rebellion*, Vol. III, p. 80.
29. Robert Surtees, *History and Antiquities of the County Palatine of Durham*, Vol. II, p. 258 and note *e*; *A Catalogue of the names of the Knights, Citizens and Burgesses that have served in the last four Parlaments*, November 21, 1656 (E.1602/6); *Royalist Compositions in Northumberland and Durham, 1643–1660*, Surtees Society Publications, Vol. III (1816), pp. 36, 237–241, 262, 277, 280, and *passim*.; H. Conyers Surtees, *History of New Shildon and East Thickley* (Newcastle, 1923), Lilburne family tree; Brunton and Pennington, *op. cit.*, pp. 64, 202.
30. *A Catalogue of the . . . Knights, etc.*; *The Common Council Book of Newcastle-upon-Tyne, 1639–1656*, for March 15, 1647, Publications of Newcastle-upon-Tyne Records Committee, Vol. I, (1920), p. 85; for the Beke family see *Visitation of Buckinghamshire, 1634*, Harleian Society Publications, Vol. LVIII. *D.N.B.* says that Margaret Beke was the daughter of Richard and Coluberry; the *Visitation* names Margaret as a granddaughter, and this accords with other dates known.
31. Lilburne, *The Legall Fundamentall Liberties*, p. 22.
32. Lilburne, *Innocency and Truth Justified*, p. 39.

Chapter Eight : Lieutenant-Colonel John Lilburne

1. *Englands weeping Spectacle*, p. 4.
2. Sir John Maynard, speech in the House of Commons, July 27, 1648, *Old Parliamentary History*, Vol. 17 (1647–48).
3. *Innocency and Truth Justified*, pp. 39–41, 65; *Englands weeping Spectacle*, p. 4.
4. *Rushworth*, VI, p. 83.
5. *History of the Rebellion*, Vol. V, p. 306.
6. *The Examination and Confession of Capt. Lilbourne*, December 10, 1642; *Heads of a Speech Spoken by Captaine Lilbourne before a Councell of War held at Oxford*, December 18, 1642.
7. *Englands weeping Spectacle*, pp. 4–5; *C.J.*, Vol. II, p. 892; *Rushworth*, VI, p. 93.
8. *A Letter from Capt. Lilburne* (1643), p. 4.
9. *Letter to D.D. in the United Provinces*, printed in *L. Colonel John Lilburne Revived*; *The Legall Fundamentall Liberties*, p. 22.
10. *A Letter from Capt. Lilburne*, p. 4.
11. *Letter written by Capt. Edward Wingate* and signed by him and seven others, including Lilburne, prisoners in the castle at Oxford, *Harley MSS.*, quoted by F. J. Varley, *Oxford Castle and its Prisoners*, Bodleian Quarterly Record, Vol. VII, pp. 420–422; *C.J.*, Vol. III, pp. 80, 84.

12. Lilburne, *A Whip for the present House of Lords*, p. 5; *The Legall Fundamentall Liberties*, p. 23; Clarendon, *History of the Rebellion*, Vol. V, p. 306.
13. *Innocency and Truth Justified*, pp. 21–22.
14. *A Whip for the present House of Lords*, p. 5.
15. *The Legall Fundamentall Liberties*, p. 23.
16. *Ibid.*, p. 23; *Innocency and Truth Justified*, p. 41.
17. *Ibid.*, p. 75.
18. *The Parliament Scout*, October 13–20, 1643 (E.71/25).
19. Gardiner, *Civil War*, Vol. I, pp. 101–102.
20. *The Parliament Scout*, October 13–20, 1643.
21. " Statement by an Opponent of Cromwell," in *Manchester's Quarrel with Cromwell* (Camden Society, 1875), pp. 71–77.
22. *Apologeticall Narration*. p. 5; *Innocency and Truth Justified*, p. 41.
23. John Weaver's Account Book for 1644 shows payments made in Suffolk to John and Robert Lilburne in April—see *Suffolk and the Great Rebellion, 1640–1660*, in Suffolk Records Society (ed. Alan Everitt), Vol. III, p. 89; *Innocency and Truth Justified*, pp. 42–46.
24. C. H. Firth, *Cromwell's Army*, pp. 123–128; A. H. Burne and P. Young, *The Great Civil War: A Military History of the First Civil War, 1642–1646*, p. 10.
25. *C.J.*, 1644, *passim*; *L.J.*, 1644, *passim*.
26. Burne and Young, *op. cit.*, p. 160.
27. *Innocency and Truth Justified*, pp. 22–25, 46; Lilburne, *Jonah's Cry out of the Whales belly*, p. 2.
28. *Cal.S.P.Dom.*, 1644–1645, pp. 148–149; *Manchester's Quarrel with Cromwell*.
29. *Innocency and Truth Justified*, p. 46.

Chapter Nine : " THE DARLING OF THE SECTARIES "

1. *A briefe Remonstrance of the Reasons of those people called Anabaptists for their separation*, July 26, 1645 (E.293/31).
2. *A Whisper in the Eare of Mr Thomas Edwards*, p. 3; and see Bibliography.
3. See Bibliography.
4. See the *Catalogue of the Thomason Tracts* for the year 1645, *passim*.
5. For example, Leonard Lee, *A Remonstrance humbly presented to Parliament touching the insupportable miseries of the poore of the Land*, March 13, 1645 (E.273/8).
6. *A Discourse consisting of Motives for the Enlargement and Freedome of Trade, especially of Cloth and other Woollen Manufactures, engrossed at present by Merchant-Adventurers* (E.260/21).

7. E.292/24.
8. Gardiner, *Civil War*, Vol. II, p. 107.
9. *Ibid.*, p. 109.
10. *C.J.*, Vol. II, p. 996.
11. *Acts and Ordinances of the Interregnum*, Vol. I, pp. 184–187.
12. *The humble Remonstrance of the Company of Stationers*, April 1643 (E.247/23).
13. *Copie of a Letter . . . to William Prynne*, p. 7.
14. *L.J.*, Vol. VII, p. 116.
15. *Ibid.*, p. 142.
16. H. R. Plomer, " Secret Printing during the Civil War," in *The Library*, New Series, Vol. 5 (1904), p. 374.
17. *MSS. House of Lords*, *H.M.Comm.*, Vol. 5, p. 46.
18. Prynne, *The Lyar Confounded*, p. 4; Edwards, *Gangræna*, II, p. 104; Vicars, *Picture of Independency*, p. 9. Lilburne, in *The resolved mans Resolution* (1647), p. 11, says: " I have but one good eye to see with, and yet for that, I am forced to use the helpe of spectacles." (*Cf.* the portrait of 1649, facing p. 288.) I know no details of the accident, which appears to have had no personal or political significance. Probably troops were exercising or practising in the Fields.
19. *Reasons of Lieu. Col. Lilbournes sending his Letter to Mr Prin*, pp. 3–7.
20. Lilburne, *Innocency and Truth Justified*, p. 4.
21. *The Lyar Confounded*, Epistle Dedicatory and pp. 4, 9.
22. *Ibid.*, p. 5; *Reasons of Lieu. Col. Lilbournes sending his Letter*, pp. 3–7.
23. *Innocency and Truth Justified*, p. 46.
24. *Copy of a Letter from Lieutenant Colonell John Lilburne to a friend*, July 25, 1645, pp. 5–6.
25. June 14, *Letters and Speeches of Oliver Cromwell* (ed. T. Carlyle), Vol. I, p. 205.
26. *A More full Relation of the great Battell* [Langport], July 10, 1645.
27. *A Fresh Discovery*, p. 9. Prynne also suggested Robinson as the author of the Marpriest tracts.
28. *The Lyar Confounded*, p. 6.
29. Lilburne, *Innocency and Truth Justified*, p. 13; Prynne, *The Lyar Confounded*, pp. 6–7; Bastwick, *A Just Defence*, pp. 2–8 *passim*.
30. *Copy of a Letter . . . to a friend*, p. 2.
31. *Innocency and Truth Justified*, p. 15.
32. *Copy of a Letter . . . to a friend*, p. 16.
33. *Ibid.*, p. 17.
34. *The Lyar Confounded*, p. 7.
35. *Innocency and Truth Justified*, p. 16.
36. *C.J.*, Vol. IV, pp. 236–237.
37. *Innocency and Truth Justified*, p. 62.

38. Lilburne, *Englands Birth-right justified*, p. 42.
39. *C.J.*, Vol. IV, p. 307.
40. *A Just Defence*, p. 15.
41. Edwards, *Gangræna*, I, p. 40.
42. *The Lyar Confounded*, pp. 2, 7.
43. *Ibid.*, The Epistle to the Reader.
44. *A Fresh Discovery*, p. 13.
45. *Gangræna*, I, p. 128.
46. *A Just Defence*, pp. 20–21, 33.
47. *The Lyar Confounded*, p. 22.
48. *A Just Defence*, pp. 16–17.

Chapter Ten : ENGLAND'S PHYSICIAN

1. *Englands Birth-right justified*, pp. 1–8.
2. *Ibid.*, pp. 8–12.
3. *Ibid.*, pp. 12–13.
4. *Ibid.*, pp. 44–45.
5. *Ibid.*, p. 29.
6. *Ibid.*, pp. 30–32.
7. *Ibid.*, pp. 30, 33.
8. *Letters of Advice touching the choice of Knights and Burgesses for the Parliament*, September 3, 1645 (E.298/32).
9. *Englands Birth-right justified*, p. 37.
10. *Ibid.*, pp. 11–12.
11. *Ibid.*, p. 43.

Chapter Eleven : "THE PEARL IN A DUNGHILL"

1. *L.J.*, Vol. VIII, *Passim ; C.J.*, Vol. IV, p. 338 ; *A true Relation of . . . Lilburnes sufferings*.
2. *The Petition and information of Joseph Hunscot*, June 11, 1646, p. 5 (E.340/15).
3. H. R. Plomer, *A Dictionary of the Booksellers and Printers who were at work in England, etc., from 1641 to 1667*; *A true Relation of all the illegall Proceedings against William Larner*, May 2, 1646 (E.335/7).
4. March 29–April 5, 1649.
5. *The Petition of Hunscot*.
6. The story of Larner's arrest and examination and subsequent events is told in *Every Man's Case* (669.f.10/52) and *A true Relation of all the illegall Proceedings against William Larner*.
7. *The Freemans Freedome vindicated*, pp. 2–5.
8. The *Protestation* is printed in *The Freemans Freedome vindicated*, pp. 5–6.
9. Lilburne, *Londons Liberty in Chains*, p. 26.

10. *John White's Defence*, September 15, 1646, pp. 2–3.
11. *The Petition of Hunscot.*
12. *Letter to Wollaston*, June 23, 1646.
13. *The Just Man in Bonds*, p. 4 (paraphrase).
14. *L.J.*, Vol. VIII, pp. 388–390.
15. *L.J.*, Vol. VIII, pp. 426–494 *passim.*
16. *An Anatomy of the Lords Tyranny*, pp. 12–15 *passim.*
17. *L.J.*, Vol. VIII, pp. 432–494 *passim.*
18. *Anatomy of the Lords Tyranny*, pp. 16–17.
19. *L.J.*, Vol. VIII, p. 491.
20. Petitions to the House of Lords from the Stationers' Company, April 13, 1646, January 23, 1647, *MSS. House of Lords, H.M.Comm.*, Vol. 5, pp. 130, 154.
21. Overton, *A Defiance against all Arbitrary Usurpations*, p. 8.
22. See Plomer, *Secret Printing during the Civil War*, for list of pamphlets he believes to have come from this press.
23. Overton, *A Defiance*, pp. 14, 17, and *passim*; *The Commoners Complaint*, pp. 13–15.
24. *L.J.*, Vol. VIII, pp. 463–465; petitions of Stationers' Company and of Eeles to the House of Lords, *MSS. House of Lords, H.M.Comm.*, Vol. 5, p. 130.
25. *The Commoners Complaint*, p. 15.
26. *The Oppressed Mans Oppressions declared*, pp. 9–12; *London's Liberty in Chains*, pp. 59 *ff.*

Chapter Twelve : " DEFENDER OF THE FAITH "

1. *L.J.*, Vol. VIII, pp. 645–648.
2. *The Appeal and Petition of Mary Overton*, March 24, 1647 (E.381/10); Overton, *The Commoners Complaint*, February 1, 1647.
3. Lilburne, *The resolved mans Resolution*, passim.
4. *Letter from Lilburne to John Goodwin*, February 13, 1646, in *Jonah's Cry*, pp. 5–6.
5. *C.J.*, Vol. V, p. 112; *Whitelocke*, p. 243.
6. E.464/19*; it was not bound up by Thomason until 1648 (see Haller, *Tracts on Liberty*, Vol. III, p. 397).
7. Lilburne, *Rash Oaths unwarrantable*, passim.
8. *Whitelocke*, p. 251.
9. *C.J.*, Vol. V, pp. 179–180.
10. Letter of Intelligence, May 27 and 31–June 3/13, 1647, *Clarendon MSS.*, Vol. 29, f. 229.
11. *Rash Oaths unwarrantable.*
12. *Ibid.*, pp. 5–6.
13. *Plaine Truth without Feare or Flattery*, pp. 10, 11, 13, 17.

Chapter Thirteen : SEDUCER OF THE ARMY

1. When all transfers were complete 5940 men were enrolled, leaving 8460 to make up the 14,400 foot required by the New Model. Little attempt seems to have been made to get these voluntarily. Instead, on February 17, 1645, an apportionment was made to certain counties, each of which was told " to raise, levy, and impress " its quota of men. The continued Ordinances for raising and impressing men—with increasing emphasis on impressment—which continued to stream from Parliament and the Committee of Both Kingdoms, were a clear indication that the efforts did not meet with immediate success. See *Cal.S.P. Dom., 1644–1645*, pp. 358, 359, 379, 564, 625; *Whitelocke*, pp. 138, 165. For an interesting *exemption* from impressment see *L.J.*, Vol. VII, pp. 256–257.
2. *Reliquiae Baxterianae* (ed. 1696), pp. 50–60 *passim*.
3. *The Juglers discovered*, p. 5.
4. *C.J.*, Vol. V, 126.
5. *A Second Apologie of all the private Souldiers*, April 1647.
6. *The Declaration of the Armie*, May 16, 1647, p. 2.
7. *Whitelocke*, p. 248.
8. Letter from Suffolk, April 20, 1647, *H.M.Comm., Portland MSS.* III (Vol. I, Harley Letters and Papers), pp. 155–156.
9. *Whitelocke*, p. 290.
10. *Rash Oaths unwarrantable*, p. 4; he uses a similar expression in *The Juglers discovered*, p. 9.
11. *An Alarum to the House of Lords*, p. 5.
12. *The Oppressed Mans Oppressions declared*, p. 17.
13. *John White's Defence*, p. 5.
14. *The Juglers discovered*, p. 1.
15. *Petition of the Officers and Souldiers in the Army*, March 21, 1647 (E.385/12), in *Book of Army Declarations*, pp. 1–2 (E.409/25).
16. *Jonah's Cry*, p. 3.
17. *Ibid.*, p. 4.
18. *Ibid.*, pp. 3, 4.
19. *The Juglers discovered*, p. 3.
20. *Jonah's Cry*, p. 9.
21. *L.J.*, Vol. IX, p. 115.
22. *H.M.Comm., Portland MSS.* III (Vol. I, Harley Letters and Papers), pp. 155–156.
23. *The Apologie of the Common Souldiers.*
24. *Rushworth*, VII, p. 474.
25. *The Apologie of the Common Souldiers.*
26. C. H. Firth, *Clarke Papers*, Vol. I, p. 24, note (*a*).
27. *Ibid.*, Vol. I, p. 24.

28. *Rushworth*, VII, p. 485.
29. See, for example, *Clarke Papers*, Vol. I, pp. 101–102, 111–113.
30. May 24, *The Armies Indempnity*.
31. *Clarke Papers*, Vol. I, pp. 108–111.
32. *Ibid.*, Vol. I, p. 116.
33. Letter of the Commissioners to the Committee of Derby House, Cary, *Memorials*, Vol. I, p. 220.
34. *Clarke Papers*, Vol. I, p. xxii.
35. *Rushworth*, VII, p. 504.
36. *Whitelocke*, p. 254.
37. *Rushworth*, VII, p. 556.

Chapter Fourteen : AGITATOR-IN-CHIEF

1. *The Character of an Agitator.*
2. *Jonah's Cry*, p. 14.
3. *Solemne Engagement of the Armie*, p. 6.
4. *Memoirs*, in *Maseres Tracts*, Vol. I, p. 240.
5. *Clarke Papers*, Vol. I, pp. 22–24.
6. *Ibid.*, p. 23.
7. *Ibid.*, p. 22.
8. *Ibid.*, p. 86.
9. *Memoirs*, in *Maseres Tracts*, Vol. I, p. 231.
10. *Reliquiae Baxterianae*, p. 61.
11. *Clarke Papers*, Vol. I, pp. 85–86.
12. *Ibid.*, Vol. I, pp. 100–101.
13. *Ibid.*, Vol. I, pp. 112, 139, and *supra*, p. 170.
14. Letter from Poyntz to the Speaker in Cary, *Memorials*, Vol. I, p. 235; *Clarke Papers*, Vol. I, pp. 142–144, 167–169.
15. E.397/24.
16. *Tower of London Letter Book of Sir Lewis Dyve, 1646–7* (ed. H. G. Tibbutt), in *Publications of the Bedfordshire Historical Record Society*, Vol. XXXVIII (1958).
17. E.397/24; E.398/7.
18. John Cosens to Alderman Adams, June 7, 1647, in *Clarke Papers*, Vol. I, pp. 125–126.
19. Cary, *Memorials*, Vol. I, pp. 237–240; *L.J.*, Vol. IX, p. 282.
20. *Clarke Papers*, Vol. I, pp. 158–160.
21. *Dictionary of National Biography*.
22. C. H. Firth, *Killing No Murder*, *Eng.Hist.Rev.*, Vol. XVII (1902), pp. 308–311.
23. *Clarke Papers*, Vol. I, p. 83.
24. October 11, 1647, *Clarendon MSS.*, Vol. 30, f. 134. See also Jo. Wilcocks (Secretary Nicholas) to Mr Edgeman, October 18/28, 1647, *Ibid.*, Vol. 30, f. 146.

Chapter Fifteen : KING'S ADVOCATE

1. *H.M.Comm.*, *Portland MSS.* III (Vol. 1, Harley Letters and Papers), pp. 155–156.
2. Relation from Walden, *Clarke Papers*, Vol. I, p. 25.
3. *Ibid.*, Gardiner, *Civil War*, Vol. III, pp. 239–240.
4. *Plaine Truth without Feare or Flattery*, pp. 21, 22, 17.
5. *Clarke Papers*, Vol. I, p. 106. Firth suggests that the letter was from either Sexby or Lieutenant-Colonel Chillenden, p. 105, note (*a*), p. 85, note (*a*).
6. *Ibid.*, Vol. I, p. 112.
7. *Ibid.*, Vol. I, p. 113.
8. Sirrahniho (*i.e.*, John Harris), *The Grand Designe*, December 8, 1647. Lilburne later asserted that he had heard " from very good hands (I will not now say from the Cornet's own mouth) that Cromwell gave Joyce orders in the garden of his house at Drury Lane, Colonel Charles Fleetwood being by " (marginal note to Huntington's statement on laying down his commission, which Lilburne printed in his *Impeachment of High Treason*, pp. 53 *ff.*).
9. *A true Impartiall Narration*, in *Rushworth*, Vol. VII, pp. 513–517. There can be little doubt that this was Joyce's own account of the affair.
10. *Clarke Papers*, Vol. I, pp. 118–119.
11. Whitacre's Diary, Add. MSS., 31, 116, fol. 312*b*, quoted by Gardiner, *Civil War*, Vol. III, p. 272, note 1.
12. *A true Impartiall Narration*. I entirely disagree with Gardiner (*Civil War*, Vol. III, pp. 271–272) that Joyce was evasive or uncertain in his answer to Charles, or that he pointed to his soldiers as a desperate last effort to explain his actions. The *Narration* shows Joyce as straightforward and dignified, consciously acting on the authority of the soldiers.
13. *Clarke Papers*, Vol. I, p. 120.
14. *Ibid.*, Preface, Vol. I, pp. xxvi–xxxi, and Gardiner, *Civil War*, Vol. III, pp. 239–242, 265–274, for accounts and discussion of the King's removal from Holmby.

Chapter Sixteen : LILBURNE'S FREEDOM—SOLDIERS' RIGHTS !

1. *Memoirs*, in *Maseres Tracts*, Vol. I, p. 272.
2. *A Short Memorial*, in *Maseres Tracts*, Vol. I, p. 444.
3. *Memoirs*, in *Maseres Tracts*, Vol. I, p. 364.
4. October 11, 1647, *Clarendon MSS.*, Vol. 30, f. 134; see also Jo. Wilcocks (Secretary Nicholas) to Mr Edgeman, October 18/28, 1647, *Clarendon MSS.*, Vol. 30, f. 146.
5. *Clarke Papers*, Vol. I, pp. 214–215.

6. The charges against the officers were expressed in many pamphlets then and later, especially Lilburne's *Jonah's Cry, Letters to Marten*, of September 1647, *Englands New Chains, Part II, An Impeachment . . . against . . . Cromwell and . . . Ireton*, and in *The Hunting of the Foxes*.

7. *An Impeachment*, p. 4.

8. *The Juglers discovered*, p. 1.

9. *E.g.*, in *Rash Oaths unwarrantable*, written May 31, 1647, published in June, such passages as " I professe it before you, and all the world, that were I rationally able, I would make no scruple of conscience to help forward with my sword in my hand, the distruction of every lawlesse, tyrannicall, treacherous man . . . that I should groundedly know to be a ring-leader in the fore-said transcendent vilenesse, then I should be help to destroy so many rats or devouring vermin " (p. 8).

10. Letter of the agitators to Trinity House, Cary, *Memorials*, Vol. I, p. 239.

11. *Jonah's Cry*, p. 7.

12. *Ibid.*, pp. 9, 10, 15.

13. *The Juglers discovered*, p. 3.

14. *Clarke Papers*, Vol. I, pp. 170–211, *passim*.

15. *Idem*.

16. *Jonah's Cry*, p. 13.

17. *An Appeale from the degenerate Representative Body, the Commons at Westminster, to the free people*, p. 29.

18. *The Juglers discovered*, p. 5.

19. *Rushworth*, VII, pp. 750–756, *passim*, for a general account of the Army's entry into London.

20. William Sanderson, *A Compleat History of the Life and Raigne of King Charles* (1658), p. 1002.

21. *C.J.*, Vol. V, p. 270.

22. *The Humble Address of the Agitators of the Army to Sir Thomas Fairfax*, signed by fifty-three agitators (E.402/8).

23. *The Declaration of the Army* (E.404/3).

24. Attached to *Letter to Marten* of September 15, 1647.

25. *Jonah's Cry*, p. 9.

26. Both published at the end of the *Letter to Marten*, pp. 7–8.

27. Published in *Jonah's Cry*.

28. *Memoirs*, in *Maseres Tracts*, Vol. I, p. 363.

29. *A Cal to all the Souldiers of the Armie*, p. 5.

30. *The Tower of London Letter Book of Sir Lewis Dyve, 1646-7* (ed. H. G. Tibbutt), in *Publications of the Bedfordshire Historical Record Society*, Vol. XXXVIII (1958), pp. 85–88; *The Additional Plea of John Lilburne*, p. 22.

31. For the progress of Lilburne's Committee see *C.J.*, Vol. 5, *passim*.

32. *Letter to Marten*, September 15, 1647.

33. Gardiner gives no date. Dyve's report indicates a date prior to September 29. See also *infra*, pp. 198–199. I assume, however, that *five* regiments, and not six, elected new agitators at this time.

Chapter Seventeen : ROYALIST INTRIGUER

1. *Dictionary of National Biography.*
2. Works of Judge Jenkins, collected and edited by William H. Terry (1929).
3. *The Tower of London Letter Book of Sir Lewis Dyve, 1646–7* (ed. H. G. Tibbutt), in *Publications of the Bedfordshire Historical Record Society*, Vol. XXXVIII (1958).
4. *Diary*, September 6, 1651. Dyve told Evelyn several ' tall ' stories—see Vol. III, pp. 40, 49–50 (ed. de Beer).
5. *The Proposition of Lieutenant-Colonel John Lilburne Prisoner in the Tower of London*, October 2, 1647.
6. *The grand Plea of Lieut. Col. John Lilburne*, October 20, 1647.
7. Speech of Sir John Maynard in the House of Commons, July 27, 1648, *Old Parliamentary History*, Vol. 17 (1647–48), p. 356.
8. *The grand Plea*, p. 16.
9. *C.J.*, Vol. V, p. 353.
10. Dyve's *Letter Book* emphasizes the quarrel between Rainsborough and Cromwell, and deduces therefrom support for the King from Rainsborough. This is contrary to the generally accepted view that Rainsborough was Republican.
11. *A Whip for the present House of Lords*, p. 5, *et al.*; Ian Lilburn.
12. The letters are in *L.J.*, Vol. IX, pp. 519–20.

Chapter Eighteen : THE AGREEMENT OF THE PEOPLE

1. *The Prisoners Plea for a Habeas Corpus*, p. A.3 (no pagination, but the mark A.3 appears at the bottom of the page); *The Lawes Funerall*, p. 9.
2. *A Defiance to Tyrants*, p. 1.
3. *The Lawes Funerall*, p. 24.
4. *Londons Liberty in Chains*, p. 41.
5. J. Warr, *The Corruption and Deficiency of the Laws of England* (1649).
6. Gardiner, *The Constitutional Documents of the Puritan Revolution*, No. 71.
7. J. Wildman, *Putney Projects.*
8. Gardiner, *Civil War*, Vol. III, p. 365.
9. M. Ashley, *John Wildman : Plotter and Postmaster* (1947), pp. 9–14.
10. *Ibid.*, p. 15.

11. *The Case of the Armie truly stated*, p. 15.

12. *Letter to the Officers and Soldiers*, Postscript.

13. *An Agreement of the People for a firme and present Peace.*

14. Putney Debates, in *Clarke Papers*, Vol. I, pp. 299–301, and A. S. P. Woodhouse, *Puritanism and Liberty*, Part I.

15. *A Letter sent from several Agitators to their Respective Regiments.*

16. *Foundations of Freedom*; *An Agreement of the Free People of England.*

17. Newsletter, July 29, 1653, *Clarendon MSS.*, Vol. 46, f. 131.

18. *Regall Tyrannie discovered.*

19. *Jonah's Cry*, Postscript, p. 13.

20. Prose works, Vol. 2, p. 111, quoted by Woodhouse, *op. cit.*, Introduction, p. 72.

21. *An Arrow against All Tyrants*, pp. 3–4.

22. *Redintegratio Amoris.*

23. *Innocency and Truth Justified*, p. 38.

24. *An Appeale from the degenerate Representative Body . . . to the Body represented*, p. 2.

25. *Letter from the agitators of Five Regiments of Horse to Fairfax*, accompanying *The Case of the Armie.*

26. *An Arrow against All Tyrants*, p. 5.

27. *Regall Tyrannie discovered*, Introduction.

28. Overton, *A Remonstrance of many Thousand Citizens*, pp. 4–5.

29. Lilburne quotes this—apparently from a pamphlet of 1642— see *Cal.S.P.Dom.*, *1641–1643*, p. 309.

30. *Clarke Papers*, Vol. I, p. 306; Woodhouse, p. 57.

31. *Clarke Papers*, Vol. I, p. 301; Woodhouse, p. 53.

32. *Clarke Papers*, Vol. I, pp. 322–323; Woodhouse, p. 69.

33. *An Apologeticall Narration*, p. 70.

34. *Reliquiae Baxterianae*, p. 61 (ed. 1696).

35. *A Manifestation from Lieut.-Col. John Lilburne . . . and others*, p. 4.

36. Lucy Hutchinson, *Memoirs of Colonel Hutchinson*, p. 316 (Bohn's ed., 1906).

37. *History of Independency.*

38. *Rushworth*, VII, p. 866.

39. Letter from London, November 15, 1647, *Clarendon MSS.*, Vol. 30, f. 182.

40. *Maseres Tracts*, Preface to Vol. I, pp. xxxiii–xxxix.

41. E.413/18.

42. " John had said to his friends, That the happy time was come (meaning the Randevouze at Ware) that he should have balme powred into his wounds, since by his stripes England was healed, and therefore big with hope Legislative John was got as far as Ware, to behold the Lords worke (as he tearmed it) effected, and himselfe made a great man, being pitched upon

by some wretched ones in the Army for their Generall, to go
before them out of the Land of Egypt, and to guide them (no
doubt) into the Land of Promise. But John and they are like
to wander forty yeares, and to tast the bitter waters of Marah,
ere they arrive in their Utopian Paradise, and now toles out the
Bell, for John Lilburne lies sick, sick at heart of the sullens,
how is the mighty fallen ! " (*Mercurius Anti-Pragmaticus*, No. 6,
November 18–25, 1647, p. 4.)

43. *C.J.*, Vol. V, p. 354.
44. *C.J.*, Vol. V, pp. 367–368.
45. 669.f.11/98.

Chapter Nineteen : PARTY LEADER

1. *C.J.*, Vol. V, pp. 436–437; *L.J.*, Vol. IX, pp. 663, 666.
2. *The poore Wise-mans Admonition unto all the plaine people of London, and the Neighbour Places*, June 10, 1647.
3. Thorold Rogers, *A History of Agriculture and Prices in England*, Vols. V and VI; Gardiner, *Civil War*, Vol. III, pp. 194–195; Margaret James, *Social Problems and Policy during the Puritan Revolution, 1640–1660*, Chapter II.
4. *A Good Motion*, January 14, 1647.
5. Henry Peacham, *The Worth of a Peny*, July 19, 1647.
6. *The mournfull Cries of many thousand Tradesmen, who are ready to famish through decay of Trade. Or the warning Tears of the Oppressed*, January 1648, printed in *A Declaration of some Proceedings of Lt.-Col. John Lilburne*, February 14, 1648.
7. J. U. Nef, " The Progress of Technology and the Growth of Large-scale Industry in Great Britain, 1540–1640," in *Economic History Review* (1934–35), Vol. V, pp. 1–24.
8. Not to be confused with Smithfield, the meat market.
9. Many seventeenth- and eighteenth-century maps show East Smithfield, Ratcliffe Highway, and the district around them. Gascoyne's map of Stepney (1703) shows Well Alley right out in the Stepney district off Ropemakers Fields, north of Limehouse Dock and close to the river. There was also a Well Close Square and a Well Street just north of Ratcliffe Highway, and much nearer to the City, where Well Yard may well have been located. Contemporary accounts speak of the meeting at " Well Yard," " Smithfield," " East Smithfield," " Ratcliffe Highway," or " Wapping." East Smithfield, or Ratcliffe Highway, may merely have described the way of getting there, but on the whole the area of Well Close seems the more likely one for the Leveller meeting, though the Limehouse Dock area would probably have contributed even more local colour.
10. M. Ashley, *John Wildman*, p. 48.

11. Accounts of the meeting and subsequent events are in G. Masterson, *The Triumph stain'd*, February 10, 1648; *Mercurius Pragmaticus*, January 18–25, 1648; *A Declaration of some Proceedings*; Lilburne, *An Impeachment of High Treason*.

12. January 18–25, 1648; *A Declaration of some Proceedings*.

Chapter Twenty : RELEASE

1. *C.J.*, Vol. V, p. 438; *Cal.S.P.Dom.*, *1648–1649*, p. 14. Elaborate instructions were issued to the Committee of Kent, the Committee of Militia of London, the Hamlets, Southwark, Westminster, etc., to suppress and prevent all meetings—*Ibid.*, pp. 14–15.

2. See Bibliography.

3. J. U. Nef, " The Progress of Technology and the Growth of Large-scale Industry in Great Britain, 1540–1640," in *Econ. Hist. Rev.* (1934–35), Vol. V, pp. 1–24.

4. Margaret James, *Social Problems and Policy during the Puritan Revolution, 1640–1660*, Chapter III.

5. *Catalogue of the Thomason Tracts.*

6. But it is often possible to pick out a Lilburne tract.

7. *L.J.*, Vol. X, pp. 345, 508; *MSS. House of Lords, H.M.Comm.*, Vol. 6, p. 53. Mabbot was associated with the Independents, having been appointed licenser on the recommendation of the Army. It is possible that he wrote for early issues of *The Moderate* and that he published the newspaper. Later issues show that it had swung leftward, and No. 12 contains, for what it is worth, an express repudiation of Mabbot's responsibility.

8. *The Lawes Funerall*, pp. 3, 4, 29 (pagination faulty).

9. January, 22–29, 1648.

10. Letter of Intelligence, May 18, 1648, *Clarendon MSS.*, Vol. 31, f. 82.

11. William Allen, *A Faithful Memorial*, April, 27, 1659.

12. *Old Parliamentary History*, Vol. 17 (1647–48), pp. 354–355; E.458/2. The *Catalogue of the Thomason Tracts* erroneously attributes the speech to the other Sir John Maynard, King's Sergeant.

13. *C.J.*, Vol. V, p. 657; *L.J.*, Vol. X, p. 407.

14. August 1–8, 1648.

15. *Sundry Reasons inducing Major Robert Huntington to lay down his Commission.*

16. August 1–9, 1648.

17. *The Legall Fundamentall Liberties*, p. 28; *Letter to D. D.* in *L. Colonel John Lilburne Revived*, p. 2.

18. *The Legall Fundamentall Liberties*, p. 28.

19. Committee of Both Houses to Colonel Wichcott, *Cal.S.P.Dom.*, *1648–49*, p. 168; *Rushworth*, VII, p. 1177.
20. Haselrig had been appointed Governor of Newcastle in December 1647, succeeding Robert Lilburne (*supra*, p. 97), *C.J.*, Vol. V, p. 410. See also petition of Henry Lilburne's widow, *Cal.S.P.Dom.*, *1660–61*, p. 250.
21. See news-sheets for the period (listed in *Catalogue of the Thomason Tracts*, Vol. II), and Index to the *Thomason Tracts.*
22. *Mercurius Pragmaticus*, September 14–21, 1647, p. 5.
23. *Ibid.*
24. *A Preparative to an Hue and Cry*; *A Just Reproof to Haberdashers Hall*; *Cal. Cttee compounding with Delinquents* (*Domestic*) *1643–1660*, Part III, p. 2239.
25. E.464/5.

Chapter Twenty-one : DISILLUSION

1. Lilburne tells the full story of the negotiations between Levellers, Independents, and the Army in *The Legall Fundamentall Liberties*, pp. 29–39.
2. *A Preparative to an Hue and Cry after Sir Arthur Haselrig*, p. 31.
3. *The Legall Fundamentall Liberties*, pp. 34–35.
4. The Whitehall debates are in *Clarke Papers*, Vol. II, and Woodhouse, *Puritanism and Liberty*, Part II.
5. *Foundations of Freedom*; *or, an Agreement of the People.*
6. *Ibid. :* " The Publisher to the Judicious Reader."
7. *An Agreement of the People for a Secure Peace.*
8. *The Legall Fundamentall Liberties*, p. 37.
9. *Ibid.*, pp. 31–32.
10. *Ibid.*, pp. 34, 42–43.
11. *Ibid.*, p. 42.
12. December 21, 1648, *C.J.*, Vol. VI, p. 102.
13. *A Preparative to an Hue and Cry*, pp. 33–36.
14. *The Legall Fundamentall Liberties*, pp. 42–63.
15. *Ibid.*, pp. 43–44.
16. *Ibid.*, pp. 65–73.
17. *Ibid.*, p. 74.

Chapter Twenty-two : " ENGLAND'S NEW CHAINS "

1. *The Moderate*, February 20–27, 1649.
2. *Whitelocke*, p. 377.
3. *Clarke Papers*, Vol. II, p. 191; *The Hunting of the Foxes*, p. 10; *Englands New Chains* (not paginated).

4. *Englands New Chains.*
5. *The Legall Fundamentall Liberties,* p. 74.
6. *The Moderate,* February 27–March 6.
7. Printed in *The Hunting of the Foxes.*
8. *Mercurius Pragmaticus,* March 20, 1649; *Cal.S.P.Dom., 1649–1650,* pp. 55, 56, 59. It is interesting that on March 19 the House of Commons ordered that it be specially recommended to the Council of State to take present care to prevent such meetings as may be dangerous and prejudicial to the safety of the Commonwealth, and at the same time ordered that letters be written and signed by Mr Speaker and sent to all the Justices of the Peace in the several counties advising them to take special care to put the laws into execution for the relief of the poor in their several divisions. (*C.J.,* Vol. VI, p. 168.)
9. In *The Picture of the Councel of State* Lilburne, Overton, and Prince gave their accounts of their arrest and examination. Walwyn gave his in *The Fountain of Slaunder discovered.*
10. *The Moderate,* March 27–April 3, 1649.
11. *C.J.,* Vol. VI, p. 178; *Whitelocke,* p. 383; *The Moderate,* March 27–April 3, 1649. Gardiner, *Commonwealth and Protectorate,* Vol. I, p. 42, says 80,000 signatures were obtained for the petition of April 2, but gives no authority other than that of *The Moderate,* which, however, does not mention the number of signatures.
12. *Mercurius Militaris,* May 8, 1649.
13. *Whitelocke,* pp. 384–385.
14. *Mercurius Pragmaticus,* April 24–May 1, 1649.
15. *To the Supreme Authority of England,* petition of Women of London, Westminster, Southwark, Hamlets, etc.
16. February 19, 1649 (E.544/5).
17. See *The Works of Gerrard Winstanley,* edited with an Introduction by George H. Sabine, 1941.
18. February 16, 1649 (669.f.13/89).
19. *Clarke Papers,* Vol. II, pp. 203–204.
20. Lilburne, Postscript to *The Picture of the Councel of State*; *The Petition of several Churches of God in London commonly, though falsly, called Anabaptists,* April 2, 1649.
21. *Mercurius Pragmaticus,* April 24–May 1, 1649.
22. *Mercurius Elencticus,* May 1–8, 1649.

Chapter Twenty-three : MUTINY

1. *A True Narrative of the late Mutiny made by several Troopers of Captain Savage's Troop, in Col. Whaley's Regiment* (E.552/18); *The Army's Martyr* (E.552/11).

2. There are many accounts of Lockier's funeral, especially in the news-sheets. The most detailed are in *Mercurius Pragmaticus* (E.552/15); *The Kingdom's Weekly Intelligencer* (E.552/21); *The Moderate Intelligencer* (E.552/26); *The Moderate* (E.552/20).
3. *Whitelocke*, p. 385.
4. April 24–May 1, 1649 (E.552/15).
5. *The Moderate Intelligencer*, April 19–26 (E.552/4).
6. April 25, 1649. Headed by Thomason " A Libbell " (E.551/21).
7. 669.f.14/28.
8. May 6, 1649 (E.553/2).
9. *A Modest Narrative of Intelligence*, May 5–12, 1649 (E.555/8).
10. E.530/3; E.555/13; E.555/12.
11. *Mercurius Elencticus*, May 7–14, 1649 (E.555/9).
12. *C.J.*, Vol. VI, p. 205; *Cal.S.P.Dom.*, *1649–1650*, p. 131; *Mercurius Elencticus*, May 7–14, 1649 (E.555/9).
13. For further pamphlets on the Burford Mutiny see Bibliography.
14. *Mercurius Pragmaticus*, May 22–29 (E.556/25).
15. *Mercurius Philo-Monarchicus*, May 14–21, 1649 (E.555/34).
16. *The Moderate*, June 12–19, 1649 (E.560/17).
17. *Ibid.*, May 22–29, 1649 (E.556/31); *Cal.S.P.Dom.*, *1649–1650*, p. 162.
18. *Cal.S.P.Dom.*, *1649–1650*, July 17, 1649, p. 237.
19. *C.J.*, Vol. VI, p. 213.
20. " An act Declaring what Offences Shall be adjudged Treason," in *Acts and Ordinances of the Interregnum*, Vol. III, p. 120.
21. " A Motion to the Parliament and Councel of State concerning the Levellers," by " an unbyassed Person," in *The Moderate*, June 26–July 3, 1649 (E.562/22).
22. *A Discourse betwixt John Lilburn and Hugh Peters*, p. 8.
23. Preface to *An Impeachment of High Treason*; *Preparative to an Hue and Cry*, pp. 38–40.

Chapter Twenty-four : AN IMPEACHMENT OF HIGH TREASON
BY JOHN LILBURNE

1. Lilburne, *An Impeachment of High Treason against Oliver Cromwell and . . . Ireton*, pp. 5–6.
2. Professor Don M. Wolfe believes that Overton was the author of this pamphlet; but I cannot feel convinced that it was not Lilburne or part Lilburne. The pamphlet is incisive—but not more so than Lilburne at his best. The imagery is rich—but not more so than Lilburne's finest. The verve it displays could be Lilburne's as well as Overton's. In March 1649 Lilburne had just come back into the struggle after his attempt to hold aloof (Chapter XXII), and the pamphlet very accurately fits his state

of mind. If it is better than many of his hurriedly penned polemics this may easily be because it came after a period of comparative rest, when his expressions had crystallized. Besides, he was closer to the Army than Overton or Wildman, and the baulked anger it expresses was more naturally his. Small straws to point to Lilburne's participation are the use of the expression " stout Capel," which he often used, and the metaphor of the foxes, which he frequently used—in reference, for example, to Haselrig, though the fox metaphor was not, of course, uncommon.

3. *The Hunting of the Foxes*, p. 7.
4. *An Impeachment*, p. 4.
5. *The Hunting of the Foxes*, pp. 7–8.
6. *Ibid.*, pp. 8, 9, 12.
7. *An Impeachment*, p. 8.
8. Evidence of John Took, Thomas Lewis, John Skinner, at Lilburne's trial.
9. July 25, 28, 1649, *Cal.S.P.Dom.*, *1649–1650*, pp. 248, 251. Eyres was to be removed to Warwick Castle (*Idem.*, pp. 251, 254).
10. Summarized in *The Moderate*, September 4–11, 1649 (E.573/7).
11. *Cal.S.P.Dom.*, *1649–1650*, p. 304.
12. *Ibid.*, pp. 303–304.
13. *Ibid.*, p. 303; also Robert Coytmor to Colonel Popham, MSS. of Leyborne Popham, *H.M.Comm.*, Vol. 51, p. 36.
14. *Cal.S.P.Dom.*, *1649–1650*, pp. 302–303.
15. Letter from " neer Oxford," September 8, in *The Moderate*, September 4–11, 1649.
16. *The Moderate*, September 18–25, 1649 (E.574/22). A narrative of the mutiny was given by Captain Wagstaff to the House of Commons and printed in *The Moderate*, September 11–18 (E.574/3). Other sources of information are *The Moderate* for the week September 4–11, the *Calendar of State Papers*, and the news-sheets in general.
17. *The Moderate*, August 21–28, September 4–11, 1649 (E.572/1).
18. *The Remonstrance of many thousands of the Free-People of England. Together with the Resolves of the Yong-men and Apprentices of the City of London, in behalf of themselves and those called Levelers*, September 21, 1649 (E.574/15).
19. *Cal.S.P.Dom.*, *1649–1650*, p. 312.
20. *Ibid.*, p. 314.
21. *Acts and Ordinances of the Interregnum*, Vol. II, pp. 245–254.
22. E.571/11, p. 10.
23. September 8, 1649, *Cal.S.P.Dom.*, *1649–1650*, p. 303.
24. September 19, 1649, *Ibid.*, pp. 314–315.
25. *Whitelocke*, p. 396.
26. *Mercurius Elencticus*, May 21–28, 1649 (E.556/19).

Chapter Twenty-five : LILBURNE ON TRIAL

1. April 24–May 1, 1649.
2. May 15–22, 1649.
3. *Strength out of Weaknesse.*
4. *Mercurius Elencticus,* September 17–24, 1649; *Mercurius Pragmaticus,* September 18–25, 1649.
5. Lilburne, *A Defensive Declaration,* pp. 10–11; narrative of William Blanke in *A Preparative to an Hue and Cry,* pp. 7–8.
6. October 20, *The Innocent Man's first Proffer*; October 22, *The innocent Man's second Proffer.*
7. *Mercurius Pragmaticus,* October 23–30, 1649.
8. *Truths Victory over Tyrants and Tyranny* (E.579/12).
9. *L. Colonel John Lilburne Revived,* p. 4.
10. *The Triall of Lieut.-Collonell John Lilburne,* by Theodorus Verax; Howell's *State Trials,* Vol. 4, p. 1270.
11. *Mercurius Pragmaticus,* October 23–30, 1649.
12. Lilburne, *The Upright Man's Vindication,* p. 14.
13. Ian Lilburn.

Chapter Twenty-six : JACK OF ALL TRADES

1. *The Engagement vindicated and explained.*
2. December 26, 1649. *C.J.,* Vol. VI, pp. 337–338.
3. *Mercurius Pragmaticus.*
4. *To the Supreme Authority the Parliament of the Common-wealth of England* (669.f.15/62).
5. *To every individuall Member,* November 1650 (669.f.15/64).
6. Ian Lilburn.
7. Lilburne, *A Just Reproof to Haberdashers Hall.*
8. Lilburne, *A Defensive Declaration,* Appendix.
9. *Portland Papers* (Longleat), Vol. II, ff. 89–90, and see illustration between pp. 328 and 329.
10. *A Defensive Declaration,* Additional Appendix.
11. *A Just Reproof to Haberdashers Hall,* p. 3.
12. *Ibid.*
13. Lilburne, *To every individuall Member,* November 26, 1651; Huntington, *A True Narrative concerning Sir Arthur Haselrig's possessing of Lieut-Colonel John Lilburne's Estate in the County of Durham,* 1653.
14. *A Defensive Declaration,* p. 4. Might this purchase have included the tenement at Greenwich ? (*Supra,* p. 20.)
15. *The Just Defence of John Lilburn,* p. 9.
16. *The Second Part of the Triall of Lieut Col. John Lilburne* (E.598/12).
17. *The Just Defence of John Lilburn,* p. 9; *Lilburne tryed and cast,* p. 81.

18. *The Case of the Tenants of the Mannor of Epworth.*

19. *Ibid., Cal.S.P.Dom., 1652–1653,* pp. 373–376; *Cal.S.P.Dom., 1654,* pp. 309–310; M. Ashley, *John Wildman,* Chapter VI.

20. *A Just Reproof to Haberdashers Hall; Lilburne tryed and cast; A Declaration of Lieutenant-Colonel John Lilburn; A Remonstrance of Lieut. Col. John Lilburn; A Defensive Declaration of Lieut. Col. John Lilburn; Mercurius Politicus,* January 15–22, 1652 (E.651/31); *C.J.,* Vol. VII, pp. 55, 64, 71–75.

21. *The Several Examinations and Confessions of Thomas Coke, Esquire, taken in the month of April, 1651,* (*H.M.Comm.,* Portland *MSS.,* I, p. 591).

22. Lilburne, *As you Were,* letter to Kiffin, p. 7; *Apologeticall Narration,* p. 50.

23. *The Just Defence of John Lilburn,* p. 10; *A Declaration of Lieutenant-Colonel John Lilburn to the Free-born People of England; A Defensive Declaration,* p. 3; *Apologeticall Narration,* p. 51.

24. *A Defensive Declaration.*

25. *Apologeticall Narration,* pp. 59–61.

26. *A Defensive Declaration,* p. 3.

27. *A Perfect Account,* January 28–February 4, 1652.

28. The address given in the letter to Kiffin in *As You Were.*

Chapter Twenty-seven : THE EXILE

1. Lilburne, *A Defensive Declaration,* pp. 5–7, 13–14, and *passim.* Lilburne was right. In 1660 Thomas Scot confessed various activities, including spying upon Lilburne and using Hugh Riley and Wendy Oxford. The confession, edited by C. H. Firth, is published in *Engl. Hist. Rev.,* No. XII (1897), p. 116. The reference to Lilburne is at p. 120.

2. Lilburne, Letter to Kiffin in *As You Were;* Letter to Scotland in *L. Colonel John Lilburne Revived; The Banished man's Suit for Protection.*

3. Lilburne, *Apologeticall Narration.*

4. Reproduced in *As You Were.*

5. *As You Were.*

6. *Ibid.; Letter to D. D.* in *L. Colonel John Lilburne Revived.*

7. *Letter to D. D.; Severall Informations,* examination of Titus, p. 7.

8. *Severall Informations,* examination of Richard Foot, p. 11.

9. *As You Were,* pp. 15–16; *The Upright Man's Vindication,* p. 7 (see Wolfe, *Modern Language Notes,* May 1941, for reference to Milton); Letter to Henry Marten and other letters in *L. Colonel John Lilburne Revived.*

10. Letter to Scotland in *L. Colonel John Lilburne Revived*; Letter to Kiffin in *As You Were*.
11. Huntington, *A True Narrative*, p. 7.
12. *A Defensive Declaration*, p. 4.
13. Letter to Scotland in *L. Colonel John Lilburne Revived*.
14. *Nicholas Papers*, Vol. I, p. 321, *Camden Society Publications* (1886), Vol. 40.
15. *A Defensive Declaration*, Additional Appendix, pp. 15–18.
16. *Severall Informations*, examination of Titus, p. 6, Captain Bartlett, pp. 7–8, and *passim*.
17. R. Watson to Edgeman, September 12, 1652, *Clarendon MSS.*, Vol. 43, f. 303.
18. *Severall Informations*, examination of Isaac Berkenhead, p. 1.
19. *Ibid.*, p. 3.
20. *A Defensive Declaration*, p. 16.
21. *Ibid.*, p. 18; *Severall Informations*, examination of Titus, p. 7; Newsletter, July 1653, *Clarendon MSS.*, Vol. 46, f. 34.
22. Nicholas to ' Mr Smith ' [Lord Hatton], *Nicholas Papers*, Vol. I, p. 301.
23. June 1653, *Clarendon MSS.*, Vol. 45, f. 442.
24. Nicholas to ' Mr Smith,' *Nicholas Papers*, Vol. I, p. 291.
25. *Clarendon MSS.*, Vol. 43, f. 277.
26. R. Watson to Edgeman, *Clarendon MSS.*, Vol. 42, f. 383.
27. *Clarendon MSS.*, Vol. 43, f. 139.
28. *Severall Informations*, examination of Isaac Berkenhead, p. 1.
29. *A Defensive Declaration*, p. 15.
30. *Malice detected.*
31. *A Defensive Declaration*, p. 19.
32. *L. Colonel John Lilburne Revived.*
33. *A Defensive Declaration*, pp. 1–2.
34. *The Upright Man's Vindication.* Was it May 14 ? New style and old style of dating become confused.
35. *Ibid.*, p. 14.
36. Letter published in *Severall Informations*, p. 10.
37. *The Upright Man's Vindication.*
38. *Ibid.*, p. 16; *Triall* (E.708/3), pp. 38–39.
39. *The Banished man's Suit for Protection. Severall Informations*, examination of John Staplehill, p. 14. One of the informers, John Staplehill, alleged that Elizabeth was with her husband, supping with the Duke of Buckingham and taking ship for England with him. But this does not fit the other evidence—that she was with William Kiffin in London when Lilburne arrived, or very shortly after; that she sent horses for her husband to Canterbury. Nor does it tally with Lilburne's own account of his journey, which never mentions his wife and was taken at great speed—Calais to London in a day, horseback from the

coast. Nor does the challenge at Canterbury which Staplehill
describes make any mention of a woman in Lilburne's company,
a fact that would surely not have escaped unnoticed. It is more
likely that Staplehill was, deliberately or otherwise, confusing
Elizabeth's previous visit to her husband.

40. *The Banished man's Suit for Protection.*
41. Clarendon, *History of the Rebellion*, Vol. III, p. 392.

Chapter Twenty-eight : " LONG LIVE LILBURNE ! "

1. Newsletter, *Clarendon MSS.*, Vol. 45, f. 499.
2. Beverning to Pensionary De Witt, *Thurloe State Papers*, Vol. I, p. 441.
3. Newsletter, *Clarendon MSS.*, Vol. 46, f. 9.
4. Newsletter, *Clarendon MSS.*, Vol. 46, ff. 132, 110.
5. Newsletter, *Clarendon MSS.*, Vol. 46, f. 9.
6. *Cal.S.P.Dom.*, *1652–1653*, p. 436.
7. *Clarendon MSS.*, Vol. 46, f. 89.
8. *The Faithful Post* (E.215/2); *The Weekly Intelligencer* (E.703/1).
9. *Mercurius Pragmaticus*, June 22–30, 1653 (E.703/10).
10. *Clarendon MSS.*, Vol. 46, f. 9.
11. Newsletter, *Clarendon MSS.*, Vol. 46, f. 131.
12. Lilburne, *The Prisoner's most mournful Cry*. They were sold to agents at 12*d.* for 25, and by them sold to hawkers at 14*d.* for 25.
13. *Ibid.*; *An Exact Relation*, p. 5 (E.729/6).
14. ' Peter Richardson ' to Mr Edwards, *Thurloe State Papers*, Vol. I, p. 367.
15. *Clarendon MSS.*, Vol. 46, f. 109.
16. *Cal.S.P.Ven.*, *1653–1654*, p. 109.
17. Newsletter, *Clarendon MSS.*, Vol. 46, f. 32.
18. ' Peter Richardson' to Mr Edwards, *Thurloe State Papers*, Vol. I, p. 367.
19. *Cal.S.P.Ven.*, *1653–1654*, p. 122.
20. *Clarendon MSS.*, Vol. 46, f. 109.
21. *Ibid.*; Lilburne, *A Conference with the Souldiers. Or, a parley with the party of horse, which with drawn sword entred the Sessions at Mr John Lilburn's trial.*
22. Pamphlets covering the trial are reproduced in Howell's *State Trials*, Vol. V, p. 407. The most important accounts of the trial are in E.708/3 and E.710/21. For supporting pamphlets see Bibliography.
23. *Severall Informations and Examinations taken concerning Lieutenant Colonell John Lilburn, concerning his apostacy to the party of Charles Stuart and his intentions in coming over*

into England out of Flanders (E.705/14); *C.J.*, Vol. VII, p. 284; *The Triall of Mr John Lilburn* (E.708/3).

24. *Petition to Parliament*, July 12, 1653 (E.708/3); *Malice detected.*
25. *A Conference with the Souldiers.*
26. Van de Perre to Pensionary Bruyne, *Thurloe State Papers*, Vol. I, p. 442.
27. Beverning to Pensionary De Witt, *Thurloe State Papers*, Vol. I, p. 441. He speaks of two *regiments* near the Old Bailey, and three *regiments* of foot and one of horse patrolling the streets—*i.e.*, over 2000 men near the court, nearer 4000 in the streets, as well as 600 horse.
28. *Cal.S.P.Ven., 1653–1654*, p. 119.
29. Newsletter, *Clarendon MSS.*, Vol. 46, f. 207. The writer said Colonel Barkstead, the Lieutenant of the Tower, but Colonel Baxter, who commanded the troops present, is obviously intended, from the reference to his previous occupation.
30. *Cal.S.P.Ven., 1653–1654*, p. 119.
31. The second part of the trial was not so well reported as the first, but see Howell, *op. cit.*, and Bibliography. It was the strength and audacity of Lilburne's argument, rather than the fact that he disputed with his judges at both his trials, that won him such approbation. Sir Fitzjames Stephens, describing criminal trials between 1550 and 1637, says: " The examination of the prisoner . . . was the very essence of the trial, and his answers regulated the production of the evidence; the whole trial, in fact, was a long argument between the prisoner and the counsel for the Crown " (*History of Criminal Law*, Vol. I, p. 325). As in other respects, Lilburne carried an admitted principle farther than anyone else.
32. Newsletter, *Clarendon MSS.*, Vol. 46, f. 208; Van de Perre to Pensionary Bruyne, *Thurloe State Papers*, Vol. I, p. 442.
33. Lorenzo Paulucci to Venetian Secretary in France, *Cal.S.P.Ven., 1653–1654*, p. 122.
34. *A Letter from the North* (669.f.17/54).
35. Lorenzo Paulucci to Venetian Secretary in France, *Cal.S.P.Ven., 1653–1654*, p. 122.
36. *Ibid.*
37. Theodorus to Lord Conway, *Cal.S.P.Dom., 1652–1653*, p. 436.
38. August 22, August 27, 1653, *C.J.*, Vol. VII, pp. 306, 309.
39. *C.J.*, Vol. VII, p. 309.
40. *Cal.S.P.Dom., 1653–1654*, pp. 105, 107; *Cal.S.P.Ven., 1653–1654*, p. 125.
41. *Cal.S.P.Dom., 1653–1654*, p. 126.
42. October 26, 1653, *C.J.*, Vol. VII, p. 358.
43. *Cal.S.P.Dom., 1653–1654*, p. 311.
44. *Clarendon MSS.*, Vol. 46, f. 131.

45. *A Charge of High Treason exhibited against Oliver Cromwell, Esq.* (669.f.17/52).
46. Newsletter, *Clarendon MSS.*, Vol. 46, f. 274.
47. *Cal.S.P.Dom.*, *1653–1654*, pp. 457–458.
48. Gardiner, *Commonwealth and Protectorate*, Vol. III, pp. 16–17.
49. *Cal.S.P.Dom.*, *1654*, pp. 33–34, 46, 50, 195; Ian Lilburn.
50. *The Just Defence of John Lilburn against such as charge him with Turbulency of Spirit*, August 25, 1653, p. 11 (E.711/10).

Chapter Twenty-nine : REQUIESCAT

1. W. Prynne, *Poeticall Description of Mont Orgueil Castle.*
2. *Cal.S.P.Ven.*, *1653–1654*, p. 217. But the rumour was not universally credited, Hyde, for example, not believing it (*Clarendon MSS.*, Vol. 48, f. 251).
3. *Clarke Papers*, Vol. III, p. 32.
4. Gibbon to Cromwell, July 4, 1655, *Thurloe State Papers*, Vol. III, p. 512, and July 7, *Rawlinson MSS.*, Vol. 28, No. 246.
5. Lilburne, *The Resurrection of John Lilburne*, p. 6.
6. Gibbon to Cromwell, July 7, 1655, *Rawlinson MSS.*, Vol. 28, No. 246.
7. July 4, 1655, *Thurloe State Papers*, Vol. III, p. 512.
8. Carlisle, *Letters and Speeches of Oliver Cromwell*, Vol. II, pp. 345, 342.
9. M. Ashley, *John Wildman*, Chapter VII.
10. Gibbon to Cromwell, July 4, 1655, *Thurloe State Papers*, Vol. III, p. 512; July 7, *Rawlinson MSS.*, Vol. 28, No. 246.
11. *Rawlinson MSS.*, Vol. 28, No. 246.
12. *Cal.S.P.Dom.*, *1655*, p. 264.
13. *Ibid.*, pp. 263–264.
14. Newsletter *Clarke Papers*, Vol. III, p. 53. But Gibbon on July 4, 1655, wrote that " yesterday "—*i.e.*, July 3—he received Cromwell's order to remove Lilburne to Deal Castle, and is preparing to send him by the first opportunity after the vessel taking that letter.
15. Lilburne, *The Resurrection of John Lilburne*, pp. 7–8.
16. *Cal.S.P.Dom.*, *1655*, p. 556.
17. *The Resurrection of John Lilburne*, pp. 1–2 and *passim.*
18. *Ibid.*, pp. 6, 5.
19. *Ibid.*, pp. 2, 3.
20. Lilburne, *Letter to Margaret Fell*, *Thirnbeck MSS.*, Vol. II, in *Journal of the Friends Historical Society*, Vol. 9 (1912), pp. 53–59. See illustration between pp. 328 and 329.
21. *The Resurrection of John Lilburne*, p. 5.
22. *Ibid.*, p. 4.

23. L. V. Hodgkin, *The Shoemaker of Dover.*
24. *Ibid.*
25. *Ibid.*
26. *Ibid.*
27. *The Resurrection of John Lilburne,* printed for Giles Calvert, first edition, May 16, 1656; second edition, May 21, 1656, pp. 1, 13.
28. *Thirnbeck MSS.,* Vol. II.
29. M. Ashley, *John Wildman,* Chapters VII, VIII.
30. Anthony Wood, *Athenae Oxoniensis,* Vol. II, p. 102.
31. L. V. Hodgkin, *op. cit.*
32. Elizabeth to the Protector, November 4, 1657, *Cal.S.P.Dom., 1657–1658,* p. 148.
33. Burton's *Diary,* Vol. III, p. 507, note; Wheatley and Cunningham, *London Past and Present,* Vol. I, p. 25; *Mercurius Politicus,* September 3, 1657 (E.505); *Mercurius Pragmaticus,* September 3, 1657; *The Public Advisor* (E.925); *The Public Intelligencer,* (E.505).
34. November 4, 1657, *Cal.S.P.Dom., 1657–1658,* p. 148.
35. Elizabeth to Richard Cromwell, January 21, 1659, *Cal.S.P.Dom., 1658–1659,* p. 261.
36. *Ibid.,* pp. 260–261.
37. *C.J.,* Vol. VII, p. 760; Burton's *Diary,* Vol. III, pp. 68, 503–509.
38. *C.J.,* Vol. VII, p. 879. There was a break on September 9, 1659, when £100 was paid in lieu of pension, *C.J.,* Vol. VII, p. 776.
39. Burton's *Diary,* Vol. III, pp. 68, 509.

Chapter Thirty: ENGLAND'S TOUCHSTONE

1. Concerning the influence of the Levellers on later generations, two points of interest may be mentioned. There is in the Guildhall Library an undated eighteenth-century pamphlet in the form of an imaginary " Epistle from Colonel John Lilburne In the Shades to John Wilkes, Esq.," in which the writer draws attention to a supposed similarity between the careers of Lilburne and Wilkes. Also in the Guildhall Library is the bound volume of tracts by Lilburne to which Pease drew attention in *The Leveller Movement.* The fly-sheet announces the tracts to have been in the possession of William Hone in 1820, and to have been bound up by Mr Jeremiah Joyce, who often read them in the Tower when prisoner on a charge of high treason. " For which reason and because Lilburne was a man exceedingly after my own heart," wrote Hone in 1820, " I greatly prize the volume."
2. *History of the Rebellion,* Vol. V, p. 307.

3. *Lieut. Colonel John Lilb. tryed and cast*, p. 23.
4. *The Self Afflicter Lively Described.*
5. September 14–21, 1647.
6. *The Last Will and Testament of Lieutenant Col. John Lilburn.*
7. *A Caveat to those that shall resolve, whether right or wrong, to destroy John Lilburne.*
8. *Animadversions upon John Lilburne's Two last Books*, p. 13.
9. *A Vindication of Lieutenant Colonel John Lilburne.*
10. *Innocency and Truth Justified.* p. 4.
11. *An Impeachment of High Treason.*
12. To Cromwell, to Margaret Fell; see illustrations between pp. 328 and 329.
13. *A Vindication.*
14. *The resolved mans Resolution*, April 1647.
15. Vol. I, p. 128.
16. *Mercurius Pragmaticus*, November 9–16, 1647.
17. *Englands New Chains.*

Lilburne-Claxton Lawsuit

Mr Ian Lilburn writes:

" The lawsuit was not resolved peacefully. The champions appeared again and again. British Museum Add. MS. 27,380, in which a lawyer tries to trace the history of the proceedings, shows that the suit was still continuing in 1654, and ends with the remark ' what further proceedings were thereupon non constat mihi.'

" The quarrel was between the heirs male and the heirs of line of Richard Lilburne's great-grand-uncle, and had its origin in 1526, when his grandfather, Bartholomew Lilburne, was serving in France.

" Bartholomew was heir male of his uncle Thomas, whose daughters wrongfully took possession of the entailed estates on the death of their father. A decision had at one time been reached in favour of Richard's grandfather, but the rival faction had subsequently raided his deed-boxes, destroyed his documents, and reopened the proceedings. In 1604, with a small army of about thirty men, they even went as far as to burn down his manor-house at Thickley, for which they received the King's pardon."

Bibliography

The first bibliography of the writings of John Lilburne was published by Edward Peacock in *Notes and Queries*, Seventh Series, (1888), Vol. V, pp. 122, 162, 242, 342, 423, 502, and Vol. X, p. 125. There was some subsequent correspondence of interest. More recently Professor Don M. Wolfe, in *Milton in the Puritan Revolution* (1941), supplemented by *Leveller Manifestoes of the Puritan Revolution* (1944), pp. 425–426, provided an up-to-date Lilburne bibliography. Professor William Haller, in *The Rise of Puritanism* (1938), pp. 432–440, discusses exhaustively Lilburne's writing between 1638 and 1640. For the convenience of readers of this biography I repeat here a short-title list of Lilburne's works which differs only slightly from the bibliography of Professor Wolfe. *Plaine Truth without Feare or Flattery* I still attribute to Lilburne, in spite of Professor Wolfe's doubts. The title-pages of copies of this tract in the Bodleian Library and South Kensington differ from that of the British Museum copy. The latter announces the author as Amon Wilbee. The others say by I. L. And on two of the Bodleian copies some one has written after the L, in a possibly eighteenth-century hand, ilburn. *The Hunting of the Foxes*, for the reasons given in note 2 to Chapter Twenty-four, I still believe to be partly, if not entirely, Lilburne's. If it were a joint work I wonder if the helping hand could have been Wildman's as well as Overton's, as some of the passages in *Putney Projects* might suggest. In general, it is possible that more of the tracts than are commonly supposed were joint works. The imprisonment of the author and the difficulty of getting copy to the printer and of checking and amending proofs alone make this likely. *Regall Tyrannie* I assume, with Professor Wolfe, to have been written partly by Overton, but believe that Lilburne had a hand in it as well. I do not believe that *A Plea or Protest, made by William Prynne* . . . published by Lionel Hurbin on March 16, 1648, is Lilburne's, in spite of the fact that Thomason wrote on his copy of the tract to this effect. I should take it to be by a Leveller friend.

An E number in the following list indicates a tract in the Thomason collection in the British Museum, and refers to the actual shelf-mark. B indicates the Bodleian Library, Oxford: many more pamphlets than Peacock or Wolfe indicates are now in the Bodleian. Other locations are given only when the pamphlet is available neither at the British Museum nor at Oxford—namely, Guildhall, London (G), or the Foster Library, South Kensington (S.K.). A Guildhall reference is, however, very uncertain, as many pamphlets were lost in air-raids during the War, and those that were retrieved have not all been sorted. American locations, which Wolfe indicates, are not given here. Works *about* Lilburne and works written in collaboration are listed separately from those entirely *by* Lilburne.

Works listed here that are not attributed by Wolfe to Lilburne or are not mentioned by him, are marked with an asterisk (*). The bibliography does not claim to be exhaustive, but I believe that nothing significant has been omitted.

Lilburne's own dating of a pamphlet, or deduction of a date from internal evidence, is indicated by an L; otherwise the date is the one given in the *Catalogue of the Thomason Tracts*. Where Thomason's date, which he frequently wrote on the pamphlet, and which was generally the day of publication, is different from Lilburne's this is indicated by the letters Th.

A. Works by John Lilburne

The Christian Mans Triall, March 12, 1638 (L). The first edition not extant; a second edition December 1641 (E.181/7; B).

A Worke of the Beast, 1638 (L) (B.M., but not Th., G.5954/1; B). (It was reprinted in the second edition of *The Christian Mans Triall*.)

Coppy of a Letter written by L. C. L. to one of his special friends when he was in his cruell close imprisonment, November 11, 1638 (L). (Printed at the end of *Innocency and Truth Justified*, 1645.)

The Poore Mans Cry, written December 20, 1638 (L), printed 1639 (G).

Letter to the Apprentices, May 10, 1639. (Reprinted at the end of *The Prisoners Plea for a Habeas Corpus*, 1648.)

A Cry for Justice, May 1639 (L). (Reprinted at pp. 22–26 of *Picture of the Councel of State* (second edition, 1649).)

These last two are the works named by Katherine Hadley, when interrogated in 1639, as the pamphlets she had flung abroad in Moorfields. They were printed in Holland (*Picture of the Councel of State*, second edition). None of the original printing survive. Apparently the authorities had done their work of discovery and destruction very thoroughly. See *supra* pp. 77–78, and note 7 to Chapter Six.

An Answer to nine Arguments, date uncertain (?1639 or 1640), published January 17, 1645 (E.25/7; B).

Come out of her my people, 1639 (B.M., but not Th., 479.a.9, printed at Amsterdam).

Coppy of a Letter . . . to James Ingram and Henry Hopkins, Wardens of the Fleet, October 4, 1640 (L) (B.M., but not Th., G.5954/2; B).

A Letter from Capt. Lilburne (from Oxford), January 3, 1643 (E.84/5; B).

Copie of a Letter . . . Lilburne to . . . Prynne, January 7, 1645 (L), January 15 (Th.) (E.24/22; B).

Reasons of Lieu. Col. Lilbournes sending his Letter to Mr Prin . . ., June 13, 1645 (L) (E.288/12; B).

A More full Relation of the great Battell [Langport], July 10, 1645 (E.293/3; B).

Copy of a Letter . . . to a Friend . . . with Letter from Oliver Cromwell, July 25, 1645 (L) (E.296/5; B).

Extract relating to the Militia with Commentary, August 30, 1645 (669.f.10/33; this also is a Th. shelf-mark).

Letter to a Friend . . . to vindicate his aspersed Reputation, September 23, 1645 (E.302/17).

Englands Birth-right justified, October 10, 1645 (E.304/17; B). (Wolfe points out (*Milton*, p. 471) that this is mentioned repeatedly by Lilburne, but not claimed as his own.)

Innocency and Truth Justified, January 6, 1646 (E.314/21; B).

The Just Mans Justification, June 6, 1646 (L) (E.340/12).

The Freemans Freedome vindicated, Postscript, June 19, 1646 (L), June 16 (Th.) (E.341/12; B).

Coppy of a Letter . . . to Mr Wollaston, Keeper of Newgate, June 23, 1646 (L), (669.f.10/26; B).

Liberty vindicated against Slavery, August 21, 1646 (E.351/2).

Londons Liberty in Chains, October 1646 (L) (E.359/17; B).

An Anatomy of the Lords Tyranny, November 6, 1646 (L) (E.362/6).

The Charters of London ; or, the Second Part of Londons Liberty in Chaines, December 18, 1646 (L) (E.356/12; B).

The Oppressed Mans Oppressions declared, January 30, 1647 (L) (E.373/1; B).

The resolved mans Resolution, April 30, 1647 (L) (E.387/4; B).

Rash Oaths unwarrantable (letter to Marten), May 31, 1647 (L) (E.393/39; B).

Copy of a Letter . . . to . . . Marten, July 20, 1647 (L) (669.f.11/46).

*Letter to Marten, with Marten's reply, July 23 and 26, 1647 (B.M., but not Th., 8122.d.69).

Jonah's Cry out of the Whales belly, July 26, 1647 (E.400/5; B).

The Just Mans Justification . . . the second edition with divers Additions, presented especially to the Private Soldiers, August 27, 1647 (E.407/26).

Two Letters . . . to . . . Marten, September 13 and 15, 1647 (L) (E.407/41; B).

The Juglers discovered, September 28, 1647 (E.409/22).

The grand Plea of Lieut. Col. John Lilburne, October 20, 1647 (L) (E.411/21; B).

The Additional Plea of Lieut. Col. John Lilburne, October 28, 1647 (L) (E.412/11).

*Plaine Truth without Feare or Flattery, 1647 (E.516/7; B).

A Defiance to Tyrants, January 28, 1648 (E.520/30; B). Also quoted in *The peoples Prerogative*, where L. gives its date as December 2, 1647.

The peoples Prerogative, February 6, 1648 (L), February 17 (Th.) (E.427/4).

A Whip for the present House of Lords, February 27, 1648 (L) (E.431/1; B).

The Prisoners Plea for a Habeas Corpus, April 4, 1648 (E.434/19).

The Oppressed Mans Importunate and Mournfull Cryes to be brought to the Barre of Justice, April 7, 1648 (L) (G).

The Prisoners Mournfull Cry, May 1, 1648 (L), May 9 (Th.) (E.441/17; B).

The Lawes Funerall, May 15, 1648 (L) (E.442/13; B).

A Plea for Common Right and Freedom, December 28, 1648 (L) (E.536/22).

Englands New Chains discovered, February 26, 1649 (L) (E.545/27; B).

The Hunting of the Foxes, March 21, 1649 (E.548/7). (? with Overton and ? Wildman.)

A Discourse betwixt John Lilburn and Hugh Peters, May 25, 1649 (L) (E.556/26; B).

The Legall Fundamentall Liberties, June 8, 1649 (L) (E.560/14; B). Second edition, corrected and amended, late July or August 1649 (E.567/1; B).

To all the Affectors and Approvers of the Petition of the eleventh of September, 1648, July 17, 1649 (L) (G).

To his honoured Friend, Mr Cornelius Holland, n.d. (S.K.).

An Impeachment of High Treason against Oliver Cromwell and . . . Ireton, August 10, 1649 (E.508/20; B).

A Preparative to an Hue and Cry after Sir Arthur Haselrig, August 18, 1649 (L) (E.573/16; B).

An Outcry of the Youngmen and Apprentices of London, August 29, 1649 (E.572/13; B).

A Salva Libertate, September 14, 1649 (L) (669.f.14/76).

Strength out of Weaknesse, September 30, 1649 (L), October 19 (Th.) (E.575/18).

The Innocent Man's first Proffer, October 20, 1649 (669.f.14/83).

The Innocent Man's second Proffer, October 22, 1649 (669.f.14/85).
These last two are also attached to the report of his trial by Theodorus Verax; see *infra*.

The Engagement vindicated and explained, December 1649 (L), January 23, 1650 (Th.) (E.590/4; B).

Letters . . . to . . . Price about . . . George Lilburne and . . . Haselrig, March 31, 1651 (E.626/19).

A Just Reproof to Haberdashers Hall, August 2, 1651 (L), July 30 (Th.) (E.638/12).

The Case of the Tenants of the Mannor of Epworth, November 18, 1651 (L) (E.644/8).

A Declaration of Lieutenant-Colonel John Lilburn to the Free-born People of England, January 22, 1652 (E.652/1).

A Remonstrance of Lieut. Col. John Lilburn : concerning the Lawes, Liberties, and Inheritances of the freeborn People of England, January 28, 1652 (E.652/5).

The Levellers Remonstrance sent in a letter to . . . Cromwell, February 1, 1652 (E.652/12).
> Both these last two repeat similar statements from earlier works. Obviously very hurriedly put together, perhaps by a friend of Lilburne's.

L. Colonel John Lilburne his Apologeticall Narration, April 3, 1652 (L), in Dutch and English (E.659/30).

As You Were, May 1652 (L) (G).

L. Colonel John Lilburne Revived, March 27, 1653 (E.689/32).

The Banished man's Suit for Protection, June 14, 1653 (669.f.17/16; B).

A Second Address directed to . . . Cromwell, June 16, 1653 (669.f. 17/20).

A Third Address directed to . . . Cromwell, June 20, 1653 (L) (669.f. 17/22).

A Defensive Declaration, June 22, 1653 (L) (E.702/2; B).

Lieut Col. Lilburn's Plea in Law, June 28, 1653, second edition, much enlarged, July 2, 1653 (E.703/12*). (? by Lilburne or a friend).

The Prisoner's most mournful Cry, July I, 1653 (E.703/12; B).

The second Letter . . . to the Lord Mayor (Fowke), July 10, 1653 (E.706/5; B).

*Letter to Chief Baron Wilde, July 14, 1653 (669.f.17/35).

*A Conference with the Souldiers, July 16, 1653 (E.705/25).

The Upright Man's Vindication, August 1, 1653 (E.708/22).

The humble and further Demand of John Lilburne, August 13, 1653 (E.710/16*; B).

The Afflicted Mans Out-cry (epistle to Mr Feake), August 19, 1653 (E.711/7*).

The Just Defence of John Lilburn against such as charge him with Turbulency of Spirit, August 25, 1653 (E.711/10; B).

An Hue and Cry after the Fundamental Lawes and Liberties of England, September 26, 1653 (E.714/1; B).

The Resurrection of John Lilburne, May 16, 1656 (E.880/2; B); second edition, with additions, May 21 (E.880/5).

B. Pamphlets relating to the Trials of John Lilburne at the Guildhall (1649) and the Old Bailey (1653)

The Triall of Lieut.-Collonell John Lilburne at the Guild-Hall of London, 24, 25, 26 Oct. [1649], published by Theodorus Varax (or Verax)—*i.e.*, Clement Walker (E.584/9; B).

The second Part of the Triall of Lieut. Col. John Lilburne, 24–26 Oct.
[1649] (E.598/12; B).

*A brief Discourse of the present power of Magistracy . . . occasioned
upon the tryall of . . . John Lilburne*, October 25, 1649 (E.575/37).

Truths Victory over Tyrants and Tyranny, October 26, 1649 (E.579/12).

*A Letter of due censure and redargution to . . . John Lilburne, touching
his triall in October last*, by Henry Parker, June 21, 1650 (E.603/14;
B).

Jurors Judges of Law and Fact (reply to *A Letter of due censure*), by
John Jones, August 2, 1650 (E.1414/2).

Certain Observations upon the Tryall of Lieut-Col. Lilburne, December 1, 1649 (S.K.).

The Triall of Mr John Lilburne, 13 to 16 July [1653] (E.708/3).

*The Tryall of Lieutenant Colonell John Lilburn at the Sessions in
the Old Bayly. With the new exceptions brought by the said John
Lilburn* (E.710/22).

*The Tryall of Mr John Lilburn at the Sessions House in the Old
Baily. Together with a diurnal of each days proceedings, in order
to his tryal, 13 July to 13 Aug. Taken in short-hand* (E.710/21; B).

The Exceptions of John Lilburne to a Bill of Indictment, July 16,
1653 (E.705/20; B).

*A Plea at large for John Lilburn. Penned for his use and benefit by
a Well-Wisher to the fundamental laws, liberties and freedoms of
the free people of England*, August 6, 1653 (E.710/3).

A Word to the Jury in the behalfe of John Lilburn, August 11, 1653
(669.f.17/44).

The humble and further Demand of John Lilburn, prisoner at the Bar,
August 13, 1653 (E.710/16*; B).

More Light to Mr John Lilburnes Jury, August 16, 1653 (E.710/23).

*The Tryall of L. Col. John Lilburn at the Session House in the Old
Baily*, August 19, 1653 (E.711/9).

    The trials themselves, and some relative pamphlets, are
reproduced in J. B. Howell's *State Trials*, Vols. IV and V.

C.   PAMPHLETS ABOUT LILBURNE (EXCLUDING THOSE WRITTEN BY THE
OTHER LEVELLER LEADERS)

ANON:

*Heads of a Speech spoken by Lilburne before Council of War at
Oxford*, December 18 and 21, 1642 (B).

*The Examination and Confession of Capt. Lilbourne and Capt.
Viviers*, December 10, 1642 (E.130/33).

*A true and most sad Relation of the cruelty used on Capt. Wingate
Capt. Vivers . . . Capt. Lilburne and others of the Parliament
Souldiers, prisoners at Oxford*, February 9, 1643 (E.89/13).

The Examination and Confession of Captaine Lilbourne and Captaine Viviers . . . sent in a letter from Mr Daniel Felton, 1643 (G).

The Presbiterian Brother and Sister ; or a Briefe Reply to Dr Bastwicks Vindication which he wrote against . . . Lilburne, November 1, 1645 (E.308/2). Reprinted as *Medico Mastix*, November 7, 1645 (E.308/22).

A true Relation of the materiall passages of Lieut. Col. John Lilburnes sufferings as they were represented before the House of Peeres, February 13, 1646 (E.324/9; B).

Animadversions upon John Lilburnes Books . . . London's Liberty in Chaines . . . An Anatomy of the Lords Cruelty, November 20, 1646 (E.362/24).

The Recantation of John Lilburne, May 13, 1647 (E.386/19).

Match me these two, July 29, 1647 (E.400/9; B).

The Devil in his Dumps, August 3, 1647 (E.400/38; B).

A Declaration of some Proceedings of L. Col. John Lilburne, February 14, 1648 (E.427/6; B). (? Walter Frost.)

A Plea or Protest, made by William Prynne, March 17, 1648 (E.432/18).

Englands weeping Spectacle, June 29, 1648 (E.450/7).

A Speech in the House of Commons by Sir John Maynard, July 27, 1648 (E.458/2).

The Discoverer, June 2, 1649 (E.558/2; B).

An Anatomy of . . . John Lilburns Spirit, October 16, 1649 (E.575/21).

A Jury-man's Judgement upon the case of . . . John Lilburne, June 22, 1653 (E.702/6; B).

Severall Informations and Examinations taken . . . concerning [Lilburne's] apostacy to the party of Charles Stuart, July 13, 1653 (E.705/14; B).

Malice detected, July 13, 1653 (E.705/19).

Oyes, Oyes, Oyes. At the Quest of Inquirie holden in the Court of common Reason . . . it is found that . . . Lilburn committed no crime in appealing to the people, July 16, 1653 (E.708/7).

A Caveat to those that shall resolve . . . to destroy J.L., July 16, 1653 (E.705/21).

John Lilburne's Anagram, July 1653 (E.703/21).

Letter to . . . John Lilburne . . . in the Tower, September 8, 1653 (E.712/14).

A Letter from the North, apparently to Lilburne, September 19, 1653 (669.f.17/54).

Lieut. Colonel John Lilb. tryed and cast, November 22, 1653 (E.720/2; B).

A Declaration to the Free-born people of England, May 23, 1654 (E.735/18).

The Last Will and Testament of . . . John Lilburne, May 27, 1654 (fictitious) (E.738/8).

The Self Afflicter Lively Described, 1657 (B).
Lilburn's Ghost, June 22, 1659 (E.988/9).

BASTWICK, JOHN: *A Just Defence . . . against the Calummies of John Lilburne*, August 30, 1645 (E.265/2; B).

CHIDLEY, SAMUEL: *The Dissembling Scot . . . a Vindication of . . . Lilburn . . . from . . . Aspersions . . . by David Brown*, February 1, 1652 (E.652/13; B).

———: *An Additional Remonstrance. . . . With a little friendly touch to L. Coll. John Lilburne*, June 22, 1653 (E.711/7).

EDWARDS, THOMAS: *Gangræna*, Part 1, February 26, 1646 (E.323/2); Part II, May 28, 1646 (E.338/12); Part III, December 28, 1646 (E.368/5). (All parts in B.)

MASTERSON, GEORGE: *The Triumph stain'd*, February 10, 1648 (E.426/18; B).

OXFORD, WENDY: *Vincit qui Patitur, or Lieutenant Colonel John Lylborne decyphered*, April 1, 1653 (E.211/6).

PRYNNE, WILLIAM: *A Fresh Discovery*, July 24, 1645 (E.261/5; B).

———: *The Lyar Confounded*, October 15, 1645 (E.267/1; B).

SHEPPARD, SAMUEL; *The Farmers Fam'd* (an answer to *The Just Man in Bonds* and *A Pearl in a Dounghill*), August 4, 1646 (E.349/5).

———: *The False Alarum*, August 15, 1646 (E.350/2).

WHITE, JOHN: *John White's Defence*, September 15, 1646 (E.354/4).

D. WORKS BY RICHARD OVERTON

Considerable uncertainty still surrounds the writings of Overton. Professor Wolfe has identified a number which are included here. Until further work has been done the following list is offered tentatively.

Articles of High Treason exhibited against Cheap-side Crosse, January 1642 (E.134/23; B).

New Lambeth Fayre, March 1642 (E.138/26; B).

Man Wholly Mortal, 1643.

Man's Mortallitie, January 19, 1644 (E.29/16; B).

England's Miserie and Remedie. In a Judicious Letter from an Utter Barrister, September 14, 1645. One edition was published merely as *Copie of a Letter from an Utter-Barrister* (E.302/5; B).

A Pearle in a Dounghill, June 23, 1646 (E.342/5). (Wolfe, *Leveller Manifestoes*, attributes this to Overton.)

A Remonstrance of many Thousand Citizens of England to their owne House of Commons, occasioned through the illegall Imprisonment of John Lilburne, July 7, 1646 (E.343/11). (I agree with Wolfe that Walwyn probably collaborated with Overton.)

An Alarum to the House of Lords, July 31, 1646 (E.346/8; B).

A Defiance against all Arbitrary Usurpations, September 9, 1646 (E.353/17).

An Unhappy Game of Scots and English, 1646 (B).

An Arrow against All Tyrants and Tyranny, October 12, 1646 (E.356/14).

Vox Plebis, November 19, 1646 (E.362/20; B). (Pease, *Leveller Movement*, attributes to Marten, Wolfe, *Milton*, to Overton. Secretary Nicholas called it " a very shrewd piece " to the compiling of which one or more much abler hands than Lilburne's had contributed (*Nicholas Papers*, Vol. I, p. 74).)

The Commoners Complaint, February 1, 1647 (E.375/7; B).

Petition to the House of Commons from Bucks and Herts, edited by Overton, February 11, 1647.

An Appeale from the degenerate Representative Body . . . to the free people, July 17, 1647 (E.398/28).

Eighteen Reasons Propounded to the Soldiers of the . . . Army, why they ought to continue the Agitators, August 11, 1647 (B).

Overton's Defiance of the Act of Pardon, July 2, 1649 (E.562/26; B).

The Baiting of the Great Bull of Bashan, July 16, 1649 (E.565/2; B).

A New Bull-Bayting, August 7, 1649 (E.568/6).

The Marpriest Pamphlets (of which Overton is the acknowledged author):

> *The Araignement of Mr Persecution*, April 8, 1645 (E.276/23).
> *A Sacred Decretall*, May 31, 1645 (E.286/15).
> *Martin's Eccho*, June 27, 1645 (E.290/2).
> *The Nativity of Sir John Presbyter*, July 2, 1645 (E.290/17).
> *The Ordinance for Tythes dismounted*, December 29, 1645 (E.313/27).
> *Divine Observations upon the London Ministers Letter against Toleration*, January 24, 1646 (E.317/15).

E. Works by William Walwyn

Professor Haller has identified several of the works of Walwyn, but, again, the following list is offered with diffidence.

Some Considerations. . . . A discourse concerning the unseasonable difference between the Protestant and the Puritan, November 10, 1642 (E.126/45).

The Power of Love, September 19, 1643 (E.1206/2).

Good Counsell, July 29, 1644 (E.1199/2).

The Compassionate Samaritane, January 5, 1645 (E.1202/1).

A Helpe to the Right Understanding of a Discourse concerning Independency lately published by William Pryn, February 6, 1645 (E.259/2).

England's Lamentable Slaverie, October 11, 1645 (E.304/18; B).

A Whisper in the Eare of Mr Thomas Edwards, March 13, 1646 (E.328/2; B).
A Word More to Mr Thomas Edwards, March 19, 1646 (E.328/20).
A Word in Season, May 18, 1646 (E.337/25).
An Antidote against Master Edwards, June 10, 1646 (E.1184/4).
The Just Man in Bonds, June 23, 1646 (E.342/2).
A Prediction of Mr Edwards his Conversion, August 11, 1646 (E.1184/5).
A Parable, October 29, 1646 (E.359/8).
Gold tried in the fire, June 14, 1647 (E.392/19).
A Still Small Voice, 1647. (See Haller.)
The Bloody Project, August 21, 1648 (E.460/4).
The Vanitie of the present Churches, March 12, 1649 (E.1367/1).
The Fountain of Slaunder, May 30, 1649 (E.557/4; B).
Walwyn's Just Defence, 1649. (See Haller.)
Juries Justified, December 2, 1651 (E.618/9; B).

Pamphlets about Walwyn

KIFFIN, WILLIAM, AND OTHERS: *Walwins Wiles*, May 10, 1649 (E.554/24; B).
BROOKS, HENRY: *The Charity of Church-Men; or, A Vindication of William Walwyn*, May 28, 1649 (E.556/20; B).
EDWARDS, THOMAS: *Gangræna* (supra).

F. WORKS BY JOHN WILDMAN

Again, there is little certainty about Wildman's pamphlets.
? *The Case of the Armie*, October 15, 1647 (E.411/9). (Maurice Ashley, *John Wildman*, gives this as Wildman's; Wolfe suggests several hands.)
? *A Cal to all the Souldiers of the Armie*, October 29, 1647 (E.412/10; B). (Ashley gives this also as Wildman's.)
Putney Projects, December 30, 1647 (E.421/19; B).
Truth's Triumph, January 18, 1648 (E.520/33). (Masterson's answer was *The Triumph stain'd*, February 10, 1648 (E.426/18). Some one called Jah Norris capped this with *A Lash for a Lyar ; or, the Stayner stayned*, February 22, 1648 (E.428/8).)
The Lawes Subversion ; or, Sir John Maynard's Case truly stated (by J. Howldin), March 6, 1648 (E.431/2; B).
London's Liberties, a discussion on London elections, December 14, 1650 (E.620/70).

For Wildman's subsequent pamphlets, which have little connexion with Lilburne or the Levellers, see Ashley, *John Wildman*.

G. JOINT WORKS OF THE LEVELLER LEADERS

? *Regall Tyrannie discovered*, January 6, 1647—Lilburne and Overton (E.370/12; B).

? *The Out-cryes of oppressed Commons*, February 28, 1647—Lilburne and Overton (E.378/13; B).

The second Part of Englands New Chaines, March 24, 1649 (some copies have merely " London, 1649 ")—Lilburne, Overton, Prince (E.548/16; B).

The Picture of the Councel of State, April 4, 1649—Lilburne, Overton, Prince (E.550/14; B).

A Manifestation, April 14, 1649—Lilburne, Overton, Prince, Walwyn (E.550/25; B). (Professor Wolfe thinks undoubtedly Walwyn.)

Copie of a Letter . . . to the General (concerning Lockier), April 27, 1649—Lilburne and Overton (669.f.14/23).

H. THE " AGREEMENTS OF THE PEOPLE "

(a) Leveller

An Agreement of the People for a firme peace, October 28, 1647, November 3 (Th) (E.412/21).

Foundations of Freedom ; or, an Agreement of the People, December 10, 1648 (E.476/26).

An Agreement of the Free People of England, May 1, 1649 (E.571/10; B).

(b) Showing Strong Leveller Influence

Severall Proposals for Peace and Freedom, by an agreement of the People, December 11, 1648 (E.477/18).

(c) The Officers' Printed Agreement

An Agreement of the People of England, and the places therewith incorporated (with *A Petition from Lord Fairfax*, etc.), January 20, 1649 (E.539/2).

I. SOME PETITIONS BY OR CONCERNING LILBURNE AND THE LEVELLERS

(Only British Museum numbers are noted here.)

June 16, 1646: *To the R. Hon. the chosen and Representative body of England assembled in Parliament . . . from J. Lilburne* (1104. a. 1/2).

September 23, 1646: *For J. Lilburne from his wife and many women* (669.f.10/86).

October 9, 1646: *Richard Overton to the House of Commons for consideration of his case* (669.f.10/91).

March 1, 1647: *For Lilburne and Mr and Mrs Overton to the House of Commons from Bucks and Herts* (669.f.10/115).

March 24, 1647: *From Mary Overton to the House of Commons* (E.381/10).

November 11, 1647 (dated 13th): *For every Individuall Member of the House of Commons from John Lilburne* (E.414/9).

November 23, 1647: *A new complaint of an old grievance from John Lilburne to the House of Commons* (E.416/25). (Reprinted in *Peoples' Prerogative.*)

August 1, 1648: *For John Lilburne, to the House of Commons* (E.457/19). (Said to be subscribed by more than 10,000 persons.)

September 4, 1648: *From John Lilburne to every individual Member of the House of Commons* (E.461/36).

March 3, 1649: *Richard Overton to the House of Commons* (E.546/1).

April 17, 1649: *To the House of Commons for the Levellers in the Tower from London and parts adjacent* (669.f.14/20).

May 5, 1649: *To the House of Commons for Lockier and other Leveller prisoners from women of London and parts adjacent* (669.f.14/27).

October 23, 1649: *To the Commons of England, Assembled in Parliament, The humble Petition of the wel-affected of London, Westminster and parts adjacent for Lilburne* (E.579/9 and E.621/12).

March 12, 1650: *To Parliament from Lilburne for payment of remains of his Reparations* (669.f.15/20).

November 7, 1650: *To every Individual member . . . esp. Geo. Thompson . . . for regulating the excise . . . of sope*, by John Lilburne (669.f.15/64).

November 28, 1651: *The humble addresse of Lilburne to Parliament in answer to Huntington's petition* (E.647/7).

January 20, 1652: *Petition to Parliament of many well affected people highly concerned in the sentence against Lilburne* (669.f.16/37).

January 22, 1652: *Petition to Parliament of David Brown and family against Lilburne* (E.651/30).

June 24, 1653: *Petition to Parliament on behalf of Lieut.-Col. Lilburne* (669.f.17/24).

June 25, 1653: *To the Parliament of the Commonwealth . . . petition of afflicted women in behalf of Mr J. Lilburne* (669.f.17/26).

July 14, 1653: *Petition of many grieved People of London, Westminster and Places adjacent on behalf of John Lilburne* (669.f.17/35).

July 29, 1653: *Unto every individual Member of Parliament, the humble Representation of afflicted Women Petitioners on behalf of Mr John Lilburne* (669.f.17/36).

August 2, 1653: *To every individual Member of Parliament from divers apprentices on behalf of Lilburne* (E.710/5 and 669.f.17/38).
August 10, 1653: *A Voyce from the Heavenly Word of God . . . to Parliament on behalf of John Lilburne* (669.f.17/43).

J. FURTHER PAMPHLETS CONCERNING THE PROGRAMME, POLICY, ETC., OF THE LEVELLERS

The " Large " Petition of March 1647 (E.464/19*).
Petition of November 25, 1647, from the " freeborn people of England " to the House of Commons in support of the *Agreement of the People* (669.f.11/98).
The Smithfield Petition, January 1648 (printed in E.508/20 and E.427/6).
The Petition of September 11, 1648 (E.464/5).
A Reply to the House of Commons . . ., September 11, 1648 (E.470/6).
The humble Representation of Divers Inhabitants of . . . London, March 10, 1649 (E.546/15).
The humble Petition of . . . the County of Leicester, March 19, 1649 (669.f.14/6).
A Declaration of the Wel-Affected in the County of Bucks, May 10, 1649 (E.555/1).
The Remonstrance of many thousands of the Free-People of England, September 21, 1649 (E.574/15).

K. ARMY TRACTS

Petition of the Officers and Souldiers in the Army, March 21, 1647 (E.385/12).
Petition and Vindication of the Officers, April 27, 1647 (E.385/19).
The Declaration of the Armie, May 16, 1647 (E.390/26).
An Humble Representation of the Dissatisfaction of the Army, June 4, 1647 (E.392/9).
The Solemne Engagement of the Armie, June 5, 1647 (E.392/9).
The Heads of the Proposals, August 1, 1647 (E.401/4).
The Humble Address of the Agitators of the Army to Fairfax, August 14, 1647 (E.402/8).
A Declaration of the Engagements of the Army, September 27, 1647 (E.409/25). (Contains a number of the statements and manifestos of the spring and summer of 1647.)
A Letter sent from the Agitators . . . to their . . . Regiments, November 11, 1647 (E.414/8).
Letter sent by the Agents of severall Regiments . . . to all the Souldiers in the . . . Armie, November 11, 1647 (E.413/18).

Englands Freedome, Souldiers Rights, December 14, 1647 (E.419/23).
The Humble Petition of the Officers and Souldiers . . . to . . . Fairfax,
November 11, 1648 (E.470/32).
The Remonstrance of the Army, November 20, 1648 (E.473/11).
A Libbell (an unheaded sheet, so headed by Thomason), April 25,
1649 (E.551/21).
The Burford mutiny. All the news-sheets for the first weeks in May
report this in considerable detail. Also,
> *The Resolutions of . . . Scroop's Regiment* (669.f.14/18).
> *The . . . Declaration of . . . Scroop's and Ireton's Regiments*
> (E.555/4).
> *The Levellers . . . Vindicated* (E.571/11).
> *England's Standard Advanced* (E.553/2).
> *A Declaration of the Proceedings . . . in . . . Reducing . . . the*
> *Revolted Troops* (E.556/1).
> *A Full Narrative of All the Proceedings betweene His Excellency*
> *. . . and the Mutineers* (E.555/27).

L.   REPRINTS OF LEVELLER TRACTS

A number of the Leveller tracts have recently been reprinted.

HALLER, WILLIAM: *Tracts on Liberty in the Puritan Revolution*
(three vols., Columbia University Press, 1934). Vol. I contains
a commentary and an appendix on the writings of Walwyn.
Vol. II includes Lilburne's *Worke of the Beast* and Walwyn's
Power of Love. Vol. III includes Lilburne's *Copie of a Letter*
and *Englands Birth-right;* Walwyn's *Compassionate Samaritane,*
Helpe to the Right Understanding, England's Lamentable Slaverie,
and *Whisper in the Eare of Mr Thomas Edwards;* and Overton's
Araignement of Mr Persecution and *Remonstrance of many*
Thousand Citizens.

HALLER, WILLIAM, AND DAVIES, GODFREY: *The Leveller Tracts,*
1647–1653 (Columbia University Press, 1944). Contains, besides
a fifty-page Introduction, *The Declaration of the Armie, The Case*
of the Armie, A Declaration of Some Proceedings, The Bloody
Project, the Petition of September 11, 1648, *Englands New Chains*
and *The Second Part of Englands New Chaines,* excerpts from *The*
Picture of the Councel of State and Walwyn's *Fountain of Slaunder,*
Walwyn's Just Defence and *The Just Defence of John Lilburne,*
excerpts from *The Legall Fundamentall Liberties,* Brooke's *Charity*
of Churchmen, the *Agreement of the Free People* of May 1, 1649,
the *Manifestation* of the Leveller Leaders, and *Walwins Wiles.*

WOLFE, DON M.: *Leveller Manifestoes of the Puritan Revolution*
(Nelson, 1944). Includes Overton's *Remonstrance of many Thou-*
sand Citizens and *Appeale from the degenerate Representative*

Body; the *Agreement of the People* of October 28/November 3, 1647, December 10, 1648, and January 20, 1649; petitions of March 1647, November 1647, January 1648, September 1648, and January 1649, and the *Mournfull Cries of many Thousand Poore Tradesmen*; a letter from the agitators to the seamen, June 1647, *The Case of the Armie, Englands Freedome, Souldiers Rights, A Defence for the Soldiers of the Armie*; and *The Hunting of the Foxes.*

WOLFE, DON M.: *Milton in the Puritan Revolution* (Nelson, 1941). Includes Walwyn's *Still Small Voice* and the second part of *Englands New Chaines.*

WOODHOUSE, A. S. P.: *Puritanism and Liberty* (Dent, 1938). Reprints the Army debates (1647–49) from the *Clarke Manuscripts*—*i.e.*, the Putney and the Whitehall debates—as well as extracts from Leveller tracts in Section VIII and from other documents in the Appendix.

Extracts from contemporary sources will also be found in Hill, J. E. C., and Dell, E.: *The Good Old Course* (Lawrence and Wishart, 1949).

M.   PREVIOUS BIOGRAPHIES OF LILBURNE

There was no full-length biography until Miss M. A. Gibb published *John Lilburne, the Leveller* in 1947 (Lindsay Drummond), although Godwin (*History of the Commonwealth of England* (four vols., 1824–28)), Bernstein (*Cromwell and Communism* (Allen and Unwin, 1930)) and, more importantly, T. C. Pease (*Leveller Movement* (American Historical Association, 1916)) devoted much attention to him. C. H. Firth's article in the *Dictionary of National Biography* was full, and Edward Peacock, in *Biographia Britannica*, Vol. V (1760), had presented much useful material.

The following three tracts also contained 'Lives' of Lilburne:
Pictorial History of England (1840).
Tract Association of the Society of Friends, No. 105 (1854).
The History of King-Killers or the Fanatick Martyrology containing the Lives of 365 Hellish Saints of that Crew . . . one for every day in the Year (two vols., 1720). (Includes Lilburne for August 29, the day of his death.)

N.   SOME OTHER RECENT WORKS ON THE LEVELLER LEADERS, THE LEVELLER MOVEMENT, AND ALLIED SUBJECTS

ASHLEY, MAURICE: *John Wildman, Plotter and Postmaster* (Cape, 1947).

FRANK, JOSEPH: *The Levellers: A History of the Writings of Three Seventeenth-century Democrats, John Lilburne, Richard Overton, and William Walwyn* (Harvard University Press, 1955).

HALLER, WILLIAM: *The Rise of Puritanism* (Columbia University Press, 1938).

——: *Liberty and Reformation in the Puritan Revolution* (Columbia University Press, 1955).

HILL, J. E. C.: *Puritanism and Revolution* (Secker and Warburg, 1958).

ROBERTSON, D. B.: *The Religious Foundations of Leveller Democracy* (King's Crown Press, New York, 1951).

SCHENK, W.: *The Concern for Social Justice in the Puritan Revolution* (Longmans, 1948).

——: "A Seventeenth-century Radical" (*i.e.*, Walwyn), in *Economic History Review*, Vol. XIV (1944), pp. 74–83.

WOLFE, DON M.: " Lilburne's Note on Milton," in *Modern Language Notes*, Vol. LVI (1941), pp. 360–363.

For students of Lilburne and the Levellers nothing can take the place of the pamphlets and news-sheets of the period, so many of which are listed in the indispensable *Catalogue of the Thomason Tracts*, compiled by G. K. Fortescue (1908). Although not absolutely accurate, it is invaluable. The *Journals* of the House of Commons and the House of Lords, *Calendars of State Papers* (Domestic and Venetian), the *Acts and Ordinances of the Interregnum* (three vols.), brought together by Firth and Rait, the *Reports of the Historical Manuscripts Commission*, the *Clarendon Manuscripts*, in the Bodleian Library, many local records, and contemporary journals like those of Whitelocke and Rushworth are all of the greatest use. In the Notes to this book many more sources are given.

Professor Firth's discovery of the *Clarke Manuscripts* (printed in Camden Society publications, 1891 and 1894, and Woodhouse (*supra*)) remains perhaps the most valuable find for seventeenth-century students, but exciting enough was the recognition by Lieutenant-Colonel Peter Young in a bookseller's shop only five years ago of the letter-book of Sir Lewis Dyve. Transcribed and edited by H. G. Tibbutt in *Publications of the Bedford Record Society*, Vol. XXXVIII (1958), it is a most valuable addition to the records of a most important year.

Of more recent publications the most important are:

BRAILSFORD, H. N.: *The Levellers and the English Revolution*, ed. C. Hill (1961).

MACPHERSON, C. B.: *The Political Theory of Possessive Individualism*, pp. 107–59 (1962)

THOMAS, KEITH: 'The Levellers and the Franchise' in *The Interregnum: the Quest for Settlement, 1646–1660*, ed. G. E. Aylmer (1972) which gives a full Levellers bibliography.

THOMPSON, CHRISTOPHER: 'Maximilian Petty and the Putney Debate on the Franchise' in *Past and Present*, no. 88 (1980), pp. 63 ff.

Index